# Contents

# INSIDE THE LEARNING SOCIETY

Patrick Ainley and Bill Bailey: *The Business of Learning*

James Avis, Martin Bloomer, Geoff Esland, Denis Gleeson and Phil Hodkinson: *Knowledge and Nationhood*

Mike Bottery: *The Ethics of Educational Management*

Mike Bottery: *Lessons for Schools?*

David Clark: *Schools as Learning Communities*

Judith Chapman and David Aspin: *The School, the Community and Lifelong Learning*

Steward Ranson: *Towards the Learning Society*

Roger Smith: *Successful School Management*

John White: *Education and the End of Work*

# INSIDE THE LEARNING SOCIETY

Edited by
Stewart Ranson

CASSELL
London and New York

Cassell
Wellington House     370 Lexington Avenue
125 Strand     New York
London WC2R 0BB     NY 10017–6550

First published 1998

**British Library Cataloguing-in-Publication Data**
A catalogue record for this book is available from the British Library.

ISBN 0-304-70181-5 (hardback)
     0-304-70182-3 (paperback)

Typeset by SetSystems Ltd, Saffron Walden, Essex
Printed and bound in Great Britain by Redwood Books, Trowbridge, Wiltshire

# Contributors

**Patrick Ainley**, Reader in Learning Policy, School of Post-Compulsory Education and Training, University of Greenwich

**Sir Christopher Ball**, Fellow, Royal Society of Arts

**David Clark**, Research Fellow, Westhill College, Birmingham

**John Field**, Professor of Lifelong Learning, Department of Continuing Education, University of Warwick

**Nickie Fonda**, Chief Executive, Prospect Centre

**Richard Hatcher**, Director of Research, Faculty of Education, University of Central England

**Chris Hayes**, Chairman, Prospect Centre

**Josh Hillman**, Senior Research Officer, Institute of Public Policy Research

**Christina Hughes**, Lecturer, Department of Continuing Education, University of Warwick

**Helena Kennedy**, Chair, Further Education Funding Council, 1994–97

**Stewart Ranson**, Professor of Education, School of Education, University of Birmingham

**Glenn Rikowski**, Research Fellow, Post-Sixteen Education and Training, School of Education, University of Birmingham

**John Stewart**, Honorary Professor of Local Government, School of Public Policy, University of Birmingham

**Michael Strain**, Senior Lecturer, School of Education, University of Ulster at Jordanstown

**Malcolm Tight**, Reader, Department of Continuing Education, University of Warwick

**Michael Young**, Professor of Education, Institute of Education, University of London

**Hendrik van der Zee**, Lecturer, Centre for Learning and Communitcation in Organisations, Leiden University

To the Memory of Helena

# Acknowledgements

The editor would like to thank the authors for contributing to this book, and the following organizations for permission to publish extracts of published work: Confederation of British Industry, Chapter 2; European Commission, Chapter 9; Labour Party, Chapter 10; HMSO, Chapter 11; Scottish Community Education Council, Chapter 12; Further Education Funding Council, Chapter 13; HMSO, Chapter 14.

A number of colleagues have been particularly helpful in providing support. Pat Ainley's correspondence has offered ideas and encouragement; Glenn Rikowski has integrated support with critical challenge; and John Stewart, as always with his comments, widens my vision. I am grateful to these colleagues and especially to Seroj Kumari whose hard work and commitment at the outset made the editorial work possible.

I would also like to thank my editors at Casell – Naomi Roth, Seth Edwards and particularly Marion Blake – for their support and patience.

# Sources

Except for the three chapters written especially for this collection (Chapters 1, 20 and 21), all others have been published previously. Permissions to include them in this collection are gratefully acknowledged.

## SOURCES OF CHAPTERS

2. Confederation of British Industry, (1991) *The Skills Revolution* (London: CBI)

3. Sir Christopher Ball (1991) *Learning Pays: The Role of Post Compulsory Education and Training* (London: Royal Society of Arts)

4. P. Ainley, (1994) *Degrees of Difference: Higher Education in the 1990s* (London: Lawrence and Wishart)

5. H. van der Zee (1991) The learning society. *International Journal of Lifelong Education* 10 (3) 213–30

6. C. Hayes, N. Fonda and J. Hillman (1995) *Learning in the New Millennium* NCE Briefing, New Series No. 5 (London: National Commission on Education, Paul Hamlyn Foundation).

7. S. Ranson (1992) Towards the learning society. *Educational Management and Administration* 20 (2) 68–79

8. D. Clark (1996) *Schools as Learning Communities* (London: Cassell)

9. European Commission (1997) *Teaching and Learning: Towards the Learning Society* (Luxembourg: EC).

10. Labour Party (1994) *Opening Doors to a Learning Society: A Policy Statement on Education* (London: Labour Party).

11. Conservative Government (1996) *Lifetime Learning: A Policy Framework*, published by the DfEE on 24 June. The policy document was published with a

press release (203/96) by the Education and Employment Minister James Paice, entitled *Framework for a Learning Society*.

12.   Scottish Community Education Council (1995) *Scotland as a Learning Society* (Glasgow: SCEC)

13.   H. Kennedy (1997) *Learning Works: Widening Participation in Further Education* (Coventry: Further Education Funding Council)

14.   Department for Education and Employment (1997) *Higher Education in the Learning Society* (London: HMSO)

15.   C. Hughes and M. Tight (1995) The myth of the learning society. *British Journal of Educational Studies*, 43 (3), 290–304.

16.   M. Young (1994) Post-compulsory education for a learning society. Paper presented to a Conference on Re-Forming Post-Compulsory Education and Training, Griffith University, Queensland, Australia

17.   R. Hatcher (1996) The limitation of the new social democratic agendas: class, inequality and agency. In R. Hatcher and K. Jones (eds.), *Education After the Conservatives: The Response to the New Agenda of Reform* Stoke-on-Trent: Trentham Books

19.   M. Strain and J. Field (1997) On 'the myth of the learning society'. *British Journal of Educational Studies* 45 (2), 141–55

# Chapter 1

# Lineages of the Learning Society[1]

*Stewart Ranson*

In periods of social transition education becomes central to our future well-being. Only if learning is placed at the centre of our experience can individuals continue to develop their skills and capacities, institutions be enabled to respond openly and imaginatively to a period of change, and the difference between communities become a source of reflective understanding. The challenge for policy makers, in this analysis, is to promote the conditions in which a 'learning society' can unfold.

This idea of a learning society has become enormously influential during the 1990s. It has provided guiding assumptions for the renewal of economy and society for national politicians, the National Commission on Education, the European Commission White Paper on education and training, city policy makers, corporate strategists and industrial trainers. Within the academic community, the Economic and Social Research Council has identified the learning society as a key issue and set up a special programme of research projects on what it is and how it works.

A considerable literature has developed, yet the concept remains 'essentially contested' (Gallie, 1964). Shared commitment to an idea often masks considerable variety of interpretation. While some writers argue that the new world of work requires a learning society to encourage training for individuals so that they can accumulate transferable skills for the changing labour market, others emphasize active participation in creating the 'wealth' of the communities in which people live and work. Altered notions of work and its social distribution suggest the need for a transformed relationship between members and their society: not as passive producers in a traditional society, nor as active individual consumers in the recent market society, but as citizens within a learning society whose creative agency will be the key to economic as well as social innovation. For another set of commentators this suggests the idea of a learning democracy, with citizens participating actively in the political arena to shape agendas, critically examine services and vote on policies.

Following a decade of writing about 'the learning society', there is now a need to take stock of the significant practices which it expresses, to critically evaluate its meanings, and to prepare an analysis which synthesizes and sharpens our under-standing of it. This is the agenda of this book. The first chapter traces the lineages of the idea, describes the companion literatures of learning organizations and learning cities and proposes an underlying theory of learning. Parts 1 and 2 present some of the key essays published in the 1990s, including the significant statements of public policy; Part 3 sets out the emerging critique. The concluding analysis seeks to critically evaluate the debate.

## UNDERSTANDING THE LEARNING SOCIETY

The idea of the learning society has, arguably, had two periods of currency. The first was in the late 1960s and early 1970s with the work, for example, of Hutchins (1968), Etzioni (1968), Schön (1971) and Husen (1974). The second has typically been in the 1990s with the work of Ranson (1991, 1994), Ball (1990, 1991), Engestrom (1991), Ainley (1994a); Ranson and Stewart (1994), Cochinaux and de Woot (1995), Nixon *et al.* (1996) and Raggatt *et al.* (1996). In both periods the idea has been conceived as a way of making sense of a period of change, yet writers have brought out different aspects of the learning society:

- a society which learns about itself and how it is changing;
- a society which needs to change the way it learns;
- a society in which all its members are learning;
- a society which learns to democratically change the conditions of learning.

These ideas will be explored in turn.

### Learning about a changing society

A learning society is a society which needs to learn about itself and the significant changes which it faces if it is to survive and flourish in the future. The great theorist of the learning society has been Donald Schön (1971), whose *Beyond the Stable State: Public and Private Learning in a Changing Society* was presented as the Reith Lecture series in 1970. His analysis sought to help a society confront transforming change by understanding that placing learning at the centre was the single key to future well-being. Our societies and institutions are, he argued, routinely characterized by 'dynamic conservatism'. The belief in the virtue of a stable, unchanging order as the best protection against the threat of destabilizing change is very deep. In an ordered world we know who we are, what our roles are, and thus how to act. Change threatens to produce crisis – we will not know how to act, we will lose the stabilizing sense of who we are. We will be plunged into uncertainty.

Social institutions embody a deep-seated orientation to resist the disturbances which change can visit upon them. This conservativism is the tendency to fight to remain the same. Social systems are typically 'self-reinforcing systems'. The beliefs, interests and structures all work together to conserve the past and prevent change. Yet our societies face unprecedented and continuing change which erodes the possibility of ever recovering the traditions of stability. The new electronic technologies are meta technologies which facilitate the processes of innovation and diffusion.

> While technological change has been continuing exponentially for the last two hundred years, it has now reached a level of pervasiveness and frequency uniquely threatening to the stable state ... the implosiveness of the vein of technology mined in the last half century has made it uniquely disruptive.
>
> (Schön, 1971, p. 28)

In this period of change stable views of occupations, religions, organizations and value systems have been lost. We must learn to live 'beyond the stable state'.

- The loss of the stable state means that our society and all its institutions are in *continuing* processes of transformation. We cannot expect new stable states that will endure even for our own lifetimes.
- We must learn to understand, guide, influence and manage these transformations. We must make the capacity for undertaking them integral to ourselves and to our institutions.
- We must, in other words, become adept at learning. We must not only be able to transform our institutions, in response to changing situations and requirements; we must invent and develop institutions which are 'learning systems', that is to say, systems capable of bringing about their own continuing transformation.
- The task which the loss of the stable state makes imperative for the person, for our institutions, for our society as a whole, is to learn about learning.
  - what is the nature of the process by which organisations, institutions and societies transform themselves?
  - what are the characteristics of effective learning systems?
  - what are the forms and limits of knowledge that can operate within processes of social learning?
  - what demands are made on a person who engages in this kind of learning? (p. 30)

What are the conditions for institutions and societies to become learning systems – 'social systems [which] learn to become capable of transforming themselves without intolerable disruption' (p. 60)? Schön finds models of learning societies in studies of social movements and constellation business firms, which present 'paradigms of learning systems for the society as a whole' (p. 61). Their characteristics include emphasis on flexibility, apparent lack of structure, no fixed centre, overlapping networks, and feedback loops which enable learning and self-transformation. Societies, like organizations, need to learn about how they learn.

## A society which needs to change the way it learns

If a society is changing, it needs to learn how it is changing and thus probably needs to change the way it learns. Modes of learning are shaped by the social structures in which they are located and by the influence of historical traditions of learning. Torsten Husén's work on the learning society (1974, 1986, 1990) has been particularly influential in educational studies and practice because of his preoccupation with reflection upon and reform of traditional forms of learning. He had, since the end of the 1940s, been at the centre of educational reform in Sweden as a researcher and government adviser. Coming to education from a background outside education, he emphasized much to the irritation of traditional professional educators, 'that education has to be viewed in a wider social context' (1974, p. xvii).

The task of reforming education to meet the needs of a changing society required, Husén argued, a critical review of the institutionalized nature of schools without moving to the excess of 'de-schooling'. The reform of education would require a number of system level conditions to enable the creation of a learning society: first, a massive expansion in participation in education; second, the appropriate technology to support the knowledge explosion and the processing, storing and retrieval of information; and third, the need to individualize instruction so that each student develops a programme of learning that suits them best. The organizing principles of the educational system would include:

- Education is going to be a life long process.
- Education will not have fixed points of entry and 'cut-off' exits. It will become a more continuous process within formal education and in its role within other functions of life.
- Education will take on a more informal character as it becomes accessible to more and more individuals. In addition to 'learning centres', facilities will be provided for learning at home and at the workplace, for example by the provision of computer terminals.
- Formal edcuation will become more meaningful and relevant in its application.
- 'To an ever-increasing extent, the education system will become dependent on large supporting organisations or supporting systems . . . to produce teaching aids, systems of information processing and multi-media instructional materials' . . . (Husén, 1974, pp. 198–9).

The learning society will need to provide a foundation of general education and vocational training. The purpose of education should be to prepare young people for 'general citizenship'. The inexorable trend in a society ruled by specialists and experts (a 'meritocracy') needs to be balanced by 'a common liberal schooling' that encourages communications skills so that citizens can speak to and understand one another. Schooling should encourage internationalism and values of a pluralistic society. Education should also prepare young people for changing careers and the continuing need for re-education, and will accomplish these purposes more effectively in the future if it concentrates on inculcating certain fundamental learning processes, 'by providing a basic repertoire of skills as well as attitudes of flexibility and a taste for more, a motivation for going on with education'. 'Work', however, will increasingly 'take on the character of self-realization' (1974, p. 199).

To facilitate these purposes, the processes of schooling in the learning society will need to be very different.

- The focus should be upon learning rather than teaching: a particular target for Husén was the overemphasis on didactic teaching strategies in the classroom.
- The technological revolution will enter schools to support the learning process.
- The emphasis in the curriculum will shift from content subjects, such as history and geography, to skill subjects such as language and mathematics.
- Pedagogy will encourage children to learn more themselves and this will 'demand more initiative and self activity on their part' (1974, p. 252).
- Class sizes and grouping will vary according to the task, incorporating more discussion and independent work.
- This individualization of learning shifts the role of the teacher from didactic communication to diagnosis of the learning needs and progress accomplished.

The process of learning needs significant reform if the learning society is to be realized. Yet the focus in this discussion is, for many, too internal to the traditional institutions of education – the schools and the young. If society is to be a learning society then the formal institutions of education need radical change to prevent them enclosing learning, separating it off artificially from the everyday processes of living, and defining the constituency of education far too narrowly.

## A society in which all its members are learning

A learning society is one which recognizes that learning cannot be separated from society and is not just for the young but for all, throughout their lives. Learning needs to be opened out to all. Radical educators of the 1970s such as Holt and Illich understood that only far-reaching reforms could facilitate the learning society and help it respond to the transformations of the late twentieth century. Adult educators have been those most likely to build upon this heritage in order to develop an analysis of a learning society for all.

For Holt (1970, 1977) learning is typically denied by the apparatus of formal education. The bureaucracy of schools prevents rather than enables education because 'learning is cut off from active life' (1977, p. 7). Learning only happens through doing: 'we learn to do something by doing it' (p. 17). Thus we 'learn about the world from living in it, working in it, and changing it, and from knowing a wide variety of people who are doing the same.' (p. 8.) The motivation for this learning springs out of interest and the opportunity to influence the process of learning:

> Children (like all people) will live better, learn more, and grow up more able to cope with the world if they are not constantly . . . bullied . . . set against each other . . . made to feel incompetent . . .; if their interests, concerns and enthusiasms are not ignored or scorned; and if instead they are allowed, encouraged, and (if they wish) helped to

work with and help each other, to learn from each other, and to think, talk, write and read about the things that most excite and interest them: in short if they are able to explore the world in their own way, and, in as many areas as possible direct and control their own lives.'

(p. 11)

For Holt this learning or 'doing society' does not yet exist but has to be created. A more radical approach might include creating 'schools without walls' which both encourage more learning to take place within the community and use members of the community more routinely as resources for learning within schools.

If, however, learning as doing is to be promoted more widely then more imaginative approaches are needed, for example develolping 'learning exchanges' which enable people to get in touch with those who have the knowledge or a skill they wish to benefit from. Public libraries, moreover, have the potential to become centres of this kind of learning exchange, and to 'make available not just books and a few audio-visual materials, but musical instruments, music practice rooms ... and the equipment needed to do a wide range of arts and crafts ... libraries might also keep and lend toys, games, elementary scientific equipment, chemistry and electronic kits, sports equipment, skates, rackets and so on' (p. 43).

Illich (1971, 1973) accentuated these ideas, arguing famously for the de-schooling of society: learning can only flourish when the ossified regimes of schooling are replaced by processes which place participation at the centre:

> Only actual participation constitutes socially valuable learning, a participation by the learner in every stage of the learning process, including not only the free choice of what is to be learned and how it is to be learned but also a free determination by each learner of his own reason for living and learning – the part that his knowledge is to play in his life.

(1973, p. 14)

Like Holt, Illich proposed to substitute living 'learning webs' to replace the arid structures of schooling, by facilitating access to things or processes for formal learning; promoting skill exchanges; peer matching – a communications network which permits persons to describe the learning activity in which they wish to engage, in the hope of finding a partner for the inquiry; and the creation of a directory of 'educators-at-large', who can be chosen by consulting their former clients (1971, p. 81).

It has typically been adult educators who have been most receptive to this radical vision of education, recognizing that different learning needs require a different understanding of pedagogy, curriculum, and institutional organization. Indeed, it is the long tradition of adult education – rooted in the Mechanics Institutes, Mutual Improvement Societies, Workers Educational Associations – which can provide models for a learning society in which members of the community organize collectively to meet their educational needs (Kohn, 1982). It is out of these traditions of adult education that the value of lifelong or recurrent or continuing education has developed to meet changing learning needs through-out a life-time. Thus Hutchins (1970) described a learning society as 'one that, in addition to offering part-time adult education to every man and woman at every stage of grown-up life, had succeeded in transforming values in such a way that learning, fulfilment, becoming human, had become its aims and all its institutions were directed to that end' (p. 134).

Reflecting upon the conditions for such continuing, lifelong education has led adult educators to develop a framework for a learning society as a society of learners, using their learning to inform their shaping of the society in which they live and work. It leads to pedagogy which advocates that according the learner the responsibility to participate in shaping the purpose and process of learning is the most effective route to motivation and personal development (Evans, 1985). The institutional arrangements need to be appropriate to the needs of a client group required to move in and out of learning at different stages of their lives and for different purposes. This suggests a flexible network of learning opportunities rather than the more bureaucratic structures of statutory age provision. Institutional flexibility is the central quality needed to respond to diverse and changing needs by developing connections across traditional boundaries of school, college, work and community. Moreover, as Robert Aitken (1983) argued, 'we need to break away from a rigid delivery system of fixed entry points, of hours in the day, terms, academic years and self-contained levels and entry qualifications' (p. 46). Diversity, accessibility, transferability, partnership and accountability become the defining characteristics of a comprehensive system of continuing education. The role of the educator changes in such a system from formal provider of given, unchangeable learning experiences, to the 'educator as impresario, as course compiler, as guide, as counsellor and link man – these will be the new specialisms in a recurrent system' (Flude and Parrott, 1979, p. 119).

## A society which learns to democratically change the conditions of learning

A society which is to learn about how it is changing has to learn the conditions of learning. These are fundamentally social and political. A learning society must be a learning democracy. Different aspects of this idea have been grasped by educators in the past. Husén (1974) was clear that the changes required to reform education to respond to the transformations of the time could not be understood in a socio-economic vacuum. The task of reforming education from an élite (selective) to a socially just (comprehensive) system can never be a purely educational or pedagogical problem, but has to be conceived as a social and political one.

> The problems facing educational planners are not just problems of pedagogy. They are problems of social justice, of national economy and of preparation for a rapidly changing society where lifelong learning becomes imperative. Educational problems in a rapidly changing society are too important to be left entirely to educators.
>
> (Husén, 1974, p. xvi)

If Husén failed to develop the political theory implied in the learning society, Schön placed a learning government at the centre of the learning society. If society is to learn to adapt to change it needs government to help it to become a learning society: government 'comes to function as facilitator of society's learning' (Schön, 1971, p. 178). Government needs to become a learning system to help society learn to identify, analyse and solve its problems.

> Government as a learning system carries with it the idea of *public* learning, a special way of acquiring new capacity for behaviour in which government learns for the society as a whole. In public learning, government undertakes a continuing, directed inquiry into the nature, causes and resolutions of our problems.
>
> The need for public learning carries with it the need for a second kind of learning. If government is to learn to solve new public problems, it must also learn to create the systems for doing so and to discard the structure and mechanisms grown up around old problems.'
>
> (Schön, 1971, p. 116)

The need is for new institutional processes to be created and old structures discarded. Governments have typically been inept at the process of public learning, at learning about the mistakes of the past. If governments are to become learning systems they must recognize that the movement of learning is not from centre to periphery, as in traditional models, but from periphery to periphery, or from periphery to the centre. Continuing adaptation is best supported through fostering new ideas, enabling local networks of learning, creating task groups responsible for projects, and providing an intelligence function which monitors and evaluates them. 'The need is for differentiated, responsive, continually changing but connected reaction' (p. 189); such constellations allow diversity at the periphery without giving up central control. The emphasis is upon networks, facilitation, co-ordination, knitting together. A central role is given to change agents.

For Schön, the challenge is to create *learning systems* to address the problem of the time – the mismatch between the present institutional map and the array of problems confronting it.

> In our society public learning has been limited to the transformation of specific organisations ... Once the mismatch between institutions and problems comes to be perceived in a very general way, we come to realise that we need to raise the level of generality at which we engage in public learning.
>
> (p. 183)

> Although the institutional map of society is always in some degree mismatched with the problems thought worth solving, the loss of the stable state makes this state of mismatch universal and endemic.
>
> In response, learning systems have begun to develop in diverse forms – business systems and constellation firms, new ways of forming and implementing policy in government, and some of the dominant social movements of our time. All these share two major themses: a shift upward in the level of generality at which organisations define themselves, and a shift from centre–periphery to network modes of growth and diffusion.
>
> (p. 190)

Yet if Schön develops a political theory based upon his systems framework it fails to provide the conditions which his learning theory requires. While his critical analysis of systems theory substitutes responsive networks for traditional hierarchies, his theory of governance remains locked in a top-down paternalism. Only an understanding of the role of democratic politics can provide answers to the purposes and conditions for the learning society he desires. The way societies learn about themselves, and the process by which they transform themselves, is through politics, and the essence of politics is learning through public deliberation, which is the characteristic of effective learning systems.

At the heart of the changes confronting the contemporary world are different and often conflicting conceptions about the values which should shape society. Learning to understand and reconcile those differences, so that communities with ostensibly incommensurable values can share the same social and institutional space, is the task of politics. A society with the capacity to learn about itself depends upon the quality of political institutions to enable that learning. A learning society can only grow out of a learning democracy. The *polis*, as Aristotle understood, is the only arena in which contending claims and interests can be deliberated, transcended and aggregated in collective decision. A society can only remake itself when the different groups within it decide they can act together, and such collective action depends upon reaching a shared understanding about the purposes of change and the conditions which will enable all to develop and realize their capacities.

The central vehicle for this learning democracy lies in the process of reasoning in public discourse. Diverse interests engage in mutual learning when they reason with each other in order to reach shared understanding and agreement. Habermas's (1984) concept of 'communicative rationality' is an explicit project to rescue this concept of uncoerced public reason. The more the patterns of life are based upon conscious argued-out adducement of reasons, the greater the possibility of establishing an accountable dialogue between different views, making politics a particularly practical activity of speaking, listening and compromising. The public sphere thus extends the scope of reasoned learning.

The open public discourse which is politics also forms and defines 'a public' as a political community. The idea of a public formed by and promoting critical political discourse has been central to a number of twentieth-century writers who believe that such a 'public' is now seriously at risk. Etzioni (1968) argued that only an active self-critical public can become the knowledgeable society able to cope with change. For C. Wright Mills (1959), publics create a space conducive to the free ebb and flow of discussion, a place where authority is grounded in discussion, where people have an effective voice in the making of those decisions which vitally affect them, where the power to make those decisions is publicly legitimated and where those who exercise power are publicly accountable. The process of reasoning in public discourse helps to discover common ends and thus to transform different groups into sharing a sense of community, to become a public.

The precursors of this idea of democratic learning, which can achieve the transvaluation of values that Hutchins (1970, p. 135) aspires to see realized in the learning society, were Eduard Lindemann (Brookfield, 1987) and John Dewey (1915). Lindemann, like Mills, believed that self-awareness for individuals could only be achieved through a democracy, which involved participating actively in the decision-making and collective action within the community. Understanding oneself and others could only be achieved through the collaborative endeavour to create the communities in which we are to live. Democracy was a lived process of trying to bring about personal or social change. The task of education was to help adults as well as the young to develop the attitudes of mind – for example, reflection, tolerance, imagination, sympathy and respect – as well as the capabilities to take part in the democratic process.

Dewey's philosophy of experience dissolved the boundaries between epistemology and democracy, thought and action, knowing and doing. The process of knowing, he argued, does not consist in grasping the truth of something from the outside looking in; rather, something can only be known by taking part in events and making sense of the experiences they offer through acting in them. Philosophy, no less than democracy, is practical and experimental. Reflection and action must explore pragmagtically what is valid. Thus the key to good science and politics is a way of life that fosters reflective deliberation amongst citizens.

For Dewey (1915, 1935) only a democratic public fosters the dialogue necessary for its members to interact freely with, and learn from, one another. Participating in a common life enables individuals to contribute to shared purposes in a way that allows them to realize their own distinctive capacities. Democracy has the unique potential to reconcile individual and collective purpose. The significance of democracy for Dewey is not that it is the instrument for weighing everyone's preferences equally, but that it provides a 'form of social organisation, extending to all the areas and ways of living,' in which the full powers of individuals can be 'fed, sustained and directed' (1935, p. 35). It lies with education to prepare citizens with the capabilities to take part in this learning democracy, 'producing the habits of mind and character, the intellectual and moral patterns' that are appropriate to citizens to develop shared responsibility for the quality of public life (1935, p. 44).

## WITHIN THE LEARNING SOCIETY: ORGANIZATIONS AND CITIES

A learning society requires public learning as the necessary condition for its growth and development. The public domain provides the arena for public learning in many settings, and distinctive literatures have grown around the companion literatures of 'learning organizations' and 'learning cities'. A learning society can only be achieved if its component parts learn to learn.

### The learning organization

Dewey's (1958) theory of learning expressed a whole philosophy of being in the world: through active experience we come to understand the world and thus to change it. Knowledge only lives and has meaning through action. Once the working of a particular system has been revealed, it then becomes amenable to change; it is the experience of change that provides the catalyst to learning. This 'action learning' perspective has been applied to modern organizations by Revans

(1982) and Handy (1989) for whom 'a theory of learning is also a theory of changing'. Learning implies understanding that will lead into action, and that ongoing practice will be transformed as a result.

The significance of these learning processes for organizations as well as for individuals, and the conditions which enable learning, have become a distinctive tradition of study. The nature of the learning organization has been explored in different sectors: in health (Attwood and Beer, 1988; Harrow and Willcocks, 1990, 1992); in planning (Friedmann, 1987); in education (Holly and Southworth, 1989; Nixon *et al.*, 1996); in business (Lessem, 1993; Pedler *et al.*, 1991) and in the public sphere (Ranson and Stewart, 1994). A distinctive framework for analysing the learning organization has become influential in this literature.

*Loops of learning*

In 1978, Argyris and Schön (see Argyris and Schön, 1993) introduced an important distinction between levels of complexity in processes of learning: single- and double-loop learning. In single-loop learning a simple change is made to an activity which is not working effectively. For example, within an incremental budgeting system overspend could be corrected by reducing the level of increment to each service. Double-loop learning questions the underlying assumptions which inform the activities, in this case perhaps reviewing the principles on which budgets are constructed.

> Single-loop learning is like a thermostat that learns when it is too hot or too cold and turns the heat on or off. The thermostat can perform this task because it can receive information (the temparature of the room) and take corrective action. Double-loop learning occurs when error is detected and corrected in ways that involve modification of an organisation's underlying norms, policies and objectives.
>
> (Argyris and Schön, 1978, p. 34)

Certain problems cannot be resolved without reflecting back on the very principles which inform practice and which are usually taken for granted. Argyris and Schön believe that whereas most organizations do quite well at the simpler learning, they have many difficulties in the more complex double-loop learning. This is because many organizations are predisposed to inhibit the processes of reflection which bring into question fundamental objectives and beliefs.

*The conditions for learning*

Different kinds of learning, Argyris and Schön argue, require different conditions. Simple problems can be resolved by forms of inquiry which enable new information to come to the surface, or connections to be made within an activity where they had not hiterto been appreciated, but recognition of their interdependence is essential for effective action to proceed. In these inquiries certain processes are vital for success: the value placed upon questioning to elucidate information;

clarity of ideas; testing ideas against the evidence; and building up patterns or trends of activity. It is helpful to perceive these learning processes as a cycle (Handy, 1989; Revans, 1982; Kolb, 1973, 1984).

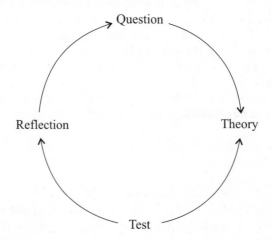

**Figure 1.1**   *The learning cycle*

Learning begins with curiosity about a particular problem or puzzle which issues in questions to be answered. These we describe as triggers for learning. The inquiry stimulated by such triggers leads us to form ideas or conjectures or 'theories' about what causes the problem, and then to test these ideas. Deliberation on the experience can illuminate the underlying processes and produce learning which changes the way we arrange an activity. It might even change the way we think about the activity or lead us to new activities.

The source of some problems, however, lies in the differences of perspective or belief which individuals or groups within an organization may have and which may prevent them reaching agreement about what counts as evidence or a relevant question. Failure of communication prevents understanding: individuals cannot understand one another because they do not grasp the meaning and significance of the others' concepts. The solution depends upon the willingness of groups to listen to opposing interpretations and reach agreement about a new framework of values and assumptions. For many organizations, however, the reality of conflicting perspectives may not be recognized or may be actively suppressed. Organizations may need to develop skills in conflict management. The task is to create the conditions for double-loop learning:

> The consequence of learning should be an emphasis on double-loop learning, by means of which individuals confront the basic assumptions behind the present views of others and invite confrontation of their own basic assumptions, and by which underlying hypotheses are tested publicly and are made disconfirmable, not self-sealing ... Where individuals function as agents of organisational learning, the consequences ... should be an enhancement of the conditions for *organisational* double-

loop learning, where assumptions and norms central to organisational theory-in-use are surfaced . . . publicly confronted, tested and restructured.

(Argyris and Schön, 1978, p. 139)

In the right conditions, people can react in different ways, so that they are more amenable to the difficult processes of questioning their own beliefs and become more receptive to the value of others' beliefs; if double-loop learning is to occur, people need to:

- feel less defensive
- feel free to take risks
- search for their own individual inconsistencies and encourage the others to confront them
- be able to state their views in ways that are disconfirmable
- believe that public testing would not be harmful.

The conditions that are most appropriate to supporting double-loop learning are those which reinforce open discussion in seach of agreement. Such a context mirrors within the organization Habermas's (1984) conditions for communicative rationality, in which speakers in public strive to make claims which are true, correct and sincere. When committed to these principles, speakers are oriented to correct mistaken perceptions and to synthesize perspectives when rationally possible:

> The correction of . . . errors requires the conditions of the good dialectic, which begins with the development of a map that provides a different perspective on the problem (e.g. a different set of governing values or norms). The opposition of ideas and persons then makes it possible to invent responses that approximate the organisation's espoused theory.

(p. 143)

For organizations, the struggles between groups present dilemmas but also opportunities which can lead to double-loop learning; they can enable an organization to unify around shared purposes. However, the dialectic which prepares for any such synthesis of perspectives may not be an easy process:

> [The good dialectic] is not a matter of smoothness of operation or elimination of error. On the contrary, its goodness is inherent in the ways in which error is continually interpreted and corrected, incompatibility and incongruity are continually engaged, and conflict is continually confronted and resolved . . . the dialectical process focuses attention on incompatibility of norms and objectives which are not resolvable by a search for the most effective means. For norms set the criteria by which effectiveness may be judged.

(p. 146)

## Learning to learn

The most effective process of learning forms a third stage of complexity: learning how to learn. Organizations experiencing change need a general predisposition to learn if they are to succeed. Bateson (1972) has called this 'deutero-learning'. Individuals become creative at learning about how they have been learning: they reflect on and analyse their previous styles of learning or failing to learn. They clarify what enabled or blocked their learning so that they can take remedial action and develop new strategies for learning. In organizations, Argyris and Schön (1978, p. 144) propose that the new strategies become encoded in mental maps that reshape organizational practice: 'learning continually questions the status quo, the theories in use people have to learn how to learn, discover how to discover, invent, generalise, learn how to establish a good dialectic'. The learning organization becomes self-aware about the cycles of learning and the conditions for learning. It becomes proficient at asking questions, developing ideas, testing them and reflecting on practice.

Awareness of the cycles of learning encourages participants to explore continually the conditions of learning, why it is that individuals and groups are open to new ideas and new ways of thinking which keep them at the front edge of change. Learning pushes back the boundaries of inquiry about the conditions which support and constrain change, laying bare the deep structures of social action. The individual explores the constraints and opportunities of the organizational context in which she works, while the organization similarly questions the limits of the wider society in which it is located. Learning continually extends the cycle of learning.

In this way the learning process explores the structures of action: the values which underlie the perspectives, the forms of interaction and the nature and distribution of power that drive action. Learning about these systems of action within organizations is best nurtured within 'action learning sets' that enable the participants, through collaborative working and reflection, to open out to, and accommodate, the value in each perspective and to develop the predisposition to change practice.

**The learning city**

The capacity for learning is the capacity for dialectic in changing practice. This is as true of cities as of organizations, and a number of them are striving to develop themselves as 'learning cities', emphasizing how citizens can learn by actively participating in creating the 'wealth' of the communities in which they live and work. Understanding of the importance of the city is reflected in the increasing number of attempts to capture its significance: the 'competitive city' (Duffy, 1995), the informational city (Castells, 1989; Webster, 1995), the 'health city' (Ashton, 1992).

In education, the interpretation given to learning cities typically focuses upon developing the opportunities for individuals to participate in education and training throughout their lives. The European Educating Cities Movement has encouraged cities to develop a culture of lifelong learning, believing that 'an educating city does not segregate the generations' (Barcelona, 1990, 1991). The movement argues that the city, and the strategies it adopts, can make a difference to lifelong learning. There are several reasons for this:

- People relate their participation in learning activities to their immediate environment. From Pittsburgh, where the collapse of the steel industry created a common need for retraining, to Vienna, where learning is related to a history of high culture and discussion, the city offers a powerful potential focus for the development of a lifelong learning culture which is hard to achieve through national initiatives alone.
- The importance of creating coherence among a very large number of actors now involved in the planning and delivery of education and training. Beyond initial schooling there is no single 'system' conveniently managed by a centralized public structure. Here, again the city can be a useful focus, as illustrated by the 'Further Education council' developed in Edmonton, which acts as co-ordinator and policy forum for the many providers of adult learning.
- The community-based nature of much adult learning. This makes it possible to build learning elements into city-led community activity – from health awareness campaigns to support for small enterprises. Conversely, learning in a city can be seen as a means of community action. In Kakegawa, Japan lifelong learning has been a way of involving citizens in the revitalisation of their city.

(CERI/OECD, 1993, p. 9)

In Britain a number of cities have formed themselves into a 'learning cities' movement. One of them, Birmingham, has been enjoying a renaissance as a result of the strategies which have been developed in the city. The Chief Education Officer, Professor Tim Brighouse, has been a particular source of inspiration. He recognizes the urgency of creating highly educated citizens who are fitted for the new age of information technology. The challenge for learning cities is 'to transform attitudes towards and achievement from education'. 'How do you help a population, old and young alike, which is used to seeing school as "a once and for all" activity, not especially important, to acquire the habits not merely of taking school seriously but of sustaining life-long habits of learning' (Brighouse, 1996, p. 3). The prospect of failure in this agenda, it is argued, does not bear contemplation if cities turn into divided enclaves of those who are educated and those who are deprived of learning. The task, Brighouse advocates, is to promote networks of learning across the city:

Ideally in a 'learning city' there would be readily available and accessible local learning networks for all people of all ages. These networks or partnerships would involve providers – whether in colleges, schools, libraries, business shops or local amenities – in facilitating access to learning resources for all the population so that the advantages of information technology are available irrespective of wealth.

(Brighouse, 1996, p. 3)

In Birmingham strategies have worked to create such partnerships. The Training and Enterprise Council, Education Business Partnership, the Chamber of Commerce, employers' organizations and particular businesses, along with the LEA, have all played a vital role in working towards local economic and social regeneration by providing stimulating education and training opportunities. A Learning

City has a thriving learning culture which builds organic links to wealth development and economic innovation. These strategies of partnership are strongly promoted by the European Learning Cities movement:

- the development of city-wide coalitions coordinating all relevant actors in both public and private sectors;
- the coordination of work-oriented and general/leisure-oriented education and training, in a way that allows all citizens easily to relate their development as individuals to their development as workers;
- the coordination of learning at different stages, for example by encouraging different generations to learn together and to learn from each other;
- the use of local media both as teaching tools in themselves and to raise awareness of learning opportunities;
- the promotion of the learning city, in which communities attempt to learn collectively as a means of changing their own futures.

(CERI/OECD, 1993, p. 10)

The importance of this last point has been brought out brilliantly by Michael Piore (1995) in a study of the significance of dialogue for local development: double-loop learning is the key to economic regeneration. The tradition of economic development has been driven by the logic of mass production – growth was perceived to depend upon highly specialized resources, dedicated capital equipment and narrowly trained semi-skilled workers. The nation–state and the large corporation were the central change agents, but now, in the context of globalization, their roles change. Subnational communities become more dependent on their own initiative and this requires them to become clear about who they are and how their traditions and resources can be developed for work markets:

> In the new environment, development is about the community finding a place for itself in world markets and thinking about how to turn its particular cultural heritage into an asset in that endeavour. It is no longer a question simply of negotiating among local interests to obtain resources . . . it is more a question of purposeful reflection and debate within the local community.

(Piore, 1995, p. 80)

The community needs to deliberate upon both the nature of the community itself and the changing form of the outside world in which it must live. In one example, small teams of community leaders drawn from different economic and social groups in the city were sent overseas to visit areas which might serve as models for economic regeneration. Piore (1995, p. 81) describes how these visits served a number of purposes, including enlarging the vision of team members and providing materials to catalyse the debate at home. For him, however, the most significant benefit is that

> the experience of travelling together in a foreign environment helps people from different, often antagonistic segments of the local community to get to know each other: it breaks down the barriers among them and provides a common set of experiences and shared knowledge base upon which to build a more cooperative relationship.

Other examples reinforce the notion of groups, businesses and communities 'learning to support each other' and develop the 'capacity for cooperation'. The role of government in this new world is 'to catalyse that learning process', to enable the creation of a denser network of collaborative relationships.

In Britain some urban regeneration projects provide illustrations of Piore's theme of dialogue as central to learning for community development. Initiatives include the setting up of local forums, or citizen panels, to promote effective dialogue between different interest groups, as well as between the community and agency or local economic developers, about the key local issues of poverty, unemployment and social exclusion. Planning partnerships are formed, or coalitions built, between local developers, voluntary associations and local communities to support credit unions, access courses, or create new jobs, because there is recognition that economic access of excluded groups (for example, the young black unemployed, or single mothers) to training and jobs develops the social and economic wealth of the community. The social capacity (and thus wealth) of disadvantaged communities has also been enhanced through organized action by local 'user groups' seeking to identify gaps in services that are vital to support women if they are to contribute to the labour market or take up learning opportunities, as well as support young children.

The unfolding local discourse acts, Piore argues, to clarify or recreate a local identity which grows naturally out of the history of the local community and 'the materials through which its people have traditionally expressed themselves', and serves as 'the fulcrum for a development strategy, fostering internal coherence and giving it direction in the world market place'.

Network organizations, which depend for their effectiveness not upon autonomous economic actors but upon the interaction of individuals embedded in their social context, provide for Piore a deeper vision of a progressive democracy. Individuals realize themselves in their social settings, through interaction with other people. The formation of the identity of the individual and of the community grow out of the same processes: 'the preeminently human capacity from this point of view is speech, the essential human creation is language, and the proto-typical human acitivity is *conversation*' (p. 84). Only through these democratic conversations which inform local networks can our society hope to address the problems of social and economic exclusion caused by the new global market forces.

> We do not, in fact, know how to integrate excluded groups ... unless it be to draw their members into the 'conversations' through which network organisations emerge and evolve over time. Some local development work is about orchestrating these conversations within the community. It provides an opportunity to experiment with modes of incorporating the economically excluded, an opportunity which is not offered in other forms of network organisation.
>
> (Piore, 1995, p. 87)

In this analysis of the learning city we end up at the same point as in the discussion of learning organizations and learning societies – with an understanding that effective learning and its conditions rest upon the quality of democratic dialogue to realize the identities of individuals and communities alike. There is a need to articulate the theory which underlies the different expressions of learning.

## TOWARDS A THEORY OF LEARNING

Learning is a process of discovery that generates new understandings about ourselves and the world around us. But is that an adequate account of learning? What does it mean to learn? Is the experience of learning best characterized as an event, or as a process which takes place over time? Where and when does learning most effectively take place? What are the outcomes and effects of learning? What conditions best support its unfolding? These are some of the questions that we need to resolve if we are to gain an understanding of the purposes and conditions of learning that can enhance the education of young people in some of the most disadvantaged contexts in the country.

Learning provides a sense of discovery. Something new enters our experience through learning and alters what we know or can do. When we learn something about the effect of soil erosion or the puncturing of the ozone layer upon the environment, knowledge is enlarged. When we learn to ride a bicycle, or use a word processor, for the first time, the skills we develop expand our capacity to engage with the world around us. When introduced to a new concept of 'radiation' in physics or of 'culture' in anthropology, our understanding of the world is enhanced, and if prejudiced attitudes to particular groups or cultures can be dissolved then appreciation of others is thereby enriched.

### The layers of learning for agency and capacity

Learning proceeds through different layers: from developing understanding of discrete events or pieces of knowledge to becoming aware of ourselves as persons and then, more significantly, of our growing capacity to shape, by ourselves and with others, the world around us.

Discovering new knowledge, concepts, skills or attitudes, however, reflects different layers of learning. A new piece of factual information may become an additional increment in my accumulating knowledge of George Eliot's novels, or a new skill may enhance profiles of world processing, but these are specific events. We associate learning with the deeper processes of influence upon our *understanding*. Learning helps us to discover why things are as they are and how they might become different. Such understanding grows from processes of reflection that reveal the connections between things which had previously been unrecognized or opaque to us. To understand why is more significant than to know what. To learn how to explain things or events is to be able to grasp the principles which underlie and make sense of their working, and thus to enable us to recognize their occurrence on some future occasion even though the surface characteristics may appear to be different.

To distinguish between knowledge and understanding deepens our grasp of the layering of learning; but the puzzles which learning resolves through understanding can, of course, vary enormously in their scope and significance. Making sense of the puzzling noise in the immersion system may resolve an irritating intrusion upon the peace of the household. However, understanding a little more clearly the limits and possibilities of ourselves as persons, for example, is a different order of learning. Plumbing the depths of the self and its relationship to others can alter the shape of a character and thus the reach of its unfolding over time. Learning may at times be experienced as a specific event; yet it can, by changing how we think about and know ourselves and others, alter our horizons and thus our sense of place.

Learning to *understand ourselves as persons* means recognizing the complex interdependence of qualities which express what is distinctive about ourselves: not just our feelings, imagination, practical or social skills and cognitive powers, but their necessary relationships. The quality of our thinking necessarily reflects our emotional maturity as well as our abstract cerebral powers (Nussbaum, 1990). Acknowledging that persons are beings, rather than just the mental mechanisms of Descartes' *cogito ergo sum*, has important implications for an education service which is still overly preoccupied with differentiating, ranking and selecting cognitive intelligence.

The work of Gardner (1984, 1991) and of Hargreaves (1984) has begun to influence our ways of thinking about the capacities of people, encouraging recognition of the multi-dimensional quality of human intelligence. Rather than reducing an individual's potential to a single score on an IQ test, Gardner has reinforced our understanding of the complexity of ability, including linguistic, musical and logical/mathematical capacities, as well as spatial and bodily intelligences, and the ability to arrive at an emotional and mental sense of self and other people. An education which does not address all the intelligences is a barren experience as, historically, too much of our education has been. The comprehensiveness of such an approach would also be revealed by recognizing the role of agency in learning. The distinctiveness of the person lies in the enacting of the qualities which define the whole.

Learning leads into action and grows out of the experience which action enables: it creates the capacity for *self-creation*. Understanding only lives and has meaning through our agency in the world. For Dewey (1958) this notion of learning expresses a philosophy of being in the world; through active experience we come to understand the world and to change it. Thus the deeper significance of learning lies, through its forming of our powers and capacities, in our unfolding agency. The purpose and outcome of active learning may be a particular 'competence' which alters our capacity to intervene in experience; but the central purpose of learning is to enable such skills to develop our distinctive agency as human beings. Learning is becoming. It is an unfolding through which we learn not only what makes us unique – what individuates us – but how we can learn to make that distinctive agency work in the world. Learning involves becoming aware of our difference but also, significantly, how to enact its distinctiveness.

Learning to develop the agency of the person is inescapably a temporal process: it takes time. We need to recover the Aristotelian conception of what it is to develop as a person over the whole of a life: the conception of life as it can be led (MacIntyre, 1981). This conception has a number of constituent elements: first, perceiving the life as a whole and the self as developing over a lifetime; second, the idea of life as a quest to discover the identity which defines the self; third, seeing the unity of a life as consisting in the quest for value, each person seeking to reach beyond the self to create something which is valued; fourth, to perfect a life which is inescapably a struggle, an experience of failure as well as success, in the quest to realize what is excellent.

There is no solitary learning: we can only create our worlds together. The unfolding agency of the self always grows out of the interaction with others. It is *inescapably a social creation*. We can only develop as persons with and through others; the conception of the self presupposes an understanding of what we are to become and this always unfolds through our relationship with others; the conditions in which the self develops and flourishes are social and political. The self can only find its identity in and through others and in membership of communities. The possibility of shared understanding requires individuals not only to value others but to create the communities in which mutuality, and thus the conditions for learning, can flourish. The telos of learning is to learn to make the communities without which individuals cannot grow and develop.

We need to recover what the Athenians understood, that human development requires recognizing the duality of values that is central to human development: a person is also a citizen, whose responsibility to contribute to the well-being of the whole is matched by the obligation of the whole polity to acknowledge the freedom of its members. Autonomy depends upon the quality of cooperative interdependence that values the difference of others. The personal exercise of a virtue cannot be separated from the same persons making a world which recognizes such values.

**The bases of learning**

To learn, then, is to develop understandings which lead into, and grow out of, action; to discover a sense of agency that enables us, not only to define and make ourselves, but to do so by actively participating in the creation of a world in which, inescapably, we live together. But what are the bases of such learning? What are the conditions and modes that allow us to enter upon this journey of learning and that sustain us on our way? In order to address these questions we shall develop our analysis of learning by examining its individual, interpersonal and public dimensions.

The examined life is the key mechanism of learning to learn, and thus the key to entering the deeper layers of learning about the nature of agency. Such learning develops as *practical reason*, which involves: deliberation upon experience to develop understanding of the situation or of the other person; judgement to determine the appropriate ends and course of action (which presupposes a community based upon sensitivity and tact); and learning through action to realize the good in practice.

Reasoning and testing ideas in this way reveals the indispensable mutuality or sociability of learning. It is not just that any competence is learnt with and through others, but that the subjectivities which define what we become as persons and therefore our agency are social creations. For learning to develop agency presupposes conceptions of what it is to be a person and thus understandings of what the self is to become over time and in relation to others. The understandings – of our sense of place and our promise – we all acquire socially through the mutuality of learning. By defining how the self is to unfold, the process also defines the nature and the reach of the motivation to learn.

Learning depends upon motivation and the empowering of internal rewards. Learning is inescapably a conscious activity. We may believe that we have unwittingly acquired some new knowledge, but it is not understood until we have exercised reflective energy upon it and made it our own. While some understanding may come easily, learning always involves some element of struggle to make sense of something of which we have been unaware. In the meaning we are giving to it – to become a person with a distinctive agency in the world – learning is never accomplished without struggle.

Learning in this view always takes effort and time – and thus motivation. Individuals cannot learn without the motivation to do so, without having the sense that it has a purpose, and thus wanting to take responsibility for achieving the ends involved in the learning process. The motivation to learn is internal to the purpose of learning in realizing the distinctive qualities of the self as agent. The rewards of learning are intrinsic to the process of enhancing personal capacities to standards of excellence. Extrinsic rewards – of money, power, status and prestige – are contingent and subordinate, and largely incompatible with the good of the unfolding self (MacIntyre, 1981). This implies something very different from 'lifelong education or training' defined simply as access to institutions. Rather, it suggests a belief that an individual is to develop comprehensively throughout her or his lifetime, and that this development should be supported and accorded value.

The purposive nature of learning presupposes a strong sense of *identity* in the learner. The purposes which grow out of learning imply a sense of self and personhood and thus the confidence to engage in the struggle of learning to create the values of the unfolding life. The identity we develop, however, and the motivation we have to unfold it are always acquired with and through others. Limited conceptions of ourselves, and limited expectation from others, seriously limit the motivation to learn.

The conditions for the unfolding self are thus social and political, depending upon *interpersonal civitas*: my space requires your recognition and your capacities demand my support (and vice versa). This emphasis recalls Aristotle's celebration of civic friendship – of sharing a life in common – as being the only possible route for creating and sustaining life in the city. Such values, arguably, are now only to be found within that literature which emphasizes an ethic of caring and responsibility in the family and community and acknowledges the dissolution of the public as a separate (male) sphere (see Gilligan, 1986; Okin, 1991; Pateman, 1987). It is only in the context of such understanding and support that mutual identities can be formed and the distinctive qualities of each person can be nurtured and asserted with confidence. Reflective interdependence remains the condition for autonomy and mutuality in learning.

Historically conditioned prejudices about capacity, reinforced by institutionalized discrimination, set the present limits of learning. The key to the transformation of prejudice lies in what Gadamer (1975) calls 'the dialogic character of understanding': through genuine conversation the participants are led beyond their initial positions, to take account of others and move towards a richer, more comprehensive view, a 'fusion of horizons', a shared understanding of what is true or valid. Discourse can lead to the *valuing of difference*. From this perspective, the possibility of mutuality in support of personal development depends on generating interpretive understanding; that is, on hermeneutic skills which can create the conditions for learning in society, in relationships within the family and the community and at work. Conversation lies at the heart of learning: learners are listeners as well as speakers, partakers of a discourse that is itself an act of social creation.

A presupposition of that discourse is *openness*: we have to learn to be open to difference, to allow our prejudgements to be challenged; in so doing we learn how to amend our assumptions, and develop an enriched understanding of others. It is precisely in confronting other beliefs and presuppositions that we are led to see the inadequacies of our own and so transcend them. Rationality, in this perspective, is the willingness to admit the existence of better options and to be aware that one's knowledge is always open to refutation or modification from the vantage point of a different perspective. For Gadamer, the concept of *bildung* describes the process through which individuals and communities enter a more and more broadly defined community; they learn through dialogue to take a wider, more differentiated view, and thus acquire sensitivity, subtlety and capacity for judgement.

Reason emerges through dialogue with others, through which we learn not necessarily 'facts' but rather a capacity for new ways of thinking, speaking and acting. It is Habermas (1984) who articulates the conditions for such communicative rationality as being 'ideal speech contexts' in which the participants feel able to speak freely, truly and sincerely. The conditions for this depend upon the creation of a more strenuous moral order. The values of learning, as much as the values which provide the conditions for learning (according dignity and respecting capacity), are moral values that express a set of virtues required of the self but also of others in relationship with the self. The values of caring and responsibility, upon which the confidence to learn ultimately depends, derive their influence from the authority of an underlying moral and social order. The civic virtues, as MacIntyre (1981) analyses them, establish standards against which individuals can evaluate their actions (as well as their longer 'quest'). Yet particular virtues derive meaning and force from their location within an overall moral framework (what MacIntyre calls a 'tradition'); it is the standards accepted by the moral community which provide the values by which each person is enabled to develop.

A moral order is a public creation and requires to be lived and recreated by all members of the community. Each person depends upon the quality of the moral order for the quality of her or his personal development; the vitality of that order depends, in turn, upon the vitality of the public life of the community. For the Athenian, the virtuous person and the good citizen were the same because the goods which informed a life were public virtues. The point of this historical reference is not to turn the clock back, but to emphasize that a moral order has authority only insofar as it involves induction into an open order rather than socialization into a closed tradition. The development of a moral community has to be a creative and collaborative process of agreeing the values of learning which are to guide and sustain life in the community.

## *The learning democracy*

We learn, in time, to recreate the public ('political') sphere which underwrites any order of values because it creates those agreements which enable individuals and their relationships to grow and develop. Such agreements constitute the foundations. Who is to be a member and what are the defining qualities? What are to be their rights and obligations? What are to be the rules for determining the distribution of status and the opportunity to develop capacities? Decisions about such matters have implications for every individual, determining the bases of identity and well-being. We fail at our peril to learn that these constitutive agreements only work *for* all if they are created *by* all. Learning to make the public world is as much about learning to create the processes which sustain it as about espousing the substantive values by which it is to take shape. Questions about who is to be involved and how (and when) those involved will participate can only be resolved together.

The reform of the political process within the public domain, Ranson and Stewart (1994) argued, is a fundamental condition for the learning society. It is only by elaborating democracy so as to allow citizens to participate, through fair rules of discourse, that they can all articulate and gain recognition for the needs and aspirations which they believe to define what they wish for themselves and the communities in which they live.

Discourse, free of distorted power (some groups imposing their will on others), enables a fair politics, through which different values and interests can be heard and negotiated. A just polity will empower different citizens (for example, women or the minority communities, or the disabled) whose voices have often not been heard until their experience is so unfair or painful that they have to shout; even then they have typically not been listened to (Lukes, 1974; Saunders, 1979). An open, involving public domain will encourage learning, a listening to and taking account of others so that public policies and the distribution of resources are made more responsive than in the past to significant differences that enrich rather than diminish society (Phillips, 1991, 1993). In this way citizens have an equal opportunity to constitute the conditions for living a life in which they can flourish because their identity is acknowledged, their values understood and their welfare sustained.

The predicaments of the time are those which can only be faced by communities in common. Those anxieties which individuals experience separately about the restructuring of work, the decay of the environment, or the fragmentation of the communities in which they live, can only be faced together with and through public institutions that encourage shared understanding of these issues and enable the appropriate action on behalf of the whole community. The urgent task of the present, as Dunn (1992) has argued, 'is to learn how to act together more effectively'.

If this task is to be realized and the eroded roots of public consent are to be restored, then a polity is needed for our time which expresses a new vision of the public domain, in which the public are conceived neither as passive clients, nor as competing consumers, but as citizens encouraged to contribute to and take a shared responsibility for the development of their society – a learning society which grasps the value of opening itself to reflective understanding of the diversity of culture within as much as to the issues which press in upon it from without. The role of this democratic polity is to develop the conditions for such a learning society to unfold. Its responsibility is not to distance itself from society but to provide the conditions for citizens to flourish as active and creative members of their communities. The quality of individual capacity, as much as the quality of life for all, will depend upon our relearning the duality of publicness, that mutual dependence of individual and community. It will depend upon renewing and developing the institutions of the public domain as the condition for the learning society.

## NOTE

1. This chapter draws directly upon Ranson *et al.* (1996) and Ranson and Stewart (1994).

# *Part 1*

---

# Perspectives on the Learning Society

If our society is to meet the challenge of economic and social regeneration then it will require a renaissance in learning. The motivation to sustain this innovation will depend upon the creation of a much wider 'learning society', one that is able to renew its members' agency and capacity to make the communities in which they live and work. The literature which has developed in the 1990s to explore this notion has tended, however, to explore different aspects of the learning society: learning for the new world of work, a changing society and a new democratic citizenship.

## The new world of work

Employment is being transformed by the experience of structural change which has accelerated since the mid-1970s (Cooley, 1993; Harvey, 1989). Substitution of new information technologies, the relocation of labour-intensive industries to low-wage economies, the shift from manufacturing to services, and the intensification of international competition, have caused unemployment, the collapse of full-time youth labour (Ashton *et al.*, 1990; Roberts *et al.*, 1990) and the growth of part-time, intermittent employment which is 'feminizing' the labour market. This restructuring and cultural redefining of work presents a profound predicament; exclusion from work denies many access to their own well-being as well as to society's process of wealth creation.

Human resources, once more, become the key to regeneration and competitive advantage, yet the changes have revealed an economy trapped in what Finegold and Soskice (1988) have called 'a low-skill equilibrium', which provides young people and firms with little incentive to invest in higher skills. In this analysis companies are as culpable as government in causing a post-compulsory education and training (PCET) system that is characterized historically by inadequate levels of investment, participation and achievement, reinforced by an institutionalized fracture of academic and vocational study. PCET has reproduced chronic inequality of opportunity when economic change now demands a massive expansion in skill levels (Finegold *et al.*, 1990; Spours, 1995; Woolhouse, 1993). Public policy has sought, but failed, to address this central predicament.

The Confederation of British Industry and Sir Christopher Ball have been leading advocates of a revolution to create 'a learning nation' (CBI, 1995) and 'learning society' (Ball, 1991). The paradigm of the CBI (1989; 1995), described in Chapter 2, has become particularly influential. If employees are to become more adaptable to a greater variety of occupational tasks then, it is argued, they will need a secure foundation of 'core' or general knowledge and skills that will allow them to transfer flexibly to different work contexts. A skills passport is needed to recognize individuals' lifetime learning, updating and accumulation of competence, and thus the capacity to progress to more complex modes of work. It is the responsibility of employers to sustain this continuing education and training by becoming 'learning businesses'. The task for Government is to 'fund all foundation learning, deal with market failure and foster lifetime learning for all'.

In 1990 Sir Christopher Ball, Fellow in Continuing Education of the Royal Society for the Encouragement of Arts, Manufactures and Commerce, launched a programme of study on 'the learning society – one in which everyone participated in education and training throughout their life. It would support them as citizens in their employment and their leisure. A learning society would also make provison to match these enhanced aspirations. It requires the cooperation, effort and enterprise of many agencies and all parts of society' (Ball, 1990, p. 6).

Following a project on *Widening Access to Higher Education, More Means Different*, the RSA began a complementary study of post-compulsory education. Chapter 3 is a section of an interim report of this project on the role of PCET. The central theme of this report is that *learning pays* – for individuals, companies and the nation – and that 'there is an urgent need to improve participation in, and the quality of, PCET in this country'. The aim of the study was to identify barriers to participation and to indicate the key areas in which action could be taken, in order that increasing numbers of young and mature people would seek PCET for themselves; colleges and other providers would offer susbstantially more places on appropriate and enabling courses; rates of participation in PCET at ages 16, 18 and for mature adults would rise; levels of achievement at 18, 21 and for mature adults would improve; and individuals, employers, educators and policy-makers would have satisfactory measures of success. Targets were set.

Patrick Ainley, in Chapter 4, offers a radical critique of 'official' versions (the CBI and the Conservative government) while retaining a refined understanding of the learning society. The claim to increase the skills of the workforce to compete in global markets seems to be undermined by the growth of insecure, intermittent and semi-skilled employment. A real learning society, Ainley argues, requires the rigour of systems theory. Closed, mechanical systems, which are locked into repeated and fixed cycles, are inappropriate to human communities. Economic systems of traditional commodity production can have these rigid features. However, if the diversity of human needs is to be supported then open systems are essential for survival, because they are responsive to complex shifts in information from the changing environment as well as to collective purpose.

## A new society

The real learning society is an information society (cf. Cooley, 1993) that eschews limited instrumentalities of vocational skill formation and accommodates the most general and richest knowledge about the changing world. A social system which is open to the widest exchange of information will be a democratic system and one which harnesses the new technologies to communicating knowledge and sustaining an informed democracy. Participation in the information society will ensure that education and training are responsive and will cultivate the broadest variety of social, cultural and political, as well as economic skills.

Other writers further develop Ainley's critique of a narrow conception of the learning society. The dominant agenda of developing flexible transferable skills for the labour market presents too limited a grasp of the paradigm shift in skills and learning required for social and economic regeneration. A much more enriched conception of work and wealth creation is needed (Giddens, 1994a, b; Offe, 1996). Not only does 'social wealth' (for example, preventative community health care, or environmental repair) add to the quality of life; it clearly adds economic value as well as saving public expenditure. Furthermore, rethinking the nature of work cannot be separated from the social and cultural relations (between the sexes, races and generations) which define who works and thus the social conditions of economic growth. In this analysis, public policy has had too impoverished a conception not only of work, but of the personal capabilities and powers needed (Moore, 1990; Spours and Young, 1990); the institutional capacity required to support the learning of new capacities (Bennett *et al.*, 1994); and the participation needed to discuss and legitimate the cultural reconstruction of wealth and work (Held, 1993; Phillips, 1991; 1993; 1995). Understanding of a wider learning society is needed.

In Chapter 5 Hendrik van der Zee develops a comprehensive map of the learning society, 'a society in which learning is the whole of life and whole of life is learning.' The whole variety of modes of learning needs to be encouraged. Guided learning, not only conventional schooling but also, for example, television courses, needs to be extended and reformed, while self-education – learning to learn – becomes a foundation of the learning society – learning how to learn and taking responsibility for learning.

> The values to which the notion of a learning society appeals will indeed have to be embodied in the various situations in which people can learn. This is precisely the strength of the chosen concept; it enables us to gather a variety of approaches and social initiatives together at a higher level of abstraction, beyond immediate self-interests and parochialism.

The reforms promoted by the National Commission on Education in its reports (NCE 1993a, 1996) and in its briefings (1993b) have been premised on the idea of a learning society. The briefing by Chris Hayes, Nickie Fonda and Josh Hillman, in Chapter 6, presents a sophisticated overview of the companion ideas in the learning society. It sees learning not only as a matter for individuals but also as a key process for facilitating the transformation of today's society into a profoundly different kind of society in the future.

## A new polity

For individuals, a foundation of compulsory learning is an essential prerequisite for self-directed learning. For this reason, it is becoming increasingly necessary for compulsory learning to avoid fostering the fear of learning for oneself and to place a high premium on the skills associated with successful self-directed learning. Self-directed learning itself, however, is not enough when people want to make a difference to a collectivity, whether it be an employing organization, a local community or a club. Self-directed learning is necessary but not sufficient to produce change through action in, and by, an organization. To achieve such change, organizations must learn as entities. Learning to prepare organizations for this future state, in an era of transformation, will be one of the preoccupations of leading senior managers and academics. Yet even the learning organization is not enough when citizens sense that existing organizations are incapable of managing change for their economic and social well-being. The learning polity advances when individuals, organizations and associations learn to build trusting relationships between themselves and develop the capability to manage change. This empowers communities to act with a shared sense of purpose and to embrace the challenges of the future.

My own work on the learning society since the mid 1980s (Chapter 7) has grown out of a concern to make sense of the economic, social and political transformations of our time and to develop an argument that proposes the creation of a learning society as the constitutive condition of a new moral and political order. Change requires a renewed valuing of and commitment to learning; as the boundaries between languages and cultures begin to dissolve, as new skills and knowledge are expected within the world of work and, most significantly, as a new generation, rejecting passivity in favour of more active participation, requires to be encouraged to exercise such qualities of discourse in the public domain. A learning society, therefore, needs to celebrate the qualities of being open to new ideas, listening to as well as expressing perspectives, reflecting on and inquiring into solutions to new dilemmas, cooperating in the practice of change and critically reviewing it. The deep learning of the learning society is thus learning the capabilities for an active and democratic citizenship.

For David Clark, in Chapter 8, a learning society is about transformation: personal, organizational, societal, global. It is a community of a political kind engaged in discourse and debate about beliefs and values. A learning society as a political community, however, is also concerned with the distribution of power. Finding the means by which power can be effectively and fairly managed for the common good is never an easy task. This is all the more reason why politics and education must go hand in hand if a learning society is not to become prisoner of its own ideological convictions. It is ideological closure which threatens all our futures.

The deliberative forum is a central vehicle for a learning society as a political community. But David Clarke is cautious about placing too much significance on the neighbourhood or autonomous schools because they cannot be self-sustaining communities, nor can they claim to represent the general public. This, for him, places considerable responsibility on government, especially local government, and makes it very important that government learns how to learn. 'In this context it is likely that, in future, forums will play a major role at national and local level in the promotion of community education and the learning society.'

*Chapter 2*

# The Skills Revolution for a Learning Nation

*Confederation of British Industry*

If we are to be internationally competitive, improve our standard of living and succeed in the world, we must do much more to ensure that we are a learning nation. The skills revolution is now well underway, but we need to intensify it. We need a concerted, continuous effort. Enhancing our education and training performance is the single most important ingredient in ensuring our sucess . . .

The world is changing, and we must change with it. In the past two decades, many of the comfortable certainties of post-war life have disappeared: full employment, a job for life, traditional industries, and the State as a major provider in all our lives. Increasingly, individuals have to make it by themselves, taking ownership of their own futures. Yet ownership means little without empowerment, and empowerment requires real choices and real opportunities.

In a world of growing uncertainty, we all need a new passport and *the best passport for the twenty-first century will be a skills passport*. A skills passport which will help to secure that first job. A passport which turns a job into a career. And a passport which helps us to move successfully from one phase in life to another; from job to family to job; from temporary to full-time to part-time work; from income earning to retirement to community work.

Only a skills passport can meet the challenge of changing technology and globalization, because individuals and employers share a need for sustained levels of competence – the ability to carry out increasingly complex roles requiring adaptability, responsibility and creativity. Business competence must be built on individual competence. That starts with foundation learning, which is the basis for our lives and careers.

Lifetime learning is essential if individual competence is to be maintained – updating our skills passport by providing new visa stamps and opening up new horizons. This vision is very different from where we are today in the UK. For many, education remains a concern of the young, and then mainly of the more able. Too many of those already in the workforce – both employed and unemployed – have skill levels which are too low, or increasingly time-expired. Training and updating of skills still receive much less attention than they should, and learning as a whole tends to be static, not dynamic; a temporary passport, not one for life.

The world is very different in the newly industrializing countries. There, where real choices and opportunities are far less available, it is ironic that there is a much stronger realization that learning is the passport to a better life. Tour an Indian village and you will find children asking for pencils more often than they ask for money; taxi drivers studying half the night for another degree. Throughout Asia you will find a thirst for learning in society, supported by a government-led national learning crusade to achieve skills targets which are well beyond our own current ambitions.

The UK needs that crusade, too. We want our young people to leave foundation learning confident and well prepared to take the world of work in their stride. We need individuals who demand lifetime learning and a society which supports them by providing the right to a skills passport and assisting with its first visa stamps. This is a major challenge for everyone in the UK. We are all stakeholders in our future – employers, individuals and government – and we must not be found wanting.

## SUMMARIZING THE CHALLENGE

The UK faces a global economic challenge. Its future prosperity depends on the skills and abilities of its people. The key to success is learning. Only by learning throughout life can individuals maintain their employability, and organizations their competitive advantage.

The UK has made real but not relative progress in education and training. The government's reforms over the last decade, and the combined efforts of educationalists, employers and individuals, have helped lay the foundations for further progress. But in comparison with its competitors, the UK fares badly. The CBI's vision of a *skills passport* rests on the need that individuals and employers have in common for sustained levels of competence.

### Foundation learning: world-class outcomes

Foundation learning extends from the early years to the first degree, and is the basis on which individuals build their careers and their lives. There needs to be clarity on the *objectives* for foundation learning, and agreement on the *outcomes* that a world-class system can be expected to deliver.

The outcomes which individuals and employers require for foundation learning are values and attitudes, including regard for others and integrity, and a positive attitude to hard work and to change; basic and core skills; national qualifications, including those taken at 16 and at higher levels; and career planning.

Inadequate outcomes from foundation learning are of concern to all employers.

Expectations are too low. High expectations assume that every young person will have the maximum opportunities to achieve at every level. Higher education should continue to expand on the basis of student demand; all those qualified and able to benefit should have a place.

All learning should develop core skills. They should be integrated into all qualifications to the appropriate level and separately assessed. A Core Skills Task Force should be set up to agree and implement a strategy for core skills in all learning. The training and development of teachers, lecturers, and managers of the system of foundation learning should be reformed. The focus should be on national standards of competence.

There should be a coherent qualifications framework for national qualifications, both academic and vocational. Standards should be explicitly defined and assessment should measure learning outcomes. The framework should offer scope to all individuals to accumulate and transfer credit, and to prepare both for employment and for further learning.

The National Record of Achievement – including individual action plans – should be used by all young people, from the age of 14 at least, to help them plan their future careers. The Standards of Advice, Guidance and Counselling Lead Body should be used for the guidance of all those involved in careers guidance.

### Lifelong learning: the employers' responsibility

Employers depend vitally on the outputs from foundation learning, and have a responsibility to support it. The growth of business education links is a UK success story and must continue to be so.

Employers are responsible for the optimum development of their employees to meet business objectives. The future lies with employers that develop their organizations as 'learning businesses'. A learning business:

- uses the Investors in People Standard to ensure training and development meet good practice standards. It seeks continuous improvement thereafter.
- accepts full financial responsibility for training and developing employees to meet business objectives, regardless of the contract status of the individual.
- ensures that all managers at all levels are aware that the skills and quality of the workforce are integral to business success, and are committed to improving their skills and those of their staff.
- promotes its training effort in company reports, and communicates this widely to key stakeholders.
- sets targets for both individual employees and the organization to raise the learning effort, drawing on the sectoral, local and national targets.
- contributes to the learning of the community in which it operates.
- recognizes the longer-term needs of its employees through providing opportunities to develop their core skills, to gain NVQs/SVQs, to own an individual learning account and to achieve broader learning goals (perhaps through an employee development scheme).

The most effective way forward is to strengthen the voluntary training framework.

Better national data is essential to ensure that national policy is soundly based, and to enable companies to benchmark their performance. Government should research the national training effort rigorously and employers should assist them by communicating their training effort better. TECs and LECs should be customer-driven, that is by local employers and individuals. Government needs to encourage this by increasing the level of their discretionary funding and ensuring they meet national standards. Industry Training Organizations should develop sector targets and implement fully the revised National Council of Industry Training Organisations' code of best practice.

Management development should be reinforced. The CBI will consult on whether there is a case for developing an instrument to stimulate more effective organizational management development.

Special effort must be made to ensure smaller firms realize skills are one of the keys to growth. Here, TECs and LECs must play a vital role. A limited voucher system to enable smaller firms to purchase a training needs analysis should be devised and piloted. Employee demand for training, and group training, should be encouraged.

Urgent improvements are needed to streamline the *assessment* of NVQs/SVQs whilst *maintaining* rigour, and to simplify Awarding Body bureaucracy. The link between NVQs and GNVQs must be clarified and strengthened.

Government should ensure that there is a top quality, impartial adult careers guidance service available to all. Current provision is patchy and varies greatly in quality. Resources should be targeted at meeting the needs of those outside employment who are unable to play.

Best practice on training and development should be disseminated rapidly, possibly through a Best Practice Forum.

**Funding lifelong learning**

The three main contributors to the funding of learning are the taxpayer through Government, employers and individuals. Together, they invest nearly £80 billion each year in learning.

A contract is needed between all parties which makes clear their respective responsibilities. For example, Government should fund all foundation learning, deal with market failure, and foster lifetime learning for all. Employers should fund the training and development of all their employees, regardless of their contract status, to meet their long-term business objectives. The individual should fund all learning throughout life which is not employment-related or part of foundation learning.

The current funding system should be improved in three ways:

- Individuals need to take greater control, acting as investors in their own futures. For example, taxpayer-funded financial credits for 16–19 learning are essential. Voluntary individual learning accounts – funded by a mixture of exployer, employee and taxpayer contributions – could reinforce lifelong learning for all.

- Managed competition between learning institutions should be used to encourage efficiency and innovation. But Government must ensure that learning remains accessible to all, and that those with special needs are not disadvantaged.
- All funding of post-compulsory learning should have an output-related element.

# Chapter 3

# Learning Pays

*Sir Christopher Ball*

Each age must determine for itself the purposes for which it needs education and the means it will use to achieve them. It must respond to changes and pressures from without: technological developments, new economic opportunities and challenges, changed political circumstances. There may also be new dynamics within: fresh social problems emerge; public opinion and pressure groups form new priorities and reshape values; more people seek to share in the benefits which education can bring. As it responds to all of these education is but one instrument of social policy; it does not work alone. And as education responds to changed circumstances it becomes part of the circumstances themselves. Change is awkward, for the *status quo* represents security; even when its utility has passed it may be preserved because it was once useful. Judging the moment when structures and concepts have outlived their usefulness is always difficult.

Throughout the world, societies are at work reassessing the contribution which education provides for them. It is a striking feature of the modern world that in many nations the people and governments are simultaneously expressing serious concerns about their systems of education and training and seeking to expand them and to improve their quality. In the developing world education is seen as a springboard for prosperity upon which can be built the health and social services, the cultural and other activities which civilization can bring. 'Education: chain breaker, nation maker' runs a motto now in use in Botswana. In many nations there is a particular contemporary focus upon the contribution made by education to economic effectiveness that supports in turn quality of social care, cultural life and personal standards of living. So education is integral to the success of such economies as (West) Germany, lies behind the successful emergence of the nations of the Pacific Rim, and is recognized as significant for those countries whose economic performance has been less successful.

It is to that last group that the United Kingdom belongs. Its response to the challenges of its present circumstances must come from within, from public conviction and commitment and from the leadership of government. The external challenges for the UK are many: a tough world economy in which existing competitors move further ahead of us and new ones emerge and overtake us; international concern to protect and conserve the environment with far higher standards of acceptable performance in the use of energy, extraction of minerals and agriculture; and changes in the very nature of work with a particular shift towards a higher thinking content in the balance of intellectual and practical activities. The internal challenges are also demanding: for a society less complacent but more at ease with itself; for higher standards of both social care and social responsibility; for a fuller intellectual and cultural life; and for higher personal incomes.

It is central theme of this report that learning pays. It pays in other societies; it already pays, but can pay far more, in the United Kingdom. This view is consistent with a growing consensus that there is an urgent need to improve participation in, and the quality of, post-compulsory education and training in this country. The report seeks to bring many strands of this consensus together and to explore new ways of looking at the national needs . . .

The RSA's vision . . . is for a learning society in the UK. A learning society would be one in which everyone participated in education and training throughout their life. It would support them as citizens in their employment and their leisure. A learning society would also make provision to match these enhanced aspirations. The translation of national aspirations into reality cannot be achieved by government alone. It requires the co-operation, effort and enterprise of many agencies and all parts of society. The project takes ideas such as these as its framework of reference. It recognizes, but does not dwell on, the failures of the past; it is more concerned to understand and build upon the advances of recent years. Its focus is the longer term. It is not primarily concerned with the details of the political and administrative issues of 1991. It seeks rather to help to lay the foundation of the learning society of the next century. It asserts that the creation of a learning society is our highest national priority.

## A LEARNING SOCIETY

### Learning . . .

Humans are learning animals. Other creatures can be trained to perform useful or amusing acts. But such a training is involuntary, limited and never engenders the process of independent learning characteristic of our species. Of course, animals can and do learn from one another. But in animals the balance between instinctive and learned behaviour is heavily weighted towards the former. In humankind it is otherwise. We are not without instincts – but after breathing and sucking probably our deepest instinct is to learn. We have to learn how to swim, fight, make love. Fortunately, we are brilliant learners. This single characteristic has given us a decisive advantage in the evolutionary process and ultimately conferred on us supremacy over all other species. Now we must learn how best to live and work with our success in a sustainable world.

Learning brings advantages. All of us benefit from learning the basic skills – how to walk and talk, dress ourselves, build with bricks, count up to ten on our fingers . . . Each benefits from learning derived skills – how to play football or dance, read and write, dress up and playact, make a raft or a dam, practise mental arithmetic . . . Everyone benefits from learning applied skills – professional sport or ballet, the uses of literacy, dress design and drama, engineering, computing and accountancy . . . Our hopes of health, wealth and happiness depend on learning – our own and that of others.

Learning is cumulative. We live on an inheritance of learning from the past: the invention of the wheel, measurement of time and space, knowledge of the sources of energy, materials, the alphabet, boat building and flying, the law and games, cooking and gardening, music and literature . . . In recent centuries the triumph of western learning, particularly in science, technology, medicine, economics and the arts, has come to dominate the whole world. English has become almost a universal second language. How far can, or should, our ideas of learning avoid the charge of being western or Eurocentric?

Learning accelerates. The dynamic of learning is a geometric, not arithmetic, progression. Centuries passed between the first idea of infection and the development of vaccination, less than 200 years between Jenner's experiments and the total control of smallpox. The first manned free balloon flight took place in Paris in 1783; the first powered flight in 1903; the first flight of a jet aircraft in 1939; Sputnik 1 was launched in 1957; the Americans reached the moon in 1969.

Learning brings change. The Renaissance changed a civilization. The advent of western influence upon Japan in the nineteenth century transformed a nation; today it is transforming an empire in Eastern Europe. Educating Rita changed a life. The acceleration of learning is inevitably matched by an increasing rate of change, economic, social, technological, political. All new learning tends to subvert. The Renaissance was followed by the Reformation; the age of reason by the French and American Revolutions. Learning anew is the only effective strategy to cope with change. Revolution typically leads to the renewal of education. Thomas Jefferson's epitaph, self-chosen, describes him as 'author of the Declaration of American Independence, of the statute of Virginia for religious freedom, and father of the University of Virginia.'

Learning is lifelong. There is no such thing as a sufficient initial education. There never was. 'When I became a man', said St Paul, 'I put away childish things.' But he didn't stop learning. Like love and play, learning is as needful for adults as for children. With enormous increase in worthwhile and relevant knowledge in the modern era and the normality of change which is characteristic of today all must be able to adapt, increase and update their learning if they are to cope with the future. The only serious and lasting failure of initial education is found in those whose instinct and appetite for learning has been dulled.

Learning is often informal. Much of what we learn – and value most highly – is achieved without teachers and outside the formal systems of education and training. Experience is often the best teacher. Our grasp of the mother-tongue, the skills of lovers or parents or chairpersons, the street-creds of the street-wise, teamwork, tolerance, compassion, courage are not primarily learned in the class-room. Obedience to the Ten Commandments, or the rules of cricket, or the conventions of good manners, are not taught as part of the national curriculum. At its best informal learning can be efficient and effective; it can also be eclectic, disorganized and incomplete.

Within the education system most learning differs from this norm and is structured, formal and controlled from outside the learner. In the workplace it is often the reverse, being unstructured, informal and controlled by the learner. In offices, for example, much learning is achieved by reading memoranda, or in conversation with colleagues. The differences between these styles are profound. In a learning society the utility of all modes will be recognized and used. But informality without structure may be narrow, leave gaps and, in particular, while taking care of immediate needs may neglect tomorrow's. Several changes may be necessary. One is for learning in employment to give more place to structure and be readier to use formal approaches when appropriate. Others affect the world of education, where there is a need to make more use of informal processess so that formal methods are reinforced by a style which is closer to our day-by-day experience of informal learning; and, even more important, to find ways of transferring control of the learning process to the learners themselves. It is a central theme of this report that the best individual learning combines informal and structured experience, and is as far as possible self-directed. Teaching is like nursing; with a little care most adults can preserve their health and continue learning on their own initiative.

All this the world well knows. The purpose of the foregoing paragraphs is to emphasize the central role of learning in human life and society, its increasing importance in the world of today, and the tension between the continuous and informal characteristics of learning at its most effective on the one hand, and, on the other, existing models of education and training which tend to over-emphasize the initial and the formal aspects of learning.

## ... Pays

Learning pays. Most nationals recognize today that the quality of the education and training of the workforce is the single most important characteristic in determining economic competitiveness. Though not by itself a sufficient condition, a world-class workforce is certainly a necessary condition for national economic success. The link between skills and knowledge, and the high quality of goods and services, in countries such as (West) Germany and Japan is well established. The competitive success of their products is evident in the houses and on the roads of Britain. By means of them these nations achieve a higher gross national product, whether measured per capita or absolutely, than we do; and are able to afford a standard of living and quality of life which we often envy but cannot at present match.

What is true for the nation is also true for companies. Effective training increases productivity and profits. Evidence is accumulating of the strong link between respect for education and commitment to training, on the one hand, and (on the other) competitive success. Companies such as GEC, Ford, Rover, Lucas, Marks & Spencer, and many others, including small companies, demonstrate both by their behaviour and their market position that learning pays in the longer term. It is difficult today to find many examples of companies which have succeeded without, or failed with, strategic investment in training.

Learning also pays the individual, who can expect to benefit through enhanced career prospects, greater self-esteem and improvement in the quality of life. Research in America shows, for example, that for every 100 disadvantaged youngsters with pre-school (nursery) education 48 managed to gain employment, and 45 were able to support themselves completely on their own earnings, when they grew up; while for every 100 without pre-school the comparable figures were 29 and 24. Research in Australia shows that early school leaving adversely affects a young person's life chances. It can result in labour market disadvantage, reduced participation in the life of the society, and poverty. The Department of Education and Science in the UK has argued that the personal rate of return in higher education is a great deal higher than the rate of return to society in general. It is also well above that available on almost all other forms of investment. The correlation between levels of qualification and average earnings is striking. The message is a simple one: the more you learn, the more you earn.

The assertion that learning pays is fundamental to the thinking of this report. It is not uncontestable. There are three difficulties. First, it is easier to demonstrate the link between learning and earning than to prove that a cause-and-effect relationship obtains. Secondly, the advantages of learning are long-term ones; short-term benefits are difficult to demonstrate. Thirdly, the benefits of learning are divided and distributed between employers, employees and society at large. This inevitably leads to argument about the allocation of the costs of learning. It sometimes results in a deadlock where the benefit for any one party is thought to be insufficient to justify the cost of education or training, but no mechanism exists to enable a co-operative approach to solve the problem of funding through the principle of partnership. These issues require more attention. In particular, there is a key role for government in bridging the gap between the obvious macro-economic arguments for learning and the apparently less compelling micro-economic incentives.

Learning also civilizes. That is, it helps us to become effective members of our own society, to enter imaginatively and sympathetically into other societies distant from our own in time and space and principle and to share in the benefits of the creative genius of the human race. One of the three great objectives of all eudcation is socialization (the others are the provision of skills and sorting for employment). This term refers to the personal and social competence required to function successfully as a member of a family, company or society. Robert Fulghum claims: 'All I really need to know about how to live and what to do and how to be I first learned in kindergarten ... share everything, play fair, don't hit people, put things back where you found them, clean up your own mess, don't take things that aren't yours, say you're sorry when you hurt somebody ...' The

Robbins Report (DE, 1963) made the same point in more measured language when it defined the fourth objective of higher education as 'the transmission of a common culture and common standards of citizenship'. In some South Asian countries the first aim of education is national unity (the second and third are wealth creation and personal fulfilment). In a multicultural society the objective and definition of national unity raises interesting problems. But in the increasingly international society of the global village, national unit (however defined) must not be bought at the expense of international disunity. The civilizing task of education in the modern world is a complex one. In particular, it is arguable that modern democracies cannot function effectively without an educated electorate.

# Chapter 4

# Rhetoric and Reality:
# Learning and Information Theory

*Patrick Ainley*

Believe it or not, the Conservative government at the beginning of the 1990s proposed to turn Britain into 'a learning society' by the year 2000. For the government endorsed the objectives of the National Education and Training Targets for Foundation and Lifetime Learning which were first formulated by the Confederation of the British Industry in 1991. These proposed to create a learning society through a process of 'skills revolution'. This would principally be a cultural revolution, creating 'a new training culture' in which individuals would be empowered with 'real buying power' for career mobility and needs satisfaction. It would involve a partnership between higher education, industry and government, in the words of the 1993 White Paper on Science, Engineering and Technology, 'to harness the knowledge and insights of all three partners to mutual advantage by encouraging and easing the increased exchange and flow of people, knowledge and ideas'.

These were the objects too of the government's 1988 education reforms, which were similarly calculated to motivate parents and pupils or students to achieve higher standards through a competitive market in schools, further and higher education. The market also requires information so that consumers – whether students, their parents or their potential employers – can make informed choices between the competing learning services offered in the education and training market place. The National Education and Training Targets that the new system is intended to meet are expressed in a new framework of National Vocational Qualifications that will be equivalent to European Union qualifications. Together these approaches will, it is intended, create a system of 'ladders and bridges' whereby learners can gain academic and vocational qualifications throughout their lives to increase personal opportunity and contribute to wealth generation. However, it is also recognized that most learning – even, or especially, in a learning society – occurs outside formal education and training.

A 'learning society' so defined is a society which systematically increases the skills and knowledge of all its members to exploit technological innovation and so gain a competitive edge for their services in fast-changing global markets. This is supposed to be now necessary because the industrial competitiveness of the UK is widely accepted as being dependent upon a highly skilled work force, able to innovate and to produce goods and services of a high marketable value. In a competitive global market developed countries like Britain can no longer compete with the newly industrializing nations, like those of the Pacific Rim – South Korea and Taiwan for example, the so-called Asian tigers – in the mass-production of the heavy industrial goods with which Britain once led the world as the first industrialized nation. Now, in order to sell, it is necessary to produce for specialized and niche markets in high-technology goods and services. These require a workforce that is computerate rather than merely functionally literate and numerate, as was needed for the first industrial revolution. At the same time the rapid pace of technical change demands workers who are flexibly able to adapt to new technology throughout their working lives. The citizens of a learning society would thus exercise an entitlement to lifelong learning and education, and training would no longer be concentrated upon the young but permeate all aspects of social life.

However, whether the UK workforce as a whole is becoming more or less skilled and knowledgeable is debatable. Indeed, the government has often been accused of following a contrary policy. In seeking to attract foreign (chiefly American but also Japanese, Arab and Far Eastern) capital looking to invest in assembling and servicing in Britain as a bridgehead to the European heartland, the government has emphasized the virtues of the low-wage, deregulated workforce that it has tried to create. Similarly, work reorganization and 'culture change' are frequently the goals of employer involvement in the education and training programmes that often accompany the introduction of new technology and new methods of working in their organizations.

As a result of these policies, it is arguable that a process of 'skill polarization' has occurred at work, together with academic differentiation in education. With permanent, structual unemployment, millions of people are relegated to insecure, intermittent and semi-skilled employment if they are lucky. And in education and training, on the one side are those with special educational needs and on programmes requiring participation in training or work experience as a condition of receipt of welfare or unemployment benefits; on the other are those whose pre-existing cultural capital is legitimated by élite higher education. Between these two groups are the mass of students and trainess, adults as well as younger people, whose participation in education and training is often prompted by unemployment. This has implications for the motivation that is widely recognized as crucial to learning.

So the rhetoric of the 'learning society' does not match the reality of the situation on the ground. Yet even at the level of rhetoric, the tremendous increase in learning required for a labour process based on the conscious involvement of all employees, together with a society of citizens active in their working and democratic lives, has hardly begun to be acknowledged. Only poets and science fiction writers have imagined what a learning society would look like and how it would differ from today's world. Long before the advent of computers, which provide most such speculations with their technical infrastructure, Hugh MacDiarmid, for example, imagined 'Glasgow 1960' in a poem written some years earlier. External appearances of the city had not changed – 'Buses and trams all labelled "To Ibrox"/Swung past packed tight'; however, the people were not going to a football match, but to listen to a debate on the conservation of energy – 'Between Professor MacFadyen and a Spanish pairty' – while the headlines on the evening papers screamed, 'Special! Turkish Poet's Abstruse New Song./ Scottish Authors' Opinions' – and, 'holy snakes,/I saw the edition sell like hot cakes.'

Whether or not the popular culture of a learning society would be as relentlessly highbrow as MacDiarmid imagined, for most people who endorse the general rhetoric of a learning society, education and training are felt to be self-evidently good things; but we have suggested that in many instances they are substituted for more fundamental economic and structural reforms. For the CBI, their proposed 'skills revolution' is part of the modernization necessary for British industry to compete in high-value, high-skill global markets. For the government, education and training (learning) is also connected to competitiveness, to creating a flexible workforce of highly motivated individuals. There are also the wider aims of 'enhancing the quality of life' for as many people as possible, boosting service sector consumption while preserving 'civilized values'; and extending the national culture. A society of 'active citizens' is also widely seen as more democratic and 'responsible'.

Similarly, to be a 'learning organization', 'Investing in People' – as many CBI-approved companies now style themselves – does not just mean more training; the entire organizational culture would have to change. This cannot be achieved in isolation, expecially if the broader society remains inimical to learning. Individuals require confidence in their ability to undertake lifelong learning and adapt to new technologies. Such confidence cannot be created by exhortation alone. Nor can people be forced to learn, though they can be forced to work. The key for research, therefore, is to identify, and for policy to overcome the economic, educational and social barriers to achieving a learning society in which individuals share high-level general knowledge and skill they can apply in different occupations throughout their lives.

Certainly, an integrated further, higher and adult education and training system has a pivotal role to play in a real learning society. In the new system as it is today, further education is already in a vital position between compulsory school education and post-compulsory or contining education and training. This has been recognized by government in the 'special new emphasis' given to further education since the 1992 Autumn Statement. Yet, despite the relative increase in its funding, the position of further education remains critical, with FE college closures and mergers threatened as a result of the competition for students between what are now independent colleges and sixth form centres.

Moreover, further and higher education is still seen as remote by many young people. Typically, the majority who feel they have 'failed' in the academic selection of a minority are discouraged by their school experience from attempting any further study, while the minority who have succeeded feel that they have nothing more to learn. Many adults also lack opportunities for learning in or out of employment. Individual motivation is allied to personal development and economic need in the context of broader culturally defined structures of employment, promotion opportunities, pay incentives and new methods of work. All these would have to change in a real skills revolution to create a true learning society.

Another critical question facing education and training policy is what knowledge and skills need to be prioritized for the future learning society, and the extent to which concentration on basic literacy and numeracy can be linked to more general, higher-level cognitive skills of reasoning and scientific/logical thinking, by qualifications systems that allow of credit accumulation and transfer. So-called 'personal and transferable skills' are also relevant, as they are the core competences required in the many employments that are becoming increasingly similar due to similar applications of new technology and similar reorganizations of work. However, the academic 'national' curriculum in schools is not necessarily contiguous with the more vocational content of much post-compulsory learning. A symbolic and practical division also persist between FE and HE.

Yet the impact of technological change potentially revolutionizes both levels of learning and the methods of its delivery. New modes of delivery, including distance and open learning, pose particular pedagogic challenges to both learners and teachers, as does widening their view of educational settings, and recognizing the importance of the workplace and the community in the social mediation of learning, to create a continuity of education and training in formal and informal settings.

There is as yet little evidence that the rapid series of changes in education and training that have taken place in recent years are underpinned by a coherent strategy, informed and monitored by rigorous analysis and research. There remains also considerable uncertainty about the benefits of education and training to the various parties involved. For some individuals it is quite rational not to enter Youth Training schemes, for instance, because they can actually depress their chances of finding waged work. And many employers simply do not require much labour that is highly qualified and certificated. This balance between public and private reward varies across commercial and industrial sectors, and in the relationship of corporate to national competitiveness. There are also market failures evident in persistent 'skill shortages' and employee 'poaching' by employers.

All this gives considerable room for scepticism regarding the government's and industry's declared aims of achieving what they call a 'learning society'. Is such a thing possible? Are not all societies learning societies? Or is our society in particular rapidly becoming not more 'learned' but more ignorant?! A glance at the day's domestic news reported by the mass media must give one grounds for doubt – as must, very often, the popular press and television that report them! To consider what a real learning society might involve requires a more rigorous approach. This is provided by what is variously called systems, information or control theory, or cybernetics.

## LEARNING AND INFORMATION THEORY

To begin with, a society is not necessarily learning just because of an increase in the amount of circulating information and in the means of distributing and presenting it. There is, as we have seen, information that may or may not be integrated as knowledge. There are also competencies and at another level there are skills. At another level again, there may also be wisdom. Information, facts, or data are nothing by themselves, although even to be considered as items for analysis they have been isolated and selected in some way. They are of value, however, only by virtue of the meanings attached to them through the preconceptions into which they are made to fit.

Information theory views all thermodynamic systems – physical, biological and social – as involving exchanges of information. Mechanical systems too can be seen in this way, and with the development of automatic control of machines a theory of engineering control has been developed to explain how to incorporate human purposes into machines. The basic distinction of this control theory is that between open and closed systems.

Closed systems are self-contained. The machine is set to perform a certain task, primed or fuelled to do so and, as long as nothing intervenes to upset the conditions of its operation, will execute it with perfect certainty of result. A closed system can however be opened to allow of self-correction by the machine so that if conditions change – if it gets too hot or too cold, for instance, or the machine goes too fast or too slow – a servomechanism with some sort of sensor to receive information from outside (like a thermostat or a 'fly-ball governor') can alter the machine's activity to keep it on its original course to complete the task it was set.

This opens the original closed system to a new and more open level of determination, one which encloses and determines the initial, more limited system of operation. A mechanical system can be regarded as an analogy or metaphor for describing more complicated systems. For whether these are physical, biological or social, these often vastly more complex and intricate systems can be viewed as exchanging information or energy (which are here regarded as synonymous) to sustain themselves. The simpler systems are open to control by the larger systems that contain them by supplying the conditions (energy or information) necessary for their continued operation, survival or reproduction. No system is completely open however; there are always larger systems of which it is a part, up to the universal set.

Information structures in the case of living systems (at least on the planet earth!) give form to cells, organs, bodies, societies and species. The circulating information exchanged with the systems environment that contains or encloses it maintains its structure. That structure or organization depends upon the finality or purpose of the system, for that is what determines the circulating information.

In this context, individual human needs are defined in terms of sustaining the necessary conditions for the proper functioning of the individual physical and psychic system. If they are not met the behaviour of the individual as system is disturbed. However, human beings are unique in not only being informed by but in forming their own environment through the use of tools. Tools transform objects not only literally but also conceptually; they distance consciousness from its immediate perceptions by forming a new purposive whole of means to end, with thought before action. A new and symbolic subsystem is thus created which is capable of self-steering, as it is called in control theory.

Unlike inherited genetic information and animal communication by signalling, symbolic consciousness, and the self-steering system it creates, is capable of learning from past mistakes to act differently in future. Therefore it is an axiom of information or control theory that 'It is a notable property of self-steering that the same state never returns in a self-steering system'.

It cannot be presumed, however, that the ways of life of which individuals of self-steering systems are a part are themselves self-steering, and have not become what information theory describes as closed systems. Such closed systems, unlike open ones, perpetually return to the state from which they started. Like a machine, they complete their operation and revert to rest or repeat it again without variation. Applied to social groups, information theory suggests that hierarchies in power over societies invariably operate solely to preserve their own power by closing systems, to prevent any further development and to lock the social system into repeated identical cycles or loops.

Looking at the capitalist economic system of commodity production as such a closed system, it is clear that the purpose or finality of the system is to produce more and more commodities for sale to rival companies or competitior countries in order to invest the profit that is realized in the sale in the production of more and more commodities and so on in an unending cycle. Whatever the incidental benefits that may accrue to some of the individuals involved in this system of competitive productivism, it is clearly necessary to break out of this particular closed system globally. Otherwise, if we extrapolate from present trends, the human species has set course for destroying the biosphere that sustains it, and which is the ultimate level of its finality or purpose, in that it is the planetary ecology which sustains human and other life and permits its ongoing reproduction.

If auto-destruction is to be avoided, the closed loop of production for profit must be opened to the larger ecological system within which it is contained and which it threatens to disrupt. It is an open question whether the capitalist corporations that now exercise undisputed control over the global economy can adapt themselves to a sustainable environment, for this would mean giving themselves over to a higher finality than the closed loop of production for profit which currently governs their operations. It would mean opening the self-contained and closed subsystem – commodity production for the sake of producing more commodities in order to maximize profits to invest them in the production of more commodities to maximize profits . . . (recurring) – to integration in a self-sustaining planetary ecology.

Such integration would mean consciously determining precisely how the mass and energy taken from the environment would have to circulate in the planetary ecology, in order to ensure the maintenance of its global organization, while at the same time ensuring the maintenance of all the individual subsystems which consititute it. This is not a call for the accumulation by a scientific technocracy of supposedly objective information in some vast database like that planned for the human genome project, upon which scientists around the world are currently working. It is a call for the availability of the information necessary for individual members of society to become informed of their own function and purpose at the global level. This information goes beyond that necessary for individuals to be aware of their contribution to the production and sale of commodities or services for the sake of (from their point of view) maintaining and reproducing their own individual and family subsystems through the wages that they earn for their services. Individual and family subsystems are in any case increasingly disrupted by the dysfunctions of the larger economic, social and ecological systems of which they are a part. Closure of information at the level of the individual or family is therefore impossible, however hard we try.

The opening of specialized information systems, which would be necessary to integrate them with the widest possible system within which they are contained, is not compatible with the level of closure of individual enterprises in competition with each other. At this level, individuals' contributions are measured only in relation to the success or failure of their firm, regardless of any other consequences of their actions. Similarly, closure at the level of national economies, or the trading blocks and military alliances of which they are parts, must be opened to the global economy and the ecosphere which sustains them. Thus what is meant by information in a real learning society is not the specialized vocational information which enables the individual to transform inanimate matter, nor the information supplied by manual or conceptual training, but a far vaster scale of information which concerns the importance of the individual as an individual within the human collectivity.

This is a considerably wider definition of information society than usual! It is, however, connected to conventional definitions by reliance upon the information technology which makes it possible. It also indicates the necessity of preserving and extending social spaces for the creation and elaboration of new ideas. It favours openness to the highest possible level against closure at the level of ideology or dogma. It is also related to the issue of democracy as self-steering.

At present, the triumphalist West has elevated one form of limited representative democracy over every other virtue, save the 'freedom' and 'equality' with which it is coupled. It is doubtful, however, that the majority rules in any self-styled democracy, beyond deciding between which of two not very different ways to accommodate itself to a global economic system perpetually balanced on the verge of crisis. This metropolitan economy of production for the sake of producing more commodities can only sustain its precarious position by further competition to impoverish the people and degrade the environment of the majority of the world's population.

Now that electronic communications and computing provide new potential for conscious planning and democratic control of self-steering, learning societies, perhaps a new historical opportunity presents itself. The goal however is no longer Utopia but simply survival. As the alternative is posed between survival and destruction, Utopia has become reality. Utopian ideals of a fixed end-state of human development, whether as 'communism', 'a free society', or any other 'state of grace', can be forsaken. Instead, we need to develop and implement the collective knowledge of what is required for human survival. New technology affords opportunities to do this by creating an information society in which meaning is given to the actions of individual members of society in relation to their most general finality at the level of planetary survival. New technology also has the potential to inform all citizens as generally as is possible to exercise democratic control towards that agreed common goal.

Telecommunications and computing could then be used not only to considerably reduce bureaucracy, but to increase participation and democracy. There are many possibilities, and local experiments could be started now to discover them and their limitations in the self-governance of as many areas of life as possible – not to mention the possibilities for the reform of an archaic national voting system popularly perceived as corrupt. Educational institutions can provide seedbeds for democracy, as the American educationalist John Dewey proposed, in order to improve the quality of political processes in a democratic society. He suggested that schools and their staff and students should be organized as democratic groups. He also suggested that students should be taught to apply scientific method to problems of concern to their communities. This combination would organize learning in democractic problem-solving groups in which students would learn democratic processes and scientific methods at the same time.

As for industrial democracy among those who work but usually exert little control over the use of their labour power, computer-integrated manufacture, which is the logical extension of the computerization presently being applied piecemeal to production, offers new opportunties to integrate the work of all employees in an enterprise. While requiring fewer operatives (or the same numbers for less time), by storing information centrally CIM ensures that it is communicated to all. The more inputs there are to the system – from designers, engineers, and managers, repairs and maintenance workers, those involved in storage and delivery, sales and marketing staff – the more information is generated and the more effectively it may be integrated for decision-making, which may also be computer-aided. The logical form of organization for optimum performance thus becomes co-operative and non-hierarchical.

Information is no longer specialized but generalized, for one part of the manufacturing process cannot act without informing and influencing all the others. As divisions between those who know and those who do, the executive and the rest, are effaced by everyone contributing and sharing information through the computerized communciations network, industry can become more responsive to the demands of consumers and to the needs of society.

But new technology extends opportunities for sharing information and decision-making beyond producer associations to the whole society. If information is power then the object must be to share information and generalize power. Power then, like knowledge, no longer exists except as it is shared. The basis for an informed democracy, in which the majority exercise power instead of handing it over to a minority who rule over them, is just that – information and the knowledge and, hopefully, wisdom to use it for the survival of society and humanity.

Education is the single most important investment in the knowledge industry that is supposed to be shifting the economy of the developed world from an industrial to an information base. Education is also, more certainly, the means of generalizing information, consciously teaching individuals their place within the largest, planetary set of which they are a part. Its purpose should be to discourage participants from seeing themselves and the purposes of their actions as set at lower levels of finality and determination – just for their own self-gratification or that of their family, or the company that employs them, or the real or imagined communities to which they belong, and which should therefore come before all others. Education at all levels must oppose such closed-system thinking and help people to develop the conceptual tools to relate the particular to the general.

However, the process of creating a learning society cannot be limited to the schools and colleges alone. The mass media and advertising also have a vital role to play. Indeed, it has been seen that with accelerating social change and to utilize new technology to its fullest potential, education can no longer be restricted to educational instituions but must be recognized as lifelong learning. This is now so generally accepted as to be a cliché, yet its implications have hardly begun to be grasped. We are in a new situation and no one seems to have realized it yet. As a part of the new social situation, however, there has been a reaction from the State which is also only dimly apprehended in society as a whole.

## LEARNING TO SURVIVE

The first priority for any government seriously committed to real modernization would be to re-establish the central purpose of education, science and the arts in society: to stimulate thought and develop new knowledge and skills to deal with a rapidly changing reality. This would be a real cultural revolution – not the partial 'skills' and 'enterprise' revolutions limited only to vocational preparation and individual competition. Nor would this new learning policy present itself only as learning for leisure. Cultural production is essential, not only for the increased education and training required for a labour process and a learning society consciously involving all its citizens, but also to encourage the restoration of the environment that the destructive productivisms of the past have already gone so far to destroy.

The economic underpinning of such an alternative modernization would be a return to full employment, but not full-time employment. The individual right to work must involve work-sharing to reduce hours worked by those in employment, to give them a chance to participate in increased learning at work as well as in cultural consumption out of work (which will increase the market for cultural products and services). Learning at all levels will be integral to such a real cultural revolution, but will not be limited to formal education but include recreation, sport and other cultural activities, especially the ecological and community improvement involved in a 'green economy'.

The right to a job in socially useful work must therefore be affirmed at the same time as the right to training, which has been substituted for it, but which is often not training at all; but as well as the right to work with proper training, there should also be the right to learning and recreation of all sorts – the right to earn and the right to learn, as the slogan has it. For training will no longer be differentiated from education and other cultural activities in a real learning society.

The fundamental cultural activity, if society is to be reconstructed from the bottom up, is democratic debate and decision-making. Just as we cannot return to the Taylorist productivism of the bureaucratically managed corporate state, so we cannot return to the professional paradigm of the welfare state, in which professionals acted on behalf of their clients. The welfare state can only be saved from its present piecemeal destruction by a resolutely decentralized reform in terms of its management and local control, even though its financing will still involve national redistribution according to priority of need.

Aside from the fact that universal nursery education is the single most effective investment in learning at any level that could be made by any government with a serious learning policy, higher education institutions, together with their associated further education colleges, have a vital role to play in the local and regional democratic reconstruction that is now so urgently required. HEIs can provide forums for the public discussion and debate which should in any case be a part of the education of all their students, and which will be the essence of the new social, political and economic compromise that is needed.

Democratic control of universities, colleges and schools, as of other public institutions, must be reasserted by the institution of local (city-wide or regional) democratic structures in place of the accountability through the market which 'free-market' philosophies advocate as the most efficient method of public accountability. The extension of democracy to localities and regions can foster learning and cultural re-creation around the economic and social regeneration of depressed areas. Vocational education must also be rescued from the market place, where it will always be low on employers' priorities. Instead of self-appointed quangos made up of local businessmen (almost invariably) on Training and Enterprise Councils, all public expenditure on education and training must be publicly reported and accounted for directly, to democratically elected bodies.

While the vital role of learning of all sorts of cultural recreation, economic regeneration and democratic reconstruction represents for higher education a reassertion of the service ideal of the polytechnics over the academic ideal of traditional humanism, teachers and lecturers at all levels, together with their students, have to have the academic freedom to pursue pure research at the generalized level that even Mrs Thatcher could see was necessary for scientific and cultural advance. But they have to recognize academic research as only one aspect of the advancement of knowledge, and they need to formulate a clearer definition of the purpose and function of academic research and its relation to other types of intellectual activity, particularly those which are taking place outside the universities, not only in industry and business but also, and more importantly, in their local communities and regions.

Academic knowledge and skills must be relevant to the local, regional, national and international communities that sustain them. Explaining their activities to others than their peers could be a good exercise in communcation for some academics engaged in more obscure research and scholarship; after all, as the

Independent Studies student quoting Einstein said, 'If an expert cannot explain the basics of his subject to a layman in five minutes, then he is not an expert.'

Participation in learning by as many people as possible is what is required for a democratic modernization, rather than the selection of a professional élite who attempt to monopolize information and knowledge. For generalized knowledge is necessary rather than specific vocational competences, not only to establish the social purposes of modernization directed towards collective survival rather than competition at the expense of others, but also for the fullest use to be made of the new information technology.

To an extent this is already recognized by those employers who call for more generalized instead of specific skills from their employees. However, we have suggested that employers are unwilling to allow the application of the new skills developed by information technology to render transparent and accessible their own prerogatives of managerial control. Middle managers may be squeezed out, but top employers prefer to sustain the hierarchies in which they are themselves advantageously placed, rather than to apply the technology to its fullest benefit for all, or even for their own firm.

Alternatively, new technology can be used to its best effect in production by charging social and economic processes with information that is accessible to the collective contributions of all involved. Its tendency then is to share knowledge and raise skills generally, multi-skilling the majority and empowering them for democratic participation, not merely enabling them to control their personal choice of the commodities presented to them, but generalizing power to control the future direction of society and its relations to the world economy and ecology of which it is a part.

The first step to generalizing the knowledge upon which to inform democracy and modernization is to establish for as many people as possible the normality and desirability of full-time education to 18, with recurring returns to learning full- and part-time thereafter. The normality of leaving general and usually full-time learning at 18 should also be used to emphasize the assumption of full citizenship rights and responsibilities for all from the age of 18, not at 25 for some, as has come to be increasingly the case.

All young people have to be brought in from the margins of society, instead of relegating a section of them to a secondary labour market in the regions and inner cities. For those who have been alienated by their previous schooling in an academic and competitive system, the opportunities afforded them by a further two years in college may need to have as little resemblance as possible to that previous schooling; and that schooling in any case will have to change, doing away with the outdated and academic 'national' curriculum and its associated competitive tests and league tables. Above all, adequate financial support should be available to students from the age of 16 onwards in order to raise participation rates and the rate of return post-18.

Student loans must be abolished as this only deters the many people who are unwilling to become indebted from entering higher education. Adequate mainten-ance is required, so that students have time to pursue their studies and do not have to work their way through college unless they wish to work and study part-time, for which option more allowances have also to be made. Access courses should be extended and people's prior experiences recognized as entitling them to pursue their cultural and intellectual interests, whether or not these are related to their employment or 'the demands of the economy'.

The recommendation of the 1963 Robbins Report, of access to higher education for all who can benefit from it, must be reaffirmed. Nor should the definition of ability to benefit be dictated by arbitrarily rising academic entry standards. Higher education must be increasing opened to all who wish as of right to enter their local college, whatever their previous qualifications or lack of them, full- or part-time, in or out of paid employment. Vouchers, which serve only to subsidize private education and training in the market-place in which they enjoy an unfair advantage, are not necessary to enforce this entitlement, which should be constitutionally and legally enforceable – unlike the empty assurances of consumer 'Charters'.

If the right of all school leavers to enter their local college is guaranteed, progression from schools and adult education will facilitate access to higher education. For those in and out of employment, tertiary/further/adult colleges are well place to become the linch-pin of the new system of education and training. Before the government cut loose into the market-place further education, tertiary and sixth form colleges, making planning and co-ordination difficult if not impossible, further education colleges in particular were well integrated with what remained of skill training in local labour markets and with their local secondary and special schools. They also increasing franchise the lower levels of higher education courses from the institutions with which they are linked.

Rather than shorten degree courses as the government now proposes, the two years which many already spend in further education before moving on to higher education can become the basis for a new two-plus-two-year degree structure. The first two years to 18 for standard-age entrants would lead to a broad-based diploma or baccalaureate embarcing both academic and vocational – or general and specific-skills. Proposals for such a unitary examination to end the division between education and training have already been published by the Institute for Public Policy Research. Subsequently many diplomates would move on, then or later in their lives, to take their study up to degree level with two further years full-time (or its part-time equivalent) in higher education, followed by two years or equivalent postgraduate study to Masters level.

Such a learning entitlement on adequate grant maintenance will be expensive, but it is a social priority that is required to raise general-level knowledge and skills among the population, which is necessary for modernization of the economy, as well as to adapt to the accelerating pace of historical and even climatic change.

The costs will be lessened by incorporating independent study into the learning programmes of all students, beginning as early as possible by building upon the project work still widely undertaken in primary schools. Instead of 'cramming' for tests which select a minority for entry to the next stage, the methods of learning and assessment associated with GCSE course work before it was restricted by government should be adopted, and made continuous from the schools through to further and higher education. In a complementary motion, the independent scholarship, research and creation of postgraduate learning should be brought down and integrated into all pre-graduate courses.

Thus all individual programmes of study in school and college will include some element of independent study, in the sense of original discovery, creation or research, with new forms of assessment and self-assessment based upon their work. (At present only art students are assessed exclusively or mainly on their creative efforts.)

Since many students in such a system will be seconded from employment or on behalf of their local communities, these creations and discoveries will return more than was invested in them, for creative artists, scientists or craftworkers (both art and science being crafts) are the only learners who give back more information than was entrusted to them by their learning. As well as the many practical tasks crying out to be undertaken, there are many unsolved theoretical problems in all fields of learning which subject specialists are too busy to resolve but which are comprehensible to students and on which they could cut their teeth.

Investigation, experiment and debate by all students and as many other people as possible is vital today when so many received ideas in the social and natural sciences are open to question. In addition, new technology can be applied at every level of learning to facilitate routine memorization and allow imagination free rein beyond the immediate necessity to earn a wage and the constraints of production for profit. This space within education for seeding new ideas must be preserved and extended by making scientific research and artistic creation an integral part of the independent study of all students, rather than separating teaching from research as the government now proposes.

Independent and individual study across traditional subject boundaries can be facilitated by the widely proposed and implemented modular systems of certification ... [T]hese facilitate access through various modes of part-time and distance learning at home and at work, through the recognition of prior experience, and they enable credit accumulation and transfer. They permit entry and exit points, from diploma level, through to the one-year certification, and to degree and Masters level, which can ease the present long haul to the final degree.

In a modular system, however, it is, as has been seen, essential not to lose sight of the divisions between disciplines as well as the interrelations between them. It is therefore important to distinguish between 'genuine' fields of study and practice corresponding to defined areas of reality on the one hand, and on the other, outdated and arbitrary academic subject divisions, which only hinder thought and dampen discovery. Whilst advances in knowledge often come from the imaginative projection from one frame of reference to another, this is not the same as a 'pick-n-mix' of modules from different areas of study. If subjects of study are chosen only on vocational (i.e. labour market) considerations, there is a loss of theoretical generalized knowledge in favour of specialized knowledge applicable only to occupational tasks not conceptually related to one another. Philosophical discussion, counselling and support is therefore required if the modular method is not to degenerate into irrelevant educational consumerism at one end, with the myopic relevant of narrow vocational goals at the other. Nor should it become a way of just packing in and processing more students, as it already has in some former polytechnics and many longer-established universities.

To ensure that other modular qualifications, like the National Vocational Qualifications, while they are employment-related are not employment-led, educational interests must have more influence in the National Council for Vocational Qualifications. Here again democratic accountability and control enter the frame, for the NCVQ should also be linked to Workplace Training Committees, as recommended by the Trades Union Congress. Work-based assessment involving workers in 'skills audits' (as also recommended by the TUC) should be an essential part of the NVQ approach, rather than assessment by outside professional 'experts'. By liaising with the WTCs, further and higher education colleges can co-ordinate the external skill setting and validation needed to maintain national and European standards if skills and knowledge are to be genuinely transferable between occupational sectors and different firms in the same sector throughout the EU.

The resources are available for the investment required if education and training are to play their part in a programme of economic modernization and social reconstruction. As stated by another former Minister, Labour Chancellor, Denis Healey,

> For Britain the first priority must be a massive switch from defence spending to economic reconstruction. Otherwise we cannot hope to repair the damage done in recent years to our economic infrastructure – our roads and railways, our schools and universities.

Such a redirection of resources can prepare the way for a culture of lifelong learning and recurrent access to further, higher and adult learning. The release of facilities in schools and colleges caused by the (temporary) demographic drop in the numbers of teenagers creates opportunities for providing education and training for the 70 per cent of the current workforce who have not acquired any worthwhile vocational qualification, as well as the four million people unemployed. With the 1991 White Paper *Employment and Training for the Twenty-first Century* (DES/DE, 1991) focused almost exclusively upon young people, the 3.4 million adults enrolled in further and adult education have been virtually abandoned. Once again, the government's free-market dogma negates its vocational training rhetoric, for the economy has been so run down that further education has become the last refuge for much skill training in local labour markets. Yet with investment in the technology, schools and colleges could respond to the gathering pace of technological change which requires a corresponding programme of retraining throughout employees' careers.

The subsidy of private schools through charitable status and the Assisted Places Scheme should be ended, as much to end the white flight and snobbery associated with the majority of them as to redistribute resources more fairly. The close connection of the élite minority of these schools with the antique univerities could, it can be suggested, also be severed by turning the Oxbridge colleges into residential adult colleges like Ruskin college, which is at present under threat of closure in Oxford; that is, instead of squeezing Ruskin out of the University,

Ruskinize the whole of Oxford! This would be widely supported by the many adults who would then be given a chance to attend such colleges. It would also nip in the bud the present moves towards setting up a superleague of semi-private élite institutions aiming to preserve their place at the top of the academic tree through marketing archaic and élite courses to those able to pay for them. It would also lay the great axe to the root of the tree of a system run for the selection of an élite. As Eric Robinson wrote in 1968 in his book *The New Polytechnics*. 'This educational conflict can be resolved only by breaking the domination of the whole educational system by universities which are devoted to the academic ideal.'

The ending of the binary divide between universities and polytechnics plus colleges would not then result in the widening of the social divisions in higher education, and the creation of the new academic division that we have predicted. Instead of the polytechnics aping the universities, the original polytechnic vision of popular universities could be spread through the new unified higher education sector. However, it is not so much polytechnicians who are required nowadays as polyconceptualists.

These are all practical proposals which could be implemented now to begin to move towards the learning society that will be required in the future. Yet a redirection of resouces to enable schools and colleges to provide all their students (as well as adults returning to and retraining for work) with the generalized knowledge necessary for full participation in a modernized and information-based economy would still only provide the technical potential to create a new and unified system of education for work. A new curriculum which facilitates, rather than prevents, transfer between its different levels is also required.

Simply, education can no longer be about selection for the employment hierarcy. We can learn from work but not necessarily just to work. The 'demands' of industry have to be set in a wider framework of human cultural and environmental need. To do this requires a greater contribution of generalized knowledge to work-related education and training. In particular, it requires theory to be related to the specific life experiences of students and trainees – 'work experience' in a deeper sense than it is habitually used. From this standpoint a progressive curriculum must lead on to an understanding of the organization of the economy as a whole, and of the relationships of power and oppression that are involved in it. Such a curriculum will insist upon international connections, on understanding 'domestic' as well as paid employment, and on opening for consideration the finality of social actions in relation to the larger political and ecological systems of which they are a part.

In a modernizing economy, education and training must raise the skills of all workers from the bottom up, much as campaigns in the Third World have aimed to raise literacy and numeracy rates. Education and training combined in lifelong learning will then integrate rather than separate manual and mental labour. If education is to build the skills and knowledge base of society to take fullest advantage of the latest developments in technology, it must begin by recognizing how new technology has been applied during the economic restructuring of the last decade, to de-skill many of the tasks involved in production, distribution and services. Resources will have to be specifically targeted at the poorest localities to overcome the disadvantage resulting from this process, reversing present priorities. New technology can now provide the potential to enable all working people to become multi-skilled and flexible in a true sense, able to undertake a wide range of specific and general tasks, including self-management of their co-operative enterprises and democratic government of their society.

In terms of knowledge and skills, the rapid diffusion of new technology throughout society, while obviating previously specialized crafts, expert professions and academic disciplines, also provides the catalyst for the majority of people to begin to think again in a generalized way about social questions. For not only are the latest applications of new technology part of the unprecedented acceleration of social change, which of itself stimulates thought and loosens the hold upon a changing reality of old mental paradigms, but new technology also presents information in new forms, and breaks down the old barriers between previously discrete bodies of information.

However, for information to be transformed, by the unique human capacity to envisage alternative futures, into the knowledge that action is necessary now to avert destruction in the near future requires a combination of widened access to information technology with the democratic forms necessary to act upon the information acquired. Only information combined with democracy can provide the knowledge and skills necessary for survival.

Unlike other species and previous civilizations we do not lack the information to predict nor the means to redirect the course of our society. The real question is then whether humanity can exercise its unique capacity to envision the future in order to open its present closed system to a level beyond its own self-destructive perpetuation.

The only historical precedent for the current challenge presented to human survival are those that faced society in the last national emergency during World War II. This time however no nation can hope to meet the challenge alone; and within countries alliance on terms of equality, co-operation and planning will be required, now as then, merely to survive. With education at all levels returned to the democratic control of localities and regions, this would serve to generalize science and raise awareness of the radical transformations required to avoid ecological catastrophe, through a real modernization of the economy and society.

All this challenges the existing hierarchy in society between those who think and those who do. Such a prospect, of overcoming the division in the working population between intellectual and manual labour, widening genuine access to all and allowing direct democratic control of a unified vocational education system by the people it serves, is daily becoming more necessary, if education and training are to contribute to, instead of hindering, human survival. Beyond individual freedom with all its limitations, free societies might then find new collective purpose in giving themselves over to securing the survival of the species.

*Chapter 5*

# The Learning Society

*Hendrik van der Zee*[1]

## CHARTING CRITERIA

Every community takes steps to ensure that its members acquire the different kinds of knowledge considered necessary for life. But societies vary considerably with respect to the importance given to learning, the specific aims that they try to satisfy through learning, and the way in which they attempt to support and reinforce learning. In the Jewish tradition learning occupies pride of place. Thus in the twelfth century Maimonides wrote (Abram, 1984, p. 64):

> Every Jew, whether rich or poor, healthy or sick, at the height of his powers or old and infirm, has the duty to study. Wood-cutters and water-bearers figured among their great scholars, even blind men. They studied day and night ... Until when should a person continue to learn? Until the day of his death ... Learning is the most important of all the rules of behaviour given in the Torah. Even stronger: learning is more important than all other rules of behaviour together ... Make learning a regular habit. Do not say: 'I'll learn if I have time'. You may never have time.

These words deserve noting in the light of the contemporary world-wide debate on education standards.[2] The pedagogical assumptions on which present-day curricula are based are increasingly coming under attack. However defective we may consider our curricula to be, we should bear in mind that criticism of education is not new. In the last century, for example, Friedrich Nietzsche (1983, pp. 133–52) complained that educational institutions, far from seeking to civilize men and society, teach people to be functionaries and make them marketable. The same and similar complaints can be heard today.

Criticism of the functioning of our educational system should be seen in the context of the societal forces that affect learning needs. These forces include:

- the explosion of knowledge and technology
- automation in companies and institutions

- attempts to make labour and labour organizations more flexible
- the economic and political unification of Europe
- the innumerable people who have to scrape an existence on the edges of the labour market
- the tendency towards individualization
- the increase in the amount of free time we have at our disposal
- the ageing of the population
- the variety in sorts of households and forms of cohabitation
- changes in the relationships between men and women and between parents and children
- the co-existence of different ethnic and cultural groups
- the revaluation of the environment.

Various suggestions are proposed to address the diverse and shifting learning needs which are emerging in response to the combined impact of these social and economic changes.

Some scholars seek the solution primarily in a *new approach to training and education*. Two different points of emphasis are discernible within this approach. In the one case, the introduction of a new or revised educational concept is stressed (self-directed learning, problem-oriented instruction, learning from experience, andragogy). In the other case, the emphasis lies on the methods that should be used in the design of instruction and for solving performance problems (instructional design, educational technology, course planning).

A second response to the new demands for education and training is the *effective school movement*. This research-driven movement takes the organization of education as its point of departure. It is maintained that such factors as strong management, regular testing of learning achievements, getting back to basics and a secure and well-ordered school environment have a vital influence on the achievements of the pupils.

A third innovation in educational thinking is the *open learning movement*. Client orientation and flexibility in the provision of learning opportunities are the main theme here. In practical terms this means the setting up of cafeteria-style arrangements for education, doing away with entrance requirements, the application of technology (television, video, telephone, computers), the use of self-instructional material, the development of a support system.

A more radical proposal for reform comes from the movement for the *de-schooling of society*. This movement, which was prominent in the 1970s, highlighted the side-effects of attempts fixated on promoting the extension and perfection of educational facilities. The de-schoolers argue that, little by little, a colossal learning factory has been created from which everything resembling education in the original meaning of the word has disappeared. Our schools have become instruments of repression: they reinforce social inequality, keep people dependent, stub out initiative and creativity, and impede common action. Moreover, what people most need to learn, schools seem least able to teach. However valid this criticism may be, it can be said that the de-schoolers have paved the way for a discussion about our educational priorities, in particular about what the basics are, about principles of self-organization, and about informal and non-informal modes of learning.

The final theme for change which I would like to mention is the idea of *recurrent education*. The term recurrent education refers to an overall strategy aimed at restructuring the educational system, so as to distribute periods of study over the total life span of the individual in a recurring way, i.e. alternating with extended periods of other sorts of activity such as work, leisure and retirement. Although recurrent education has been a political hobby-horse for many years in The Netherlands, statistics on participation and time–budget studies show that the idea has not been put to work.

Of course, the above is not an exhaustive catalogue of new directions for education. None the less, the survey does give an impression of the variety of proposals for reform. It is clear that the changes in society's demand for education have produced divergent reactions.

The more miscellaneous the chorus of critics and reformers, the more dire the need for an overall score, a concept which stresses the importance of harmony between the multitude of separate approaches. A preferred score would provide room for a variety of initiatives to renewal, without justifying every proposal beforehand and so circumventing the need to choose. Rather, it would act as a common source of inspiration. The metaphor of a *learning society* has the potential to fulfil this need.

However, at the present moment it is customary to sketch the society of the future as an *information society*. Why do I not take the availability of information (i.e. knowledge), but the acquisition of knowledge (i.e. learning) as the primary consideration? The reason is that an information society is still not an informed society. The evidence is otherwise. What is envisaged is a society in which the pressure from technology and the economy is so great that people, the users of the information, feel defeated. If we don't take action, an inhuman, highly technocratic society lies ahead of us (see, for example, Martin, 1988 and Roszak, 1986).

No matter how one regards an information society, one thing is missing in this metaphor: people. Kidd (1983, p. 530) maintains that an important linking operation is needed which enables us to make our own sense out of information. The word 'learning' guarantees this sort of linking operation. It directs attention to the dynamics of the relations between information and information technology on the one side, and the individual and the community on the other.

'The learning society is growing because it must', is the opening of Patricia Cross's inspiring survey of literature *Adults as Learners* (1986, p. 1). This makes us curious about the characteristics of a learning society, or rather about the ideas and values to which the concept appeals. Defining a concept that has engendered a world-wide debate is tricky. Nevertheless, in this chapter five criteria (strategic issues) for the development of a learning society are pin-pointed. These are:

- The need to broaden the definition of learning (education as dimension of society)
- The need to redirect the goal of learning (growth towards completeness)

- The need to go beyond learning and instruction (increasing collective competence)
- The need to foster autonomy in learning (self-education)
- The need to stress a political approach to learning (the right to learn)

## DIMENSION OF SOCIETY

A learning society stimulates and allows all its members and groups continually to develop their knowledge, skills and attitudes. Education is anchored in culture as a primary condition of existence. It is high on the agenda of many societal institutions. Besides the educational system proper, numerous other agencies are involved – the mass media, the unions, industry and commerce, the health services, travel organization public information outlets, prisons, and so on. This is what I mean by education as a dimension of society.[3]

Education can be described as the manner in which persons and groups gain skills, extend their knowledge, receive impulses, define their attitudes: in short, learn things. I believe that a comprehensive strategy aimed at opening up new opportunities for people to learn, should consist of the following three steps. First, it is necessary to chart the existing forms of learning. Then we should examine how the potential of the suggested types of learning can be further developed. Finally, we should take into account the unique contributions as well as the interdependencies of the many agencies of education and other learning resources. I will now discuss these three steps in order.

### Forms of learning

The bewildering variety of modes in which human learning occurs can be viewed from various angles. The context determines what constitutes a meaningful classification and terminology. Here the first priority is to clarify the possibilities for strengthening the educational dimension of society. From this point of view it is essential to distinguish between three basic forms of learning.

The first, but not necessarily most powerful mode of learning is *guided learning*. By guided learning I mean all sorts of learning activities which involve a measure of instruction or tuition. This includes following occupational training, attending a management seminar, taking part in a course via the television or going to dancing lessons.

The second basic form can be referred to by the term *do-it-yourself learning*. It covers all activities people undertake on their own initiative, without the mediation of teachers or course-makers, with the intention of broadening their horizons or improving their capacity to accomplish some task. Ferreting something out in the public library, doing a job 'with the social sciences', cracking a computer with the aid of a manual and mastering a physical handicap with the support of a patients' association are examples of do-it-yourself learning. It should be noted that self-learners often do not regard their behaviour as 'learning', and that only a fraction of their initiatives take the form of learning projects.[4]

The third basic form is *spontaneous learning*. Like do-it-yourself learning, spontaneous learning, as a rule, takes place without organized instruction. However, whereas do-it-yourself learning is deliberately designed to cope with a problem or to summon inspiration, one bumps into spontaneous learning without meaning to, as in the case of a serious accident (through which daily worries are put in perspective), a conflict at work (through which scales drop from the eyes), and a love affair (through which we come to look at ourselves and to reassess old relationships). At other times learning happens by the way, as a by-product of an activity which is primarily guided by other motives. Watching television, starting an own company and practising a sport are examples of activities from which a lot can be learnt in an unselfconscious fashion.[5]

To say that much learning takes place without recourse to teachers or producers of instructional materials is to state the obvious. Everyone concerned with the training and education of young people and adults acknowledges this phenomenon. Nevertheless, professional practitioners, policy makers and researchers continue to regard the school system as 'too separate, too all-sufficient and too effective an organisation of provisions' (Fletcher, 1984, p. 406).

## Promoting learning

The forms of learning mentioned above offer us many points of contact for education reform. With respect to the area of guided learning, at least three groups of initiatives deserve special attention.

- Improving the quality of the existing school system. This category includes all activities which aim at more effective, efficient and appealing methods of instruction, improved instructional materials, greater differentiation, more skilful teachers, innovative management and better amenities.
- Developing new programmes and types of education, especially around questions and needs for which the present range of educational facilities does not, or does not fully, provide.
- Enlarging access to courses and training by getting rid of all sorts of impediments which prevent people from taking part. Examples of such impediments can be: irregular working hours, transportation problems, not being able to afford the registration fee, lack of self-confidence, ignorance of the opportunities, insufficient studying skills, not satisfying the entrance requirements.

The problem of how to cope with the two remaining types of learning is less easily answered. This is due to a lack of knowledge about the processes involved. A framework for examining the tasks facing us in our daily practices is needed before more conscious action can be taken. Which tasks question our ways of thinking and behaving? How do we respond to the difficulties and opportunities these tasks represent? What sort of competence and wisdom will help us move ahead? In what way can the required proficiencies be obtained? With regard to the last question, I advocate keeping the perspective as open as possible. A multitude of sources and means deserve consideration.

- Informal contacts: friends, neighbours, members of the family
- The mass media: books, radio, television, newspapers, magazines, audio- and video-cassettes
- Labour organizations: the place of work as place of learning
- Cultural institutions: museums, libraries, theatres, cinemas, creative centres
- Utilitarian facilities: trade fairs, labour exchanges, banks, do-it-yourself shops.

Uncovering this education potential is a daunting task. Recent studies on learning in the workplace, the public library as an open-learning centre, learning through television, and the education possibilities of museums indicate a basis upon which we may proceed.

**Harmony**

Let flowers flower everywhere. However, the situation in which the diverse 'agencies of education' only care about their own back yard must be avoided. As Houle (1972, p. 6) sketched:

> The typical career worker in adult education is still concerned only with an institutional pattern of service or a methodology, seldom or never catching a glimpse of the total terrain of which he is cultivating one corner, and content to be, for example, a farm or home consultant, museum curator, public librarian, or industrial trainer.

The many sources and means available to learners must be brought into harmony. This requires co-operation, the formation of networks, the division of duties, a realization of the unique contributions one agency can make that other agencies cannot, continuous innovation and a common perspective. There may be no misunderstanding about who should judge the harmony: in the last analysis, the user of the facilities.

The fact that there is a negative side to teaching should never be forgotten. Resnick (1987, pp. 13–20) has unravelled how knowledge gained at school relates to knowledge required in everyday life and at work. She discovered four differences.

- At school individual achievements are tested, while in life you are judged by what you can contribute in a social context.
- In school it is what is in your head that counts, while in life what matters is if you are good at using technology, aids and appliances and sources.
- At school you learn to use meaningless symbols, while in life inventiveness in approaching meaningful problem situations is required.
- At school you learn general skills and subject-dependent understanding, while in life you need knowledge and experience which is relevant to specific problem situations.

These findings may not be revolutionary; but it does not hurt to think about them once again. The failure of our schools to teach proficiencies that are essential for living challenges the pedagogical assumptions on which a lot of today's curricula are based. It is a great mistake, however, to equate a society's broad educational goals with instrumental learning and an utilitarian bias. Genuine education teaches people to stand 'above the machine'. Moreover, schools share this responsibility with the media, literature and the arts, the public library, and many other institutions. This brings us to the second foundation of the learning society: education as the growth towards completion.

## GROWTH TOWARDS COMPLETION

Now we proceed from the ferment in the learning society, its sources, means and institutions, to the consideration of what is learnt. The creation of the opportunity to learn, irrespective of content, is not necessarily a positive virtue. At school and elsewhere we often learn things that do nobody any good, either directly or in the long run. Narrow-minded opinions, antiquated theories, ossified working methods, empty skills, disturbances of the motorial system, callous behaviour, ungrounded fears, docility – all are examples of the wrong kind of learning. In such cases education degenerates into, to use a word introduced by John Dewey, mis-education. But it is even worse than that. Much of the knowledge that would be most valuable to us no doubt goes unlearned, as Hirsch (1988) sets forth in his book *Cultural Literacy: What Every American Needs to Know*. How, then, do we settle our educational priorities?

Here it is only possible to talk about the direction in which I think the answer should be sought. I am not really happy about the wording but am as yet unable to do better: we learn to become a *complete* person. The justification for an educational activity, therefore, lies in the following question: in what degree does the learning contribute to a person's completeness? All learning objectives are subordinate to this ultimate test. The concern for completeness has far-reaching implications, as Abram (1984, p. 69), who has made an extensive study on the role of learning in the Jewish community, indicates:

> The permanent pupil does not learn to be able to practise a profession, not even that of rabbi, in order to obtain power or authority, but to improve himself and his behaviour and thereby the world. The purpose of his learning is, in other words, to become a complete person ... But what is 'a complete person'? There is no straight-forward answer to this question. The answer depends on the picture of the world and especially of humanity in the mind of the permanent pupil, on what he studies and appreciates in the culture, on how he digests the past and sees the future ... Each pupil has his own learning journey to make and the true significance and personal implications of the desired result, completeness, can only be revealed to him in the course of the learning process. The Torah rejects imitation both of learning method and of learning result.

This – selective – description of what 'completeness' means, of course, can only be a starting point. A conjection must be made with the formation of present-day opinion on the purpose of education. When we make this connection, we notice that the concept of 'completeness' consists of two components: it encompasses a double aspiration.

## Pursuit of quality

The first component is the pursuit of quality, an attempt to achieve improvement and ultimately excellence. In a certain sense this aim serves as a counterpoint to a point of view which dominated the discussion on the relations between education and society in the 1960s and 1970s: the ideal of equal opportunities. I am in no way advocating that the topic of social inequality and justice should disappear from the agenda. Further on the opposite will become apparent . . .

The passion for quality is *in no way* connected with the formation of an élite and *hardly* with assessments and tests, inspection committees, diplomas and examinations. On the other hand, it is *very much* related to recognizing potential and the continous search for conditions which stimulate potential.

## Pursuit of all-round development

There is a second side to the emphasis on 'completeness': the pursuit of all-round development. This striving can be seen as a counterpoint to another dominant educational trend, i.e. the concentration of attention on the cognitive development only of human beings. Other aspects of personality – including the aesthetic, social, moral, emotional, physical and even technical/manual – are regarded by western culture as more or less peripheral to education.

The British education philosopher, Louis Arnaud Reid, is one of those who has repeatedly denounced this one-sidedness. In *Ways of Understanding and Education* Reid (1986) stresses that there are two basic forms of knowledge. One form is discursive. It involves propositional statements of fact about the world around us. The other form, which covers the area of intuitive experience, is called non-discursive. The arts are excellently suited as media for expressing non-discursive knowledge. According to Reid, there should be an interchange between these ways of knowing, since the rational–intellectual and the intuitive–creative need each other. However, in western culture in general, and in curricula in particular, human knowledge is identified with what can be expressed in propositional statements. This has led to a separation of the world of the intellect, science and technology from the world of feelings, values, emotions and creativity. A disastrous schism, as Reid (1986, p. 2) writes:

> The life of personal subjects, the life of feelings and emotions, of the creative urges, of obscure symbolisms, of moral urges and intimations, religion, personal relations – all these, cut off, on this divisive assumption, from the critical purgings of thinking and intellect, remain raw, chaotic, often infantile. The personal self is split down the middle.

More attention for the training of 'eye, hand and heart' and more recognition of the importance of history, languages and literature will not, it is true, halt the increasing encroachment of specialisms, but it could nevertheless provide some counterbalance. To put it more positively, education is concerned with the whole human being and the whole culture. Does this mean that the medieval idea of the *homo universalis* is about to be reinstated? However much this idea may appeal to us, circumstances are now very different to those of our distant forefathers. There is no demand for a *homo universalis* in the present day because of the abundance of collective competence constantly around us.

## COLLECTIVE COMPETENCE

The expression 'collective competence' is taken from De Zeeuw (1984, 1985). Put simply, collective competence is the ability to act, given the availability of support systems. What, then, is a support system?

In this context I take the concept of a support system in its widest sense. Support systems are of all times and are part of the human tradition. Cultural artefacts, such as songs, fairy stories, the Bible and a hammer, can be regarded as support systems. The same can be said of manuals, spreadsheets, self-help groups, planning procedures, consultancy bureaux, radar installations and data-banks. Thus, support systems are means, tools, sources, facilities, technology.

Some support systems augment our physical strength, others reinforce our senses or our thinking powers. Some support systems enable us to act collectively (forms of social organization), others inspire us and shake us awake (art, literature). But all support systems have one thing in common: they embody the understanding, ideas and values of the past and in this respect they are human projections. Thus, using a source or aid, or some other appliance, implies calling on experience which has often been built up painfully from generation to generation in tackling the problem with which the facility is intended to cope . . . There can be no dispute that an approach to education which ignores today's support systems is out of touch with reality and, therefore, undesirable. A countervailing approach that stresses the importance of appropriating the human achievement embodied within support systems is badly needed. De Zeeuw (1984) suggests such an approach, and calls it the *participation model*. His model relies on the tacit knowledge that sources, tools and other facilities represent. We reveal this knowledge by using it, i.e. by participating in the culture in which we all have our stake.[6]

Currently there are, however, human, economic and technological obstacles to realizing this model. Let us look at some practical measures that could be taken to increase participation, thereby putting human achievement to work. These measures are centred around five critical points: (a) enriching the school environment, (b) redesigning the curriculum, (c) incorporating an educational element in the design of facilities, (d) making facilities more intelligent, and (e) removing restriction on access to facilities. I do not have room to discuss these points at length here but will limit myself to a short explanation. In each case the explanation is confined to a single example of a support system: the community or office database.

### Enriching the school environment

The school is still too much of an island. The sources from which pupils learn for the most part remain restricted to material that has been specially designed for educational purposes, and to teachers and fellow-pupils. Facilities which are available in society still do not penetrate far enough into schools. However, here and there things are changing. For example, new technology is now welcomed enthusiastically in vocational training, as are simulations of practice. But the situation is still unsatisfactory in more generally orientated educational institutions. As society moves into the micro-electronic environment of the future, the installation of computers giving access to databases relevant to the subject being handled in classrooms would be a step in the right direction.

### Redesigning the curriculum

Redesigning the curriculum is even more vital than the mere presence of present-day technological facilities in the school environment. Students need to be taught how to work from and with facilities. So, no mental arithmetic, but a task performed with the calculator. No handwritten business correspondence, but straight into the computer. No prefabricated teaching material but 'real life' sources should be used.

The community and office database is such a source. As computerized knowledge systems become more accepted in educational settings, students will have to acquire new skills in order to cope with them. What can teachers do to help students in this respect? The solution which schools are beginning to develop is the provision of special programmes on subjects with names such as study skills, information skills, computer literacy, library skills and communication skills. An alternative is to integrate the training in the normal discipline-centred courses, which involves a different kind of pedagogy. In whatever way they are organized, the perspective – what are the lessons for? – must be clear. Explanation (of why), broadening (of the possibilities for application), coupling (of the various forms of computer applications in daily life) and recognizing 'the meaning of meaning' should be key areas of attention.

### Embedded training

Few individuals like to invest a lot of time and energy in learning how to use facilities such as libraries or computers. By incorporating an educational element into the design of such facilities it is possible to avoid forcing the beginner to struggle through all sorts of manuals and instructions, or even to attend training courses before being able to start off. It makes instruction available when and where needed, on the job, in everyday settings. Furthermore, building education into a support system ensures that actors keep on developing their skills to a 'professional' level. Indeed, embedded training can best be seen as a form of learning by doing.

What are the implications for our case study, the computerized knowledge system? First, the information offered and the retrieval procedures must be clear. Second, support must be available at critical moments when decisions have to be made and steps taken. Third, this support facilitates reflection on the user's actions and the development of an own perspective on the subject. Fourth, the data file must contain valuable information which is attractively presented and tempts the user to proceed further. Fifth, there should be room for several methods of working.

## Making facilities more intelligent

This measure lies in the extension of the previous one. However, here we are concerned not so much with the educational aspect, but rather with the desire for something that is referred to as 'user friendliness'. The criteria are, then, simplicity in use, accessibility, the appeal of working with the facility, efficiency. But there is more. The facility must not only be 'friendly' towards the user, it should also be designed from the user's perspective and not proceed from the demands of a specialized discipline or a programming language. There is even a further criterion. Most facilities are inclined to deteriorate over the years as, for example, when professionals come to dominate their use or when insufficient attention is paid to changing needs and circumstances. For this reason, facilities should be designed with mechanisms that ensure a permanent dialogue between the (projected) user and the professional.

Despite the fact that they may be regarded as wonders of sophistication by some, all the automated information facilities with which I am familiar seem depressingly inadquate with respect to the criteria just mentioned. Take one example from my own experience. I discovered part of the documentation for this study using the Online Public Catalogue which the Library of the University of Amsterdam recently installed. It had something to offer, undoubtedly. But, to begin with, the layout on the monitor was so primitive: no pictograms, far too many words and codes, no attempt at all at a pleasing graphical presentation. And to think that this is a relatively advanced system. Contrary to the shining visions of the computer enthusiast, it is obviously still a long time till the micro-electronic era. Lessons on how to use information often deal chiefly with problems which would not exist if the system had been built more intelligently in the first place.

**Increasing the availability of facilities**

Modern society is rich in facilities. But not everything is within everyone's reach. Wealth – and consequently opportunities to learn – is unevenly distributed . . .

With regard to computerized knowledge systems there are signs that in the coming years increasingly more information on the most diverse topics will be (exclusively) stored in computers. But the public at large has no, or no easy, access to these electronic publications. It is a good thing that in several countries the public library is trying to do something about this problem. Two Dutch projects are worth mentioning: TACO (a national data-bank) and Biblitel (a local data-bank). However, the context in which a project such as TACO must function deserves more attention. Taking repercussions on existing ways of working, establishing responsibilities and hierarchies into account, there are three basic possibilities. First, the data-bank leaves everything as it is (and is probably hardly ever used). Second, the introduction of the data-bank requires some adjustments to be made in its environment (until a new equilibrium is reached). Third, the introduction of the data-bank leads to a restructuring of intelligence work and to adjustments at other levels of the institution and this, in turn, leads to special design requirements for the data-bank, and so on. Only in the last case can we speak of a true innovation, in the sense of a long-term increase in the collective competence embedded in public libraries.

So much for a number of measures connected with collective competence. I would add this: by regarding sources, equipment and other facilities as support systems, terms of reference are set within which a constructive discussion of our culture can be held. Such a discussion is constructive because it is directed to transforming our culture into a living possession with everyone participating in it. The notion of collective competence has brought the third premise for the learning society into focus. But more is involved in such a society.

## SELF-EDUCATION

The achievement of self-education is the fourth key to the advancement of a learning society. Although different writers mean different things when they use the word self-education, the insight that the concept contains two elements is gradually emerging. First, self-education is the objective aimed at: encouraging people to keep on learning of their own volition. A general heading that applies to this aim is *learning to learn*. Second, self-education is a recommended *way of teaching*, an approach for helping people to learn. In educational practice self-education can be both the objective and the vehicle. However, to avoid confusion, I have unravelled these two strands.

## Learning to learn

Learning to learn seeks to emphasize that, throughout life, human beings are what they are because of learning. The concept assumes a 'recursive framework', one that sees actors as potentially creative. At its heart is the achievement of autonomy: people taking the responsibility for their own learning.

Libraries could be filled with what has been written on these ideas, though not every writer goes under the same banner. Because of its utilitarian flavour, Smith (1982, p. 19) prefers the phrase learning *how to* learn. His effort to come to terms with the slippery concept starts from the following definition: 'Learning how to learn involves possessing, or acquiring, the knowledge and skill to learn effectively in whatever learning situation one encounters.'

Such a general definition looks attractive, but it is not adequate in this case, since it ignores the fact that the concept can be approached from various angles. Thus, learning to learn is variously described as:

- acquiring skills in tracing and making sense of information
- becoming proficient in solving problems in varying situations
- obtaining a grasp of the principles of good research
- reinforcing self-regulation in school and training settings
- practising study techniques
- developing 'higher order' skills
- increasing one's ability to learn from experience
- nurturing the desire to become a complete person.

Admirable as these goals are, instruction to increase people's competence in learning is usually simplified into courses or lessons in studying skills. Often such efforts are dominated by a school-bound mentality, by helping students to survive in the education arena. The chief concern is about coping with the system: tricks on how to get through examinations, learning material by heart, doing homework, marking study texts, making notes. In my opinion, the study-skills movement should broaden its perspective and shift its focus from the reproductive to the productive aspects of knowledge. For that a link should be sought with the other approaches to improving the capacity to learn.

In addition, it is necessary to emphasize the crucial importance of the environments in which the skills one has learnt are applied. What I advocate is an ecology of learning to learn. The ecological view may be premised with some thoughts on the problem of transfer, which is indeed a major deficiency in many study-skills programmes (Nisbet and Shucksmith, 1986). But the ecology of learning implies more than simply taking care of transfer. It also involves being fully alive to the power relationships within the social structure. To paraphrase the Czech-born novelist Milan Kundera (see McEwan, 1984, pp. 26–32), we can say that in a world which has become a trap the struggle for inward independence (and against the monster within) should coincide with the struggle for outward independence (against the monster from outside).

How can this look at learning to learn be implemented in practical situations? Various suggestions have been made. Some, for example Boud (1988, p. 8),

**Table 5. 1**   *Basic ways of increasing knowledge*

| The school approach | The adult approach |
| --- | --- |
| Transmitting a given body of knowledge | Developing an own perspective on a subject |
| The teacher decides | The learner decides |
| A semantically poor context | A semantically rich context |
| Learning without facilities | Learning with facilities |
| Learning as drilling | Learning as a conscious activity |
| Experience as condition | Experience as foundation |
| Directed to subject-matter | Directed to problems |
| Evaluation as a check | Evaluation as a means of improving |
| Compulsion and duty | Voluntary basis, pleasure in learning |
| Directed at achievement | Directed towards completion |
| Closed tasks | Open tasks |

advocate changes in the regular curriculum: 'They believe that it is the responsibility of all teachers to ensure that they construct their courses to foster autonomy and that this goal is compatible with the discipline-centred goals which often predominate'. Others take the existing curriculum as a fact of life but think that it should be enriched with supportive lessons, optional or otherwise, on subjects such as coping with self-instructional materials, working through projects, writing a thesis, using a library, and 'reading' media constructions. A third group maintains that measures outside education are also needed; there is a task for broadcasting organizations, museums, libraries, publishers and creativity centres.

As I see it, a learning society will explore all possible avenues of promoting learning to learn. With one reservation, I have very little faith in initiatives determined from on high which do not take the day-to-day experiences of those involved into account. Emancipation – meaning inner and outer independence – is not granted, it has to be fought for and won.

## Ways of teaching

As I said, the word self-education stands not only for something to strive for, but also for a means, a way of teaching. This is another topic which has fuelled a lot of controversy and, again, polemicists do not all share the same background. This is expressed in the variety of concepts denoting the principles of good practice. Perhaps the issues at stake can be clarified by identifying two basic ways of helping people to increase their knowledge and improve their qualifications. I have labelled these contrasting views the 'school approach' and the 'adult approach' (Table 5.1).[7]

It has to be admitted that this scheme is full of crass contradictions. But the descriptions help us to cut out the proverbial rigmarole that is so typical of the age-old discussion about the most appropriate ways of meeting learners' needs. It goes without saying that the approach advocated here is the adult approach. Its principles characterize the spirit in which pupils – of any age – and teachers deal with each other in a learning society.

For clarity's sake: an adult approach is also possible outside general forming and development work and group teaching. Its principles are viable everywhere: in study at a distance, in computer-assisted learning, in mathematical education, in in-house company training programmes, in occupational training, at universities, in museums, in public libraries and elsewhere.

## RIGHT TO LEARN

As a social issue education is the responsibility of the community. In a learning society, therefore, learning should be a right and not a privilege. All citizens – regardless of social status, income, initial training, descent, sex and affiliations – should be given equal opportunities to develop themselves and to improve proficiencies throughout their lives. This goal is music to democratic ears. Is it then any wonder that since the 1960s terms such as lifelong learning, permanent education and recurrent education have occurred regularly in the introductions of official educational documents? Enough rhetoric to sink a ship.

But what are the implications for educational practice? Which attitude should the government adopt? What is entirely private domain, and how far should state interference reach? Kidd (1983, p. 530) sketches the alternatives:

> Is there a basic education that a citizen should have as a birthright and would the provision of such constitute the main conditions of a learning society? Or would something more be needed, such as national declarations or law, or an ethos of learning, or an environment for learning?

It seems that, as far as the right of learning is concerned, the Dutch government does not wish to commit itself to more than guaranteeing a sort of minimum programme, and even that is under review. The most important policy instrument is the general-proficiency schooling for 12- to 15- or 16-year-olds. In addition there are plans for an educational voucher system.

### General-proficiency schooling versus basic education

According to the Dutch Scientific Council for Government Policy (1986, p. 81) general-proficiency schooling is concerned with:

- *basic* skills: proficiencies (knowledge, attainments, understanding) that are vital to be able to function as a member of society and which are the essential foundation and nucleus for further development;
- education for *everyone*: in principle, the contents of the basic forming are the same for all groups;
- *common* education: in principle, the schooling is directed to the common acquisition of the contents of a curriculum that is equally valid for all. Forms

of differentiation between pupils in anticipation of their further education are, in principle, to be avoided.

How does this renewed interest in the myth of 'the common school, common programme, common core' (Holmes, 1988, p. 246) fit in with the notion of a learning society? Getting back to basics, in keeping with the diversity of tasks that life has set aside for people, seems to me a viable idea, provided that general schooling allows for differential educational provisions to accommodate inequalities in pupils' capacities and backgrounds. As far as the belief in common public education appeals to the idea of equality as a principle of justice it cannot possibly mean equality of treatment. Rather, it has to come to terms with the principles of equal consideration and equal opportunity (Fletcher, 1984).

Whatever general-proficiency schooling may mean, my greatest fear is that we may claim to be achieving quality if everyone in the Netherlands can neatly answer a barrage of pre-set questions drawn up by experts in different fields. We will then be even further from the mark. Our educational system will not be truly worthwhile until schools succeed in motivating youngsters to keep on learning and asking critical questions about the world.

Another point which prompts criticism and concern is that adult education has been left out of the discussion. It is an obvious step to give not only young people but also adults the opportunity to acquire and cultivate basic proficiencies. The State Regulation on Adult Elementary Education could be applied to this end. In addition to higher priority for this branch of adult education, a more differentiated package of lessons with more choice, more quality and less utilitarian bias is needed.

A third isssue is also important. It must be recognized in word and in deed that it is not just schools that enable citizens to function in contemporary society. The involvement of companies, television, newspapers, museums, public libraries and other 'socializing contexts' is essential. A *national newspaper literacy day*, an American initiative, could be held up as an example.


**Educational vouchers?**

The second policy instrument that is expected to strengthen the right to learn is the educational bond. The idea has been broached that all young people should be presented with an educational bond at the end of their compulsory schooling at 16. The bond would consist of a fixed number of vouchers which would entitle each holder to the same number of years of full-time day education, to be filled in as they chose. The personalized vouchers would remain valid indefinitely, but when they are used up, that is it. Precursors of such a voucher system exist already. We only have to think of the time limits in higher education.

Much as support must be given (with reservations) to the idea of general-proficiency schooling, so the idea of an educational bond is hopeless. The introduction of a voucher system does not lead to an enlargement but to a contraction of the opportunities for learning. Will schooling soon only be available to ticket holders? Whatever ends this regulation meets, it certainly does not serve that of lifelong learning, even leaving aside the question of practicality. Social security has proved to be beyond our reach in many ways; would educational security fare better? (Not to mention the containment of the expectations roused by the voucher system.) Should government credulity be trusted this time?

**Looking further**

A government which takes the right to learn seriously cannot limit actions to seeing to it that skills 'which are an essential foundation and form the nucleus for further development' are taught. Attention must also be given to the quality of the learning environment. For this is often the difficulty, as can be seen from research into the background and reasons for (non-)participation in educational activities. Lists of the large number of barriers to learning have been drawn up time and time again. However, we are still waiting for a plan of campaign for tackling these obstacles. Unless it is accompanied by free access to the relevant sources of learning, the right to learn is just so many words.

CONCLUSION

The disturbing question of the future of education led an American government commission in 1983 to shake the American people awake with the report *A Nation at Risk* (US Congress, 1983). The typical Dutch reaction was to conduct a 'trial investigation to establish if a periodical assessment study into the level of education in the Netherlands' was feasible. This unsentimental attitude appeals to me; but at the same time, I hope that a more creative answer will be found, based on a sense of direction concerning the future of our culture and not on mourning for a lost past. An answer, moreover, which takes learning human beings and not educational institutions as its starting point.

The concept 'learning society', a society in which learning is the whole of life and the whole of life is learning, is a powerful stimulation to the formation of opinion. In this chapter I have outlined what the cornerstones of such a society could be. I realize the risks involved in working with an abstract, even utopian, idea such as that of a learning society. On the other hand, it has to be said that it is impossible to work without a perspective – without sources of inspiration, aims, guidelines and norms.

A lack of commitment is one of the risks of the approach proposed above. Dimensions of society, growth to completeness, collective competence, self-education, right to learn – all good publishers' blurb. But what are the practical implications of this way of thinking? The values to which the notion of a learning society appeals will indeed have to be embodied in the various situations in which people can learn. This is precisely the strength of the chosen concept: it enables us to gather a variety of approaches and social initiatives together at a higher level of abstraction beyond immediate self-interests and parochialism.

Time is of the essence. The general climate has not become more hospitable to human learning in the last twenty years. Today the criterion is the return from educational institutions and not the contribution made to stimulating potential. Training courses increasingly benefit ambitious men in senior and top functions, while the training chances for those with only elementary education, for the unemployed and for women are decreasing. The school approach to learning and teaching is gaining the whip hand. Consumerism and cafeteria-style education is encroaching on all sides. But the cause for most concern is probably that the discussion about such a crucial public issue as educational reform is being conducted by the civil service, industry and commerce and educational specialists; there are no organized counterforces. Is this the culture we want?

## NOTES

1 This chapter is an edited version of an article in the *International Journal of Lifelong Education*, 10 (3), 1991, pp. 210–30.
2 Here I am concerned with the organization principle, without the restrictions on contents. For a Jewish believer the sources are fixed (the Torah); he only has to dig things out. In this chapter, on the other hand, the selection of sources is under discussion.
3 As defined here, the *educational* dimension coincides with the *cultural* dimension (Zijderveld, 1983) and the *moral* dimension (Etzioni, 1988). Politics and the economy are examples of alternative perspectives for viewing societal processes. My position is quite close to that of Fletcher (1984).
4 The concept 'learning projects' has gained some popularity through the writings of Penland and Tough (see, for example, Penland and Mathai, 1987, and Neehal and Tough, 1983). But two related terms are increasingly found now: self-directed learning and independent learning. Strictly speaking, the phrase 'learning project' refers to sustained, planned and voluntarily chosen major efforts to learn something that is fairly well defined. This meaning has been eroded. The idea that people are the active agents of their own education has led to a plethora of empirical studies. Yet the findings are still very modest. Cross (1986, p. 199) states 'So far, most pioneer researchers on self-directed learning have left what happens during the learning project as virtually unexplored territory. Whether one wants to know how to facilitate learning or how to present information to adults, more in-depth study of how learning takes place in everyday settings is a necessity, one that should receive first priority in the 1980s.' Cross has put her finger on the sore spot; but more work has to be done. There is also a pressing need for clarity about the theoretical basis of this line of thought and practice.
5 The unintentional lessons which accompany taking part in training programmes and courses are a special case of spontaneous learning. Asserting yourself in a group, waiting your turn, getting used to discipline, and experiencing company culture are examples of this phenomenon. The occurrence of such side-effects, whose importance should not be underestimated, is called the 'hidden curriculum'.
6 A theoretical framework that has kinship with De Zeeuw's ideas is Donald Schön's concept of *knowing-in-action*. Schön (1987) uses this term to refer to the sorts of know-how skilled practitioners display in their judgements, decisions and other complex actions, usually without being able to state the rules or procedures they followed. The knowing is part of the action.

7 There are many other terms in circulation at the moment which denote the polarization of ways of (thinking about) teaching. To name but a few: pedagogy *versus* andragogy; the dissemination orientation *versus* orientation *versus* the development orientation; the didactic model *versus* the communication model; the behavioural paradigm *versus* the normative paradigm.

# Chapter 6

# Learning in the New Millennium

*Chris Hayes, Nickie Fonda and Josh Hillman*

## INTRODUCTION: THE ARGUMENT

In discussing the future of education and training it has become almost obligatory to use the phrase 'learning society'. It gives the impression that arguments for change are embedded within a broad-ranging vision. Yet most would-be reformers using it as a thematic umbrella have a limited view of the concept of a 'learning society', as something that can be achieved through adaptation of the current institutional framework to increase individuals' access to educational opportunities.

This briefing adopts a radically different starring point. *It sees learning not only as a matter for individuals but also as a key process for facilitating the transformation of today's society into a profoundly different kind of society in the future.* The skilful management of that transformation is critical if the risk of serious conflict is to be minimized. The briefing offers a framework for placing and evaluating policies for the development of learning processes, the organization of work and communities.

The shift from an agricultural to an industrial society 200 years ago caused a revolution in all aspects of British life. It is becoming clear, from examination of broad trends and from day-to-day experience, that our society is currently undergoing another historic transformation. A clear picture will only emerge when the transformation has reached a more advanced state, but there are some harbingers (see Panel 6.1).

In this period, the abyss between the emerging imperatives and society's capacity to adapt presents a raft of new challenges: to individuals, to organizations, to communities, and to society as a whole. Learning, in particular, assumes a crucial role: first, in understanding and managing change; second, in discovering and implementing solutions to immediate problems; third, in anticipating further developments; and fourth, in being effective in a new world.

The problem that society faces is now to prepare for this crossing. In order that it should be best positioned it will require four essential bridges into the

**Panel 6.1** *Harbingers of the transformation*

- The nation state in the developed West is declining as a locus of power.
- There is an ongoing shift from mass-production work to work in organizations based on responsiveness and customization.
- The economy is increasingly organized around the processing of information.
- The increasing accessibility of information is helping to break monopolies of power. How more dispersed power is used and how information is manipulated, will depend on the new economic, political and social structures which are bound to arise.
- Effective action is no longer possible on the traditional military, industrial, political and public service model, with thinkers and planners instructing and controlling implementers and doers.
- Active participation is demanded from ever-wider sections of society, with each individual developing the capability to bring about change at individual, organizational and collective levels, in other words, individuals can make a difference.
- Problem-solving capabilities based on the the use of concepts rather than on experience are becoming essential when facing new and unfamiliar situations. Knowledge and skills are necessary, but insufficient, prerequisites for effective action.
- Information technology is coming to be seen not simply as a tool but as a new and intrinsic dimension in learning.

post-transformation society: two patterns of collective learning and two patterns of individual learning. These are shown in Panel 6.2.

These patterns of learning form a continuous spectrum, in which they are interdependent and overlapping. For each, we discuss:

- its features and benefits
- what 'doing it well' could mean

**Panel 6.2** *Patterns of Learning*

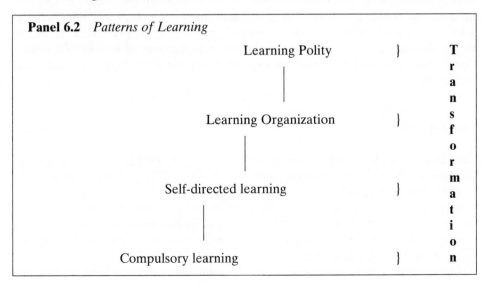

- what active steps might be taken to prepare most effectively for the uncertainties of the transformation
- its limits
- at the end of the chapter (in Panel 6.4), some of its prominent chroniclers and advocates.

## COMPULSORY LEARNING

### Features and benefits

Between the ages of 5 and 16 everybody attends primary and secondary school, and the national curriculum and its associated assessment arrangements now prescribe in detail what is to be taught. Later on, when education becomes voluntary, those acquiring general or professional qualifications are expected to study certain subjects or develop particular skills. In the workplace, employees are often required to undergo job-specific training. National Vocational Qualifications verify competence to perform specific tasks in a specific occupation.

These are all examples of compulsory learning. In each case, what is to be learnt is decided by an authority rather than the learner. Such decisions are diffuse and complex in the case of publicly provided education services, with a multitude of interest groups, all with very different expectations, staking their claims. As a consequence, there is protracted discussion before any major changes in the curriculum take place, followed by a long time-lag before implementation at a satisfactory level of quality. In the case of training, both in private and public sector organizations, the process of change is usually more straightforward; however, time-lags can have more rapid practical repercussions, for example with training provided for tasks or responsibilities that have ceased to exist.

Historically, compulsory learning has tended to expand, reflecting the fact that modern societies cannot function without learning foundations, which continue to grow and change. Modern societies depend increasingly on process skills and an understanding and use of concepts. The increasing sophistication of both manufacturing and services also requires an ever widening range of skills, knowledge and understanding.

### Doing it well

The first requirement for doing it well is to keep compulsory education and training in line with the demands of current realities. The removal of items from learning programmes are as essential in this as the addition of new ones.

Second, it is not enough for compulsory learning to respond to changes that have already occurred. Its aims and processes must anticipate future needs. These include learning to manage change and diversity, and developing the foundation skills for self-directed learning.

Third, new technologies can be used to facilitate the learning process, by responding to the preferences of learners for where, when, and how learning takes place. They can also help to reduce the unit costs of high-quality delivery.

Fourth, assessment is needed to ensure that learning has taken place to required standards and also to promote the improvement of the learning process itself.

## Into the transformation

For individuals, a foundation of compulsory learning is an essential prerequisite for self-directed learning. For this reason, it is becoming increasingly necessary for compulsory learning to avoid fostering the fear of learning for oneself and to place a high premium on the skills associated with successful self-directed learning:

- the ability to navigate in an ever-increasing flow of data in order to produce usable information
- understanding one's immediate and more distant environment
- looking out for, and seizing, opportunities
- clarifying one's own hopes and intentions
- learning to learn on a continuous basis
- Since information to technology will be one of the core technologies of the future, learners will need to use whatever IT can be made avilable as a tool for an ever-widening range of tasks and explorations.

## Limits

Compulsory learning is not enough when:

- individuals cannot rely on political and economic authorities to provide continuous employment and career opportunities.
- individuals want to learn primarily for personal satisfaction.

## SELF-DIRECTED LEARNING

### Features and benefits

Self-directed learning is driven by a range of purposes:

- for its own sake
- for family or leisure pursuits
- for better positioning in the labour market
- for carrying out work assignments or fulfilling work responsibilities.

These may overlap and pursuit of one may stimulate interest in another. For example, a person may learn the basics of a language for its own sake, be motivated to take it a step further for travel, and then continue learning at a more advanced level for use at work.

Choice is also affected by the variety of means of learning at the disposal of the individual:

- formal learning institutions and centres, either through modular programmes or custom-built courses, which may or may not lead to qualifications
- assessment of prior experience learning
- books, packages, computer networks
- personal contacts
- informal learning opportunities, whether aided or unaided, such as experimentation, reviewing experience, evaluating and drawing conclusions.

Making the right choice is often a matter of luck since many learners lack access to independent advice, guidance and information.

Some of the large employers are keen to develop a learning culture in their enterprises, as a stop on the road to becoming a 'learning organization', and are prepared to pay for their employees to participate in almost any self-directed learning programme. These are the exceptions to the rule. Most employers in Britain will not make any contribution towards a course unless first, they consider its content to be directly relevant to their perception of the employee's role, and second, they believe it will not unduly increase the mobility of the employee. In organizations of all types, employees are increasingly having to find both their own time and money, even in some cases for training as a precondition of employment.

This lack of a will to invest is founded on the assumption that employers will not get a return on their investment. But it is worth reminding ourselves of one of the central tenets of human capital theory: education and training develop the assets of knowledge and skills and can increase workplace productivity, just as investment in and updating of machinery can increase productivity in physical capital. A critical difference between the two, of course, lies in the mobility of people. These points were documented in the 1960s, but continue to increase in importance. A recent study showed that in Germany the value ratio of material capital stock (material assets such as buildings, equipment, communications) to human capital stock (spending on education and training) fell from 3.2 : 1 to 2.2 : 1 between 1970 and 1989. This ratio will continue to fall in every country for the foreseeable future.

## Doing it well

By its very nature, self-directed learning is not determined by authorities on behalf of the learner. Learners are motivated by their own purposes and choose both the content and the means of learning. These choices are part of the excitement and the satisfaction of this pattern of learning, but they are associated with its biggest risk. Four issues confront the learners at various stages in the learning process.

- *Information.* Impartial advice about what is available is essential. In addition to being disinterested, information should offer a strategic perspective on the value of particular learning opportunities and a consumer perspective on its quality. Information technology could enhance the availability of this information at the time when choices are being made.
- *Financing.* Detailed information about costs of learning opportunities needs to be complemented by access to a range of financing options and concessions, and to self-learning materials.
- *Quality.* The public education system has a long tradition of quality inspection, but there is great room for improvement, even in the compulsory learning sectors. Evaluations of quality will inevitably need to go beyond what can be simply measured, to assessments which are meaningful to learners.
- *Relevance.* Self-directed learners may not be fully aware of changes in the labour market and choose, or be encouraged, to acquire knowledge and skills the utility of which is fast disappearing. Equally, they may be offered inflexible and out-of-date learning methods which could hinder their ability to learn in the future.

## Into the transformation

As we move into a period of greater uncertainty, burgeoning demand for self-directed learning will lead to a series of developments.

- Increasing amounts of time and money will be spent by increasing numbers of individuals on learning. This trend will be accentuated by the ever-growing expansion of knowledge.
- To feed this growth, the infrastructure of learning facilities will grow apace: materials, equipment, examinations and tests, software, learning facilitators, counsellors and guides.
- There will thus be a further shift in investment from physical assets towards resources to support learning. Learning outside organized learning institutions will assume much greater importance.
- There will be a shortening life-cycle of learning products. To be economically viable, they will either have to be taken up in high volumes and in quick succession, or be based on new and cheaper forms of development and delivery.
- Behind the widely accessible and 'transparent' opportunities for self-directed learning, there will be a proliferation of networks of 'virtual' communities for the development of new learning products. Such virtual groupings will bring together specialists from various organizations all over the world for specific projects. Examples of this kind already exist.
- Guide 'books', written by people with knowledge of areas of learning, will help learners to select what they are looking for in the plethora of freely available data and information.

**Limits**

Self-directed learning is not enough when people want to make a difference to a collectivity, whether it be an employing organization, a local community or a club. Self-directed learning is necessary but not sufficient to produce change through action in, and by, an organization. To achieve such change, organizations must learn as entities.

## THE LEARNING ORGANIZATION

Up to now the focus has been on individual learning. In the following section, the organization as an organic entity becomes the centre of the learning process.

**Features and benefits**

Organizations exist for a collective purpose: schools for teaching and learning; banks for lending money to organizations and individuals; hospitals for diagnosis and treatment of patients; and tennis clubs for managing facilities for members.

Organizations could continue in perpetuity what they do, how they do it and to what standards they do it, if their environments were constant. However, expectations of users of products or services do not remain unchanged; nor do buying power and preferences; nor competition or technology. Greater stability in politics and in international relations is also unlikely.

In competitive private sectors, organizations disappear when they fail to anticipate, capitalize on, and adapt to changes in the environment. Unless an organization has been purposely set up with a finite life in view, it has to take active steps to survive.

Until recently, public services have remained relatively unaffected even by substantial changes in their environment – except for technological change in their core activities. In the past few years, government has begun to insist that public services develop the YAII, which has not always been matched by the ability, to respond to change. 'Re-inventing' public services has become much discussed in many countries.

The implication is that to achieve their purpose, organizations have to learn to think differently, to do things differently and to do new and different things. For example:

- Manufacturers of cars, exposed to global competition, must achieve new standards of quality, master radically new manufacturing technology, and reduce unit costs and product development cycles. They must also respond to environmental protection measures, incorporate more sophisticated safety features, and adapt to traffic management systems.
- As a result of the National Health Service reform, hospitals are becoming concerned with the outcomes of treatments for patients and with living up to

the public standards of patients' charters; medical consultants are now offering clinics close to patients, as well as in hospital locations; doctors are expected to manage budgets. Keeping up to date with the technology (e.g. in key-hole surgery) continues as before.

'When the wind of change blows, some build walls, others build windmills'. The latter are learning organizations and they are defined in Panel 6.3 by contrasting them with non-learning organizations.

In the private sector, if the environment is changing, and particularly if it is turbulent, survival, growth and profits depend on organization learning. Public services can only maintain trust and goodwill by meeting ever-rising public expectations. This, and the continuous improvement in the well-being of citizens, can only be accomplished by organizational learning.

**Doing it well**

There are a number of dimensions to successful 'organizational learning':

- The rate of learning of the organization is greater or equal to the rate of relevant change in its environment.
- The organization not only demonstrates the will to manage change but also takes the necessary steps to acquire or develop the capability to do so.
- The organization learns to improve its performance on a continuous basis.
- Everybody is expected to add value through their work, and is supported in so doing.
- A general learning culture is valued, recognized and rewarded.

**Into the transformation**

Organizations are increasingly becoming the locus for knowledge work. Individuals by themselves will always lack the infrastructure of access to new developments, which only organizations can offer. The management and continuous renewal of this infrastructure is likely to become a major preoccupation of organizations which can hope to survive. To become a leader requires industry foresight, for example, into the trends in technology, demographics, regulation and lifestyles that can be harnessed to rewrite industry rules and create new competititve space.

None the less, as the rate of innovation increases, it becomes harder for organizations to keep up. Projects can no longer be paced in order to accumulate finance and knowledge, but must be completed quickly and be 'right first time'. Even the largest companies are finding it difficult to draw on adequate resources, both money and expertise, and to keep up to date with developments in the outside world. An increasingly common response has been the formation of partnerships and joint ventures, often across industrial sectors as well as national and cultural boundaries. Some examples are the European Airbus enterprise,

---

**Panel 6.3**   *What is a learning organization?*

**Learning organization**
Anticipates future problems
Pays attention to external environment
Continuously seeks improvement
Problem-solving based on conceptual analysis and understanding
Problem-solving is organization-wide and problem-centred
Rewards for growth, initiative and creativity
Job definitions encourage exploration, initiative and information-sharing

**Non-learning organization**
Reacts to current problems
Pays attention only to internal operations
Responds to accumulation of poor performance
Problem-solving is based on trial and error
Problem-solving is compartmentalized and hierarchical
Rewards for historical performance
Jobs are narrowly circumscribed and risk-taking is discouraged

---

multi-media consortia, industry research partnerships, public/private sector joint ventures and 'one-stop shops' for public services. There are some important implications of these developments:

- the demands of managing extreme cultural diversity
- the proliferation of temporary and permanent webs of relationships within and across organizations
- the challenge of boosting the commitment of knowledge workers, in a context of complex and continuously shifting alliances.

All of these will generate new learning challenges and new learning needs. The culture, systems and structures of organizations will undergo dramatic changes, many of which are currently unknown and unknowable. Learning to prepare organizations for this future state, in an era of transformation, will be one of the preoccupations of leading senior managers and academics.

**Limits**

The learning organization is not enough when citizens sense that existing organizations are incapable of managing change for their economic and social well-being.

## THE LEARNING POLITY

### Features and benefits

The polity, that is the organization of government and the way in which citizens participate in opinion-forming and decision-making, is under increasingly heavy fire. Politics and public administration are suffering a loss of trust and esteem. Public services are often considered to be failing to meet the (rising) expectations of citizens.

There are two common responses. One attempts to make past and present institutions and systems of public management work 'better', for example, through accountability by local elected representation, enforcement of law and order, the 'Charter' initiative, or through advocacy of greater collective responsibility, as in the communitarian movement.

The second response is for citizens to associate in more or less transient interest groups, often around single issues, and outside the established political and institutional framework. Some single-issue groups become action groups which seek to achieve their goals through more or less legal remedies. They can be seen as part of a process of the dispersal of power, often accompanied by the more general availability of knowledge and information. Some of these groups or movements can be thought of as angry reactions without longer-term concerns, but others can be considered as forerunners of a transformation to a new polity.

For us in Britain, it is important to separate underlying trends which point towards more fundamental changes, and the particular interpretations of such trends by governments. Command and control by government of business processes, of task objectives of the flow of resources and the nature and quality of arrangements to ensure accountability to stakeholders often hinder rather than enhance inevitable long-term trends.

### Doing it well

For instance, the trend towards individuals exercising greater control over their lives, and the decentralization, devolution and delegation of decision-making responsibilities in organizations are undoubtedly historic trends. In industry they show themselves as a 'transformation of production units into business units', in the Health Service in the development of Trusts, and in education in the greater responsibilities of schools and colleges. These developments can only lead to effective performance and high-quality services if self-directed learning and understanding by individuals, and learning by organizational entities, grow faster than changes in their environment.

The time-lag between technological, industrial, ecological and social change and subsequent changes in the political and public-service systems can be seen clearly by the pain which the new responsibilities are causing in public life. Moreover, the benefits which could be gained from this devolutionary trend are held back by the hierarchical command and control system and the behaviour of politicians and government institutions. They may be the last in the learning chain to understand the fundamental changes in our environment and to see the need for building capability for practical response.

Decentralization of decision-making is associated with more widespread participation and shared responsibility, giving a key role to stakeholders who have a direct interest in a body or organization. Governance should guide the behaviour and performance of units of public life so as to earn the trust and esteem of those who work within them and the public. Politically elected or nominated representatives are losing public confidence. The growth of quangos is no substitute for a search for new forms of equitable governance. We are not sufficiently advanced down the road to transformation to know how the voice of stakeholders will be heard but current processes are ineffective.

Similarly, the only attempts to explore new forms of funding are initiatives for joint ventures between the public and private sectors. Outside of these, the traditional Treasury model has hardly been touched.


**Into the transformation**

Although there is a long way to go, hesitant steps are being taken towards greater transparency of public systems and activities. More local or regional taxes, perhaps hypothecated, and systems of credits and vouchers might add to transparency and encourage individuals and interest groups to undertake responsible initiatives.

Where national strategic aims have found resonance, local initiatives are growing in numbers and effectiveness. They may be within or outside the official institutional structures. For instance, the vision of 'health gain' has brought together different local organizations and interest groups which are learning, albeit by trial and error, to design and manage processes leading to health gain. Such initiatives have to break down the functional separation of organizations and replace them with processes needed to achieve the purpose of the wider vision. Similar early developments can be found in the fields of crime reduction, regeneration and other areas. Raising and managing money and other resources is often an important part of the learning process.

Without national aims, self-help systems are emerging which focus on areas of needs, for example the *Big Issue* network for the homeless.

The learning polity advances when individuals, organizations and associations learn to build trusting relationships between themselves and develop the capability to manage change. This empowers communities to act with a shared sense of purpose and to embrace the challenges of the future.


CONCLUSION

The burden of the case made in this briefing is that we are in the early parts of a historic transition to a new form of society and that 'learning' is one of the keys to progressing through the transformation and achieving it with the minimum of social upheaval.

Those who expect at the conclusion of this briefing a series of policy prescriptions or practical hints for better learning processes will be disappointed. The National Commission on Education and others have already contributed to a substantial literature on these subjects. Nor is the conclusion a plea for further research.

The sheer scope and magnitude of the tasks of moving through a historic transformation with uncertain outcomes calls for everybody's imaginative participation. We therefore suggest that readers use the framework in this briefing in order to assume responsibility for:

- evaluating what we – individually and collectively – are doing now
- considering how this positions us on the route through the transformation
- envisaging what needs to be different and better
- deciding how each one of us can contribute to making this difference as:
  - a citizen in a community
  - a worker, whether employee or self employed
  - a member of a profession, trade union or other common interest group
  - a voter, policy maker or leader

---

**Panel 6.4**  *Prominent chroniclers and advocates*

**Introduction**
Boyer, F. (1991) *Ready to Learn*, Carnegie Foundation for the Advancement of Teaching.
Husen, T. (1986) *The Learning Society Revisited*. Oxford: Pergamon.
Hutchins, R. (1968) *The Learning Society*. London: Pall Mall.
OECD (1992) *High Quality Education and Training for All*. Paris: OECD.
OECD (1992) *New Technology and its Impact on Education Buildings*. Paris: OECD.

**Compulsory learning**
Dearing, R. (1994) *The National Curriculum and its Assessment*. London: School Curriculum and Assessment Authority.
Further Education Unit, (1992) *Core Skills in Action*. London: FEU.
Jessop, G. (1991) *Outcomes; NVQs and the Emerging Model of Education and Training*. London: Falmer Press.
Lawton, D. (1989) *Education, Culture and the National Curriculum*. London: Hodder and Stoughton.

**Self-directed learning**
Ball, C. (1993) *Towards a Learning Society*. London: Royal Society of Arts.
Gardner, H. (1993) *Multiple Intelligence: The Theory in Practice*. New York: Basic Books.
Handy, C. (1994) *The Empty Raincoat*. London: Hutchinson.
Wood, D. (1993) *The Classroom of 2015*. In National Commission on Education Briefings. London: Heinemann.
Zuboff, S. (1988) *In the Age of the Smart Machine*. London: Heinemann.

**The learning organisation**
Ansoff, I. (1984) *Implanting Strategic Management*. London: Prentice Hall International.
Botkin, J., Elmandjra, M., and Malitza, M. (1970) *No Limits to Learning: Bridging the Human Gap*. Oxford: Pergamon.
Drucker, P. (1993) *Post-Capitalist Society*. London: Butterworth-Heinemann.
Fullan, M. (1993) *Change Forces*. London: Falmer Press.
Hamel, G. and Prahalad, C. (1994) *Competing for the Future*. Boston: Harvard Business School Press.
Hammer, M. and Champy, J. (1993) *Reengineering the Corporation*. New York: Harper Business.
Senge, P. (1990) *The Fifth Discipline: The Art and Practice of the Learning Organisation*. New York: Doubleday.

**The learning polity**
Etzioni, A. (1993) *The Spirit of Community*. New York: Touchstone.
Giddens, A. (1994) *Beyond Left and Right: The Future of Radical Politics*. Oxford: Polity Press.
Hirst, P. (1994) *Associative Democracy: New Forms of Economic and Social Governence*. Oxford: Polity Press.
Hobsbawm, E. (1994) *Age of Extremes*. London: Michael Joseph.
MacIntyre, A. (1987) *The Idea of an Educated Public*. In Haydon, G.[ed.] *Education and Values: The Richard Peters Lectures*. London: Institute of Education.
Mulgan, G. (1994) *Politics in an Antipolitical Age*. Oxford: Polity Press.
Osborne, D. and Gaebler, T. (1993) *Reinventing Government*. New York: Plume.
Ranson, S. (1994) *Towards a Learning Society*. London: Cassell.

*Chapter 7*

# Towards the Learning Society

*Stewart Ranson*[1]

## INTRODUCTION

Education has, once more, become a national issue and priority during a period of great social, economic and political change. The intention of this chapter is to identify the argument surrounding education, to develop an analysis of its needs, and to propose organizing principles upon which to base education and society for the twenty-first century. My purpose is to argue for the centrality of education by tying it into the large and unique issues of the time.

It is not possible to assume that the reform of the service can be taken for granted. Indeed, it is central to my argument that the principles upon which the present reforms of education are being based are themselves the problem: education is being made a priority to serve the needs of the nation's economy. It is good that there is a window of opportunity for education based on economic need, but if we value education then we need to discover firmer ground than an instrumental economic imperative. Tomorrow that need may have evaporated. In any event it mistakes the central needs of our time, which are moral and political. My argument is that if society is to seriously address the problems facing education then the solution requires more than a quantitative expansion or a mere adaptation of existing systems; rather, it will need a reform of the organizing principles of learning: from instrumental and technical rationality to moral and political principles of the learning society; from learning for economic interest to learning for citizenship. This chapter seeks to develop the framework for a political theory of education for the twenty-first century, defining the purposes and conditions for a learning society which can enable all to develop their powers and capacities.

## EDUCATION IN QUESTION: A BELEAGUERED SERVICE

Education has, once more, become the subject of criticism in recent speeches, papers, inquiries and leader articles which express concern about declining standards and the exodus from education at sixteen. Indeed, Britain was 'in danger of becoming the worst educated of all the advanced countries'.[2] Such a view is countered in Glennerster and Low's (1990) meticulous review of education since 1974, which is able to conclude that 'major improvements in exam performance were achieved by the average ability students and they were mostly achieved in comprehensive schools . . . It is a tribute to the state schools that they produced more qualified leavers and the structural changes' required by the nation.

Yet it is in the final report of HM Senior Chief Inspector (1990) that the achievements and failings of the service are most judiciously held in balance. Mr Bolton censured the indiscriminate attacks, finding much to applaud in teaching, including levels of achievement and increased rates of participation beyond sixteen. Moreover, there was no evidence that standards were falling and there were early signs of improvement following the 1988 reforms. He acknowledged, however, that nearly one-third of 5- to 16-year-old (2 million children) were still receiving a limited experience and that one-third of all primary and secondary schools had been performing poorly (two thirds of 9- to 11-year-olds were underachieving and reading standards were unsatisfactory in one school in five. Long-term failings continued to confront schools, in particular poor standards of achievement amongst specific groups, especially inner-city children and the less academically able. In the more deprived parts of the education service high proportions of children (68 per cent) leave at sixteen, they learn in poorly maintained buildings and experience the poverty of resources more than others. There is a stubborn statistic, the SCI concluded, of one child in three receiving a poor education.

While any concluding analysis, therefore, must point to considerable improvement in the face of daunting constraints of resource, nevertheless deep seated problems remain. The task is to establish a clearer identification of the problem and its cause. The SCI account provides the basis for an analysis of the entrenched pattern of disadvantage and underachievemenent. It is not lack of capacity or educability of the disadvantaged which explain underachievement: it is more the conditions which have eroded the motivation to learn, or to take seriously an education that all too clearly has provided little meaning or purpose to their lives. An understanding of these factors requires an analysis of the deep social and political structures of our society which define the subjectivity, self-esteem and capacity of individuals and their communities.

### Analysing the deep structures of underachievement

The cause of underachievement lies in the long cultural tradition of educating a minority. Only a few succeed because that is what our society has preferred. Any analysis of the dominant characteristics of the educational and political systems reveals the institutionalizing of underachievement.

### Characteristics of education

Young people fail to fulfil their potential, develop their powers because of principles and assumptions which are constitutive of the education system.

*Assumptions about who education is for.* Boundaries typically surround the process of learning. Education is too often regarded as a stage in life. To be in education is to be young, to be successful academically, and to be located within an institution – traditionally a school – because colleges specialize in 'training'. Such boundaries express a narrow conception of who education is for, excluding most people and limiting the possibilities of achievement.

*Assumptions about the learning process.* Traditional conceptions of teaching and learning – insisting upon the didactic transmission of knowledge to passive and solitary individual pupils – have almost certainly diminished rather than enhanced the motivation of most young people, inculcating anxiety rather than joy at the prospect of learning.

*Assumptions about the curriculum.* These have usually involved the introduction of unnecessary barriers: organizing learning into bounded subjects (Bernstein's 'classification code') and defining 'an education' as the accumulation of abstract understanding, and bifurcating knowledge between theory and practice. More recently, a curriculum has been imposed upon the majority of young people which reverses this traditional emphasis and now insists upon a narrow concept of vocational preparation for work determined instrumentally by the needs of the labour market.

*Assumptions about educational institutions.* Not only has education been 'institutionalized', the schools and colleges have typically been conceived as enclosed institutions controlled by their professional communities. Parents, employers and the wider community – the sources of complementary support and motivation – have usually been held at bay. The organizing rules and structures of educational institutions have, moreover, rarely been responsive to the needs of the clients they are designed to serve. As Aitken (1983, p. 46) argued, they have been rigid systems: 'we need to break away from such a rigid delivery system of fixed entry points, of hours in the day, terms, academic years and self contained levels and entry qualifications.'

*Assumptions about the organizing principles of the system.* The determining principle of the education system is, paradoxically, more accurately described as a system of failure rather than of enabling, recording and celebrating achievement, because it has been designed primarily for the purposes of differentiation and selection. Peter Mortimore[3] has argued recently that although GCSE was likely to raise standards amongst both teachers and pupils, nevertheless, the new system was still geared to make almost 70 per cent of pupils believe they were failures and this contributed to Britain's poor staying-on rates compared with those of other European countries. Education has characteristically been a race, a race to ensure entry into types of education (indeed, an education). It has been a race because an education has been a privilege from which most are excluded. The dominant instrumental assumptions are tied to the labour market and the education system has provided mechanisms for 'cooling people out', or down, from 'education' to 'training' to 'work'. Society has set limits on the numbers it has been willing to educate, passing off the failure of the majority in terms of their own failure (blaming the victim) or the inescapable limits of resources. While the principles governing the race were more open in the period of social democracy (late 1950s to early 1970s) and were more restrictive in the period of corporatism (late 1970s) or the neo-liberalism of the 1980s, the principles nevertheless remained the same: of utilitarian social selection. Thus an education has denied what the conditions of learning require: a sense of purpose, commitment to and responsibility for personal development, rather than generating for many a pervasive sense of futility. The assumptions of social selection are deeply inscribed in society and the polity.

## Characteristics of the polity

These determine and reinforce those of education because, as Weber (1978) argued, social structures come to exhibit a 'dominant order' of beliefs and values which legitimate a pattern of power and organization. Thus the source of under-achievement and lack of motivation lies in the underlying structures which have characterized the post-war polity, providing neither the purposes nor the conditions to empower most people. While the period of liberal democracy provided services and opportunities that were indispensable for many, it was also a meritocracy which measured the numbers it wished to motivate. The programmes of post-war modernization and reform in time ran up against the limiting beliefs informing that dominant order.

*The belief in the essential atomism of society* composed of private and self-sufficient individuals (this is the ontology of the dominant order). This doctrine seeks to oppose and undermine the belief that human nature is essentially social and that our distinctive capacities and potential can only be realized through collaborative endeavour within society (Taylor, 1985). Thus the welfare state identified with and served the needs of individual clients rather than enabled the collective development of whole communities.

*The belief of a liberal order in being neutral about the good.*   Moral values are to be a matter for private reflection and choice and the state should eschew any prescription of virtue in the public domain. Thus the development of the welfare state was bereft of any moral foundation that articulated the public good, apart from an exiguous utilitarianism.

*The dominance of instrumental rationality* of scientific knowledge, in any understanding of the world (the epistemology of the dominant order). This 'positivist' ideology created an overdetermined account of reality that resisted the possibility of alternative constructions of meaning or action. The world, and knowledge of it, is given to members of society rather than created by them (Habermas, 1972). The hidden curriculum of the welfare state expressed determinism and dependence rather than agency and emancipation.

*Professional domination.* The handing down of knowledge was part of the more general vision of how society was to be developed. Liberal democracy believed that the just and open society could be *provided* and, as it were, handed down to a passive public by professionals and administrators, the controllers of knowledge. An educated public was something to be *delivered* by specialists rather than lived and created by citizens with the support of professionals. We lived, as Perkin (1989) has called it, within 'the professional society' underwritten and monitored by the more detached system of elective representation. Post-war social democracy arguably atrophied because of its limited conception of the public domain. An educated public cannot be delivered by specialists. It can only emerge from the meaning and by the agency of the people themselves.

These interdependent values defined the dominant mode of organizing the relationship of people to their society: lack of motivation reflected unequal opportunities and power. The polity did not provide the purposes and conditions to motivate all as equal members. It made some active members, but most were passive dependents, thus depriving the majority of the motivation for learning, to achieve more than a menial job, to become something more than an instrument in the labour market.

This order, of the professional society, has been in doubt since the mid-1970s. There is a need for a consensus about a new political and moral order in which solutions to problems of underachievement will reflect broader conceptions about the nature of power and purpose in society. The vacuum in the post-war polity has been the lack of any involvement of the public; the challenge is to empower that public. Although there may be growing agreement about the aim, the debate surrounds the means. The argument so far has proposed that the sources of underachievement lie in the structures which have eroded the conditions for motivation: people do not take learning seriously because they are not encouraged to take their lives and capacities seriously. The limits of an old order, as much as the prerequisites of the new one, have since the mid-1970s been increasingly illuminated by a period of change in our society.

## The transformations and the challenge

The economic, social and political transformations of our time are fundamentally altering the structure of experience: the capacities each person needs to flourish, what it is to live in society, the nature of work and the form taken by polity. The changes raise deep questions for the government of education and for the polity in general about: *what is it to be a person?* Is a person a passive being or possessed of powers that define his or her essential agency? *Is there any such thing as a society?* What is it? An aggregation of individuals or some form of social and linguistic community? *What should be the nature of the polity?* What is it to be a member and with what rights and duties? What distribution of power and wealth is consistent with justice and freedom? Who should take decisions and how? What forms of accountability and representation define our democracy? Any effective response will require a capacity for renewal, for learning – from the institutions of our society as much as from each individual confronting the changed circumstances in private life. From either perspective, the problems of the time are public and require public solutions, and yet it is the public institutions which are being eroded.

There is an urgent need for fundamental change, to create a common purpose and the conditions for individuals and their communities to flourish by empowering their sense of agency and responsibility for the future. The foregoing analysis suggests that realizing such aims will depend upon the creation of a new moral and political order, both to support the development of individual powers and to create an open, public culture responsive to change. The defining quality of such a new order, and the key to change, is a society which has learning as its organizing principle. There is a need for reforms that will rescue us from the mistakes of the past and prepare us more adequately for the future. Our priority must be both to change the purposes of education and to embody in the reform of social and political institutions the organizing principle of learning.

During the past decade there have in fact been two principal strategies for reforming education. The first, emanating from Whitehall, has promoted a philosophy of the administered market; the second has reflected the analysis of local professionals and elected members, striving to create a context for learning that will revive motivation in disadvantaged inner-city dwellers. Both have some of the conditions which prepare the basis for a model that can promote the learning society.

## STRATEGIES FOR RECONSTRUCTION

### Model 1 from Whitehall: the market solution

The 1988 Education Reform Act created the most radical recasting of the government of education since 1944, now further reinforced by the 1991 White Paper on *Education and Training for the Twenty-first Century*. The intention of those at the centre is not only to redefine the roles and responsibilities of the partners in education but to do so as part of a broader reconstituting of the social and political order. They present a vision of an active consumer democracy which is intended to replace the purportedly weary assumptions of the liberal democratic state.

While aspects of both reforms are to be commended and will probably survive electoral change, nevertheless as a whole their underlying organizing principles are flawed responses to the needs of the time and contradict their own objectives. First, the preoccupation with instrumental vocational objectives for education provides too limited a vision of the needs of individuals and society for the twenty-first century; the commitment to 'parity of esteem' between vocational and academic routes only serves to confirm the intention to stratify them into separate channels.

Second, the Government's avowed commitment to empower the public in its relationship with state bureaucracies expresses tendencies which have a broader appeal. However, the belief in market competition as the principal vehicle for public choice and accountability not only appears to contradict other more traditionally 'universal' objectives (such as entitlement) which are internal to the legislative plans, but also creates a mechanism which can only disempower many. The market is formally netural but substantively interested. Individuals (or institutions) come together in competitive exchange to acquire possession of scarce goods and services. Within the market place all are free and equal, only differentiated by the capacity to calculate their self-interest. Yet the market of course masks it social bias. It elides but also reproduces the inequalities which consumers bring to the market-place. Under the guise of neutrality, the institution of the market actively confirms and reinforces the pre-existing social order of wealth, privilege and prejudice. The market, let us be clear, is a crude mechanism of social selection and intended as such. It will provide more effective social engineering than anything we have previously witnessed in the post-war period. The effect of the market mechanism in education can only be to create a social, and selective, hierarchy of institutions.

## Model 2 from the inner city: the empowerment curriculum

This model[4] for reconstruction was developed by local professionals and their councils, who were required very directly to address the issues of disadvantage and hopelessness in 'the inner city'. The distinctive characteristics of such entrenched disadvantage and underachievement caused these LEAs to turn away from the post-war model of putting their faith solely in increased resources, towards recognizing the need for a more fundamental review of the purposes and conditions of learning. They defined the problem as an entrenched loss of self-esteem, dignity and confidence. In this context, the task was understood as 'the long term process of transforming the way people think about themselves and what they are capable of, and of shaping our methods of implementation accordingly'. Initially, the LEAs perceived the management challenge as one of clarifying their vision of education, in the direction of enabling local people to develop the confidence and capacity to handle their own futures. Subsequently, they attempted to articulate this vision in development plans that could both manage change and help to regenerate education. Such plans often began by expressing the new values and principles which would shape the reform of provision, teaching and learning, the curriculum and relations with parents. I shall summarize these in turn.

## Valuing capacity

Values were carefully chosen to celebrate a distinctive vision about the reservoirs of capacity in individuals, the purpose of education being to create active rather than passive learners, empowered with the skills to make responsible choices about the direction of their own lives as well as to co-operate with others to improve the quality of life for all in the community. The LEAs believed in:

- *Valuing the identity and dignity of each*: to develop the self-esteem which is a precondition for learning. Education helps young people to form positive attitudes to themselves as well as others and thus to dissolve prejudice.
- *Belief in individual capacity and achievement*: 'that no limit should be assumed to the individual's capacity for achievement: this must be the basis of expectations of all children and young people from all backgrounds'.
- *Valuing agency, assertiveness, self-confidence*: to learn is to reach out, to examine something beyond the self; to encounter a different environment and the strangers within it. The value of self-confidence is especially important for those groups – girls and women, black and ethnic minorities – which have, traditionally, been disadvantaged by education.
- *Empowerment for autonomy and responsibility (agency)*: enables children to become independent learners: they manage what they are doing, make decisions about the best way of doing it and have access to resources.
- *Responsibility for others and the wider community*: the LEAs wished to encourage an outward looking education: 'schools and colleges should help young people to form constructive and cooperative attitudes to each other, to their work and to the community so that they can play an active and responsible role in society'. There was also some movement towards active citizenship and an understanding of the importance of taking decisions.

## Provision for entitlement

A number of values established objectives for schools and colleges: what is offered in terms of opportunities, resources and facilities. Thus it was argued that provision should enable the principles of: *entitlement* to a comprehensive and continuing education for all to achieve personal growth throughout their lives; *responsiveness* to the expressed educational needs of all in the community; *accessibility* to enable members of the community to take up learning opportunities, which require *flexibility* of provision in schools and especially in further and higher education to enable students to transfer courses and maintain *progression* in learning. *Resources* remain a vital condition for educational quality and these LEAs invested considerably in staff development; indeed they strove to protect expenditure in the face of pressure to contract it. A belief in *quality development* was expressed in the growing commitment to the monitoring and evaluation of provision. Teachers and advisers sought to develop principles which would encourage a *comprehensive curriculum* that would be *relevant* to learners, enabling them to draw upon their experience of living within the community. This proposed curriculum should be broad and balanced in the learning offered, *modular* in its form, though ensuring *coherence* and integration across the experience of learning, enabling *continuity and progression*, and supporting young people with *formative and positive assessment* to help them understand their achievements and progress.

## Active learning

If learning is to be effective it should motivate young people by engaging their interests and by being related to their experience. The process of teaching, moreover, should seek to involve students in, and negotiate with them, a process of active and collaborative learning: 'we must shift from a teaching approach to a learning approach'. The values emphasized:

- *Student-centred learning*: Education should begin from the needs and strengths of the individual and not merely the benchmarks of preconceived standards; 'learning should be appropriate to the needs of individual pupils and provide a challenge to each one . . .' 'We must take time and involve students, to share the ownership of learning. It is no good if the "problem" is ours and we tell the answers. It is only when the child owns a problem in learning that they will really want to learn "to write" or "to read". We need to listen to children'.
- *Participation and dialogue*: motivation is more likely if learning grows out of a process of agreeing with pupils the tasks to be undertaken.
- *Active learning*: there is a strong belief among educators in disadvantaged LEAs that if the learning process is to be involving it needs to be a more active experience than it has proved traditional in most schools. Active learning can encourage students to *take responsibility* for their own learning experience and that of others.
- *Learning can serve others:* learning, even within the traditional subject curriculum, can be given purpose by serving the needs of others in the community.
- *Collaborative learning:* if students are to achieve the educational value of respecting other persons and cultures, then the very process of learning must encourage collaborative as well as individual activity. Pupils need to be given the responsibility of developing projects together so that they decide the ends and plan the means: 'learning is most fulfilling as a co-operative activity rather than a solitary or competitive enterprise. Your ideas and knowledge provide the spark to my discovery, your progress is necessary to mine.
- *Learning as enjoyment*: 'learning should be interesting and challenging, it should be an exciting experience: it should be fun: too many schools are still boring environments.'

*Partnership with parents and the community*

Partnership with parents is regarded as the key to improving pupil motivation and achievement, while service to and involvement of the public reflects the broader responsibility of school and college to promote education within the community. Characteristics of partnership for improving learning quality include:

- *Welcoming parents into the life of the school as partners*: establishing a new style in which schools will listen to and respond to parents: 'as teachers we need to listen, learn and respect: the great mystique about teacher automony needs to be unmasked.'
- *Parents as complementary educators – in the home*: parental contribution to schemes of reading is encouraged because of its acknowledged influence upon motivation, confidence and attainment scores; and – *in school*: they increasingly recognize the wide range of skills and experience among parents which can support the learning process.
- *Developing shared understanding of the curriculum*: establishing a closer match of understanding within the partnership takes time, given the differences of perception, but 'teachers, pupils and parents as well as others need to know what is intended, how it is to be pursued and achieved.'
- *Dialogue in curriculum design*: listening to parents and members of the community about how the curriculum, enriched by local knowledge and experience, can enhance a school's multicultural and anti-racist understanding.
- *Partners in assessment of learning progress*: establishing regular communication with parents about the progress their child is making; involving the parent in assessment and in agreeing a strategy about future development.
- *Partners in evaluation and accountability*: schools having the confidence to report to parents about performance, to listen to the 'accounts' of parents and to involve them in evaluating achievement.

What we learn from the strategies pursued by disadvantaged authorities is, however important resources are, and they are very important, how much more significant it is to hold a new conception of the purposes and conditions of learning; that we cannot learn without being active and motivated; without others (i.e. the support of society); and without shared understanding about justice and rights to equal dignity. This suggests that if we are to establish the conditions for all to flourish, to be motivated and to take their learning and lives seriously, then reform needs to address the wider public purposes and conditions of learning. The challenge is vast: it implies no less than the re-enchantment of the world with the learning society, whose principles can dissolve and supplant the dominant para-digm of instrumental rationality, the drive to competitive self-interest, prejudice, accumulation and bureaucracy that embody Weber's iron cage of icy darkness, stifling the conditions for most individuals and communities to flourish. Our task is to re-enchant the world with a moral and political order, the defining principle of which is learning as inquiry, understanding and discourse. This could provide the possibility – which Rorty (1989) denies – of linking together a morality of personal development, setting out principles about how we are to live, with a just polity, which can constitute how we are to agree a future.


## THE LEARNING SOCIETY

This sketch for a theory of the Learning Society builds upon the ideas and practice being developed 'from the inner city'. Reforms do not begin *de novo*; they have their origins in local communities which are discovering solutions to dilemmas they confront. Our task is to develop understanding of underlying principles in order to create the basis for their more general application.


### Key components of the theory of the learning society

The theory builds upon three axes: of presupposition, principles and purposes. The *presupposition* establishes an overarching proposition about the need for and purpose of the learning society; the *principles* establish the primary organizing characteristics of the theory; while *purposes and conditions* establish the agenda for change that can create the values and conditions for a learning society.


#### *Presupposition*

There is a need for the creation of a learning society as the constitutive condition of a new moral and political order. It is only when the values and processes of learning are placed at the centre of the polity that the conditions can be established for all individuals to develop their capacities, and that institutions can respond openly and imaginatively to a period of change. The transformations of the time require a renewed valuing of and commitment to learning; as the boundaries between languages and cultures begin to dissolve, as new skills and knowledge are expected within the world of work and, most significantly, as a new generation, rejecting passivity in favour of more active participation, requires to be encouraged to exercise such qualities of discourse in the public domain. A learning society, therefore, needs to celebrate the qualities of being open to new ideas, listening to as well as expressing perspectives, reflecting on and inquiring into solutions to new dilemmas, co-operating in the practice of change and critically reviewing it.


#### *Principles*

Two organizing principles provide the framework for the learning society: that its essential structure of *citizenship* should be developed through the processes of *practical reason*.

*Citizenship: establishes the ontology, the mode of being in the learning society.*    The notion of being a citizen ideally expresses our inescapably dual identity as both individual and member of the whole, the public; our duality as autonomous persons who bear responsibilities within the public domain. Citizenship establishes the right to the conditions for self-development, but also a responsibility that the emerging powers should serve the well-being of the commonwealth. 'Citizenship' I define (cf. Held, 1989) as the status of membership of national and local communities, which thereby bestows upon all individuals equally reciprocal rights and duties, liberties and constraints, powers and responsibilities. Citizens express the right as well as the obligation to participate in determining the purposes and form of community and thus the conditions of their own association.

*Practical reason: establishes the epistemology, the mode of knowing and acting, of the citizen in the learning society.*    Practical wisdom (or what Aristotle called *phronesis*) describes a number of qualities which enable us to understand the duality of citizenship in the learning society: knowing what is required and how to judge or act in particular situations; knowing which virtues should be called upon. Practical reason, therefore, presents a comprehensive moral capacity because it involves seeing the particular in the light of the universal; a general understanding of what good is required, as well as what proper ends might be pursued in the particular circumstances. Practical reason thus involves deliberation, judgement and action: *deliberation* upon experience to develop understanding of the situation, or the other person; *judgement* to determine the appropriate ends and course of action, which presupposes a community based upon sensitivity and tact; and learning through *action* to realize the good in practice.

### Purposes, values and conditions

To provide such purposes and conditions, new values and conceptions of learning are valued within the public domain at the level of *the self* (a quest of self-discovery); at the level of *society* (in the learning of mutuality within a moral order); and at the level of the *polity* (in learning the qualities of a participative democracy). These conditions for learning within the self, society and the polity are discussed in turn.

## Conditions for a learning self

At the centre of educational reforms within the inner city, as much as those emerging from the polity itself, is a belief in the power of agency: only an active self or public provides the purposes and conditions for learning and development. Three conditions are proposed for developing purpose within the self: a sense of agency; a revived conception of discovery through a life perceived as a unity; and an acknowledgement of the self in relation to others.

*The self as agent*

Learning requires individuals to progress from the post-war tradition of passivity, of the self as spectator to the action on a distant stage, to a conception of the self as agent both in personal development and active participation within the public domain. Such a transformation requires a new understanding from self-development for occupation to self-development for autonomy, choice and responsibility across all spheres of experience. The change also presupposes moving from our prevailing preoccupation with cognitive growth to a proper concern for development of the person as a whole – feeling, imagination and practical/social skills as much as the life of the mind. An empowering of the image of the self presupposes unfolding capacities over (a life-) time. This implies something deeper than mere 'lifelong education or training' (referred to as access institutions). Rather, it suggests an essential belief than an individual is to develop comprehensively throughout his or her lifetime and that this should be accorded value and supported.

*The unity of a life*

We need to recover the Aristotelian conception of what it is to be and to develop as a person over the whole of a life, and of a life as it can be led (cf. MacIntyre, 1981; Temple[5]) This has a number of constituent developments: first, perceive the life as a whole; the self as developing over a lifetime. Second, therefore, a conception of being as developing over time: life as a quest with learning at the centre of the quest to discover the identity which defines the self. Third, seeing the unity of a life as consisting in the quest for value, each person seeking to reach beyond the self to create something of value, which is valued. Fourth, developing as a person towards the excellences; perfecting a life which is inescapably a struggle, an experience of failure as well as success. Fifth, accepting that the struggle needs to be guided by virtues, which support the development of the self; dispositions which strengthen and uplift (character); valued dispositions. Lastly, acknowledging that the most important virtue is that of deliberation, a life of questioning and inquiry committed to revising both beliefs and action; learning, from being a means, becomes the end in itself, the defining purpose creatively shaping the whole of a life.

*The self as persons in relation*

But we can only develop as persons with and through others; the conception of the self presupposes an understanding of how we live a life with each other, of the relationship of the self to others. The conditions in which the self develops and flourishes are social and political. The self can only find its moral identity in and through others and membership of communities. Self-learning needs to be confirmed, given meaning by others, the wider community; what is of value will be contested; therefore we need to agree with others what is to be considered valuable; to deliberate, argue, provide reasons.

## The social conditions for learning

The unfolding of the self depends upon developing the necessary social conditions which can provide a sense of purpose within society, both for the self and others. These conditions are *civitas*; active participation in creating the moral and social order; and a capacity for interpretative understanding.

### Virtues of civitas: *the civic virtues of recognizing and valuing others, of friendship*

The conditions for the unfolding self are social and political: my space requires your recognition and your capacities demand my support (and vice versa). Jordan (1989) emphasizes the importance of mutual responsibility in developing conditions for all individuals to develop their unique qualities. It recalls Aristotle's celebration of civic friendship – of sharing a life in common – as being the only possible route for creating and sustaining life in the city. Such values, arguably, are now only to be found within feminist literature which emphasizes an ethic of caring and responsibility in the family and community, and the dissolution of the public as a separate (male) sphere (cf. Gilligan, 1986; Okin, 1991; Pateman, 1987). It is only in the context of such understanding and support that mutual identities can be formed and the distinctive qualities of each person can be nurtured and asserted with confidence.

### Creating a moral community

The post-war world was silent about the good, holding it to be a matter for private discretion rather than public discourse. But the unfolding of a learning society will depend upon the creation of a more strenuous moral order. The values of learning (understanding), as much as the values which provide the conditions for learning (according dignity and respecting capacity), are actually moral values that express a set of virtues required of the self but also of others in relationship with the self. The values of caring or responsibility, upon which can depend the confidence to learn, derive any influence they may have from the authority of an underlying moral and social order. The civic virtues, as MacIntyre (1981) analyses, establish standards against which individuals can evaluate their actions (as well as their longer 'quest'); yet particular virtues derive meaning and force from their location within overall moral framework (what MacIntyre calls a 'tradition'). A moral framework is needed to order relationships because it is the standards accepted by the moral community which provide the values by which each person is enabled to develop.

Yet a moral order is a public creation and requires to be lived and re-created by all members of the community. Each person depends upon the quality of the moral order for the quality of his or her personal development, and the vitality of that order depends upon the vitality of the public life of the community. For the Athenian, the virtuous person and the good citizen were the same because the goods which informed a life were public virtues. But the authority of a moral order for the modern world will grow if it is an open morality rather than a socialization into a tradition. The development of a moral community has to be a creative and collaborative process of agreeing the values of learning which are to guide and sustain life in the community. Simey (1985) and Titmuss (1971) have recorded the emergence of communal virtues which reflect the process of citizens taking ownership and responsibility for their lives.

*Interpretative understanding: learning to widen horizons*

Taylor (1985) has argued that the forms of knowing and understanding, as much as, or at least as part of a shared moral order, are the necessary basis of civic virtue. Historically conditioned prejudices about capacity, reinforced by institutions of discrimination, set the present context for the learning society. The possibility of mutuality in support of personal development will depend upon generating interpretative understanding, that is on hermeneutic skills which can create the conditions for learning in society: in relationships within the family, in the community and at work. In society we are confronted by different perspectives, alternative life-forms and views of the world. The key to the transformation of prejudice lies in what Gadamer (1975) calls '*the dialogic character of understanding*': through genuine conversation the participants are led beyond their initial positions to take account of others and move towards a richer, more comprehensive view, a 'fusion of horizons', a shared understanding of what is true or valid. Conversation lies at the heart of learning: learners are listeners as well as speakers.

The presupposition of such agreement is *openness*: we have to learn to be open to difference, to allow our prejudgements to be challenged; in so doing we learn how to amend our assumptions, and develop an enriched understanding of others. It is precisely in confronting other beliefs and presuppositions that we are led to see the inadequacies of our own and transcend them. Rationality, in this perspective, is the willingness to admit the existence of better options, to be aware that one's knowledge is always open to refutation or modification from the vantage point of a different perspective. For Gadamer, the concept of *bildung* describes the process through which individuals and communities enter a more and more widely defined community – they learn through dialogue to take a wider, more differentiated view, and thus acquire sensitivity, subtlety and capacity for judgement.

Reason emerges through dialogue with others, through which we learn not necessarily 'facts' but rather a capacity for learning, for new ways of thinking, speaking, and acting. It is Habermas (1984) who articulates the conditions for such communicative rationality as being 'ideal speech contexts' in which the participants feel able to speak freely, truly, sincerely. The conditions for this depend upon the creation of arenas for public discourse – the final and most significant condition for the creation of the learning society.

## Conditions in the polity

The conditions for a learning society are, in the last resort, fundamentally political, requiring the creation of a polity which provides the foundation for personal and collective empowerment. The personal and social conditions described above will be hollow unless bedded in a conception of a reformed, more accountable, and thus more legitimate, political order. The connection between individual well-being and the vitality of the moral community is made in the public domain of the polity: the good (learning) person is a good citizen. Without political structures which bring together communities of discourse, the conditions for learning will not exist: it is not possible to create the virtues of learning without the forms of life and institutions which sustain them. The preconditions of the good polity are:

### Justice: a contract for the basic structure

The conditions for agency of self and society depend upon agreement about its value as well as about allocating the means for private and public self-determination. Freedom rests upon justice, as Rawls (1971) and Barry (1989) argue. But this makes the most rigorous demands upon the polity, which has to determine the very conditions of which life can be lived at all: membership, the distribution of rights and duties, the allocation of scarce resources, the ends to be pursued – the good polity must strive to establish the conditions for virtue in all its citizens. These issues are intrinsically political and will be intensely contested, especially in a period of transformation that disturbs traditions and conventions.

### Participative democracy

Basing the new order upon the presupposition of agency leads to the principle of the equal rights of citizens both to participate in determining what conditions the expansion of their powers and to share responsibility for the common good. The political task of our time is to develop the polity as a vehicle for the active involvement of its citizens, enabling them to make their contribution to the development of the learning society. There is a need, in this age of transition, to fashion a stronger, more active democracy than the post-war period has allowed. The post-war polity specialized politics and held the public at bay, except periodically and passively. By providing forums for participation the new polity can create the conditions for public discourse and for mutual accountability, so that citizens can take one another's needs and claims into account. Learning as discourse must underpin the learning society as the defining condition of the public domain.

*Public action*

A more active citizenship, Mill believed, would be a civilizing force in society. Through participation citizens would be educated in intellect, in virtue and in practical activity. The upshot of participation should now be public action based upon deeper consent than that obtained from earlier generations. For Sen (1990; Dreze and Sen, 1989) the possibility of producing a fairer world, one which will enrich the capacities and entitlements of all citizens, depends upon the vitality of public, democratic action. The creation of a learning society expresses a belief in the virtue of the public domain and will depend upon the vitality of public action for its realization.

## CONCLUSION

A beleaguered service is variously accused of failing young people who leave school at the earliest opportunity with much of their potential unrecognized and underdeveloped. This happens, it is argued, because education is committed to perpetuating an élite culture which offers little connection with the lives of ordinary children; a more practical curriculum tied to the world of work is proposed as the solution most likely to provide the required motivation to learning for those pupils. But this proposal turns an effect (the school curriculum) into the focus of policy, thus obscuring the real (social and political) causes. Moreover, the proposal is confused, for unless the vocational reform is for all children then it becomes another policy which will reinforce the social selection it is purportedly designed to overcome.

Education will always 'fail' if the capacity of young people has to be sectioned off to match a pyramidal, hierarchical society (the hidden curriculum of which is learned very early by young people), underpinned by a political system that encourages passive rather than active participation in the public domain. A different polity, enabling all people to make a purpose of their lives, will create the conditions for motivation in the classroom. Only a new moral and political order can provide the foundation for sustaining the personal development of all. It will encourage individuals to value their active role as citizens and thus their shared responsibility for the commonwealth. Active learning in the classroom needs, therefore, to be informed by and lead towards active citizenship within a participative democracy. Teachers and educational managers, with their deep understanding of the processes of learning, can, I believe, play a leading role in *enabling* such a vision to unfold not only among young people but also across the public domain.

## NOTES

1 This chapter is derived from an Inaugural Lecture given in the School of Education at the Unviersity of Birmingham on 19 June 1991. Now, as then, I would like to thank Professors Meredydd Hughes and John Stewart for their development of management studies within the university. This chapter is dedicated to Helena, who has also made sense of its grammatical structure!

2 The critiques include Sir Claus Moser, Prince Charles, Sir Christopher Ball, Corelli Barnett, Peter Morgan and *The Times*. To this list might now be added the *Independent*'s *School Charter*, the Channel Four Commission, *Every Child in Britain* and BBC2's *Learning to Fail*.

3 Peter Mortimore, quoted in *Times Educational Supplement*, 15 February 1991.

4 This model is based upon a synthesis of studies in Haringey, Knowsley, Manchester, Strathclyde and Waltham Forest. I am grateful to a number of colleagues who contributed to these studies: Clyde Chitty, John Gray, Valerie Hannon, Peter Ribbins, Kathryn Riley and Kieron Walsh. They are not of course responsible for the construction here.

5 Archbishop Temple's speech in 1942: 'Are you going to treat a man as what he is or what he might be? That is the whole work of education'. Quoted in R. A. Butler, *The Art of Memory*, London, Hodder and Stoughton, 1982.

# Chapter 8

# The Political Community as a Learning Community

*David Clark*

To transform learning communities into a learning society, and indeed into a learning world, we are talking not just about a process of personal self-actualization (though that potentially volcanic thrust from below is immensely important). We are drawing attention to a process that needs encouraging, fostering, promoting and, at times, moving forward in the face of considerable collective resistance (the 'communal dilemma'). Here questions of power and conflict are ever present, and the role of politics and the nature of government, at different levels, become paramount. We shall examine these issues from two complementary perspectives: society as a political community, and society as a learning community.

## SOCIETY AS A POLITICAL COMMUNITY

In a societal as well as global context, therefore, we are faced with an urgent search for sustainable communal forms which can offer people what Handy (1994, p. 100) calls 'twin citizenship', but what might more appropriately be called 'multi-citizenship'. People must be able to find their communal sustenance not just in one but in numerous groupings of differing function and scale. Thus one critical task societies now face is enabling their members to develop and maintain this new kind of ciizenship without becoming lost in the lonely crowd or made captive in the ghetto.

The other fundamental question is: how are such pluralistic societies to be governed? Where politics has now become what Westwood (1992, p. 243) calls 'the politics of difference', how can a political community be fashioned which is able to encompass immense diversity while fostering coherence?

The search for sustaining and sustainable forms of community has of course always been one facing humankind. But in our age the population explosion, increased longevity, greater affluence and thus choice, the information revolution and the explosion of networking and, not least, the threat of nuclear war or ecological disaster, have all immeasurably raised the stakes. Thus right at the top of the agenda of all societies is the question of how a new political community with any hope of seeing us through the next century can be born. As Martin (1992, p. 6) puts it: 'The project is ultimately to reconstitute the wider meaning of community as society, and to show through our actions that there is such a thing.' In this particular context, our own communal task – that of creating an increasingly strong sense of security, significance and solidarity within and across social systems – becomes not a cross-curricular theme to weave into other focal tasks but the very core of the focal task itself.

It is government in the end which has to manage or, rather, orchestrate this communal task as a focal concern. But the success of such an undertaking depends increasingly on the creation of a political community which, at the level of its participants' beliefs and values, Berger and Luckmann's (1967, pp. 110f) 'symbolic universe', is sufficiently coherent and sustainable to make government possible. All nations, internally and in relation to one another, must now engage with urgency in pursuit of this new and sustainable political paradigm.

**'The heart of the matter'**

If a new sense of political community is to be born, then we have to return to the heart of what community is all about. We here want to suggest not an 'answer' to the challenge of fragmentation and fundamentalism but a new perspective. If community is rooted in the values of life, liberty and love, and the feelings of security, significance and solidarity, then these must also be the foundations of political community.

'What can be a more fundamental human right than the right to survival?' writes Kingdom (1992, p. 98). For all of us a sense of security is fundamental. The response of the world, albeit half-hearted and unsustained, to the crises of famine ... poverty in the Ethiopias and Somalias of our generation indicate that there is at least a glimmer of hope that a political community might emerge which acknowledges, in practice as well as principle, that life and security are due to all human beings by right of their humanity. And there are signs that this right is increasingly acknowledged, as in our Rwandas, even where such insecurity is the direct result of anarchic human conflict.

Beyond these high-profile flash-points on the world scene, political community needs to embrace a more holistic and long-term appreciation of survival. Our planet's physical well-being must form a key part of the communal agenda if humanity is to continue. Here the emergence of 'green politics', however tenuous as yet, has pin-pointed one fundamental principle of community-building, that of the affirmation of life and an adequate means of living for all, which must come increasingly centre stage. 'The survival of the species' depends upon it.

However, political community, like all community, is not only about survival and a sense of security. Indeed, we have argued that unless liberty and love, a sense of significance and solidarity, are also present, then our attempts to build ecologically aware and economically sustainable societies will collapse. The bottom line is not the material but the human.

What is important is that the next century will necessitate the development of a new kind of politics, rooted in a new political philosophy and founded on a new kind of political community, if humankind is to see it through. Such a community will have to emerge not only within societies but between them.

### Focal systems and forums

If a new political community is to be built around a more creative synthesis of the values and sentiments at 'the heart of the matter', its scope and operation are likely to reflect, at all societal levels, our guidelines. This means, for a start, the inclusion of a far broader range of focal systems than has hitherto been engaged in matters political. We are in search of a new form of democracy which can embrace the concerns, interests and resources of a much wider spectrum of public life than has ever been dreamt of before.

This is not just the consequence of new centrifugal forces at work. The shrinkage of our world is also generating centripetal forces, already compelling us to hammer out new systems of government. The issue facing societies is not whether the politics of difference will become a reality but how we handle what is already upon us. In this context many systems, such as those embracing the unemployed, the disabled and the single parent, remain relatively weak and, in the light of our guidelines, need to be given hugely greater affirmation, support and authority. But ways now need to be found of enabling all types of social system to develop solidarity with, and find significance within, a new kind of identifiable but open political entity.

The key to this quest is what happens at the boundary of these systems or, as Münch (1932, p. 67) describes it, within the 'zone of mutual penetration'. For though centripetal forces may be turning many social systems in on themselves, centrifugal forces are necessitating complex patterns of external engagement however temporary. Münch writes (pp. 67–8):

> Larger and larger zones of interpenetration are developing between discourses, markets, associations and political decision-making procedures, in which an increasing proportion of events in society take place. At the same time, the subsystems are becoming increasingly interwoven in processes of networking, communication, negotiation and compromise formation. This requires the building up of new institutions with the function of mediating between societal subsystems.

This 'function of mediating' describes what government is now all about. Government has to offer identity and coherence to a society whose future development can only be understood 'in terms of interpenetration, overlaying, communication, networking, negotiation and compromise formation, all of these occurring in ever more wide-ranging zones of an intermeshing fabric of different societal subsystems' (Münch, p. 57). It is a task which, on the global scene, now faces challenges such as those typified by 'the internet society' (Kelly, 1994, p. 464) which, 'as its users are proud to boast, [is] the largest functioning anarchy in the world'.

For a form of government to emerge which can promote synergy rather than segregation or assimilation, the growth of an overarching political community rooted in the kind of views and sentiments outlined above is a *sine qua non*. This means that alongside, as well as within, institutionalized politics, 'connecting systems' with a political role are needed which can forge new links, 'hold the circle'; and facilitate a negotiated response to conflict. Sciulli and Bould (1992, p. 260) argue that such a development is 'to break out of the authoritarianism–liberal bifurcation (of Hobbesian centralisation *v.* normative consensus) altogether and also to abandon the undifferentiated concept of social control', in favour of 'collegial formations ... capable of specifying unambiguously when possibilities of social integration are either increasing or decreasing'. One particularly significant type of collegial formation, from our perspective, is the so-called 'forum'.

The concept of forums is not new. They have existed since the days of Rome and well before. What is new is the possibility, in a mass pluralistic society, of once again bringing meaningful and sustainable human-scale democratic structures into being. Boswell (1990, pp. 131–40) has begun to delineate some qualitative characteristics of forums which could give them a critical role in the reconstruction of society as a political community.

He stresses that forums must be cross-sectional, encompassing a far wider membership than peers or even market competitors, and genuinely representative of the public they serve. He argues that 'because forums exist in "the economy"' it is quite inadequate to judge them 'by the conventional criteria of economics'. Their key functions are not just the obvious ones of 'information transfer', 'consultation', 'collective research' and even 'group bargaining', but 'quieter, more diffuse and less discussed attributes'. The more subtle, but communally more vital, functions of forums Boswell distinguishes as 'mutual source surveillance', akin to our guideline relating to mutually supportive accountability (pp. 78–9), 'socio-economic learning' and 'morally extending their members'.

These last two characteristics pin-point the essence of what forums can contribute to the creation of a political community. It is their 'collegial style' expressed through debate, their potential to restructure society through discourse, which offers hope for the future. What matters most, however, is not the quantity of debate and discourse, but the quality, the distinctive nature of such dialogue as portrayed in our own guidelines on communication (p. 76).

To promote discourse of quality, Boswell (1990, pp. 16f.) argues for 'organisational transparency', closely related to the 'concepts of "open government" and "accountability"'. For Mayhew (1992, p. 193), the issue is ensuring 'authentic debate within a forum that gives true influence to the public'. Münch (1992, p. 63) believes that such authenticity can only emerge 'if, apart from developing effective strategies to fight economic inflation and recession, [society] builds up corresponding strategies to deal with discursive inflation and recession, and the breakdown of universal public discourse'. This can only be achieved if 'the tokens of public discourse ... the rhetorical symbols of influence' (Mayhew, pp. 198–9) are related to 'true persuasion, unadulterated by threat or by inducements appealing solely to self-interest, [and are] based upon convincing others of common interests' (p. 194).

Forums typified by debate and discourse of this sort are the bedrock of an overarching political community, which is so essential if societies are to cohere in the modern world. Forums are gathering momentum, but will need to develop further at all levels of 'government'. They can be seen, often in embryonic form, in such phenomena as neighbourhood committees, area associations, affinity groups, single-issue groups, quality circles, focus groups, tele-cottages, teleconferences, and of course across the whole of the media – press, radio (phone-in programmes) and television (informal and formalized debates and discussions of all kinds, with interactive television approaching fast over the horizon).

More institutionalized forms of government will only find a credible communal role in future if they take on many of the features of such forums, and the changing nature of the new political community which they reflect. This requires not only that government, at both local and national levels, commits itself to 'organizational transparency', but that it addresses the reality of an increasingly educated public. One outcome has to be a growing acceptance of the principle of 'subsidiarity', a situation, as Handy (1994, p. 115) defines it, of 'reverse delegation'; where the parts are the ultimate guardians of the rights and responsibilities delegated in trust to the centre, rather than vice versa. And this will demand 'a free political community outside the state to which the state is accountable' (Mayhew, 1992, p. 191).

Such a lateral shift in much traditional political thinking, let alone practice, is very hard for most of us, not least politicians, to make. It requires a huge investment in 'the negotiation of meanings' (Shotter, 1993, p. 118), not least wrestling with how the values and sentiments we have distinguished as the hallmarks of community can be distinctively affirmed yet synthesized, as well as operationalized. It means a much more explicit recognition of the fact that very often 'it is only through compromise that decisions can be made at all' (Münch, 1992, p. 68), and of the primacy of negotiation and the skills to undertake it. It will necessitate much greater weight being accorded to what Boswell (1990, pp. 177f.) calls 'social monitoring' to encourage 'transparency'. It will also mean much greater influence being given to 'para-intermediaries' (pp. 130f.) who 'exercise leadership by perceiving needs and opportunities for public co-operation, influencing sectional organisations towards it, innovating methods for achieving it, and organising it operationally'.

## The political community as a learning community

The politics of difference means that the old landmarks have gone for ever. Centrifugal forces create a pluralistic society and an unending search for 'symbolic universes' which can facilitate community-building. Such forces also bring conflict over meanings and purposes, frequent compromise, and the necessity of continuous negotiation. For a new political community to overcome what Berger (1980, p. 9) called this 'vertigo of relativity', it must thus become a dynamic learning community. At the same time, centripetal forces are at work which can lead to the domination of vested interests, the hegemony of political ideologies and the corruption of the media undermining emerging forms of political community. The most potent weapon against such potential domination is again an educated and articulate public.

In this context, a re-framed understanding and implementation of community education becomes imperative. This will require more than 'education for democracy', though important contributions to the debate have been made under that heading. It will call on all the wisdom and skills we possess to enable society to become a community of learning communities. It will mean our 'rediscovering education's social and political purpose' (Benn, 1992, p. 162).

Community education re-framed in this way will set the agenda for all organizations across all sectors of society as they respond to the need to become 'learning organizations', with the characteristics we have explored in previous chapters. It will require us to learn a new language which 'is not that of engineering but of politics, with talks of cultures and networks, of teams and coalitions, of influence or power rather than control, of leadership not management' (Handy, 1989, p. 71). It will need the training of a new type of community educator, networker, negotiator and intermediary with skills drawn from a diversity of professions. Such training few so-called community education courses have even begun to address at any depth.

Community edcuation, if re-framed along these lines, will also require what Baron (1989, p. 83) describes as 'a political strategy'. If it is to give impetus to the new political community so urgently required, community education will have to pay particular attention to the political sphere. Here its concerns must be publicly legitimized, here its contribution has to be nurtured and developed, and here its development needs to be adequately resourced. It is, therefore, to the political aspects of the education system that we must turn to see whether our society is grasping the nettle of its future survival.

## Politicial and educational connecting systems

A learning society is about transformation: personal, organizational, societal, global. It is a community of a political kind engaged in discourse and debate about beliefs and values. But a learning society as a political community is also concerned with the distribution of power. Finding the means by which power can be effectively and fairly managed for the common good is never an easy task. This is all the more reason why politics and education must go hand in hand if a learning society is not to become prisoner of its own ideological convictions. It is ideological closure which threatens all our futures.

Creating a learning society, however, requires knowledge, experience and skills which have to be delivered by an education system which itself exercises power and influence. Thus, just as the political system needs to be educational, the education system has a political responsibility. The challenge for a would-be learning society is how it integrates the contribution and influence of the political system on the one hand, and that of the education system on the other.

The means of sustaining this creative tension might best be met by the establishment of two major kinds of 'connecting system', one having a more explicitly political and the other a more explicitly educational function. The former would be primarily concerned with the well-being of every citizen. Its political power and expertise might be considerable but educational expertise incidental. The latter would be mainly concerned with the maintenance of more specialized educational organizations and associations. Its educational experience might be considerable but political power and skill more limited.

The political system, as a connecting system, should be concerned with the whole of public life. It must operate at a level where public life can be given an identifiable and sustainable identity. At present this is at the level of the nation-state, on the one hand, and at the level of the city and its region on the other. Some, such as Handy (1994, pp. 251f.), argue that the city is the future's most viable form of community. It would seem, therefore, communally as well as politically destructive to follow the trend of recent government legislation which diminishes the importance of local authorities. Whatever their precise form and responsibilities, only the latter can represent the general public and the common good in a way that gives at least some power to local people in relation to local concerns, not least in relation to local manifestations of a national education system. Provided local authorities themselves become learning communities, and that is a major proviso, there is no reason to be rid of them, and every reason to retain them. Nor should they have to delegate their power to quangos (such as the Education and Training Boards recommended by the National Commission on Education in *Learning to Succeed* (NCE, 1993a, pp. 350f.), which can only represent a more specialized and élitist public.

It is doubtful, however, whether much political power should, or could, be given to neighbourhood (or parish) councils. The principle of subsidiarity may indicate the right of such councils to control local neighbourhood resources but, as we have argued at length, the neighbourhood can no longer be viewed as an easily definable or self-sustaining community, simply because of the social, physical and cognitive mobility of modern life. This also means that neighbourhood schools and governing bodies cannot claim to represent the general public, even on educational matters. Despite the local management of schools, their political rights relating to educational policy, even at a neighbourhood level, are circumscribed by the social systems they serve.

Thus, in the total political context, we must uphold the importance of both national and local government as the main means by which the affairs of a learning society are shaped and governed. This makes it all the more important that government itself, local and national, learns how to learn. The medium must be the message.

Where then lies the significance of 'the forum', whose praises we sang earlier in this chapter? It will, we believe, become increasingly significant as the prototype of connecting systems of a more explicitly educational kind. In this context, it is likely that in future forums will play a major role, at national and local level, in the promotion of community education and the learning society.

There have been varieties of educational forum in existence for many years.

The teaching unions could be said to come into this category. The churches have acted as educational forums, national and local. Parents too, through parent–teacher and parent associations, have networked along these lines. But there is now a pressing need to reconstruct such forums, or create new ones, to represent wider interests and coalitions, with the vision of the learning society much more to the fore.

Steffy and Lindle (1994, p. 13), for example, see their 'future school' as constituted by a variety of forums connecting up legal services, health care, social services, businesses, government, as well as education services and students and their families. Ranson (1993a) suggests: 'A stronger democracy suggests the need for community forums with a wider remit to cover all services enabling parents, employers and community groups to express local needs and share in decision making about [educational] provisions to meet them.' But, as we have observed, 'the spirit of corporate management in a really local community has yet to find appropriate forms of management' (Sayer, 1989b, p. 7). We would add 'and a strong common purpose'. It is, therefore, likely that the most valuable educational forums in future will gather people together, across a wider area and constituency than the neighbourhood, to be channels through which informed educational opinion can enable political decision-makers to pursue more enlightened policies on behalf of all. As Maden (1994) puts it:

> It is time to search urgently for ... a structure which ensures that the necessary expertise located in business, in trade unions, schools, colleges, local government departments and so on, is brought to bear on the decision-making processes of those citizens we elect to take [educational] decisions on our behalf.

We urgently need a wide range of educationally articulate forums to be advocates for a learning society. A General Teaching Council would greatly help here. But we also require inter-agency and cross-sector forums of both a macro and micro kind if a re-framed and reformed philosophy of community education, and the learning society to which that philosophy points, are to become a reality.

## COMMUNITY EDUCATION RE-FRAMED – THE NEW AGENDA

It is always a great temptation to assume that one lives at a major turning-point in human history. But it is more than just a naïve judgement that those who have lived through this century have probably witnessed changes as far-reaching and as rapid as any so far experienced in the history of human civilization. In a tiny moment of life on earth, our world has shrunk to a fraction of its previous size, while the number of those jostling for a place to stand has suddenly exploded. All of us are caught between centrifugal pressures forcing us out into the great beyond and centripetal pressures drawing us into social systems which we can still, even if tenuously, call our own. However, one thing is certain. We are now 'one world' in a way that previous generations have never been. The name of the game for the century on the horizon is not the survival of some, even the fittest, but the survival of all.

Whatever our particular religious beliefs or political creeds, the search for a way of life, and an ideology to empower it, which can embrace pluralism without destroying identity, is at the very top of the agenda. In our terminology, the search which in the end makes us human beings, is the search for community. Kingdom's words (1992, p. 118) are worth repeating:

> The need for a future predicated upon a communal culture goes beyond natural economic recovery, the moral claims of egalitarians, the cry for justice by socialists or even the quest for the good life. It is linked to the sustainability of life on the planet.

We have argued that our greatest resource in ensuring 'the survival of the species' is community itself; not that vague and unctuous version of community which is used to cover a multitude of sins (and conflicts), but that magnetic power which can hold people together through thick and thin and offer them life, liberty and love. If community is the gateway to a sustainable future, it is only this interpretation of community that will suffice.

All forms of power can be creative or corrupting. Community is no exception. 'Community is a way of thinking and working which contains both radical and reactionary possibilities', writes Martin (1994, p. 25). If community were not such a hugely potent force for renewal, it would not have latent within it such massive powers of destruction. There is always the danger that community will be used to further what Paulo Freire has called 'neophilic' not 'biophilic' ends. This happens when usurpers use religion to turn community into a community of cult, use wealth to turn it into a community of privilege, use the market and the media to turn it into a community of consumers, and use deprivation or immobility to imprison it within a community of place.

In all these cases, the debasement of community is characterized by one overriding feature – that of closure. What should be universal becomes parochial, what should be ecumenical becomes sectarian, and what should be inclusive becomes exclusive. Beliefs, values and feelings are employed to set system against system, for the protection of those within and the denigration of those without. No shrinking planet, no 'global village' can hope or deserve to survive if such distortion and manipulation of the nature of community continues.

If these powers of disfiguration and destruction are to be countered, then we have to put real community education, not the insipid substitute which has gone by that name, at the top of the agenda. We have to discover infinitely more about the rich nature of community itself, not only about its many forms and expressions but about those experiences, values and beliefs which are at the very heart of the matter.

Such learning goes far beyond nurture, instruction or training. It requires education at its richest, at its most profound; education as a challenging journey of discovery into the meaning of being human and the nature of the common good. It requires education as nothing less than transformation. This journey of discovery will be one bringing many surprises, involving many risks, traversing many cultures and continuing over many years. But it is a journey to which it is now imperative that all of us commit ourselves wholeheartedly for the sake of all our futures.

# Part 2

---

# The Learning Society and Public Policy

The idea of a learning society has appealed not only to academics, who seek to analyse how society might develop a way through the changes it confronts, but also to policy makers who have a responsibility to carry ideas and policies into practice. This section of the book sets out the influence of the idea of the learning society on education policy makers in the European Commission, in the Conservative and Labour Parties and in Scotland.

The influence of the idea on policy makers has been international in scope. In America in 1983 the National Commission on Excellence in Education prepared a report, *A Nation at Risk: The Imperative for Educational Reform*, which had a section on 'The Learning Society':

> In a world of ever-accelerating competition and change in the condition of the workplace, of ever greater danger, and of ever-larger opportunities for those prepared to meet them, educational reform should focus on the goal of creating a Learning Society. At the heart of such a society is the commitment to a set of values and to a system of education that affords all the members the opportunity to stretch their minds to full capacity, from early childhood through adulthood, learning more as the world itself changes. Such a society has as a basic foundation the idea that education is important not only because of what it contributes to one's career goals but also because of the value it adds to the general quality of one's life. Also at the heart of the Learning Society are educational opportunities extending far beyond the traditional institutions of learning, our schools and colleges. They extend into homes and workplaces, into libraries, art galleries and science centres: indeed into every place where the individual can develop and mature in work and life. In our view formal schooling in youth is the essential foundation of learning throughout one's life. But without life-long learning, one's skills will become rapidly dated.
>
> pp. 13–15 quoted in Gokulsing *et al.*, 1996)

In 1993 the Swedish Ministry of Education published *The Swedish Way Towards a Learning Society*, which described the national reforms to education. During the

1980s, Swedish education policies had been oriented, as in many other countries, to increasing decentralization and encouraging choice for individuals and institutions. These strategies within formal education built upon a strong tradition of recurrent education.

> Various metaphors have been used to describe Sweden and its endeavours on the way towards a learning society. The notion of recurrent education, introduced in the OECD vocabulary in the late 60s, has strongly affected educational policies in Sweden during the last two decades. (p. 14).

The report believed that raising the level of education in society influenced the capacity of individuals to contribute to public issues at various levels of society. This fundamental change was caused not only by the extension of education but also by styles of teaching and learning 'where participatory learning and the development of critical individuals play a major role.'

Another typical feature of Swedish society has been the role of popular movements and popular adult education through study circles and folk high schools. Thus Sweden has been labelled a study-circle democracy. Today, almost half the adult population is active in various forms of organized adult learning (from full-time studies to participation in a study-circle a couple of hours per week). Women have been the principal beneficiaries of this policy commitment to recurrent education. 'Women are in a majority in adult and higher education. It seems likely adult and recurrent education have had a significant impact on the transition of women from unpaid housework to the labour market during the last decades.'

To coincide with the launch of the 1996 European Year of Lifelong Learning, the Commissioner for research, education and training, Mrs Edith Cresson, with Mr Padraig Flynn, Commissioner for employment and social affairs, and in agreement with Mr Martin Bangemann, Commissioner responsible for industrial affairs, information and telecommunications technologies, published a White Paper on *Teaching and Learning: Towards the Learning Society*. Its objective, expressed in Chapter 9, is to help Europe move towards 'the knowledge-based society' (p. 11) by mapping a more flexible system of opportunities for lifelong learning. The White Paper developed strategies for:

- encouraging the acquisition of new knowledge and proposing new ways of accrediting technical and vocational skills;
- bringing schools and the business sector closer together and encouraging networking and mobility of apprentices across Europe;
- combating exclusion by offering a second chance through school;
- encouraging proficiency in three Community languages;
- treating material investment and investment in training on an equal basis.

Radical changes will be needed because there is 'too much inflexibility, too much compartmentalisation of education and training systems and not enough bridges or enough possibilities to let in new patterns of lifelong learning' (p. 74). The White Paper concludes that only by building up the learning society of Europe can a forward-looking society be developed capable of 'helping to change the nature of things globally and of maintaining full awareness of itself' (p. 74).

Clearly the idea of the learning society is believed to provide the foundation for a new consensus of policy makers in education and training for a changing world. Not only has the idea been conceived as one around which European countries might converge, but also different political parties and national regions in the UK have promoted its value. In 1994 the Labour Party published a policy statement on education entitled *Opening Doors to a Learning Society* (Chapter 10). The statement begins by celebrating the rich possibilities that can open up in the twenty-first century:

> We stand at the threshold of a society in which everybody will have the chance to learn and achieve as never before. A whole series of changes – economic, technological and cultural – has presented us with the opportunity of building a genuinely learning society – a society in which all individuals can fulfil their potential as active citizens in a prosperous, civilized, and caring community.
>
> A learning society is one that continually extends the skills and knowledge of all its people; is one in which education has become a lifelong process of the discovery and development of the talents of each and every individual; is one in which the education system is dynamic and rewarding, capable of providing all the opportunities for understanding and achievement that young people and adults will need in the twenty-first century,
>
> (p. 1)

Developing a framework for lifetime learning, the Labour Party proposed:

- We will set in place a coherent 14–19+ *framework* for education and training.
- Labour will develop a genuine parity of esteem between the academic and the vocational.
- Labour will respond to the universal call to replace the present over-specialized narrow A level.
- We will introduce a unified qualification structure that will incorporate the best practice from existing qualifications, whether academically orientated or geared to vocational skills.
- We will create a General Certificate of Further Education (GCFE), building on the strengths and experience of the present GCSE. We will integrate GCSE and the new GCFE and part of a continuous structure for the 14 to 19+ group. (p. 22)

Labour proposed to reverse the falling level of skills within the workforce by raising the standards of education and training of young people, widening access to retraining for those in work and providing training for real skills for those out of work. To enhance the world of training, Labour advocated a skills audit of the nation, which would enable the identification of the skills that are available and those in short supply, with a view to targeting training resources.

> Labour will open up greater opportunities for the retraining of those in work by introducing a national training levy to ensure that every company provides its workforce with the chance to upgrade its skills. The objective will be to encourage

companies to focus on the training appropriate within their own business rather than treating training as an external function that is somebody else's responsibility.

(p. 25)

Enabling adults to gain access to worthwhile and satisfying learning experiences is vital to realizing the aims of lifelong learning 'because it not only increases confidence and skills but also provides routes back into work. It is a valuable resource for enhancing the quality of people's lives.' But adult education and training had been neglected both by central government and by employers and needed to be rejuvenated.

If the Labour Party was first to proclaim a learning society, the Conservative Government (Chapter 11) was not far behind. In December 1995 the Government published *Lifetime Learning: A Consultation Document* (DfEE, 1995a). Following consultation, in June 1996 the Education and Employment Minister, James Paice, published *A Framework For a Learning Society*, aimed at creating a culture of lifetime learning for all. The policy framework described six key elements:

- employers investing in the training and development of employees
- gaining the commitment of individuals
- developing an effective and high quality infrastructure of information, advice and guidance in every area
- improving access to learning
- giving people of all ages the opportunity to acquire the basic skills on which to build further learning and
- developing effective partnerships nationally and locally to give practical effect to shared responsibility and to make the best use of resources.

The Minister emphasized the importance of lifetime learning to the economic success and competitiveness of business and individuals. While the Government had an important role to play in advancing the lifetime learning agenda, it was recognized that this could only be achieved with the active co-operation of many others – including employers, individuals, providers of education and training, careers services, TECs and local authorities. The policy framework set out a number of the Government's initiatives:

- reviewing basic skills provision;
- giving the Campaign for Learning a key role in the national lifetime learning strategy (the Campaign, to which the Government is contributing, brings together a national alliance of companies and organizations such as NIACE, the TEC National Council and the Open University);
- developing learning towns and cities;
- examining the scope for introducing a national help-line to provide easy access to information and advice;
- considering the possibility of running 'learning on benefit' pilots, i.e. piloting different arrangements under the Job Seekers Act; and
- working with providers to develop national standards so that individuals, wherever they live, can be assured that the advice they receive is up to date, relevant, informed and worth listening to.

Lifetime learning is not a single programme owned by one institution. We shall only create a learning society if we all work together. Policies such as Investors in People, employee development schemes, sectoral strategies and Skills for Small Businesses can – and are – making a real difference. We need national, sectoral, regional and local partnerships. They may have individual aims, policies and activies, but they will share the common goal of the learning society and be able to work within a common framework. The strategic challenge before us is to weave the threads of lifetime learning into a coherent, bold and long-lasting pattern. That is how we shall achieve our aim of a learning society in the 21st century.

(DfEEb, 1996b, press release 203/96)

The Scottish Community Education Council present, in Chapter 12, a vision of the learning society as a 'a society whose citizens value, support and engage in learning as a matter of course in all areas of activity'. Though education in Scotland has a reputation for greater democracy that in other regions of the United Kingdom, SCEC argue the case for extending the practice of a participatory learning democracy in an active society. Responsibility for the building of a learning society lies not only with the education providers but with the whole range of organizations and institutions in Scotland. They propose that:

- Parental involvement in schools, measured by the number and quality (in terms of levels of participation in decision-making, etc.) of parent-teacher associations, parents' associations and school boards, should be increased.
- Educational broadcasting to encourage and support learning should be increased.
- Increased use of libraries, theatres, museums, cinemas, leisure and sports centres should be actively promoted among hitherto under-represented groups.
- The growth of self-help groups, e.g. study-circles, and community-based learning groups providing networking, mutual support and learning should be encouraged.
- New communications technology should be put at the service of adult learners and teachers.
- The level of involvement in voluntary service and community work should be increased.
- All local authority departments (not just education departments) should be encouraged to recognize their role in stimulating and supporting learning.
- The proportion of the population voting in local, national and European elections should increase.

SCEC believe that

we have the real possibility of creating, in Scotland, a Learning Society ... The challenge confronting us is to recapture the positive and enthusiastic belief in the power of learning and in the worth and potential of all our people. The practical promotion of Scotland as a Learning Society would be a significant step towards releasing the creative capacities of this nation.

The chapters so far in this section of the book propose wide-ranging educational reforms in order to achieve the goal of a learning society. Public policy has more recently begun to focus upon particular sectors of education which have a strategic contribution to make to the formation of a learning society. The important Kennedy Report (Chapter 13) argues that drawing a much broader cross-section of the population into education will create the 'self-perpetuating learning society' which is required to sustain economic success and social cohesion though a period of unprecedented global change. The Dearing Report (Chapter 14) also perceives the vision of the learning society as providing necessary conditions for maintaining social, cultural and economic change. The distinctive contribution of higher education to this vision will lie in 'the pursuit of teaching at its highest level, the pursuit of scholarship and research, and increasingly through its contribution to lifelong learning'.

# Chapter 9

# Moving Towards the Learning Society

## The European Commission White Paper

### TEACHING AND LEARNING – TOWARDS THE LEARNING SOCIETY

Presented by the European Commission at the instigation of Mrs Edith Cresson, Commissioner for research, education and training, Mr Padraig Flynn, Commissioner for employment and social affairs, in agreement with Mr Martin Bangemann, Commissioner responsible for industrial affairs, information and telecommunications technologies, this White Paper stems from the observation that the changes currently in progress have improved everyone's access to information and knowledge, but have at the same time made considerable adjustments necessary in the skills required and in working patterns. It is a trend which has increased uncertainty all round and for some has led to intolerable situations of exclusion. Everyone's position in society will increasingly be determined by the knowledge he or she has built up. Tomorrow's society will be a society which invests in knowledge, a society of teaching and learning, in which each individual will build up his or her own qualifications. In other words, a learning society.

### THREE FACTORS OF UPHEAVAL

Among the many complex changes taking place in European society, three major trends, three 'factors of upheaval', are particularly manifest. These are the internationalization of trade, the dawning of the information society and the relentless march of science and technology.

- *The impact of the information society*. The main effect of this is to transform the nature of work and the organization of production. Routine and repetitive tasks which used to be the daily lot of most workers are tending to disappear as more autonomous, more varied activities take their place. The result is a different sort of relationship with the company. The role of the human factor is increasing but the worker is also more vulnerable to changes in the pattern of work organization because he has become a mere individual within a complex network. Everyone therefore has to adapt not only to new technical tools but also to changes in working conditions.

- *The impact of internationalization* radically affects the situation as regards job creation. After initially affecting only commercial, technological and financial trade, the internationalization is now bringing down the borders between the labour markets, thus making a global employment market closer than is generally thought. The Commission, in its White Paper on growth, competitiveness and employment, took a clear option to open up to the world, while stressing the importance of preserving the European social model. This means raising the level of qualifications in general if the social rift is not to widen still further and spread the feeling of insecurity among our citizens.

- *The impact of the scientific and technical world.* The growth in scientific knowledge, its application to production methods, the increasingly sophisticated products which thus emerge, give rise to a paradox. Despite its generally beneficial effect, scientific and technical progress engenders a feeling of unease and even irrational misgivings in society. Many European countries have endeavoured to allay these misgivings by promoting scientific and technical culture from a very early stage at school, by defining ethical rules, particularly in the areas of biotechnology and information technology.

## THE ANSWERS: BROAD-BASED KNOWLEDGE AND EMPLOYABILITY

What solutions can education and training provide in eliminating the pernicious effects these three sources of upheaval are expected to bring? While not purporting to provide exhaustive answers, the White Paper proposes two.

### (a)  Reintroducing the merits of a broad base of knowledge

The first of these involves reintroducing the merits of a *broad base of knowledge*. In a society in which the individual will be called upon to understand complex situations which fluctuate unpredictably, in which he will also be inundated with a vast quantity of varied information, there is a risk of a rift appearing between those who are able to interpret, those who can only use, and those who can do neither. In other words, between those who know and those who do not know. Building up a broad base of knowledge, i.e. the wherewithal to grasp the meaning of things, to understand and to create, is the essential function of school. This is also the first factor in adjusting to the economic and employment situation.

Also increasingly evident is the strong re-emergence of a broad base of knowledge in vocational training establishments, in programmes for the retraining of low-qualified or very specialized workers, as the key to acquiring new technical skills.

## (b) Building up employability

Second route: *building up employability*. How can education and training enable the countries of Europe to create a number of lasting jobs comparable to that which the new technologies have caused to disappear?

The *traditional route* generally pursued by the individual is the quest for a *paper qualification*. The result is a general tendency throughout Europe to prolong studies, accompanied by considerable social pressure to broaden access to higher education. While the paper qualification is still the most effective passport to employment, it nevertheless has perverse effects in that it devaluates the vocational channels (which are considered as second-best options), overqualifies young people in relation to the jobs open to them as they enter the world of work, and, lastly, conveys an image of the paper qualification as the near-absolute reference point in terms of skills, making it possible to filter out the élite at the top and, more generally, to classify the worker in his job. This intensifies the lack of flexibility of the labour market and causes substantial wastage by locking out talent which does not correspond to standard profiles.

Although it does not call into question this traditional route as such, this White Paper advocates that a more open, *more flexible* approach be adopted alongside it. This approach would in particular encourage the *mobility* of workers, employees, teachers, researchers – and students. It is today striking to observe how much easier it is for goods, capital and services to move around Europe than it is for people and knowledge!

Establishing this mobility depends on genuine recognition of knowledge within the European Union, not only recognition of paper qualifications, but also recognition of the different components of which they are comprised. For instance, a student having completed six months of studies in another European country should automatically be entitled to the recognition of this period by his university of origin, without having to resit the corresponding examinations. The fact is that this is not possible at present unless the two establishments concerned have reached a partnership agreement. Genuine mobility also presupposes the removal of administrative and legal obstacles (arising out of right of residence or social protection schemes applicable) and fiscal obstacles (taxation of study grants).

Another key point is that access to *training* should be developed *throughout life*. While the need for such access is recognized by everybody, public authorities and the business sector alike, there has been little progress in this area. This is all the more inadequate as changes in the pattern of work organization, particularly those generated by the information technologies, making training in these new tools more urgent. The year 1996, as the European Year of Lifelong Learning, should help to raise awareness in this area.

The information society does not only change the way the company works, it also offers fresh horizons for education and training. However, we have to be properly equipped to fully exploit this potential. Unfortunately, the fragmentation of the European market in the educational multimedia sector and the – as yet – inadequate quality of the teaching products on offer, along with the low level of computer equipment available in the classroom (one for 30 pupils in Europe compared with one for 10 pupils in the USA), means that these tools are very slow to appear in our schools. The commission has accordingly made it a priority to develop multimedia educational software by strengthening co-ordination of research conducted in this area within the European Union. This mission has been delegated to a task force drawn from the departments of Mrs Cresson and Mr Bangemann.

Mobility, lifelong learning, the use of new technical instruments . . . this greater flexibility in acquiring knowledge elicits the question of new ways of *validating skills acquired* irrespective of whether or not they were acquired via *a paper qualification*. This approach has already been used: the Teaching English as a Foreign Language (TEFL) test, which makes it possible to evaluate knowledge of English, and the Kangaroo test for maths, are well-established systems.

So why not 'personal skills cards', which would provide a record of what the holder knows in terms of fundamental (languages, maths, law, informatics, economics, etc.) or technical or vocational (accounting, finance, etc.) knowledge? A young person having no paper qualification could thus apply for a job on the basis of his card, which attests to his ability in terms of written skills, language proficiency and word processing . . . This scheme would allow an immediate assessment of people's qualifications throughout their lives, in contrast to diplomas which lose their value as years go by, at an ever-increasing pace.

## GUIDELINES FOR ACTION

The knowledge-based society cannot come about by proclamation. It has to emerge from an ongoing process. The White Paper's purpose is not to put forward a programme of measures, for the Commission has no miracle remedies to propound. It purports merely to provide food for thought and pointers. The White Paper in no way sets out to impinge on national responsibilities and suggests five general objectives for action, setting out for each of them one or more support projects at Community level.

*(1) Encourage the acquisition of new knowledge*: i.e. raise the general level of knowledge. The commission accordingly invites thought as to how skills not necessarily acquired via a paper qualification may be recognized. The White Paper proposes a *new way of accrediting technical and vocational skills*.

How can this approach be introduced? First of all by creating European networks of research centres and centres of vocational training, companies, business sectors which will make it possible to identify the areas of knowledge in greatest demand and the essential key skills. The next stage will be to define the best accreditation methods (tests, software packages for evaluation, evaluators, etc.). This could ultimately produce personal skills cards which would enable everyone to have their skills and know-how recognized throughout the European Union.

The White Paper is also intended to make student mobility easier. The Commission will propose that every student who has obtained a study grant in his own country be authorized to use it for courses in a higher education establishment in another Member State if he/she so wishes. It will also propose that the mutual recognition of 'course credits', i.e. the different component parts of a diploma, be generally introduced (European course credit transfer system – ECTS). It will also propose the removal of obstacles of an administrative, legal and social security nature which are a hindrance to the exchange of students, trainees, teachers and researchers. Lastly, it will instigate joint calls for tenders across the relevant Community programmes in order to develop multimedia educational software.

*(2) Bringing school and the business sector closer together:* developing apprenticeship in Europe in all its forms. The White Paper proposes networking apprenticeship centres in different European countries, to help apprentice mobility along the lines of the Erasmus programme, and to introduce a European apprentice's charter, in line with the forthcoming Green Paper on the obstacles to transnational mobility of people in training.

*(3) Combat exclusion:* offer a second chance through school. Some of the major conurbations have tens of thousands of young people who have failed at school. Schools located in the 'problem' areas are increasingly reorganizing to provide a 'second chance'. What these schools are trying to achieve is to improve access to knowledge by using the best teachers, better paid than elsewhere, an appropriate teaching pace, in-company placements, multimedia equipment and smaller classes. They are also trying to make school a community environment once again at a time when social and family links are breaking down in these sensitive districts.

How is this to be achieved? The White Paper proposes that complementary European funding be redeployed from existing programmes such as Socrates and Leonardo in support of national and regional funding. It also advocates acting in conjunction and partnership with the economic players; schools could, for instance, be sponsored by a company, if possible with the pledge to recruit if the relevant qualifications or skills recognition are obtained. The families would also be closely involved in the approach to and running of training. Lastly, the use of new teaching methods, information technology and multimedia would be strongly encouraged. This 'second chance' scheme has been successfully tested in the USA, with the 'accelerated schools' project, and in Israel with the 'Alyat Hanoar' institution.

*(4) Proficiency in three Community languages:* a quality label. Proficiency in several langages has today become essential for getting a job. This is particularly true in a single European market without frontiers. It is also an asset which makes it easier to move towards others, to discover different cultures and mentalities, to stimulate one's intellectual agility. While being a factor of European identity and citizenship, multilingualism is at the same time a cornerstone of the knowledge-based society.

This is why the White Paper proposes to define a 'School of Europe' quality label which would be bestowed – as a function of certain criteria – on those schools which have pursued language learning to greatest effect. These schools would then be united in a network. In addition, the mobility of mother-tongue teachers in other schools in other countries would be systematically encouraged.

*(5) Treat material investment and investment in training on an equal basis.*   Making education and training a priority as regards European competitiveness is not enough. Concrete measures are needed whereby firms or public authorities which have made substantial 'intangible' investment are encouraged to continue to do so. This presupposes a change of approach to how expenditure on training is viewed in taxation and accounting terms. It should therefore be made possible for firms investing heavily in training to have part of such investment written into their balance sheets on the intangible assets side. In parallel with this, 'training funds' should be developed for the benefit of persons wishing to add to their knowledge or resume training after a break in their studies.

A wide-ranging debate will be instigated in 1966 – European Year of Lifelong Learning – with the main players around all the issues raised in this White Paper. This debate could take place, for instance, at 'jumbo' Council meetings bringing together the social affairs, education and industry ministers. The Commission will take stock of these discussions at the end of 1996 and then submit its proposals for future action.

This is not, of course, to say that these few recommendations can solve all the issues currently outstanding. The White Paper's objective is a more modest one, namely in conjunction with the education and training policies of the Member States, to help Europe move towards the knowledge-based society. It also hopes to start a broader debate in the years ahead, for radical changes are going to be needed. As Mrs Cresson has stressed, what education and training systems all too often achieve is to map out an occupational pathway on a once-and-for-all basis; there is too little flexibility and too much compartmentalization between these systems, too few bridges and too few opportunities for taking on board new patterns of lifelong learning.

Lastly, the White Paper can help to show that if it is to secure its place and future in the world, Europe has to place at least as much emphasis on the personal fulfilment of its citizens, men and women alike, as it has up to now placed on economic and monetary issues. That is how Europe will prove that it is not merely a free trade area, but a coherent political whole capable of coming successfully to terms with internationalization instead of being dominated by it.

## GENERAL CONCLUSION

The world is going through a period of transition and profound change and the signs are that in Europe, as elsewhere, a new age is about to dawn which is more variable and unpredictable than those which went before.

There is no doubt that this new age – one of internationalization of trade, of the information society, of scientific and technical upheaval – brings uncertainties and concerns, primarily because it is difficult to see the direction of the future.

These uncertainties and concerns are without doubt stronger in Europe than elsewhere. European civilization has a long history and is very complex. It is today divided between a deep thirst for research and knowledge, the legacy of a tradition which made Europe the first to bring about a technical and industrial revolution and thus change the world, and a deep-seated call for stability and collective security. This is a perfectly understandable aspiration for a continent so long torn apart by wars and divided by political and social conflicts. Unfortunately, it is also one which can engender a reactionary reflex to change.

Yet this age of change is a historical opportunity for Europe, because such periods in which one society gives birth to the next are the only ones conducive to radical reform without violent change. The increase in trade across the world, scientific discoveries, new technologies, in fact open up new potential for development and progress. An eminent European historian (Le Goff, 1994), co-director of the *Annales* and well-placed to compare this period of change with those that preceded it, particularly the transition from the Middle Ages to the Renaissance, said:

> The Europe of the Middle Ages and post-medieval times had to face up to the Byzantine world, the Arab world and the Ottoman Empire. The struggle today is fortunately set in a more pacific context. Nevertheless, the existence of protagonists in history gigantic by their size or by their economic strength, or indeed both, means Europe has to achieve a comparable scale if it is to exist, progress and retain its identity. Facing up to America, Japan, and soon China, Europe must have the economic, demographic and political mass capable of securing its independence.
>
> Fortunately, Europe has the weight of its civilization and its common heritage behind it. Over 25 centuries European civilization has, in successive stages, been creative; and even today, as one slogan goes, Europe's main raw material is unquestionably its grey matter.

It is in the European dimension that a forward-looking society can be built, capable at the same time of helping to change the nature of things globally and of maintaining full awareness of itself.

This White Paper contends that it is by building up the learning society of Europe as quickly as possible, that this objective can be attained. This move entails radical change. All too often education and training systems map out career paths on a once-and-for-all basis. There is too much inflexibility, too much compartmentalization of education and training systems and not enough bridges, or enough possibilities to let in new patterns of lifelong learning.

Education and training provide the reference points needed to affirm collective identity, while at the same time permitting futher advances in science and technology. The independence they give, if shared by everyone, strengthens the sense of cohesion and anchors the feeling of belonging. Europe's cultural diversity, its long existence and the mobility between different cultures are invaluable assets for adapting to the new world on the horizon.

Being European is to have the advantage of a cultural background of unparalleled variety and depth. It should also mean having full access to knowledge and skill. The purpose of the White Paper is to make it possible to exploit these possibilities further; the recommendations it contains cannot claim to provide an exhaustive response to the question.

Their aim is much more modest, namely to help, in conjunction with the education and training policies of the Member States, to put Europe on the road to the learning society. They are also intended to pave the way for a broader debate in the years ahead. Lastly, they can help to show that the future of Europe and its place in the world depend on its ability to give as much room for the personal fulfilment of its citizens, men and women alike, as it has up to now given to economic and monetary issues. It is in this way that Europe will prove that it is not simply a free trade area, but an organized political entity, and a way of coming successfully to terms with, rather than being subject to, internationalization.

# Chapter 10

# Opening Doors to a Learning Society

*The Labour Party*

## INTRODUCTION

The twenty-first century will be rich with possibilities. We stand at the threshold of a society in which everybody will have the chance to learn and achieve as never before. A whole series of changes – economic, technological and cultural – has presented us with the opportunity of building a genuinely learning society – a society in which all individuals can fulfil their potential as active citizens in a prosperous, civilized, and caring community.

A learning society is one that continually extends the skills and knowledge of all its people; is one in which education has become a lifelong process of the discovery and development of the talents of each and every individual; is one in which the education system is dynamic and rewarding, capable of providing all the opportunities for understanding and achievement that young people and adults will need in the twenty-first century.

Britain's international competitors have long recognized that, in the knowledge-based economies of the modern world, education forms the basis of national wealth in much the same way that physical resources did in the past. Nations well positioned for the future – Japan, Germany, the Scandinavian countries – have in common excellent education systems for all young people, a highly skilled workforce and good retraining systems. In these countries it is recognized that education is the key to personal fulfilment for the individual, to economic success for the nation, and to the creation of a more just and cohesive society.

The Labour Party believes that Britain can also aspire to excellence. Our task is to persuade the whole of British society that we can no longer tolerate mediocrity and decline. We must recognize that our national wealth lies in the talents of us all, and that the exploration and development of those talents should be a national crusade.

This is the challenge of a new era: to provide high quality education for all our citizens. That will be the central ambition of the next Labour government. Of course, we recognize that we must put a stop to the bewildering range of experiments currently being carried out on the nation's children and the institutions which serve them. The chopping and changing must certainly cease. But that cannot mean a static system; however fatigued we are with the pace of change we cannot simply freeze our education system where it is now. There must be change – constructive change, based on consent.

This document is the outcome of a wide-ranging and extensive consultative exercise by the Labour Party on education issues. It sets out a vision for education in a learning society, and outlines our objectives and priorities in major areas of education policy.

## Labour's vision of education

Labour's vision is of an educated democracy in which good education ceases to be restricted as a competitive prize at arbitrary points throughout life but becomes the very basis for economic, political, and cultural success.

To achieve this vision we must start to advance the importance of education. Government cannot do this alone. What it must do is provide inspiration and leadership. As a society we must understand that education is not just about learning facts and passing tests, it is about empowering individuals. It is the foundation of a healthy democracy, and central to overcoming the notion that citizens are no more than passive consumers.

Individuals need to be empowered to make their own decisions about their own lives. This requires not only a broad and balanced education but, even more importantly, that individuals are equipped with self-confidence and self-esteem necessary for full participation in the democratic life of this country and of the European Union of which it is a part.

Our education system must also respond to the challenges of technological change and the development of new communications infrastructures. Across the globe, governments are exploring how best to exploit the enormous educational potential of technological developments. In the United States, the Clinton administration has embarked on a high profile campaign to connect every classroom in every school to the new information superhighways by the year 2000. It has placed at the top of the policy agenda the goal of ensuring equitable and lifelong access to learning technologies for all Americans.

A Labour government will require the telecommunications industry to provide a universal service for the connection of subscribers to the national communications network. It will pursue the long-term aim of offering every child and adult in the country access to the educational benefits that this network can provide. We will promote the development of new, imaginative methods of delivering educational services and the use of collaborative learning opportunities provided by new technologies. In addition, we will work to promote the cost-effective use of technology in schools, stimulate educational access to libraries and databases, and ensure that schools receive equal treatment in the provision of resources for information technology education.

The Labour Party believes that everyone has an entitlement to a high-quality, lifelong education. We also recognize that without this entitlement individuals will be unable to be part of the multi-skilled, creative, and adaptable workforce we will need in the twenty-first century. We are convinced that a new framework is required in the education services of this country: a new understanding of the purposes of education and new mechanisms for constructive dialogue and change.

## *A British Association for the Advancement of Education*

At present there is no independent body to articulate the long-term, non-sectional interests of education, across all its sectors. The time has come to look to the establishment of such a body, one endowed with the status of a national or royal academy of scholarship. This should not be a quango but on a par with, for example, the RSA or the British Association for the Advancement of Science.

Labour proposes that discussions take place with interested parties with a view to establishing a British Association for the Advancement of Education. The creation of such a body, while not able to override the wishes of Parliament, would provide a non-partisan arena for the promotion of education. Membership could come from any group involved in education, such as a national parents' voice, a national governor's forum, teachers, commerce and industry, and representatives from the field of early years, special needs, HE, and FE. This body would decide its owns terms of reference but we envisage that it would make an annual or biennial report to the Secretary of State or to the Select Committee on Education.

The association could collate research, promote good practice, increase awareness of international best practice in education, and act as an advocate for the role of education in our national life. The importance of education for individuals and society is such that a new initiative on this scale is needed. We must make the British education system second to none. The establishment of an associaton would help achieve this objective.

## *Principles for education policy making*

Labour asserts five key principles guiding education policy:

*Access for all.*   Education should be about opening doors and keeping them open as wide as possible for as long as possible. At the moment too much of educational provision is concerned with excluding people and providing a prize for the few. We reject this approach. Education is central to personal fulfilment and satisfaction. It is the key means by which individuals fulfil their ambitions, improve their own economic and social well-being, and put their talents and capacities at the service of society.

*Quality and equity.* Every individual, at every stage of the learning process, deserves a high quality education. This depends on both the individual and the educational institution having high aspirations, high expectations, and high levels of motivation. The existence of widespread underachievement in Britain today is an indictment of the educational 'reforms' of the last fifteen years. We must expect the best from our children and students, and we must give them the best in return. To achieve this there must a be a fair distribution of resources, countering disadvantage not reinforcing privilege.

Priority in education provision must be assessed according to need. That is why we will put such great emphasis on nursery education. Early learning not only gives all youngsters the best start in education but strengthens social cohesion and the sense of community so lacking in many areas. Our current system is based on low expectations and the assumption that the vast majority lack ability. Labour believes that quality education demands comprehensive provision for all stages, and rejects any system in which a few are selected at the expense of the vast majority.

*Continuity.*   Labour believes we need a system of education that extends horizons, increases expectations and enhances the aspirations of each person. Education is a lifelong process and it should not be terminated at arbitrary points. Individuals must be able to continue in, and return to, a flexible system of education over the course of their lives. This will become increasingly important in the twenty-first century as changes in work patterns require greater flexibility and changes in life expectancy increase learning in retirement.

*Accountability.*   Education services belong to the whole community, and until recently it had always been accepted that they were accountable to the whole community. Recent legislation, however, has concentrated power in the hands of the Secretary of State and a proliferation of unelected, unaccountable quangos. Education is too important for decisions to be made on this basis. There must be proper public scrutiny of education spending and clarity of responsibility for policy decisions. Everyone must feel they have a stake in the system. Without that sense of ownership we will not extend the aspirations and achievements of all our citizens.

*Partnership.*   A civilized society cannot operate when its education system is undermined by confrontation. Policies should be determined after consultation and decision-making should be shared. Central government should create the frameworks for education, whilst the local delivery of services must be the responsibility of those who are democratically and professionally accountable. Professionals must be recognized as such. Parents must be actively involved in their children's educational lives. Last, but not least, the wishes and needs of pupils themselves must be recognized and respected, and they must be central to its partnership. Confrontation must be replaced by co-operation.

## TOWARDS LIFETIME LEARNING

Labour believes that every young person should be able to continue in mainstream education, training, or training in work for two years after 16.

* We will set in place a coherent 14–19+ *framework* for education and training.
* Labour will develop a genuine parity of esteem between the academic and the vocational.
* Labour will respond to the universal call to replace the present over-specialized narrow A level.
* We will introduce a unified qualification structure that will incorporate the best practice from existing qualifications, whether academically orientated or geared to vocational skills.
* We will create a General Cetificate of Further Education (GCFE), building on the strengths and experience of the present GCSE. We will integrate GCSE and the new GCFE as part of a continuous structure for the 14 to 19+ group.

Labour's longer-term target is for 80 per cent of the nation's young people to matriculate at GCFE. At the local level Labour will encourage individual targets for pupils, schools, and LEAs.

Labour will ensure that the governing structures of colleges are accountable and reflect the different social partners and the wider public interest. Labour will review the role, functions, and accountability of the TECs. Labour will review existing structures to offer an education and careers service that will provide lifetime advice and guidance.

In the modern world Britain's future is either as a knowledge-based economy built around the skills and talents of all our people, or the low-skill, low-tech, low-wage economy of the present government. Labour believes Britain must and can have the best-educated and trained workforce in the world. We must develop structures that encourage the acquisition of knowledge and skills as a lifelong process, and continuing access to learning.

Our education system is a failure system for too many people and at too many stages. Over a quarter of young people fail to continue in education and training at the age of 16, and dropout rates are high thereafter. Between 30 and 40 per cent of starters on further education courses fail to complete their courses – a massive drain on resources as well as a waste of human potential. A significantly lower proportion of 16- to 19-year-old is in full-time or part-time education in this country compared with other major advanced countries. In 1991 only 24 per cent of 18-year-olds were in full-time education compared with more than 60 per cent in France and Japan.

The present system creates and emphasizes an unreal division between education as a high-status academic exercise and training as a lower-status set of activities geared to the world of work. This is a split which has become irrelevant to a modern technological society and one which is increasingly being challenged in other countries. However, in Britain it continues to act as an inhibition on vocational training. According to the European Commission, in 1990 only 38 per cent of the UK workforce had undergone skilled vocational training compared with 58 per cent in Spain, 67 per cent in West Germany, 79 per cent in Italy and 80 per cent in France.

When we compare the standards of achievement in Britain, the rest of Europe, and other advanced and emerging industrial countries, Britain's achievements are alarmingly low. Whilst our top achievers compare with any country in the world, we suffer from a long tail of underachievement and a shortage of technological and vocational skills.

The training available for the unemployed is often of very low quality. Only one-third of Youth Trainees gain a vocational qualification. Only 27 per cent of adult trainees on Training for Work, and its predecessor schemes like ET, gained qualifications or credits towards one, and only 19 per cent were taken on in employment.

Labour will develop a system which motivates young people to stay in a broad-based eductional and training structure and one which encourages people who presently do not do so to return to education and training at a later stage. We will set in place a coherent 14–19+ framework for education and training.

Labour will develop a genuine parity of esteem between the academic and the vocational by ensuring that all young people continue to have experience of a broad and balanced curriculum.

We will set targets to improve our performance, increase the numbers of young people in education and training and improve their achievements. We must also create pathways back for those who drop out.

**The qualifications system**

Labour believes the GCSE approach has been beneficial to young people and is widely supported. However, there is now almost universal agreement that there needs to be a change in the nature of the post-16 qualification system in Britain. The present plethora of qualification systems, described aptly by the CBI as a 'jungle', needs rationalization. Neither young people nor employers can make sense of the present structures, so access to courses is inhibited, the usefulness of qualifications as passports into employment is reduced, and transfer to different areas and progress to different levels is made more difficult.

We will introduce a unified qualification structure that will incorporate the best practice from existing qualifications, whether academically orientated or geared to vocational skills. Such a structure, once in place, will serve as the accreditation base for education and training initiatives undertaken in the workplace or in further education and leading to higher education. It will also provide one of the yardsticks by which to judge the merits of private providers, whose role has grown in recent years, notably in providing courses for the unemployed.

Such a unified structure must build on the innovations of recent times in both further and higher education. Amongst these has been the introduction of GNVQs as a basis for full-time vocational education for the majority for whom the present A/AS level is inappropriate.

Building on current best practice we will ensure an overarching framework for all qualifications based on the principle of credit accumulation systems and on modular courses. This modularization of courses depends on identifying core skills and breaking down courses into units which represent well-defined and well-understood levels of learning and attainment. In further education this process has undoubtedly been held back by the government's clear hostility to modular A levels, but it is widely regarded as successful and advantageous for the student.

Such a unified qualification system will allow the individual to define clearly how he or she wishes to progress. For employers it provides a better picture of the capacities and potential of their workforce. In this way we will break down the increasingly artificial divide between academic and vocational qualifications by recognizing the value of both.

## A General Certificate of Further Education

The GCSE has been widely accepted as a qualification that has both maintained standards and improved attainment, but we can still do better. Our initial target is for 80 per cent of our young people to be able to achieve the equivalent of GCSE grades A–C in core subjects.

Labour believes that every young person should be able to continue in mainstream education, training, or training in work for two years after 16. We want to prevent GCSE marking the end-point of school life in a way that limits the achievements of the overwhelming majority. Accordingly, we will integrate the GCSE examination into part of a modular structure for all post-16 qualifications. This would involve turning GCSE into a series of major and minor credits. The GCSE should serve as a record of achievement for each student to give entry into appropriate post-16 education and training and work opportunities.

We will create a new General Certificate of Further Education (GCFE), building on the strengths and experience of the present GCSE. There is much to learn, in this regard, from the long tradition of academic education post-16 and the recent emergence of vocational qualifications like NVQs and GNVQs. This background can help us decide what organizations and structures are needed to guarantee that GCFE matches the best achievements of the past and builds on them to achieve the different aspirations of a changing world. We will integrate GCSE and the new GCFE as part of a continuous structure for the 14–19+ group.

Core elements of all GCFE courses would have to ensure that a balance was maintained between academic and vocational courses and between classroom contact and the world of work. Every young person should have the opportunity to combine education and training in a way that suits their individual needs. To do less would simply condemn us to replicate the futile split in attitude and status which exists at present between A levels and NVQs.

Definition of the core elements of GCFE must be a matter for wide consultation, following acceptance of the principle of a unified qualification to be gained through credit accumulation.

The clearest possible relationship has to be established between levels of achievement at GCFE and the best qualification systems emerging in the international arena. Labour wants the best for all our young people. High achievements at GCFE should be easily identifiable with qualifications like the International Baccalaureate, and we will ensure that increasing numbers of our young people will attain these high-status qualifications. Labour's longer-term target is for 80 per cent of the nation's young people to matriculate at GCFE.

For GCFE students pursuing a workplace-based series of courses, the traditional craft apprenticeship model holds important lessons. The standards in our craft trades should be as high as anywhere in the world, and our craftsmen and women should be trained to the highest standards and be competitive with the best in the world. But GCFE will only be the start of craft-based training.

We will ensure that every employer makes available appropriate structured training for 16- to 19-year-old employees.

For young people in school or college, we recognize the need to expand their experience of the outside world, and especially the world of work, in order to help develop the social and interpersonal skills which are largely absent from current educational experience.

All the main employers' organizations, further and higher education institutions, and public and private school groups alike agree that A levels are a real barrier to the development of further and higher education.

Labour will respond to the universal call to replace the present over-specialized narrow A level.


**Learning for life**

Labour is determined to reverse the falling level of skills within our workforce by raising the standards of education and training of our young people, widening access to retraining for those in work and providing training for real skills for those out of work.

Adult education and training not only increases confidence and skills but also provides routes back into work. It is a valuable resource for enhancing the quality of people's lives. The Cinderella status of adult education has been exacerbated by government cuts. There are many barriers that have prevented, and continue to prevent, acccess to worthwhile and satisfying learning experiences for many adults. Adult education and training has been neglected both by central government and by employers.

This government has neither a long-term nor a short-term strategy for adult learning. The market has not provided a system which can meet and stretch the aspirations of the individual or serve the needs of the nation.

We will review the financing of further education so that the range of courses is designed on educational and training grounds. Equally we will provide a structure within which further education colleges and other agencies can plan course provision in co-operation to serve the wider community interest.

Further education colleges are the backbone of adult education and much vocational training. However, the freedoms offered to colleges through incorporation have not been matched by adequate levels of accountability. Labour will therefore ensure the governing structures of colleges are accountable and reflect the different social partners and the wider public interest.

Those on benefit are also barred from full-time study. The social security regulations, which insist on claimants actively seeking and being available for non-existent jobs, debar anyone from receiving benefit who is engaged in studying for more than 21 hours a week. We will review the barriers that prevent those on benefit from undertaking study and improving their employment prospects. These and other issues relating to further and higher education will be discussed in greater detail in a forthcoming consultative document. In addition, a consultative document will be produced on the issue of the Youth Service.

## A National Training Strategy

The Training and Enterprise Councils (TECs) were supposed to usher in a new wave of training investment both for those in work and for the unemployed. The TECs have become entrenched in delivering low-standard training for the medium and long-term unemployed which simply fails to open the pathways to skills that ought to exist.

The TECs have the potential to make a valuable contribution to local and regional economies by matching skills to jobs. However, we are aware of the widespread frustration with their present role, which has been expressed in the large number of resignations of directors from their boards.

Labour will review the role, functions, and accountability of the TECs in order to ensure: that their structure provides a balanced membership from the local community; that where public money is invested it is spent on high-quality training; that they offer high-quality training to the unemployed to equip them with the skills and qualifications needed to find work; and that there is investment in retraining the existing workforce in the skills needed for industrial expansion.

Labour will establish local mechanisms whereby all agencies involved in vocational training are brought together to plan and provide for the local labour market. Amongst employers there are many who do train their employees and resent the fact that amongst their competitors are those who prefer to freeload, making no effort to train, and who exist by poaching those who have been trained elsewhere. Equally some companies which do not train, especially among the smaller firms, simply do not know how to assess the benefits of training or how to go about accessing relevant programmes.

Labour will open up greater opportunities for the retraining of those in work by introducing a national training levy to ensure that every company provides its workforce with the chance to upgrade its skills. The objective will be to encourage companies to focus on the training appropriate within their own business rather than treating training as an external function that is somebody else's responsibility.

Labour will undertake a skills audit of the nation which will enable the identification of the skills that are available and those in short supply, with a view to targeting training resources.

Labour will introduce new and extended anti-discrimination legislation to create the framework for tackling discrimination in training. Training providers will be required to take positive measures to eliminate discrimination and bias and to promote equity in the delivery of training.

The Labour Party document, Winning for Britain, also deals with skills and training and outlines Labour's strategy for industrial success.


*An Education and Careers Guidance Service*

Good quality, impartial, and accurate careers advice must be provided to young people and adults so they are able to make informed curriculum and careers choices. Many LEA careers services have been run down in recent years in response to central government cut-backs in local government spending. This is a false economy. An Audit Commission/OFSTED report made it clear that there is massive waste involved in students making the wrong choices where such a service is absent or inadequate.

It is clear that other groups in society, such as the unemployed or adult returners, can benefit from a similar type of service. The Department of Employment used to offer a range of services providing a counselling role. Inevitably in recent years the credibility of DE schemes like Restart has suffered because they were more concerned with manipulating the unemployment claimant figures than offering independent advice. The CBI report *Routes for Success* emphasized the 'critical role' of independent education and careers guidance, and went on to make a powerful case for a service which recognizes the need to offer high-quality guidance at the earliest point where young people begin to make choices.

It is vital that adequate contact be maintained with the education and guidance services throughout life. We will define exactly what services should be available for people, not just through their years of formal education and training, but also in later stages of career and life.

Labour will review existing structures to offer an education and careers service that will provide lifetime advice and guidance.

# Chapter 11

# Framework for a Learning Society[1]

## *The Conservative Government* (1996)

Lifetime learning is not a Government programme, or the property of one institution. It is a shared goal relating to the attitudes and behaviour of many employers, individuals and organizations. Government has a part to play but governments alone cannot achieve the cultural changes involved in making a reality of lifetime learning. The goal of a *learning society* will be achieved through many changes over a period of time. The framework described here puts particular policies and initiatives in the context of this goal.

### THE CONTEXT

Lifetime learning matters to the economy, to businesses, to communities and to individuals. It is important socially, culturally and economically:

- Economic borders have largely disappeared. Capital, products, skill and know-how all move between countries but skills tend to be less mobile than capital or technology.
- The Skills Audit clearly shows the continuing challenges we as a country have to meet to make sure that we have a workforce to sustain our competitiveness in international markets.
- The labour market is changing rapidly. Manual and unskilled jobs are increasingly scarce while the number of skilled jobs increases. Part-time employment has grown by nearly a quarter over the last decade. Self-employment has doubled since 1979. People need up-to-date skills to grasp new employment opportunities through their working lives.
- Those people who participate in learning (including learning to learn and the other skills valued by employers) and who get skills and qualifications, are more likely to get jobs and earn higher wages than those who do not.

- The pace of technological change in the workplace and in daily life means that those who do not acquire relevant skills will find it harder to cope and to compete.
- Businesses which invest in their people and encourage learning achieve real benefits in productivity and profitability.
- Children who are encouraged by their parents to learn grow into people who make learning a way of life.
- Older people with a background of continuing learning are likely to remain active in the economy and community for longer.
- Learning can help overcome social disadvantage and exclusion; it can help build positive and productive communities.
- Learning offers individuals personal fulfilment.

Recent surveys[2] show that most young people and adults believe that learning is important. But only about a third of adults have actually done any learning in the last three years and a third have done none since leaving school. Of those who left school at 16 or 17, 60 per cent have done no learning in the last three years. More generally, four out of five who have done no learning since school do not expect to do any in the future.

Our aim must be that more people of all ages and from all backgrounds acquire the learning habit. The National Targets for Education and Training will help us measure our success to the year 2000. Achieving them depends on embedding a habit of learning, acquiring skills, and gaining qualifications among employers, individuals and families. The Government is committed to promoting, encouraging and supporting the Targets and, in that process, to help people take more responsibility for their learning.

## FIRM FOUNDATIONS – ACHIEVEMENTS TO DATE

Learning must start early. Attitudes to learning are formed very early in life. Young people need to grow up with a personal commitment to continuing learning and with an expectation that they will acquire new skills throughout their working life. High-quality early and compulsory education for young people is the rock on which lifetime learning must be built. From 1997, the Nursery Education Voucher Scheme will enable parents to choose a high-quality place from an increasingly diverse range.

Schools provide the foundations. These foundations are being strengthened by the National Curriculum and testing pupils at key stages. This is supported by wide-ranging reforms to school management, inspection of schools and action to ensure high teaching standards. The Technical and Vocational Education Initiative (TVEI) has helped young people to develop and put to use learning skills which are relevant throughout life.

Less than 40 per cent of those who left school at 16 or 17 have done any formal learning in the last three years.[3] Learning must not stop at the school leaving age. As *Competitiveness: Creating the Enterprise Centre of Europe* (DTI, 1996) makes clear, we have now put in place policies and action that offer all young people the opportunities to build successfully on their school experiences and make the transition from compulsory education to the school sixth form, further education sector or work-based training and eventually into jobs:

- The vast majority of young people now continue education and training beyond the age of 16.
- Reforms to the provision of careers education and guidance are improving the quality of the information and support available to young people to help them make important choices about their learning and increase their chances of success. This helps to broaden understanding about opportunities in the future and sets the foundations for lifetime learning.
- The choice of high-quality *qualifications* has been extended. A levels are well respected. General National Vocational Qualifications (GNVQs) are increasingly popular.
- Modern Apprenticeships are now being undertaken by more than 25,000 young people. Well over 100,000 should be in training by the end of the century, if employers and young poeple continue to expand opportunities and take them up as they have to date.
- Sir Ron Dearing's proposals for developing and strengthening qualifications will ensure that standards are maintained and more young people – and adults – fulfil their potential. Sir Ron also stresses that young people must learn to manage and improve their own learning by the process of reviewing, recording and action planning – a skill they will need for life.
- The Government's policies for stimulating fair competition between providers, rigorous inspection and other quality assurance arrangements and the publication of performance tables for schools and colleges are all enhancing choice and standards, and ensuring that 16–19 learning is an effective launchpad for lifetime learning.

Reforms in further and higher education funding and management have helped to ensure that we have excellent opportunities for more students of all ages. Further education has grown significantly in recent years and will continue to offer more opportunities in coming years:

- Public expenditure plans allow for 20 per cent growth between 1993–4 and 1998–9 in student numbers in further education. On 1 November 1995, 2.4 million students were enrolled in the further education sector. Around 70 per cent of these were 19 years or over and around 50 per cent were 25 years or over.
- The total number of higher education students in Great Britain more than doubled between 1979–80 and 1994–5, from 779,000 to 1.6 million, with fastest expansion occurring in the period from 1988–9. As participation has increased, so has the diversity of the student body in terms of background and needs. Mature students now outnumber young people going straight to university from school. Half of these mature students study on a part-time basis. We have over 500,000 part-time students, of all ages, at all stages of life. The number of

students studying part-time has grown at an even faster rate than for full-time students. Fifteen per cent of all students are now post-graduates, and there has been significant growth in the number of people following short, post-degree, vocational courses to update their skills and knowledge, mainly in science, business and education;

• the Government's emphasis on diversity, together with a funding approach which encourages innovation and entrepreneurial activity has led to much greater activity, by universities in lifetime learning than can be seen in the rest of Europe and elsewhere.

In today's world learning is about the medium as well as the message. New technology is increasingly and effectively used in schools, colleges and universities, and by companies and individuals to help people learn in their workplace and at home at times that suit themselves. The Government is supporting the use of new technology through a wide-ranging programme of innovative projects in schools and across the education service, looking at the opportunities *superhighways* can bring. This will provide practical help and advice for those in education and will build on the support for teacher training and equipping made possible under Grants for Educational Support and Training (GEST) and other programmes. Through these and other initiatives, we are investing in the future delivery of learning on an unprecedented scale.

Learning will only become part of the accepted approach to work and to life where there is a widespread determination to make it happen:

• More employers are committed to training as central to their competitiveness and profitability. Investors in People is now widely accepted as the standard all organizations should achieve – some 22,000 are now Investors in People or are committed to reaching the national standard, covering almost 25 per cent of the workforce. The Government, through Training and Enterprise Councils (TECs) and Business Links, is providing substantial support for smaller firms to become Investors in People.

• More individuals are investing in their own learning and development. Some 80,000 people have taken out Career Development Loans (CDLs) over the last 10 years. Additionally, in 1995–6 some £21.2 million was claimed in tax relief for vocational training by individuals, representing a total personal investment of £84.8 million.

• Colleges, universities and training providers have developed ways of delivering learning to individuals and employers in ways that help overcome the difficulties – time, location, childcare, entry requirements – that some face when they want to get involved.

• TECs and careers services have worked with their local partners to develop further information, advice and gudiance services for adults that encourage the development of a market. Local partnerships have been developed that support a range of opportunities for young people and adults to take part in learning.

## BUILDING SUCCESS

There is more to be done – by the Government, employers, education and training providers, TECs, local authorities and individuals. It is important that each of these is aware of what the others are doing and is able to contribute. Recognition that lifetime learning is a joint venture will encourage all the parties to participate.

The policy framework described here seeks to bring together the many and varied developments that will help to open up learning to a far wider range of the population and, in the process, to achieve the challenging National Targets that we have set ourselves. It identifies six main strands of development for the years ahead. They are:

- Investing in the training and development of employees. This is critical to business growth, community prosperity and national competitiveness.
- Gaining the commitment of individuals to return to and continue learning. It is crucial to find ways of promoting new attitudes to learning and bring back those who no longer see learning as relevant to them.
- Developing an effective and high-quality infrastructure of information, advice and guidance for individuals in every area.
- Improving access to learning. More work is required to help break down barriers – real or perceived – to participation.
- Giving people of all ages the opportunity to acquire the basic skills on which to build further learning.
- Developing effective partnerships nationally and locally to give practical effect to shared responsibility and to make the best use of resources.

## TRAINING AND DEVELOPMENT OF EMPLOYEES

Successful businesses use education and training as a competitive weapon. Firms of all sizes are recognizing increasingly that training and developing people are critical to business success. But investment in training by employers cannot be achieved by statute or government regulation. Experience in Britain and abroad has shown that compulsion does not work. Effective and lasting investment will result only from an appreciation by employers themselves that a skilled and learning workforce brings about greater productivity, competitiveness and profitability.

The Government has a major role to play. It will continue to invest in helping employers, particularly small and medium-sized firms, to recognize and tackle the need for a planned approach to skills and learning.

Key elements in the Government's strategy include:

- funding the work of Investors in People UK, TECs and the Management Charter Initiative (MCI)
- reforming the network of national sector training organizations
- the promotion of exemplars through the National Training Awards. 1996 is the Awards' tenth year.

This year Investors in People UK will be:

- developing support for Industry Training Organizations (ITOs) so that they can maximize their role in promoting Investors in People and facilitating sector initiatives in specific, targeted industries
- working with other bodies such as the BSI on strengthening the relationship between the Investors in People Standard and other quality initiatives
- working with a group of large, multi-site companies and TECs to accelerate progress in those companies across the country
- establishing a national network of employers which are recognized Investors in People to share good practice on their continued development
- developing a toolkit targeted at small businesses
- working to increase the awareness of Investors in People among employees.

The Government will continue to provide substantial funding to TECs to promote learning strategies with employers and to help them move towards the Investors in People Standard. TECs' work with employers includes:

- specific tailored help in moving to recognition as Investors in People
- advice and funding for small firms in initial approaches to their training plans and capability through the Skills for Small Businesses programme and local initiatives
- schemes to bring small companies together so that they can share their work on skills and training, including the wide range of successful projects from the recent Skills Challenge.

TECs and Business Links will be supported in their efforts to promote improved management development by employers through the MCI with funding from the Government. MCI, TECs, Investors in People UK, the Confederation of British Industry (CBI) and others are working together to develop a support framework for companies to address their management development needs in the context of Investors in People.

This support for employers at national and local level will be complemented by the Government's proposals for a single network of National Training Organisations (NTOs) at sector level. The Department for Education and Employment (DfEE) proposes to recognize through a quality mark those sector organizations which can most effectively help the employers and/or occupational groups in their industries to meet their training and education needs. They might do this by, for example, defining occupational standards and promoting them for use in National and Scottish Vocational Qualfiications (N/SVQs) and other applications; setting sector skills targets; and promoting Investors in People and skills benchmarking.

The Government plans now to build further on the framework of local and sectoral support for businesses in addressing skills issues. The review of Government support for businesses, which was announced by the Prime Minister in March 1996, position people, their know-how and skills as one of the four key areas for work to improve businesses' competitiveness and profitability. The focus on support, which is locally designed and which integrates skills and learning into the core of work with firms on technology, marketing and other business issues, will take forward work done already by TECs. It will ensure that the Business Link network and such key local partners as Chambers of Commerce play a full part in developing firms' competitiveness through their people.

The Government does not have the only role in encouraging employers to realize the competitive benefits from training. The CBI has consistently promoted this message. Its recent documents, *Realising a Vision: A Skills Passport* (CBI, 1995) said:

> The Investors in People Standard is a key lever in raising the competence levels of the workforce. It is a powerful force for change in developing learning businesses in every sector of economic life. The CBI recommends that all organizations should be Investors in People.

This message has been echoed by the Institute of Directors and other bodies. The Government believes that employers' bodies have a vital role in communicating the clear business benefits of their members' investment in learning for their employees. Recent statements from the Trades Union Congress (TUC) have reinforced the message: 'The TUC supports Investors in People because it has the potential to transform attitudes to employee development and skills training. Effective training and development has to be linked to organizations' business objectives.'

Action by Government and other bodies can motivate and support employers. However, it is the actions of employers themselves which results in more training and education at work. The take-up of Investors in People by employers of all sizes in both the private and public sectors, and the sustained levels of business expenditure on training in recent years show that many managers are hearing the message. Over 400 companies have introduced Employee Development Schemes providing broad-based learning opportunities. The Government will continue to promote the development of effective schemes of this kind and ensure that good practice is made widely known. Some companies are building on Investors in People and seeking to become *learning companies or learning organisations*. We will draw on these developments and explore with others ways in which these ideas and activities can contribute further to employer investment and individual take-up of learning opportunities. Many employers are using links with education as a powerful means of promoting and reinforcing a learning culture within their organizations. Involvement in initiatives such as providing work experience for pupils and students, teacher placements in industry, mentoring programmes, and membership of local school or college governing bodies can provide excellent opportunities to support staff development and motivate employees at all levels. Education business partnerships provide a network for facilitating these links at local level. Employer involvement in the training of young people, in particular their enthusiastic take-up of Modern Apprenticeships, is helping to build a company culture of lifetime learning.

The Government is itself a major employer and is committed to developing a Civil Service with the skills to meet the significant programme of change set out in its White Paper, *The Civil Service: Continuity and Change* (DE, 1994). The forthcoming White Paper on training and development in the Civil Service will set out the Government's commitment to Investors in People in all Departments and Agencies and establish a culture in which every one of its employees expects continuing encouragement in his or her learning.

## GETTING INDIVIDUAL COMMITMENT

Convincing individuals to get involved in learning is critical. While the majority of people agree that learning continues throughout life and that it leads to more interesting work and better prospects, the main reason they do not participate is lack of understanding or motivation.

The five-year Campaign for Learning was launched by the Royal Society of Arts (RSA) in April 1996. The Campaign brings together a national alliance of companies, organizations such as the National Institute for Adult Continuing Education (NIACE), the TEC National Council, the Open University and many others. It aims to:

- increase awareness of the importance of personal learning, raise expectations and change attitudes towards learning
- get more individuals taking part in learning
- get more companies and other organizations actively working towards the principles of a learning organization.

To those ends the Campaign, to which the Government is contributing, will develop and support a wide range of national, regional and local initiatives.

In addition, the Government will continue to:

- support the work of NIACE and its partners in running the annual and highly successful Adult Learners' Week
- co-operate with broadcasters on particular projects. The contribution broadcasters can make in providing easily accessible information as well as learning materials is recognized and valued.
- commission and support research and development directly or by others, for example under the Economic and Social Research Council (ESRC) *Learning Society* programme, and internationally under the five-year programme of work *Implementing Lifelong Learning for All*, undertaken by the Organization for Economic Co-operation and Development (OECD).

To encourage individuals' own investment in learning, the Government will:

- work in partnership with the four banks which currently offer CDLs to promote such loans as a simple and affordable means of paying for continuing education and training. Development to meet the needs of the market will continue. Special arrangements for CDLs for unemployed people are now being piloted. From September 1996 CDLs will also be available to individuals on three-year sandwich courses including up to a twelve-month period of work placement.
- keep under review the scope and effectiveness of the tax relief available to individuals investing in vocational education and training.

Many people who are unemployed and receiving benefits undertake learning. Some people argue that the benefit rules are a barrier to this learning. There is however little evidence about the link between learning while unemployed and receiving benefits and success in securing work or qualifications. The new rules on study which Jobseekers' Allowance will introduce on 7 October 1996 are designed to allow broadly the same number of people to study part-time as do so under the current rules, to make the arrangemens clearer for individuals and colleges and to reflect changes in the way that the education sector designs its courses. We intend to collect more and better information on this issue. As part of this, we shall be looking at the possiblity of running pilots to test the effectiveness of different arrangements for part-time study while receiving Jobseekers' Allowance.

The responses to the consultation document showed a range of views on individual training (or learning) accounts but overall these confirm the difficulties which would lie in any nationally prescribed or funded scheme. Those who might readily make use of such a scheme are likely to be those who already invest in their own learning. There is little support from the financial institutions and this would be critical to any TESSA-type or other accounts that were to be portable between employers. The administrative complexities of any national model would be huge and costly. Such a scheme would be difficult to apply for those with flexible working patterns – short-term contracts, part-time and portfolio workers – as well as the unemployed or returners to the labour market. Overall a scheme of this kind would be unlikely to tackle cost-effectively the central aim of providing incentives and motivation for non-learners to participate in education and training. Schemes run by employers for their own employees need not suffer from the same degree of difficulty and may be an effective part of an organization's overall approach to investing in their people.

## INFORMATION, ADVICE AND GUIDANCE

Individuals need information and advice to identify courses and learning materials relevant to their needs. They may also need help in recognizing their existing achievements and constructing realistic action plans to take advantage of appropriate learning opportunities. Careers services deliver comprehensive provision for young people. However, existing provision for adults is variable both in its quality and its coverage. In some areas, local partnerships are giving information and advice. TECs, careers services, higher and further education institutions, the Employment Service and other bodies have set up local networks to provide easily accessible services for individuals. In other areas it may be difficult for an individual to know where to go to get objective information or difficult to get any such service. The Government will be looking to:

- work with providers to develop national standards so that individuals, wherever they live, can be assured that the advice available to them is up to date, relevant, informed and worth listening to;
- further develop and stimulate local partnerships to provide well signposted and

co-ordinated services using new technology where possible; within such services to encourage systems of charging for some guidance services for those who can afford to pay;

- examine the scope for introducing a helpline service building on the pilots undertaken by some local partnerships, and the experience of national helplines run from time to time by the BBC and in support of Adult Learners' Week over the last five years.

## RELEVANT AND ACCESSIBLE OPPORTUNITIES

More individuals are likely to take up and continue learning if they can recognize their existing achievements and if they find that more formal learning can be done easily within the demands of everyday life. Providers of education and training opportunities must continue to develop ways of responding to the different needs of actual and potential learners. Many colleges and others responding to the consultation document gave useful examples.

More needs to be done to provide opportunities where people live or work rather than in existing institutions. To do this many colleges and other providers are developing new partnerships with community and voluntary organizations and with employers. These are delivering, for example:

- courses tailored to meet the needs of particular groups of learners, including ex-offenders and single parents
- opportunities to learn in familiar environments (e.g. community centres) and with support from peers
- appropriate childcare
- additional work-based learning relevant to the needs of firms and their employees.
- development and improvement of a robust and recognized system of qualfica-tions, accessible to those at work and founded on the occupational skills needed by employers. NVQs are now offered by 40 per cent of employers with more than 25 employees – a very significant growth in opportunities over the past two years.

The Government welcomes the advice of the Further Education Funding Council (FEFC) to colleges on the controls they should have in place when delivering education away from college premises by and with the assistance of a third party. Colleges which follow this advice should be able to continue or develop imaginative partnerships with employers, while securing effective use of taxpayers' money.

The Government is also supporting TEC development projects and is consider-ing how best to contribute to the wider goals of improving the awareness of new technology throughout the UK. It welcomes the contribution of the FEFC's Learning and Technology Committee to the debate on the use of information technology in and by the further education sector. In this area, progress is likely to benefit particularly from new and innovative partnerships with industry.

Action resulting from a review of NVQs and SVQs will update NVQs, make them easier to use and introduce a wider range of assessment methods. This should enable the growth of NVQs among firms to continue and should also increase the attractions to individual employees of improving their skills to nationally recognized standards. Sir Ron Dearing's proposals for qualifications for 16- to 19-year-olds and for improving their learning will, among other things, give a wider base of accomplishment for young people. This will act as a platform for future skill acquisition and generate a continued motivation to learn in future. Action being taken on Sir Ron Dearing's report will help provide qualifications relevant to adults as well as 16- to 19-year-olds.

Sir Ron's proposal that the NRA should be reviewed and restructured to make it a more effective tool for helping adults plan and record their learning is welcomed by the Government. The review will examine both the use and design of the NRA document, with the intention of gaining employer support for its use through all stages of education, training, employment and lifetime learning.

The FEFC's Committee on Widening Participation chaired by Helena Kennedy QC is considering many of these issues and the ways in which colleges and others and the FEFC through its funding methodology and strategic guidance might respond to get more individuals involved in learning. The Government looks forward with interest to the Committee's report to FEFC.

The higher education sector has also shown much enterprise and innovation in its response to lifetime learners' needs. This response arises, in part, as a result of the government's commitment to diversity in higher education, and of an approach to funding which encourages universities to be more involved in lifetime learning than would be the norm in the rest of Europe and elsewhere. There have been impressive increases in recent years in higher education participation at all ages. The growth in the number of mature, part-time and post-graduate students provides encouraging evidence of the willingness of the sector to respond to an increasing demand for lifetime learning. Universities and colleges have responded to demands from lifetime learners by opening more post-graduate centres and business and management schools, and by providing flexible courses that allow students to combine study with work and other adult commitments. The Government will continue to encourage the higher education sector to become even more accessible to lifetime learners, for example by its support of the development of work-based learning and of credit accumulation and transfer systems. The terms of reference for the National Committee of Inquiry into Higher Education, chaired by Sir Ron Dearing, state that there should be maximum participation in lifetime learning in the context of the needs of individuals, the nation and the future labour market. The Committee will take this into account in making its recommendations on how the purposes, shape, structure, size and funding of higher education should develop to meet the needs of the UK over the next twenty years.

## BASIC SKILLS

Our policies for lifetime learning must also secure that everyone has the basic skills of functional literacy and numeracy, which are necessary for living and working in today's complex and fast changing society. To that end, the Government is setting in hand a review of its policies to tackle low achievement in basic skills.

The review will examine the effectiveness and coherence of a wide range of current measures and initiatives. These include:

- setting learning goals in language, literacy and numeracy skills for young children leaving nursery education
- the National Curriculum and testing of pupils' achievements at key stages
- support for teachers, particularly in primary schools, through the development of literacy and numeracy centres
- the family literacy demonstration programmes run by the Basic Skills Agency which show that bringing children and parents together can help both make real progress
- the current Training for Work pilot programmes providing prevocational and basic skills training for unemployed adults who need them before pursuing vocational training and/or jobsearch,
- developing the new entry arrangements for young people at 16 and 17 who are underachieving, or not engaged in learning at all.

## EFFECTIVE PARTNERSHIP

Because lifetime learning is not about a single programme of activity by one institution, policies aimed at creating a learning society will only be effective if all those concerned work together. New and more effective partnerships at national, regional and local level need to be forged to give full effect to all the strands of the policy framework outlined here.

At *national* level, organizations representing employers and employees need to work together to promote lifetime learning. They need to support those working towards the Investors in People Standard and, more generally, to encourage individual companies and trade unions developing effective strategies for learning in the workplace. As part of this, they need to work with broadcasters, national bodies like NIACE, RSA, the TEC National Council and others to promote the need for and benefits of learning. New industrial training organizations will need to develop effective lifetime learning strategies for their sectors.

At *regional* level Government Offices working with the local authorities, TECs, employers and others can do much to encourage effective partnerships. Regional competitiveness plans all include aspects of lifetime learning as critical. The Single Regeneration Budget has supported, and will continue to help a wide range of relevant development and activities.

*Locally*, colleges and Local Education Authorities need to work together to plan and deliver co-ordinated programmes of learning opportunities of all kinds. TECs and careers services need to continue to work together and with others to put in place high-quality information, advice and guidance for adults and to develop and deliver relevant and accessible education and training opportunities. TECs' partnerships in Business Link with Chambers of Commerce and others need to make sure that skills issues are integrated in their advice on business development to local firms. Partnerships with employers, Chambers of Commerce and others are needed to ensure the demand for learning is matched with relevant opportunities. All local partners need to work together to develop challenging local targets for education and training. In some places, they are working to develop the idea of a learning city or town and the Government will support the development of models to help such initiatives.

The Government is playing its part by supporting such partnership activity through, for example, contributing to particular development projects and in helping to make effective practice well known across the country.

## CONCLUSION

All the elements of the policy framework described here will contribute to establishing a society in which learning throughout life becomes a way of life. The Government has taken many initiatives to lay the foundations and build towards this goal. But *responsbililty is shared*, and the goal will only be achieved if employers, individuals, providers and many others continue, jointly and severally, to take steps to turn it into reality.

## NOTES

1 This chapter is taken from the 1996 Conservative Government document *Lifetime Learning: A Policy Framework*, published by DfEE, 24 June 1996 (paragraphs 1.1 to 1.3 have been omitted). The policy document was published in a press release (203/96) by the Education and Employment Minister, James Paice, entitled *Framework for a Learning Society*.
2 *Creating Two Nations?* NIACE/Gallup, 1996; *Attitudes to Learning: MORI State of the Nation Poll – Summary Report*, Campaign for Learning, 1996.
3 *Creating Two Nations?* NIACE/Gallup, 1996.

# Chapter 12

---

# Scotland as a Learning Society
## Scottish Community Education Council

People learn in many different contexts, and they learn better and more effectively if the whole society in which they live regards learning as a natural activity for people of all ages. In such a society:

- It would be taken for granted that virtually everyone would wish to engage in some form of learning at different stages of their lives.
- Education would no longer be regarded as an activity largely confined to schools and colleges and appropriate only for children and young people.
- Structures, working hours and other aspects of employment, and social life, both nationally and within local communities, would be adapted to encourage learning and provide everyone with ready access to the facilities they require to pursue the kind of learning they need or want.

Knowledge, skills, understanding, curiosity and wisdom cannot be kept in separate boxes, depending simply on who is paying for or providing them. Neither training systems nor educational institutions, nor informal learning opportunities – no matter how high the quality – will be enough on their own to meet the learning needs of society. This report uses the term 'learning', in preference to 'education' in many instances, in order to emphasize the natural and lifelong nature of learning and to avoid the widespread tendency to equate education with only the work done in schools and colleges.

It may have been this kind of realization that led Robert Hutchins, writing in 1968, to define a Learning Society as

> one that, in addition to offering part-time adult education to every man and woman at evey stage of grown-up life, [has] succeeded in transforming its values in such a way that learning, fulfilment [and] becoming human [have] become its aims, and all its institutions [are] directed to this end.

An updated version might read: 'A society whose citizens value, support and engage in learning, as a matter of course, in all areas of activity'. It is a vision of Scotland as that kind of society which forms the basis of this report.

Contrary to much popular belief, there is not single set of 'roots, values and traditions' at the heart of education in Scotland. Enthusiasts for the Scottish tradition have made much of the poor but talented 'lad o' pairts' whose eventual success in our educational system is presented as the proof of its openness and essential fairness. In practice, the picture is less impressive. The present system:

- is arguably less 'democratic' than is often claimed;
- is individualistic in emphasis and tends to reinforce gender stereotypes in its treatment of young people;
- creates a sense of failure in many young people who do not succeed in climbing the competitive ladder it provides;
- fails to sustain beyond school the relatively high levels of academic achievement attained in comparison with England;
- results in relatively high levels of employee related training offered to young people in comparison with England, but low levels of workplace training offered to adults over the age of 20 in comparison with England;
- resutls in only 20 per cent of the adult population in Scotland engaging in organized learning, compared with 24 per cent for Britain as a whole

(NIACE, 1994)

Any attempt to reform Scotish education has to contend with the contrast between the high value which Scottish people often place on education, and the mixed feelings and reactions which many of them display towards it in practice.

Nevertheless the current education scene in Scotland is characterized by good community-based adult learning initiatives, which succeed in engaging adults who do not normally seek out learning opportunities. A further strength of the present system in recent years has been the growth of cross-sectoral adult educational guidance networks. Adult Learners' Week has played an important part in their development. Both these features, however, are highly vulnerable to *ad hoc* and short-term present funding arrangements and to the imminent changes in the structure and organization of the education system.

This report reaffirms the existing good practice and the reputed value of education held within Scottish society, but challenges individuals and organizations to give greater substance to the valuing of learning.

The main reasons are:

- because knowledge and skills inevitably go out of date and are currently doing so at an increasing rate. This is true not only in economic and work areas but also in the social arena. Much attention is rightly focused on how employees are to keep up with technical change in their work situations: it is no less important, however, to equip parents to keep in touch with their children and young people, and to enable citizens in general to cope with political and cultural change.
- because a great deal of human potential is being neglected by the present

system. This neglect affects people as learners and, less obviously, as learning resources for each other. The wasted potential is of many kinds, not just intellectual. It restricts and reduces individuals' economic performance, as well as their contribution to the social and cultural life of their communities and the country as a whole.

- because a healthy modern society needs its people to possess a high degree of critical awareness. Unless they acquire the critical skills to cope with the power advertising, media manipulation, and floods of information and disinformation, and to interpret and respond to social, political and economic trends, society and the individuals within it will suffer. The damage will be of many kinds, ranging from financial fraud to impoverishment of the whole culture.
- because learning is a profoundly social activity, as well as an individual one, and our social relations need strengthening. Learning alongside other people assists social communication and promotes collective understanding: it is especially vital in the present era of increasing privatization of what have hitherto been public services.
- because the protection of the environment depends on people acquiring levels of knowledge and understanding of our world well beyond their current levels. What is more, learning itself can lead to active ways of living in a society which make more modest demands on the world's natural resources than the high-consumption, mainly passive, lifestyles of many people today.
- because even the most progressive schools are not able to meet all the learning needs of our young people and communities. In our vision of a Learning Society effective schools would be a vital element in the lifelong education process.
- because we need to build capacity. People need support to develop their potential to contribute to the economic growth of their society.

How would we recognize a Learning Society if we saw one, or more to the point, if we found ourselves part of one? It would be relatively easy to describe it in material terms alone, by referring to levels of financial and physical resources and other easily measured features. A full description, however, must also include less tangible factors, such as prevailing attitudes and values, levels of participation, etc. We believe that a Learning Society would have the following essential characteristics:

- Learning would be a crucial element in people's sense of personal and community identity, encouraging positive attitudes to their communities and to society as a whole, a willingness to accept their responsibilities for determining its future, and a dynamic understanding of tradition.
- Levels of resourcing would match and confirm the importance given to learning. A society's commitment to learning is not measured by rhetoric but by the priority it receives in the allocation of limited resources. This applies at all levels of society, national, local and domestic. It applies to the distribution of resources among different areas of need, including geographical areas, as well as their overall volume.
- There would be a high-quality infrastructure – buildings, and communications

systems – capable of supporting and encouraging the pursuit of learning, by providing real access for all citizens, and the best achievable physical environment and facilities for the purpose.

- A supportive legal and administrative framework would be designed to encourage learning and to remove barriers and disincentives to would-be learners. This would involve not only establishing individual rights and entitlements, but also framing obligations on employers and other organizations to ensure minimum standards of provision and/or financial commitment.
- Good industrial practice would be encouraged and supported, including formal commitments by employers, of the kind encouraged by Investors in People. Human resource development would be positively valued and explicitly included in a company's statement of accounts.
- People would find it easy to move through successive stages of a learning process and from one learning opportunity to another. They would receive appropriate incentives and rewards for learning achievements, which need not be material.
- A place would be found for a positive valuation of human growth through learning in the assessment of the society's economic and financial progress.
- The whole society would be notable for the high degree of participation of its citizens in all areas of activity. Measures of this kind would include the uptake of existing learning opportunities in different geographcial areas and among all sections of the population.

We believe it important, as well as articulating the main features of the vision of Scotland as a Learning Society, to offer some specific targets, which we see as practical goals to work towards within an identified timescale. Progress can be assessed in a number of ways, by comparing present with past performance within our own society and by looking at the levels of success achieved in comparable societies, in Western Europe and elsewhere.

We present here a list of target arenas and, within each, a number of national targets in pursuit of the long-term goal of establishing Scotland as a Learning Society. We wish to avoid painting an idealized picture and consider these targets to be realistic and achievable, although we acknowledge that their attainment will present a serious challenge to many established priorities and assumptions in Scottish education and in the wider society. Within the proposed framework, councils, companies and local organizations are invited to adapt and adjust the targets to take account of their own priorities.

## PARTICIPATION

One of our main aims is to increase the total number of people taking part in adult education in Scotland and to attract them from a wider cross-secton of the population and, in particular, from groups who have traditionally been under-represented among adult learners.

In order to do this we need a broader debate on the meaning of learning and its place in society. A comprehensive study of people's attitudes to learning, with the findings regularly monitored and updated, would be a major step towards both stimulating and informing such a debate. The material produced would be useful both for promoting learning opportunities and for planning programmes and activities. Specifically we propose that:

(a) The percentage of all adults taking part in education should be increased by at least 3 per cent in each of the next five years.
(b) The number of students in adult education drawn from hitherto under-represented groups – including the long-term unemployed, unskilled and semi-skilled men, the over 50s , the unskilled employed, members of ethnic minority communities and disabled people – should be increased disproportionately to the total.
(c) The number of adults engaged in part-time further and higher education should be increased in absolute terms and as a proportion of the total number engaged in education.
(d) The support and guidance infrastructure in further and higher education institutions should be expanded and strengthened to assist student retention rates.

## INVESTMENT IN EMPLOYEES

The need for employers – in the public, private and voluntary sectors – to see their employees as their most important assets and to invest resources in their development is, we believe, central to the creation of a Learning Society. Personal development combines employement-related skills with learning based on individual's own interests, to the mutual benefit of employers and employees. To this end, we propose that:

(a) Every working adult should be guaranteed a small group guidance meeting in the workplace, at least once every two years.
(b) The proportion of corporate budgets spent on employee development schemes, staff development and paid leave for educational purposes should be increased.
(c) A sponsored consultancy service should be set up to support the expansion of employee development schemes, especially among small and medium-sized employers.

## GOVERNMENT INVESTMENT

Central government will have a key supportive role in the creation of a Learning Society, in enacting appropriate legislation and increasing the level of investment necessary to make the concept of lifelong learning a reality. In particular, we propose that:

(a) The percentage of the Gross Domestic Product (GDP) spent on education should be increased and a greater proportion of the total allocated to broadening the base of participation in learning by hitherto under-represented groups.
(b) The number of nursery school places should be increased so as to achieve the target of places for all 3- and 4-year-olds by the year 1999.
(c) There should be equity of funding for full-time and part-time students in post-school education
(d) The allocation of additional resources should be aimed at increasing participation in education in areas/among groups where uptake of learning provision is low.

## NATIONAL INITIATIVES

We recognize the need for certain steps to be taken at national level, in order to bring about some of the key changes in the political and economic climate that are required for the creation of a Learning Society. Specifically, we propose that:

(a) Every long-term unemployed person should be guaranteed a free, two-hour impartial guidance interview annually.
(b) The percentage of adults lacking essential skills, such as literacy, numeracy, communication skills and basic familiarity with information technology should be halved over the next ten years.
(c) A National Human Resources Audit should be undertaken by the Advisory Scottish Council for Education and Training Targets and conducted at regular intervals.
(d) The Advisory Scottish Council for Education and Training Targets should develop a target for general vocational training and non-vocational programmes which are designed, as a first step, to rekindle the desire and ability to participate in post-school education and training.

## THE ACTIVE SOCIETY

Targets for society as a whole are more difficult to formulate, but they are crucial to the creation of a Learning Society. Responsibility for the building of a Learning Society lies not only with the education providers but with the whole range of organizations and institutions in Scotland. We propose that:

(a) Parental involvement in schools, measured by the number and quality (in terms of levels of participation in decision-making, etc.) of Parent-Teacher Associations, Parents' Associations and School Boards, should be increased.
(b) Educational broadcasting to encourage and support learning should be increased.

(c) Increased use of libraries, theatres, museums, cinemas, leisure and sports centres should be actively promoted amongst hitherto under-represented groups.
(d) The growth of self-help groups, e.g. study circles and community-based learning groups providing networking, mutual support and learning should be encouraged.
(e) New communications technology should be put at the service of adult learners and teachers.
(f) The level of involvement in voluntary service and community work should be increased.
(g) All local authority departments (not just education departments) should be encouraged to recognize their role in stimulating and supporting learning.
(h) The proportion of the population voting in local, national and European elections should increase.

We have the real possibility of creating, in Scotland, a Learning Society. Many of the constituent elements are already in place – an increasingly effective primary and secondary schools sector; a revamped further education college structure, a Community Education Service that uniquely in Europe offers an integrated structure for the promotion of lifelong learning; a progressive library and information service; and a small but significant voluntary sector. There is growing evidence of increasing business and education partnerships. There is, however, much still to be done if the vision of Scotland as a Learning Society is to be realized.

We hope this paper will stimulate a debate and subsequent action. The targets that we have identified are an initial list and we would fully expect these to be re-worked, expanded and made more specific by each company, organization or authority.

We also hope that the sense of urgency expressed by many in the group may be shared by those who receive this document. We believe that the forthcoming European Year of Lifelong Learning in 1996 will be a further stimulus to future action.

The challenge confronting us is to recapture the positive and enthusiastic belief in the power of learning and in the worth and potential of all our people. The practical promotion of Scotland as a Learning Society would be a significant step towards releasing the creative capacities of this nation.

# Chapter 13

# A Self-perpetuating Learning Society: A Report on Participation in Further Education

*Helena Kennedy QC*

Learning is central to economic success and social cohesion. As we approach the twenty-first century and the immense challenges of the global economy and unprecedented technological change, achieving these inseparable national goals will depend more and more on the knowledge, understanding and skills of the whole population. Recent policies to increase participation and achievement in learning have achieved some success, but mainly in providing opportunities for those who have already achieved to continue to do so. Those who are disadvantaged educationally are also disadvantaged economically and socially; equity and viability dictate that all should have the opportunity to succeed. To continue with current policy at a time of rapid change will widen the gulf between those who succeed in learning and those who do not, and puts at risk both social unity and economic prosperity. We are convinced that national leadership is required to place learning at the heart of our national common purpose. We must widen participation, not simply increase it. Widening participation means increasing access to learning and providing opportunities for success and progression to a much wider cross-section of the population than now. All those who are not fulfilling their potential or who have underachieved in the past must be drawn into successful learning. Widening participation in post-16 learning will create a self-perpetuating learning society.

## LEARNING FOR WORK AND LEARNING FOR LIFE ARE INSEPARABLE

Our work over the last two years has confirmed our conviction that learning is central to both economic prosperity and the health of society. We believe that the achievement of economic goals and social cohesion are intertwined. A healthy society is a necessary condition for a thriving economy: where parents encourage and support their children's education; where people in employment can adapt to change; where enterprise can flourish and where those seeking employment can acquire the skills they need for economic activity. Equally, economic prosperity is a major factor in enabling individuals, families and communities to play a full part in the personal, social and cultural dimensions of life.

Many of the skills and qualities required for success at work are the same as those required for success in personal, social and community terms. Literacy, numeracy, communication and information technology, together with problem-solving skills and effective team working are recognized as key skills for employment. These capabilities are learned and developed in a wide variety of ways over a lifetime. Participation in community life, be it working in a charity shop, serving as a school governor, managing a local football group, provides rich, diverse and accessible routes for learning. Those without these key capabilities will find themselves at a disadvantage in social and public life as well as in the labour market.

## ALL LEARNING IS VALUABLE

We believe that all types of learning are valuable. It has always been difficult to define 'vocational' and 'non-vocational' learning and these concepts are fast becoming less and less valid. The growth of lesure, tourism and entertainment industries means that more and more people are making their living from other people's leisure pursuits. Many of them may have discovered a new career direction through their own leisure interests. Equally, many people pursue formal qualifications for personal satisfaction whereas the student in the conversational Spanish class may really have an eye on applying for a job in the export section of their organization. The student taking an upholstery course to re-cover the family's old sofa may later set up a business using such newly acquired skills. The distinction between training by employers, and education by educational institutions has also become blurred by the growth of work-based learning and employee development schemes.

## THE CHALLENGE OF CHANGE

Even a glimpse of the future provides incontrovertible evidence that we must widen our horizons. The pace of technological innovation within the world of work continues to accelerate phenomenally quickly. Changes in information technology are akin to the introduction of the printing press and the industrial revolution, both of which precipitated revolutions in the spread of learning. More and more people need to achieve higher-level knowledge, understanding and skills. Everyone must acquire different knowledge, improved understanding and new skills throughout their working lives. Failure to take this agenda will worsen the already wide gap between those people and their families who know and can do, and those who do not know and cannot do.

Conventional structures of work are changing at a rapid rate. More people are working in small organizations, on part-time or fixed-term contracts, or on a self-employed basis. Long-term trends identified by the Confederation of British Industry and the Institute of Employment Studies indicate that an increasing proportion of the workforce, currently almost one in four, will become part-time or temporary workers. New and more flexible styles of working will bring with them different or additional demands for learning opportunities for self-management, work and business planning as these groups of workers become increasingly common. More people will work from home and will need to learn how to manage their own activities or to plan their own business.

Developments in new technology impact on domestic and community life as well as on the workplace. Next year, more personal computers will be sold in the world than television sets. Multi-media computers will soon be available for the same price as video recorders and many more people will be able to afford them. Routine activities such as shopping, booking appointments for health care and other services may soon commonly be carried out using home-based computers. Social changes also precipitate new learning needs; for example, the growth of private pensions and the introduction of self-assessment of income tax will bring with them a need for increased knowledge and skills. Technology, both in the home and the workplace, provides new and powerful ways to develop more widely the demand and the opportunity for learning.

**Meeting the challenge**

The 'National Targets for Education and Training' were launched by the Confederation of British Industry in 1991. In 1995, the National Advisory Council for Education and Training Targets (NACETT)) published revised national foundation and lifetime targets for the year 2000 under the banner, 'Developing skills for a successful future'. Despite recent increases in participation, achieving the national targets is still an enormous challenge. NACETT reported in July 1996 that an additional 100,000 young people under 19 would need to achieve Foundation Target 1 if the 85 per cent target was to be met by the year 2000.[1] Lifetime target 1 is that three out of five of the adult workforce should be qualified to at least the equivalent of NVQ level 3. Only two in five of the workforce were qualified to this level in autumn 1995. To meet the targets for the year 2000, we need over a million adults to achieve level 3 qualifications each year between now and the end of the century.[2]

Achieving the current targets remains a significant challenge. The urgency of the task is plain. The United Kingdom's partners and competitors are not standing still. If we wish even to maintain our competitive position, we will soon have to achieve levels of training which are way beyond the present national and local targets.

**Measuring participation and achievement**

Measuring participation and achievement in post-16 education and training is not straightforward. Schools, colleges and private training providers have different systems for collecting data. There is little detailed information on the training carried out by employers. It is not possible to get a comprehensive picture of levels of participation and achievement, or of changes in these over time. The government's plans to improve the collection of national data should be accelerated. Comprehensive reports on participation and achievement should be published annually.

Participation in post-16 learning has increased significantly in recent years. However, there is clear evidence that policies which are directed solely at increasing participation will not achieve the levels of learning and achievement now required, and certainly not those to which we aspire:

- In 1995 under half of 15-year-olds achieved five GCSEs at grade C or above.[3]
- Although more than four in five 16-year-olds stayed on in full-time or part-time education, or were involved in work-based training, this applied to only three out of five 18-year-olds'.[4]
- Just over two out of five young people left 'Youth Training' with a qualification in 1995–6.[5]
- Over four out of five students in the college sector completed courses in 1994–5; two in three of those who completed their courses achieved a qualification.
- Less than 44 per cent of employees receive training.[6]

**Groups not participating and not achieving**

There is no single source of evidence to identify those who do not participate in learning and those who fail to achieve. However, an accumulation of evidence points in the same direction.

There are two ways of identifying the groups which do not participate. One way is to look at specific characteristics such as age, sex, or ethnicity. We know that employers provide less training to older workers than younger workers, and that women and members of some ethnic minority groups generally have fewer qualifications. Participation by these groups is changing. More women than men now participate in post-16 education and young people from certain ethnic groups are more likely to be in full-time education than their white peers.[7] Furthermore, there are very different patterns of participation in some localities. In some communities, the most significant under-representation may be among white working-class males; in others, it may be older women from ethnic minority groups. The other ways of identifying such groups is to look at general character-istics such as levels of previous educational achievement, or levels of income, or where people live. We discovered that this method applies both locally and nationally. It also stands the test of time.

All the evidence suggests that it is those who are already well qualified who go on to earn more and to demand and get more learning; many of those who fail the first time round never make up the lost ground, educationally or economically. There are clear links between previous educational achievement and economic and social disadvantage. The link between staying on in education, GCSE results and economic and social disadvantage at 16 is well established, though the link does not apply for the work-based route. Council statistics show that, for both adults and young people, there are strong links between economic disadvantage and low income on the one hand and poor retention rates and low levels of achievement on the other.[8]

We are convinced by the wide-ranging and detailed evidence presented to us that there exists an immense and diverse body of people in this country which should be encouraged and welcomed into post-16 learning.

**Participation must be widened, not simply increased**

Equity dictates that all should have the opportunity to succeed in personal, social and economic spheres. Collective economic success will depend on maximizing the potential of all; it will not be enough to draw on the talents of an educated élite or even of an educated majority. As prosperity comes to depend more and more on knowledge and skills, any economy in which 30 per cent of its people fail to maximize their potential or do not develop learning skills will, in the long run, lose out in competition with those who take a more comprehensive approach. Developing the capacity of everyone to contribute to and benefit from the economic, personal, social and cultural dimensions of their lives is central to achieving the whole range of goals we set ourselves as a nation. In our view, public policy for post-compulsory learning must be dramatically, systematically and consistently redirected towards widening rather than simply increasing participation and achievement. A much wider cross-section of the population needs to be involved than now.

We found that while recent policy acknowledges both the economic and social benefits of learning, it does not recognize sufficiently their interdependence. The result is that priority in further education is given to economic goals at the expense of learning for life. We believe there are two major weaknesses in this approach; there is too limited a definition of learners, and too narrow a focus on the range of learning opportunities. Despite their inclusive aims, the national targets for lifetime education apply only to the workforce, not to those who are unemployed and economically inactive. The acquisition of basic skills, study units which lead to qualifications, and uncertificated learning are the ladders leading to the achievement of these targets. New and comprehensive 'National Learning Targets'; are required which include these important steps and are supported by local participation targets.

## A SELF-PERPETUATING LEARNING SOCIETY

The pace of change in the economy, and in society more widely, is such that we will all need to develop and add to our work skills. The ability to learn is the most important skill and the central thrust of public policy for learning should be the development of the capacity to learn throughout life. The key to developing a society of learners is the recognition of a universal entitlement for all to acquire a level 3 qualification, including appropriate key skills. Such an entitlement could provide a platform for lifelong learning and for employment.

### National leadership

Government must apply imaginative national leadership in creating a learning society at the heart of its common purpose for the nation. There must be a national strategy to re-energize the efforts of the key stakeholders in learning.

A national strategy should be underpinned by a framework designed to measure whether participation in learning is being widened. The framework should provide a consistent method of measuring progress, while at the same time allowing enough flexibility to take account of local priorities. We have developed a specific framework for the Council to use in measuring progress in the further education sector.

## RECOMMENDATIONS

The government should:

- provide leadership to place the creation of a self-perpetuating learning society at the heart of the national common purpose
- create a national strategy for post-16 learning to widen, not simply increase, participation
- state its aspiration for all to achieve a level 3 qualification, including key skills to provide the platform for the creation of a self-perpetuating learning society
- set new and comprehensive 'National Learning Targets'
- expect local partnerships to set local participation targets
- accelerate its activities to harmonize systems for measuring participation and achievement in post-16 learning and publish an annual report on progress in participation and achievement.

The Council should:

- publish an annual report on progress in widening participation in the futher education sector using the new framework for measurement that has been developed by the committee.

## NOTES

1 Five GCSEs at grade C or above, intermediate GNVQ or NVQ level 2.
2 National Advisory Council for Education and Training Targets (1996) *Skills for 2000: Supplement to the Report on Progress Towards the National Targets for Education and Training*. London. (Hereafter 'Skills for 2000'.)
3 Department for Education and Employment (1995) *Secondary School Performance Tables 1995*. DfEE, London.
4 Skills for 2000.
5 DFEE (1977) *Financial Control of Payments Made Under the Training for Work and Youth Training Programmes in England*. London: The Stationery Office.
6 Skills for 2000.
7 Skills for 2000.
8 Council statistical evidence commissioned by the Committee.

# Chapter 14

---

# Higher Education in the Learning Society

*The Dearing Report*

1.1  The purpose of education is life-enhancing: it contributes to the whole quality of life. This recognition of the purpose of higher education in the development of our people, our society, and our economy is central to our vision. In the next century, the economically successful nations will be those which become learning societies: where all are committed, through effective education and training, to lifelong learning.

1.2  So, to be a successful national in a competitive world, and to maintain a cohesive society and a rich culture, we must invest in education to develop our greatest resource, our people. The challenge to achieve this through the excellence and effectiveness of education is great. As Members of the National Committee of Inquiry we have been privileged to have the opportunity to review and recommend the direction of higher education policy over the next twenty years. None of us doubts the importance or difficulty of our task.

## A VISION FOR HIGHER EDUCATION

1.3  Over the next twenty years, we see higher education gaining in strength through the pursuit of quality and a commitment to standards. Central to our vision of the future is a judgement that the United Kingdom (UK) will need to develop as a learning society. In that learning society, higher education will make a distinctive contribution through teaching at its highest level, the pursuit of scholarship and research, and increasingly through its contribution to lifelong learning. National need and demand from students will require a resumed expansion of student numbers, young and mature, full-time and part-time. But over the next decade, higher education will face challenges as well as opportunities. The effectiveness of its responses to these, and its commitment to quality and standards, will shape its future.

1.4   We believe that the country must have higher education which, through excellence in its diverse purposes, can justifiably claim to be world class. As institutions will increasingly have to operate within an international market for education, they will all be judged by international standards. UK higher education must:

- encourage and enable all students – whether they demonstrate the highest intellectual potential or whether they have struggled to reach the threshold of higher education – to achieve beyond their expectations;
- safeguard the rigour of its awards, ensuring that UK qualifications meet the needs of UK students and have standing throughout the world;
- be at the leading edge of world practice in effective learning and teaching;
- undertake research that matches the best in the world, and make its benefits available to the nation;
- ensure that its support for regional and local communities is at least comparable to that provided by higher education in competitor nations;
- sustain a culture which demands disciplined thinking, encourages curiosity, challenges existing ideas and generates new ones;
- be part of the conscience of a democratic society, founded on respect for the rights of the individual and the responsibilities of the individual to society as a whole;
- be explicit and clear in how it goes about its business, be accountable to students and to society and seek continuously to improve its own performance.

1.5   To achieve this, higher education will depend on:

- professional, committed members of staff who are appropriately trained, respected and rewarded;
- a diverse range of autonomous, well-managed institutions with commitment to excellence in the achievement of their distinctive missions.

1.6   Institutions of higher education do not and will not fit into simple categories: they do and will emphasize different elements in their chosen purposes and activities: they are and will be diverse. Those which already have an established world reputation should be able to retain their distinct characters: there should be no pressure on them to change their character. Their aim should be to sustain their outstanding achievements in research, scholarship and teaching. There will also be specialist institutions and individual departments which achieve distinction in the world community of scholars.

1.7   Many institutions will see their distinctive contribution in offering first-class teaching. They will find innovative and effective ways to extend the opportunity for learning to a larger and broader section of the community. Some institutions will seek to interact creatively with local and regional communities. Some will see a distinctive role in applying the knowledge gained from research to addressing practical problems. Yet others will challenge their peers in other countries with ideas on some of the world's most profound and challenging problems.

1.8   Such diversity and distinctive missions should be encouraged, valued and fostered by national funding schemes. While there will continue to be competition between institutions, diversity will become the basis for collaboration between complementary institutions to their mutual advantage, and to the advantage of the communities of which they are part.

1.9   Higher education needs continuity in the framework within which it operates to support its achievement of quality and distinctiveness. Government should avoid sudden changes in the funding or scope and direction of higher education. In return, the community, as represented by the government, has a right to expect higher education to be responsive to the developing needs of society and to be as zealous in the use of resources as it is in the pursuit of excellence in teaching and research. In this, higher education should be as ready to question conventions about what is desirable or possible in the way it operates, as it is to question established wisdom through academic enquiry.


## THE LEARNING SOCIETY

1.10   The expansion of higher education in the last ten years has contributed greatly to the creation of a learning society, that is, a society in which people in all walks of life recognize the need to continue in education and training throughout their working lives and who see learning as enhancing the quality of life throughout all its stages. But, looking twenty years ahead, the UK must progress further and faster in the creation of such a society to sustain a competitive economy.

1.11   In a global economy, the manufacturers of goods and providers of services can locate or relocate their operations wherever in the world gives them greatest competitive advantage. Competitive pressures are reinforced by the swift pace of innovation and the immediate availability of information through communications technology. When capital, manufacturing processes and service bases can be transferred internationally, the only stable source of competitive advantage (other than natural resources) is a nation's people. Education and training must enable people in an advanced society to compete with the best in the world.

1.12   The pace of change in the workplace will require people to re-equip themselves, as new knowledge and new skills are needed for economies to compete, survive and prosper. A lifelong career in one organization will become increasingly the exception. People will need the knowledge and skills to control and maanage their own working lives.

1.13   This requires a learning society, which embraces both education and training, for people at all levels of achievement, before, during and, for continued personal fulfilment, after working life.

1.14   Experience suggests that the long-term demand from industry and commerce will be for higher levels of education and training for their present and future workforce. The UK cannot afford to lag behind its competitiors in investing in the intellect and skills of its people. While the United States of America is a strong investor in higher education, and has high rates of participation, the Far East is increasingly setting the pace. In Japan, participation in higher education is already more than ten percentage points higher than in the UK and, with demographic changes, participation by young people there will exceed 50 per cent in 2000–10 without an increase in total expenditure on higher education. A significant proportion of such participation is at levels below first degree.

1.15   The economic imperative is, therefore, to resume growth. In a twenty-year context, participation rates by young people of 40 per cent or beyond have been canvassed by those giving evidence to us. This has already been achieved in Northern Ireland and in Scotland, with participation rates by young people of around 45 per cent. Much of the increase may be among people seeking qualifications below degree level, as in Scotland. Whatever the means of delivery and level of achievement, however, it is clear that growth in participation by traditional young entrants will need to resume. The present cap on continued expansion must be seen as a temporary pause following several years of very fast growth.

1.16   Traditional entry by young people is only one aspect of the need. The other, for the members of a learning society, is the requirement to renew, update and widen their knowledge and skills throughout life. This will influence the system, character and scope of higher education in very many institutions.

1.17   Apart from the economic imperative, there are other influences pointing to resumed growth. Unless we address the under-representation of those from lower socio-economic groups we may face increasingly socially divisive consequences. As a matter of equity, we need to reduce the under-representation of certain ethnic groups and of those with disabilities. Not least, there will be increasing demand for higher education for its own sake by individuals seeking personal development, intellectual challenge, preparation for career change, or refreshment in later life.

## THE CHARACTERISTICS OF HIGHER EDUCATION IN THE LEARNING SOCIETY

1.18   Lifelong learning points to the need, overall, for higher education to:

- be increasingly responsive to the needs of students and of clients (such as employers and those who commission research);
- structure qualifications which can be either free-standing or built up over time, and which are commonly accepted and widely recognized;
- offer opportunities for credit transfer between courses and institutions;
- adopt a national framework of awards with rigorously maintained standards, with the academic community recognizing that the autonomy of institutions can be sustained only within a framework of collective responsibility for standards, supported by the active involvement of professional bodies;
- work in partnership with public and private sector employers;
- respond fully to the need for active policies for developing, retraining and rewarding its own staff;
- maintains its distinctiveness and vitality through linking research and scholarship to teaching;
- take full advantage of the advances in communications and information technology, which will radically alter the shape and delivery of learning throughout the world;

- be explicit about what it is providing through learning programmes, and their expected outcomes, so that students and employers have a better understanding of their purposes and benefits.

## A VISION FOR TWENTY YEARS: THE LEARNING SOCIETY

2   Our title, 'Higher Education in the Learning Society', reflects the vision that informs this report. Over the next twenty years, the United Kingdom must create a society committed to learning throughout life. That commitment will be required from individuals, the state, employers and providers of education and training. Education is life-enriching and desirable in its own right. It is fundamental to the achievement of an improved quality of life in the UK.

3   It should, therefore, be a national policy objective to be world class both in learning at all levels and in a range of research of different kinds. In higher education, this aspiration should be realized through a new compact involving institutions and their staff, students, government, employers and society in general. We see the historic boundaries between vocational and academic education breaking down, with increasingly active partnerships between higher education institutions and the worlds of industry, commerce and public service. In such a compact, each party should recognize its obligation to the others.

4   Over the next twenty years, we see higher education gaining in strength through the pursuit of quality and a commitment to high standards. Higher education will make a distinctive contribution to the development of a learning society through teaching, scholarship and research. National need and demand for higher education will drive a resumed expansion of student numbers – young and mature, full-time and part-time. But over the next two decades, higher education will face challenges as well as opportunities. The effectiveness of its response will determine its future.

5   That future will require higher education in the UK to:

- encourage and enable all students – whether they demonstrate the highest intellectual potential or whether they have struggled to reach the threshold of higher education – to achieve beyond their expectations;
- safeguard the rigour of its awards, ensuring that UK qualifications meet the needs of UK students and have standing throughout the world;
- be at the leading edge of world practice in effective learning and teaching;
- undertake research that matches the best in the world, and make its benefits available to the nation;
- ensure that its support for regional and local communities is at least comparable to that provided by higher education in competitior nations;
- sustain a culture which demands disciplined thinking, encourages curiosity, challenges existing ideas and generates new ones;
- be part of the conscience of a democratic society, founded on respect for the rights of the individual and the responsibilities of the individual to society as a whole;

- be explicit and clear in how it goes about its business, be accountable to students and to society, and seek continuously to improve its own performance.

6   To achieve this, higher education will depend on:

- professional, committed members of staff who are appropriately trained, respected and rewarded; and
- a diverse range of autonomous, well-managed institutions with commitment to excellence in the achievement of their distinctive missions

7   The higher education sector will comprise a community of free-standing institutions dedicated to the creation of a learning society and the pursuit of excellence in their diverse missions. It will include institutions of world renown and it must be a conscious objective of national policy that the UK should continue to have such institutions. Other institutions will see their role as supporting regional or local needs. Some will see themselves as essentially research oriented; others will be predominantly engaged in teaching. But all will be committed to scholarship and to excellence in the management of learning and teaching.

8   Higher education is fundamental to the social, economic and cultural health of the nation. It will contribute not only through the intellectual development of students and by equipping them for work, but also by adding to the world's store of knowledge and understanding, fostering culture for its own sake, and promoting the values that characterize higher education: respect for evidence; respect for individuals and their views; and the search for truth. Equally, part of its task will be to accept a duty of care for the well-being of our democratic civilization, based on respect for the individual and respect by the individual for the conventions and laws which provide the basis of a civilized society.

9   There is growing interdependence between students, institutions, the economy, employers and the state. We believe that this bond needs to be more clearly recognised by each party, as a compact which makes clear what each contributes and what each gains . . .

# *Part 3*

# **The Critical Debate**

The concept of the learning society has achieved considerable recognition within the academic community as an idea which can help to interpret and respond to the transformations of our time. The Economic and Social Research Council has established a research programme on *The Learning Society: Knowledge and Skills for Employment* under the direction of Professor Frank Coffield (1995a, b; 1997a, b, c, d). The aim of the programme:

> is to examine the nature of what has been called a learning society and to explore the ways in which it can contribute to the development of knowledge and skills for employment and other areas of adult life.
>
> (ESRC, 1996, p.1)

This book, by providing the background debates and policy developments, can be seen to complement the empirical research that will emerge from the ESRC programme.

A number of academics have taken up the idea of the learning society and have been influential in their fields: Schuller (1992) in Scottish education policy making as well as in the field of adult and continuing education (see also Raggatt *et al.*, 1996); Ainley (1994a, b) in educational research as well as the field of further and higher education (see also Hyland, 1994, and Avis *et al.*, 1996); Barnett (1994; 1997) in the field of higher education; Lawton (1992) and Green (1996; 1997) in educational theory; and Hargreaves (1997) and Quicke (1997) in educational reform. Barber's (1996) *The Learning Game* has been particularly influential in public policy with the election of New Labour in 1997 and his appointment as a special adviser to the Secretary of State for Education and Employment.

Inevitably there is a healthy critical debate about the value of the concept or the way that it is typically defined. A number of critics reject its validity, believing that it lacks credibility (Hughes and Tight, 1995), or clarity (Edwards, 1995b; White 1997), or critical analysis (Gleeson, 1996), or is just utopian. Others believe that the concept of the learning society has value but needs significant reformulation if it is to be rescued (Hatcher, 1996; Rikowski, forthcoming; Young, 1995b). Clark (1996) and Strain and Field (1997) have recently responded to the critiques with a vigorous defence of the critical value of the learning society.

This section of the book presents some of the key interventions in the debate about the meaning and value of the learning society. This is followed by a response and analysis.

# Chapter 15

# The Myth of the Learning Society

*Christina Hughes and Malcolm Tight*

## INTRODUCTION

Many politicians, industrialists and educators now appear to share an underlying belief that the learning society – which places education, learning and training at the centre of its concerns – is the answer to current economic, political and social problems. These decision-makers undoubtedly have both varied beliefs on which they base their understanding of the term 'learning society', and different means for assessing whether it is achievable or has been achieved. Their common concern is impressive, and forces us to take the idea of the learning society seriously. Yet we also need to be questioning and cautious in greeting this 'new' idea. This chapter attempts to assess critically the concept, its application and potential by considering it as a modern-day myth.

Many of the social, economic and political assumptions on which we base our lives, or within which our lives are located by others, have the nature of myths. That is, whether or not these particular notions are actually true, they appear to represent, at least for some, a reasonable basis on which to think, operate and plan ahead.

Although the appeal may be largely emotional, it is cast in at least a semblance of a rational form (Sykes, 1965, p. 334). But, more than that, myths can be held up as self-evident realities and slogans for the rest of the society to follow: 'Once a way of feeling or a mode of action has been embodied in the mythology of a large group of people it acquires an incalculable power' (Tillyard, 1962, p. 27). In this way, myths can become very powerful for developing alternative visions, mobilizing rhetoric and leading people through change. Such myths may then become organizing principles on which policy and practice are based.

In our view, this is achieved in part by the process of myth interconnection and development. These processes have at least two elements. First, they may involve the use of other myths as component parts of a new myth. Or, second, a new myth may be a redevelopment of an existing, precursor myth. Of course, in many cases, as here, these distinctions may not be so clear. However, it is important to recognize the dialectical nature of myth construction.

In the case of the learning society, we can recognize two levels or stages of myth development, and thus two sets of component or precursor myths. The first is provided by the myths of productivity and change; the second by the myths of lifelong education and the learning organization, which themselves incorporate the productivity and change myths. The interconnections between these four myths provide a strong framework for creating and sustaining the learning society myth. The myths referred to may be summarized as follows:

- The *productivity myth* argues that there is continuing need to increase productivity; and that there is a more or less direct linkage between, on the one hand, educational preparation and initial training, or continuing education and re-training, and, on the other hand, individual earnings, organizational productivity and national economic performance.
- The *change myth* suggests that social, economic and technological changes are accelerating at an increasing rate, such that we are currently living in a period of unprecedented change.
- The *lifelong education myth* proposes that education, training and learning should be available and engaged in throughout the whole lifespan, not just in childhood and adolescence.
- The *learning organization myth* envisages that the only, or the most successful organizations will be those which continually involve their members in worth-while individual and group learning activities.
- The *learning society myth* suggests a resolution of the productivity and change myths through the productive involvement of individuals in education through-out their lives, to the benefit of themselves, their employing organizations and society.

Each of these myths can readily be revealed as offering only a partial or inadequate basis on which to understand the complex relations between learning, work and life, and to plan policy and practice in these areas. In this chapter, we well discuss and criticize in turn each of the five myths identified, focusing in particular on the learning society, and then consider their roles as myths.

It should be stressed at this point that, in labelling and characterizing each of these ideas or concepts as 'myths', we are not denying that they have any truth or validity. What we are suggesting is that their mythic qualities raise them above everyday considerations. We need to appreciate and understand these concepts in their role as myths if we are to handle them appropriately as policy options.

## PRODUCTIVITY AND CHANGE

We will start by exploring in more detail the ideas of productivity and change. As myths, these ideas can stand alone, and in recent history have done so in much policy discourse, as self-perpetuating and inviolable truths. Here, however, they will be considered principally as essential parts of a further myth, that of the learning society, which cannot be effectively sustained without them.

*Productivity* has been one of the most powerful myths in developed and developing societies since the industrial revolution and the rise of capitalism. It invokes the work ethic, perpetuates a sense of unlimited potential, and drives individuals, organizations and nations towards more competitive endeavours. It affirms that continuing economic growth is not just achievable but desirable and necessary. Investment in education or training is then seen as one of the driving forces for productivity and economic growth. Productivity is typically assessed by using a range of quantitative measures or techniques. These techniques effectively reinforce the myth, backing up its assumptions with what appears to be 'hard' data.

The productivity myth takes consistent but differing forms at different levels of activity. For individuals, it acts as a spur towards self-help, personal betterment and career development. In educational terms, it suggests that personal expenditure on education or training, funded by a loan if necessary, will have a probable, if by no means certain, pay-off in terms of enhanced future earnings and career prospects.

At the level of the firm, the myth supports expenditure on training and human resource development as an investment in the future of the organization. This may be held to be true almost regardless of the state of the economy and of the markets in which the firm is operating. Indeed, though training expenditure is typically among the first cutbacks at times of crisis, these can be seen to be the times at which it is most justified. At the level of national policy, the productivity myth supports the many measures which have been taken to encourage increased participation in further, higher and continuing education, and in vocational preparation and updating.

*Change,* like productivity, is widely illustrated and justified using quantitative data. This is often presented in the form of graphs, frequently showing exponential growth in just about any quantity you care to mention: birth rates, divorces, numbers of scientific journals, patents applied for. There is a wide popular literature which expounds and supports the myth of the present time as a period of unprecedented change (e.g. Bell, 1973; Toffler, 1970).

These changes are seen as having major implications for education and training, in their relation to employment, family and social life. We may point to, for example, the development of successive or parallel careers, the regular need for updating knowledge, and the attempted use of initial education to inculcate flexible transferable skills. As with the productivity myth, the change myth impacts at individual, organizational and societal levels.

Taken together, the productivity and change myths can be seen to underpin the idea of modernization as progress. Conversely, they may also lead to the interpretation of our present position as being a 'crisis', whether in economic or social terms (Tight, 1994a). Our educational response to these positions in developed societies involves a varying mix of individualized or collectivized solutions (e.g.

career development loans or an employers' tax for training), which substantially effect how we view the underlying myths.

## LIFELONG EDUCATION AND THE LEARNING ORGANIZATION

The ideal of lifelong education was developed at international meetings during the 1960s in response to perceived inadequacies in existing educational provision and practice, though it has antecedents which may be traced back to the writings of Dewey, Lindeman and Yeaxlee in the early twentieth century (Jarvis, 1983). Lifelong education was adopted as a 'master' [*sic*] concept by the United Nations Educational, Scientific and Cultural Organization (UNESCO) in 1970 (Fauré *et al.*, 1972; Lengrand, 1989).

The implications of lifelong education have been summarized in a way which emphasizes its individual development focus.

> Lifelong education, conceptualized as a means for facilitating lifelong learning, would:
>
> 1 last the whole life of each individual;
> 2 lead to the systematic acquisition, renewal, upgrading and completion of knowledge, skills and attitudes, as became necessary in response to the constantly changing conditions of modern life, with the ultimate goal of promoting the self-fulfilment of each individual;
> 3 be dependent for its successful implementation on people's increasing ability and motivation to engage in self-directed learning activities;
> 4 acknowledge the contribution of all available educational influences including formal, non-formal and informal.
>
> (Cropley, 1980, pp. 3–4).

While this particular definition makes no direct reference to issues of productivity, though it does to change, it allows for a more economic interpretation. It leaves unspoken the question of how individual self-fulfilment might manifest itself: e.g. in increased earnings as well as self-awareness. The openness of the concept has allowed its use by a wide variety of interests: 'Both totalitarian and liberal regimes express their support of lifelong education, as do technologically more developed as well as technologically less developed societies' (Cropley, 1979, p. 1).

The notion of the learning organization is of similar vintage, and arises from the same kinds of concerns about change, crisis and survival. It draws on the continuing interest in the idea of organizational learning (e.g. Argyris and Schön, 1978), as well as on trends in industrial relations, such as the advance of employee development schemes (Forrester *et al.*, 1993). It applies many of the ideas incorporated in the myth of lifelong education, but at the organizational or company (rather than the individual) level:

> The Learning Company is a vision of what might be possible. It is not brought about simply by training individuals; it can only happen as a result of *learning at the whole*

*organisation* level. A Learning Company is an organisation that facilitates the learning of all its members and continuously transforms itself.

(Pedler *et al.*, 1991, p. 1).

Like lifelong education, the learning organization has been the subject of varied interpretations. The rather top-down, managerially imposed view just quoted may, for example, be contrasted with more democratic, bottom-up approaches: 'Learning organisations are characterised by total employee involvement in a process of collaboratively initiated, collaboratively conducted, collectively accountable change directed towards shared values or principles' (Watkins and Marsick, 1992, p. 118). Many organizations have been held up as learning organizations, including, in the United Kingdom, Nabisco, Rover, Sheerness Steel and Sun Alliance (Jones and Hendry, 1992).

While these two concepts have many similarities, it may be noted that the first is essentially reactive and the second is more proactive. Thus, lifelong education is presented as a necessary response to changing demands, but largely at the individual (or state) level, while the learning organization is offered as a strategy for creating change so as to survive in a competitive world.

## THE LEARNING SOCIETY MYTH

While the learning society has only recently become the subject of considerable debate in the United Kingdom, it has a longer history in other countries with a stronger post-war tradition of encouraging greater educational participation. These include, for example, Canada, New Zealand, Sweden and the United States of America (Boshier *et al.*, 1980; Carnegie Commission on Higher Education, 1973; Commission on Post-secondary Education in Ontario, 1972; Husen, 1974). The learning society was recently defined in a briefing paper by the United Kingdom Economic and Social Research Council (ESRC) in the following terms:

> A learning society would be one in which all citizens acquire a high quality general education, appropriate vocational training and a job (or series of jobs) worthy of a human being while continuing to participate in education and training throughout their lives. A learning society would combine excellence with equity and would equip all its citizens with the knowledge, understanding and skills to ensure national economic prosperity and much more besides ... Citizens of a learning society would, by means of their continuing education and training, be able to engage in critical dialogue and action to improve the quality of life for the whole community and to ensure social integration as well as economic success.
>
> (ESRC, 1994, p. 2)

This definition suggests the potentially all-encompassing nature of the learning society, which spans both vocational concerns (the link between education and economy) and quality of life issues (the link between education and personal and social development). Others might, of course, define the learning society rather more narrowly, focusing on just one of these concerns. As defined here, the myth clearly builds upon the notions of lifelong learning and the learning organization, and makes use of the ideas of productivity and change. They are used as the justification for a radical change in the structure, extent and linkage of economy, society and education. In this way, a continuing process of myth development forms part of the way we understand and respond to these concerns.

In addition to its vocational and personal elements, there are a number of other tensions apparent within existing discussions on the learning society. Thus, though the concept suggests a concern with the productive learning of all members of society, many of those writing on this topic have focused largely on school education (e.g. Husén, 1974, 1986; Ranson, 1994). Further, as the following two quotes illustrate, there is a division between analysts and visionaries:

> Only poets and science fiction writers have imagined what a learning society would look like and how it would differ from today's world.
>
> (Ainley, 1994a, p. 156)

> Modern statecraft is becoming little more than the proper management of learning.
>
> (Thomas, 1991, p. 160).

The learning society can be seen as in part a description and in part an aspiration. It is an expression of the perceived need, in an increasingly competitive global economy, for the effective development and availability of all human resources. Yet, at the same time, there may also be a concern for the growth of the individual and the community. While this vision can be seen as an improvement on strict vocationalism, it does represent something of an unhappy and unstable compromise. As a banner under which a diversity of interests – politicians, educators, industrialists – can gather, the learning society embodies an alliance between state, professions and capital. Such an alliance seems likely to marginalize the interests of the individual in pursuing learning for their own self-fulfilment.

## CHALLENGING THE MYTHS

There is a conflict between myth in practice and myth as story. For example, when we consider the linkages made between education and training, on the one hand, and economic productivity and individual development, on the other hand, they appear to most to be obvious and strong. This demonstrates the importance and power of myth as story. It provides a simplistic truth that captures the imagination in a populist and transmittable form.

However, when we look at myth in practice, the linkages made may appear to be neither obvious nor strong. For example, one examination of the productivity myth concluded that 'there is little evidence to support the view that the total quantity of training is closely correlated to a country's economic performance and ... there is no necessary connection between stocks of skilled labour and productivity' (Shackleton, 1992, p. 80; see also Murphy, 1993).

We will focus the remainder of this critique on the three related myths of lifelong education, the learning organization and the learning society. The concept of lifelong education has been the subject of a great deal of discussion, comparison and critique since its original formulation. This is in part because it has been used very loosely to refer to a wide range of ideas:

> The term 'lifelong education' has been used in recent education literature variously to advocate or denote the function of education as being: the preparation of individuals *for* the management of their adult lives, the distribution of education *throughout* individual lifespans, the educative function *of* the whole of one's life experience, and the identification of education *with* the whole of life.
>
> (Bagnall, 1990, p. 1) (emphasis in original)

It may be argued that the idea of lifelong education was, and remains, utopian in nature (Tight, 1994b). This was recognized at the time of its development by at least some of its proponents:

> Reference to the concept met with many reservations, if not hostile attitudes. Some educators expressed the view that lifelong education was nothing more than a new term to designate adult education and that its use led to confusion. Others, while recognizing the rationality underlying the concept, looked upon it as Utopian, reaching far beyond the possibilities of implementation of a great number of countries.
>
> (Lengrand, 1989, p. 8)

Indeed, there is not a society which is anywhere near achieving the kind of system of educational provision advocated in the 1970s by UNESCO, the Organization for Economic Co-operation and Development (OECD) and others; not the United States of America with its mass educational system built on a mix of public support and private investment; not Sweden, with its high participation rates and traditions of community and social provision; and certainly not the failed Soviet system. While some of the richer nations are naturally much closer than others to creating something like a lifelong learning society, in all cases substantial proportions of the population remain excluded or under-involved.

When we shift our focus from the level of the nation to that of the individual adult, we can identify major cultural, political and economic obstacles which profoundly inhibit the development of lifelong education (Blaxter and Tight, 1994). National surveys indicate that, in Britain, the majority of adults are not involved in lifelong learning, primarily because they lack support, interest or motivation (Sargent, 1991). Those that are, and are responding to the opportunities and challenges which lifelong learning presents, readily come up with lists of the financial, situational, institutional and attitudinal barriers to their effective participation. Many believe that 'education is for other people' (McGivney, 1990).

The criticisms which may be levelled at the idea of the learning organization are in some ways similar, but in others different. Thus, only a minority of organizations would or could call themselves learning organizations. Amongst those that have so labelled themselves, there are substantial variations in practice and experience. This can readily be demonstrated by, for example, the differences in who is included within the ambit of the learning organization: full-time staff? permanent staff? part-timers? all grades? customers? suppliers? all plants? subsidiaries? This listing raises again the alternative visions illustrated by the two definitions quoted earlier. Is the learning organization about empowerment or exploitation? Is it in the business of creatively seeking and using the views and learning of all of its members, or is it about squeezing as much value as possible out of each unit of production?

Further, there is the question of whether learning organizations actually do any better at their business than comparable 'non-learning' organizations. Here the evidence, as with that on general linkages between educational participation and economic productivity, is both partial and difficult to interpret. We lack the sizeable, longitudinal studies which are needed to demonstrate and measure linkages. Most existing studies have used cross-sectional data for particular time periods, and have not been able to control for all the possible factors affecting the relationship.

> The learning organization concept may provide the catalyst which is needed to push forward, in an holistic way, the many strands, ideas and values with which organizations must now concern themselves ... However, there are dangers. First, there is no detailed research work completed which can confirm or deny, over time, whether such ideas and practices genuinely create fitter and better organizations for both the people who work in them and the society they seek to serve. Secondly, there is the need to know how far the learning organization is simply yet another 'vision' propounded by management and educational idealists or whether it is an idea capable of reality ... the learning organization can itself become the 'myth' which obscures its own nature and prevents advance towards other levels or learning and change.
>
> (Jones and Hendry, 1992, pp. 58–9)

In other words, the consensual nature of idealizations such as the learning organization, which become seen as the solution to problems or organizational survival and competitiveness, can act in counterproductive ways. They may deny the possibility of other solutions or progressions.

When we turn to the learning society myth itself, most of the criticisms levelled at both lifelong education and the learning organization still apply. To their credit, in their briefing paper the ESRC (1994) went on to question the notion of the learning society:

> Some of the claims made on behalf of the learning society need to be subjected to empirical test: for example, does learning pay? does it empower and enable? does it help to equalise life chances? Will the purposes of education and training for the learning society need to encompass more than selection, socialisation, and minimal levels of literacy and numeracy in preparation for the world of work? What changes in education and training will be needed for all to participate fully in the learning society? Is there a set of values or guiding principles underpinning the notion of a learning society which need to be made explicit if a culture of education and training is to be created in the UK? What would a coherent and co-ordinated policy to help the UK become a learning society look like?
>
> (ESRC, 1994, p. 4)

Other commentators have pointed out the vast disparity between the rhetoric and present reality. Thus, the National Institute of Adult Continuing Education (NIACE) of England and Wales commissioned a survey which found that only 10 per cent of those aged 17 or more were currently studying anything. Some 24 per cent had studied within the last three years, but the majority, 52 per cent, claimed not to have studied at all since they left school. The NIACE's conclusion was that 'There is still a massive gap between the government's vision of a learning society where people invest in updating their own skills throughout their lives, and the actual amount of learning adults undertake' (NIACE, 1994, p. 1).

Clearly, participation rates do not match the rhetoric associated with the concept of the learning society. On this basis, there is little to support the notion that we have already achieved in the United Kingdom, in any real sense, a learning society. Overall participation rates are not, of course, the only possible indicator of the achievement of a learning society. Other measures might include, for example, levels of qualification, expenditure on education and training, availability of support and guidance services, and public attitudes towards learning. It would be difficult to claim, however, that the United Kingdom did not have a long way to go in all of these areas. Further, when consideration is given to the embedded nature of the structural inequalities associated with access to education and training, we are left with a sense of disillusionment that a learning society in its fullest sense will ever be achieved in a society like ours.

Yet, whilst we may raise concern at the possibility of meaningful, society-wide participation in education, learning and training, we need also to encourage debate and analysis of the assumed causal relationship between education, economic prosperity and quality-of-life issues. The hopes and promises which underpin the myth of the learning society, offering a superficially simple solution to what are manifestly extremely complex economic and social issues, illustrate the persuasive force of myth construction.

## THE ROLE OF MYTH

The idea of the learning society has no current empirical validity, therefore, in a country like the United Kingdom. We must also, for the reasons just enumerated, doubt that it can be practically developed in the foreseeable future. But does this myth still have residual value as a myth? This is the question to which we will now turn. To answer this question we need to consider the role and working of myths.

A functionalist perspective on the learning society myth would argue that its purpose is to maintain a false consciousness about the structural positions of labour and capital. By suggesting that there are opportunities available to individuals for development and advancement, the myth in effect blames powerless members of the community for their 'failure' to get on.

From this perspective, the way in which the learning society myth builds upon, or recycles, earlier myths is of significance. This enables the myth to extend its life across generations, despite its practical lack of achievement. Similarly, the appeal of the myth to populist and common-sense reasoning helps to explain its continuing power. Both the proponents and recipients of such myths can readily think of illustrative examples, chiefly at the level of the individual, without concerning themselves too much about the societal level and the vast numbers of people who cannot be fitted within such examples (e.g. Lunneborg, 1994). In this way, the negative implications may be conveniently ignored.

A further important aspect of the way in which a myth, like that of the learning society, works is the way in which it draws upon the energies of disparate power groups. In this case, we can see an alliance between the interests of educators, employers and politicians. Each of these groups (and the sub-groups with them) will have differing interpretations of the meaning and objectives of the myth and will be seeking somewhat varied outcomes, but they have little difficulty in sharing the terminology. The learning society myth fits in with the idea of new working contracts between managers and employees, which can be seen to herald the end of 'us' and 'them' divisions and offer instead a mutuality of benefit.

In short, we may conclude that the function of the learning society myth is to provide a convenient and palatable rationale and packaging for the current and future policies of different power groups within society. As such, it has little impact on the nature, content or implementation of those policies, yet makes those policies appear different and more interesting, giving the impression to interested outsiders that things are improving. Overall, we may understand the learning society as an ideological concept serving ideological purposes.

## SOME CONCLUSIONS

We have argued in this chapter that the idea of the learning society be viewed as a myth. Nothing approaching a learning society currently exists, and there is no real practical prospect of one coming into existence in the foreseeable future.

Yet this myth has power. It has power because it is believed by many to be achievable, and is seen as an answer to profound economic and social problems. It can, therefore, be used by a range of interest groups to better articulate and promote their policies. This can be done without supporting emotional evidence or critical analysis; indeed, given the emotional appeal of myth in general, such rationality may be better left out.

An important part of our analysis in this chapter has concerned the continuing nature of myth construction. We have argued that the learning society myth is a product of, and also embodies, earlier myths which link education, productivity and change. The question, therefore, arises: 'What comes after the learning society?'

# Chapter 16

# Post-compulsory Education for a Learning Society

*Michael Young*

## POST-COMPULSORY EDUCATION IN ENGLAND AND WALES: A DUAL CRISIS?

In all countries in Western Europe post-compulsory education is either, as in England and Wales, in a crisis, or, as in the Nordic countries and Germany, the subject of increasing questioning and critique. This is manifest in a variety of attempts that can be found in all countries to introduce greater flexibility within the curriculum, increase the opportunities for students to make choices and bridge the traditional divisions between academic and vocational learning. This pressure for change, while expressed in educational terms, is not educational in origin. It is a consequence of two outcomes of developments in the global economy and, more specifically, of the manufacturing and trading success of the new Asian economies. The first is the disappearance of a youth labour market and the consequent massive increases in the numbers of full-time students in post-compulsory education, and the second is the continuing failure of European countries to return to the full employment of 25 years ago, even when, on conventional indicators, it is claimed that the economic recession is over. Despite the availability of labour as a result of persistent high unemployment and, at least in the UK, the introduction of legislation that restricts the role of trade unions, European production has shown no signs of competing in terms of the labour costs of mass-production with the new Asian economies such as China. On the other hand, it has not been able to draw on the familial collectivism and 'firm loyalty' associated with the advanced Asian economies of South Korea and Japan, which many see as the reason for their success in high value-added markets such as consumer electronics. Western European cultures, and especially the Anglo-Saxon variant found in the UK, are traditionally associated with individualism and independence, rewards for creativity and a capacity for innovation associated with European science, humanities and arts, and the systematic thinking and practice needed to convert ideas into products and services poses both a considerable intellectual and educational challenge. The challenge is nowhere felt more strongly than in the post-compulsory sector, with its distinctive features of learner choice and specialization, and as the sector with closest links to the labour market. With its traditional links with training and apprenticeships, it is not surprising that post-compulsory education has been seen as providing solutions to problems that appear at least in part as labour-market problems.

Post-compulsory education in the UK, however (and for the rest of this chapter the UK will refer to England and Wales, as Scotland has more in common with continental Europe), also suffers from a crisis of its own history. The UK faces the economic and cultural challenges shared by all European countries that I have referred to. However, it also inherits a weak system of compulsory education (Steadman and Green, 1993), and low levels of participation and attainment (except in the private sector) in a post-compulsory sector that is over-specialized, sharply divided and with vocational provision that carries little credibility (Spours, 1995). Three kinds of reform strategy have emerged that claim to tackle these weaknesses, one from government and two arising from the professional debate that has developed in response to the inadequacy of the government's proposals. Successive initiatives by governments throughout the 1980s focused on providing an alternative to the over-specialized and highly selective academic track (A levels). They culminated in the 1991 White Paper *Education and Training for the Twenty-first Century*, which clarified the two main elements of government strategy. The first strategy was to establish a national tripartite qualifications framework based on an academic track (GCSEs and A and AS Levels), a full-time general vocational track (GNVQs), and a work-based track (NVQs), each expressed in terms of agreed levels and at least the rhetoric of parity of esteem. The second strategy was to introduce a performance-related approach to funding that encourages institutional competition as a way of getting value for money and raising standards.

Two kinds of alternatives to the government proposals have emerged. There are those, first expressed in the IPPR report *A British Baccalauréate* (Finegold *et al.*, 1990), which have stressed the damaging effects of academic/vocational divisions at 16+, and argued the case for a unified system which links qualifications and curriculum and which guarantees a high level of general education for all students. In the UK its nearest practical expression of these ideas are in the recent White Paper from the Scottish Office, *Higher Still* (SOED, 1994). The other alternative is less easy to define and brings together three groups: those business interests that stress the importance of individual skills as the source of economic growth (CBI, 1991, 1993); those educational professionals associated with the pre-vocational tradition who stress the alienating effects of the academic curriculum, especially for disadvantaged learners with low achievements; and those with a background in adult education who have emphasized the way existing qualifications deny access to so many adults, and the importance of validating experience (FEU, 1991). These groups, though not necessarily together, have put their faith in flexibility of access, modularization of the curriculum and credit transfer of assessment, and played down the determining effect on provision of a divided system of qualifications.

The crisis in post-compulsory education in the UK, however, is not just a product of government policy or the determination of the élite to maintain a narrow and exclusive academic curriculum as the main selective route to higher education. It also reflects the doubling of participation in full-time education after 16 in a system which, both in its curriculum and its form of organization, was designed for a minority. The question then becomes whether to diversify the old curriculum and include the new learners (something the French have successfully done but which has been resisted in the UK), or to leave the old curriculum unchanged and develop an alternative (the UK government strategy), or whether to adopt one of the two approaches proposed by the reformers that have been alluded to above.

If we bear in mind that the crisis in post-compulsory education, while manifest in educational terms, has its origins in the economy, then any framework for assessing proposals for reconstruction cannot be education-bound, at least in the institutional sense. It has to be a framework that conceptualizes education–economy relationships in the context of a view of society as a whole. There are a number of options. First, we could start from the view that has dominated the economics and sociology of education: that whether we like it or not, economies do determine education systems, whether in terms of their reproductive role (as would be argued by Bowles and Gintis and Althusser in the Marxist tradition), or because people are fundamentally economic actors as assumed by human capital theory. The problem with such a strategy is that while such analyses stress issues of importance, they say little about how specific economy–education relationships work and provide little guide to policy alternatives. The second possibility is to replace rational economic man [*sic*] with status-seeking man in the Weberian tradition. While it provides a useful and probably more accurate account of the expansion of mass education than the economic theories, it relies, in effect, on a notion of consumer demand, and like the economic theories can say little about policy options. A third alternative is the one adopted by Ranson (1992), who argues that we should not be taken in by fashionable views that the future of the economy should be the primary determinant of our educational priorities. He asserts that society is fundamentally about values, and therefore our educational priorities should be moral and political, not economic. This is important as a critique of recent government policy in the UK. However, the danger of such an approach is that while correctly characterizing the current focus on the links between education and the economy as instrumental, it provides no basis for a concept of education that integrates personal development and economic life. The fourth possibility is not to separate education and the economy as Ranson does, but to explore the idea of a learning-led economy that is reflected in the works of writers such as Reich and Marshall and Tucker. They not only stress the economic significance of high-quality education but give priority to learning as a feature of the society as a whole, being a condition for a successful economy of the future. There are problems with such analyses, especially in the case of countries such as the USA and the UK where the enthusiasm for monetarist economics and markets has led them to eschew any industrial policy. They either end up allowing education take all the blame for our economic ills, as Noble (1993) has pointed out, or remain so general that as Ainley (1994b) says, they do little more than state the obvious that, at least in some sense, all societies are learning societies. However, the idea that a concept of the learning-led or learning society might be developed that could provide the criteria for judging institutions, including those with a specialist educational role, may be useful as a framework for re-conceptualizing education, particularly in the post-compulsory phase that finds itself at the intersection of many different sectors of society.

It may not be insignificant that in the UK the Economic and Social Research Council has decided to launch a major research initiative on post-compulsory education within the theme of *A Learning Society; Skills and Knowledge for Employment.* I therefore intend to assess recent reform strategies and consider the options for reconstructing post-compulsory education from the point of view of the idea of a learning society. In doing so I have two aims: first, through submitting existing reform proposals to a learning society analysis, I want to identify some criteria for evaluating different reform strategies; and second, I want to develop a concept of a learning society that is distinct from some of the sloganized ways in which it has been used. A clearer and more grounded concept of a learning society will, I suggest, supply criteria for a curriculum of the future that provides bridges and coherence in a phase of education currently characterized by diversity and fragmentation.

## THE IDEA OF A LEARNING SOCIETY AS A CONTESTED CONCEPT

There are many definitions of a learning society. Ainley (1994b) starts from Hutchins (1970), who defines a learning society as one which

> in addition to offering part time adult education to every man and woman at every stage of their life, has transformed its values in such a way that learning, fulfilment, becoming human . . . becomes its aim and all its institutions are directed to that end.

At one level this is little more than another idealistic utopia – the kind that educationalists are so fond of. Its generalized view of the future can be celebrated at international conferences when participants are freed from the pressures of implementation, and when neither the contradictions embedded in them nor the variety of ways in which they can be used are of great significance. However, as Ainley (1994b) points out, it is not chance that it was in the 1990s that the idea of a learning society began to be used not only by educational philosophers but as an example, it could be said, of a utopia becoming an ideology. In linking the idea of a learning society to notions such as skill ownership and educational or training markets, these theorists present a view of society in which social classes no longer exist and divisions are based not, as in the past, on wealth and property, but on the distribution of knowledge and skill. According to such a view, the wealth of a society is the skills and knowledge of its people. The idea of a learning society is powerful both as a concept and as an ideology. As an ideology it provides a justification for inequalities by masking the extent to which modern societies, as well as depending on the population's knowledge and skills, are also based on inequalities of power and wealth. However, as a concept it also provides a rationale for lifelong learning, the democratization of education and broadening access to learning opportunities. To put a similar point in another way, there are material reasons why the utopian visions of Hutchins and others have been appropriated both by progressive educationalists and by business and management theorists nearly twenty years after they were first published. Ideas such as a *learning society*, as well as the associated ideas of an *information society* and a *skills revolution*, reflect real economic changes and at least a partial recognition that the mode of production and the conditions for the profitability of European companies have changed. Successful companies are not just those who have displaced and controlled labour with technology, but those who have found ways of enhancing the value produced by the labour they employ. In distinguishing the concept from the ideology, the crucial question becomes: which kind of learning society and for whom? I propose, therefore, to view it as a *contested concept*, in which the different meanings given to it not only reflect different interests but imply different visions of the future and different strategies for getting there.

The strength of the idea of a learning society as a concept is that in linking learning explicitly to the idea of a future society, it provides the basis for a critique of the minimal learning demands of much work and other activities in our present society, not excluding the sector specializing in education. Its weakness is that so far the criteria for the critique remain very general and therefore, like many terms of contemporary educational discourse such as partnership and collaboration, it can take on a variety of contradictory meanings. The different interpretations of the concept need to be examined in terms of their assumptions and the groups identified with them, as well as their priorities and their limitations for assessing different solutions to the problems that beset post-compulsory education. I shall, initially, describe three models, which I shall distinguish according to the emphasis they place on different educational strategies. Implicit in each are different models of social and economic development. These issues are discussed at some length by Ainley (1994b). In this chapter I am primarily concerned with using the models to examine different priorities for educational policy. The three models each represent clearly different foci and priorities. The different countries will reflect the particular circumstances and history of the country concerned. The first model starts from the criterion of high participation in full-time post-compulsory education as a feature of a learning society. I will therefore refer to it as the *schooling model*. The second model takes as the criterion of a learning society the notion that everyone should, if possible, be qualified. I will refer to this as the *credentialist model*. The third model focuses on the individual learner and his or her opportunities for access to learning. I will refer to this as the *access model* of a learning society. In the next sections I shall analyse these models in terms of current trends in post-compulsory education, drawing largely on UK examples. From this analysis I shall develop a fourth model which I will refer to as the *educative model* of a learning society. This model focuses on the *form of learning*, and in particular the relationship between learning and economic life, which I shall argue needs to underpin a curriculum of the future. The model will also provide a way of supplying some conceptual clarification of the concept of the learning society that will hopefully prove useful to curriculum designers and practitioners.

## THE SCHOOLING MODEL

The schooling model stresses high participation in post-compulsory schooling as a way of ensuring that the maximum proportion of the population reach as far beyond a minimum level of education as possible. The Nordic countries and some South East Asian countries represent examples of strong versions of the schooling model in societies that in other ways are very different. Weak versions of the schooling model are those that retain the ideal of high participation but vary from the UK, in which participation appears to have 'peaked' at 70 per cent (Spours, 1995), with a steady drop-out to 35 per cent by the age of 18, to 'third world' countries which lose half the students of every cohort after two or three years of compulsory schooling. The schooling model has democratic origins in the popular demand for schooling in Europe in the nineteenth century and in the pressure to expand schooling in the former colonies after World War II. It has set a standard for virtually all countries and takes its most advanced form in a country like Sweden, where schools have responsibility for the learning and progression of all their pupils up to the age of 20, *even if they are no longer full-time students.*

In recent years, countries with successful schooling models, such as the Nordic countries, have begun to challenge the model as an adequate basis for a learning society of the future (Young, 1993a). This partly reflects economic factors; an extended schooling model is expensive, and as a result of global competition and liberalization of trade even the Nordic countries have begun to examine public sector costs. However, the challenges also reflect more fundamental limitations of a model which is based on the separation and insulation of education from productive and community life. In the nineteenth century, the fastest-expanding sectors of employment were industrial, and much of the work that was generated was heavy and dangerous and demanded much effort but little specialized skill. Much work was dehumanizing and there was a powerful case for protecting young people from such contexts, as well as assuming that they would learn better if not involved in work at all. The schooling model, therefore, was built on both the positive values of the academy and a desire to protect young people from the negative features of industrial production. Despite changes in production there has been little disenchantment with academic education and the schooling model has come to dominate educational policy.

However, there are a number of other problems that even the strong versions of the schooling model face, especially from the point of view of a learning society. First, they continue to represent a view of education 'as an end in itself' and therefore the curriculum tends to reflect the immediate interests of the producers (teachers and lecturers) rather than the communities that they claim to serve. It follows that standards and values of schooling models tend to be internal and implicit rather than external and explicit. Second, schooling systems are, as Ivan Illich (1971) pointed out, addictive; they tend to induce a demand for more schooling rather than for opportunities to continue learning after leaving school. Evidence of this tendency, especially when economies are contracting, is provided by the way students in Nordic countries who graduate from upper secondary school but do not gain access to university do not seek employment but re-enter the cycle of upper secondary school for a further two or three years. Third, they are 'front-loading' rather than continuous development models – in other words, they assume that education is predominantly a preparatory activity associated with the first 20–25 years of a person's life, rather than something that continues throughout life. Fourth, the insulation of education as schooling not only turns teachers away from thinking about the relationship between school learning and how learning is used, but it allows other organizations (especially in commerce and manufacturing) to avoid responsibility for education and to put the blame for their employees' lack of skills and knowledge onto the school system.

The strong schooling model exhibits a number of features of a learning society. There is no doubt that it is an expression of a 'learning culture' (with a strong popular commitment to the *public* provision of schools and colleges) and provides a powerful example to set against weak systems with medium-to-low participation, such as the UK. Whether it *offers* an appropriate model for developing countries with limited resources, and whether its institutionalized concept of learning being linked to participation as full-time students in schools or colleges is the best way of linking education to economic reconstruction and development, is much more doubtful. These questions are considered in the context of post-apartheid South Africa in another paper (Unterhalter and Young, 1995). What the schooling model clearly fails to do is to address the issues of connectivity between different types of learning – in workplaces, in communities and in specialized educational institutions. That is an issue that I shall return to in a later section.

## THE CREDENTIALIST MODEL

The credentialist model has as long a history as the schooling model. It gives priority to ensuring that the vast majority of the population have qualifications or certificated skills and knowledge and that the qualifications people achieve are related to their future employment. Unlike the schooling model, it allows for the possibility that qualifications may be achieved in other ways than through full-time study, though in practice this is rarely possible for qualifications that give entry to high-status occupations. The European countries that follow the German tradition of *gymnasia* and a dual system of vocational education are the leading examples of the strong version of this model. Other countries, including the UK in efforts during the 1980s to create a Youth Training System, have attempted unsuccessfully to copy the German model. The result, at least in the case of the UK, is what at best could be described as a very weak version of a credentialist model, with links between qualifications and employment not established and public funding being used as incentives for achieving qualification targets. In other words, what in the

German case is an employment-led system has, in the UK, become a state-led system with no direct links to employment at all. Government agencies are left trying to market to employers qualifications that were designed to be employer-led!

Strong versions of the credentialist model give priority to learning that leads to qualifications for occupations and involve legislation that restricts recruitment for nearly all occupations to those with appropriate qualifications. Such models depend on a form of corporatism within which the state, employer organizations and trade unions collaborate, and the latter 'police' their members in relation to both wages and training. Such a system worked well in the context of an incrementally growing economy with well controlled national markets and is typified by West Germany after World War II. However, as with the schooling model, just as countries such as the UK with weak education systems attempt to credentialize their labour forces, the credentialist model is being questioned in the face of changing economic circumstances just where it has been most successful. As a result, a number of its more fundamental weaknesses as a model for a learning society have become apparent.

Credentialist models are expensive to employers and the state, and they are inflexible (here there is a parallel with the factories of mass-production, in that change is an extremely onerous task and not undertaken very frequently). The credentialist model links qualifications to occupations and is based on an increasingly out-of-date division of labour that depends on clear and relatively specific statements about the skills and knowledge associated with particular occupations. A consequence is that credentialist models are prone to a form of 'vocational inertia' when specific skills are taught long after they have ceased to be used in industry or commerce, or to 'academic drift' as increasing numbers of students opt for 'the royal road' that takes them from an abitur to university. It is only in rare cases, such as the 'learnerrangements' scheme associated with Volkswagen (FEU, 1991) that new kinds of relationships between colleges and employers are established.

The more fundamental problem of credentialist models is that they have not re-examined the role of qualifications in societies where more and more people gain certificates even though the jobs associated with those certificates are diminishing in number. The result is likely to be that the function of qualifications, both in occupational selection and in their capacity as a motivator for learning, has to change. The conventional sociological argument is that the expansion of qualifications gives rise to a process of credential inflation when a more extended hierarchy of qualifications is developed and older (and lower-level) qualifications are devalued. There is some truth in this view, though it misses the fundamental point that in a learning society learning needs to be tied to production (in the broadest sense) not selection. It may well be that qualifications, as terminal outcomes of learning and as gateways to jobs, are replaced by a shift to qualifying as a continuous and lifelong process. Standard-setting, which has traditionally been another function of qualifications, will need to be carried out in new ways. The issue of qualifications in a learning society is returned to in the last section of this chapter.

## THE ACCESS MODEL

The *access model* represents a vision of a society of the future in which learning, after the phase of compulsory schooling, is increasingly freed from its ties with specialized educational institutions such as schools, colleges and universities. It is a vision of a learning society in the sense that as a model it envisages that people will learn, if free to do so, in any context they find themselves in, by picking up skills and knowledge as their needs change at different times of their lives. The model has complex and often contradictory political and cultural origins. It has affinity with the ideas of neo-liberalism, which is suspicious of professional educators, who are seen as excluding people rather than as sources of expertise. Furthermore, the neo-liberal version of the access model extends this view to all educational institutions unless they are supported by the market. The access model elevates one of the key liberal ideas of individual choice to a primary principle, even in relation to learning. However, the access model is also attractive to progressives, particularly those associated with adult education, who have spent much of their working lives finding ways round the barriers provided by institutional education. Both liberal and progressive versions of the access model link the freeing of learning from institutions to the potential of new technology, which, at least in theory, allows everyone to be 'on line' and with access to a learning network. More specifically, it casts doubt on the assumption that most learning after compulsory schooling needs teachers and therefore also specialized educational institutions.

Despite its emphasis on access and opportunities for learning, the model represents, if carried through towards its logical conclusion, a reversal of the progressive extension of formal education that has been a feature of every society that has modernized since the nineteenth century. It seems unlikely that the access model will be attractive to the growing numbers of students with wealthy parents who opt for the private sector, or the 20–30 per cent of middle-class parents who can provide the cultural capital to support their children successfully through schools and colleges. For the remainder, pressure from funding restrictions (colleges in England and Wales have been required to increase their student numbers by 25 per cent with a funding increase of only 8 per cent!) will lead to more learning centres, distance learning and assessment on demand, but less and less opportunities for the interaction and dialogue with teachers and their peers on which real learning depends. In other words it is difficult to see the access model as other than a basis for new divisions.

Access model developments such as APL (Accreditation of Prior Learning) and APEL (Accreditation of Prior Experience and Learning) schemes, the setting up of Open Learning Centres and the shift in resources towards careers guidance and learning materials and away from teaching, all attempt to tackle the question of access to learning by placing the learner at the centre of curriculum policies. Proponents argue that institutions, through their admissions policies, their timetables, their school terms and their academic structures, as well as through the more subtle epistemological processes of the hidden curriculum, exclude rather than include new and especially the more disadvantaged learners. The access model, on the other hand, not only sees people as having a right to choose where and when as well as what to study and be assessed on, but that if more and more people do choose they will take more responsibility for their own learning, so that learning becomes an attitude throughout their whole life.

The access model is about promoting learning through its de-institutionalization (though its protagonists would not necessarily endorse the association, it has many features in common with the radical utopianism of Ivan Illich's (1971) de-schooling ideas of the 1970's). By some, as in the recent experiments with learning credits, where qualifications are linked to vouchers for hamburgers, a vision is presented of people buying learning in much the same way as any product on a supermarket shelf – on demand at every stage of a person's life. In aiming to make learning as normal to everyday life as shopping, the access model represents a powerful idea. First, it addresses the reality that many people experience major barriers in trying to access current institutional provision for education. Second, the stress it gives to supporting learners in the management of their own learning is likely to be part of any strategy for achieving a learning society. Third, and unlike the earlier versions of de-institutionalized education of the 1970s, it has powerful forces behind it – both the software companies, who see it as a lucrative new market, and those politicians for whom it appears as a way, not only of cutting the costs of public education, but of weakening what some see as the sectional power of professional or producer interests.

On the other hand, the *access model* has two kinds of weakness that are exaggerated by aspects of the English context. The focus on learner choice and flexibility and the recognition of prior experience and learning makes sense in the context of adults returning to study. However, its extension to those between the ages of 16 and 25 is far more open to question, when many of those in England who find themselves on such 'access' courses will have achieved very little in their compulsory schooling. It is difficult to see how the problems facing such learners will be solved by making the curriculum more flexible and giving them more choice.

The second kind of problem applies more generally to the *access model*. I want to briefly consider two of these problems. As an alternative to institutionalized provision for learning, and one that aims to maximize learner choice and flexibility, the access model can be seen as a further step on a road that is begun by the process of curriculum modularization. However, the international experience of modularization, especially in the USA, where it has become the norm in post-compulsory education, is that if the curriculum is left entirely to student choice this leads to fragmentation and the absence of intellectual development. Intellectual development depends on individuals developing responsibility for their own learning but also on establishing agreed curriculum guidelines and strategies for promoting continuity of learning; inevitably constraints on learner autonomy and choice are involved. The access model, of which a modularized curriculum is one expression, is, in effect, placing the major responsibility for planning and coherence on the learner. However, the learner in question is often one who is least equipped for such a responsibility. It is not surprising, nor does it imply a rejection of the potential of modularization, that it has, at least in Europe, been largely associated with low-status courses.

The second issue for the access model involves the question of how learning links to modern forms of production (I am using the term production in its broadest sense). A whole series of recent books and papers (Reich (1991), Zuboff (1988) and Sparkes (1995) are just a few examples) stress the emergence of new production or delivery. The demands of work will therefore be increasingly opaque to direct experience and more and more dependent on those involved developing new concepts, skills and knowledge. These combinations of skill and knowledge are referred to by a variety of terms such as 'connective', 'conceptual' or 'intellec- tive'. Despite the fact that their operational meaning is far from clear, it is increasingly argued that they will be at the centre of any solution to the crisis of European production that triggered the business interest in the idea of a learning society. It is impossible to see how the skills and knowledge associated with advanced forms of production and services will be developed on the basis of the access model when APL or work-based learning may be quite separate from the sources of conceptual innovation developed in specialized educational institutions. Combining conceptualization and execution will need planning and design of learning assignments based upon close collaboration between production workers and learning specialists in colleges and companies. The access model's focus on learner choice, access to IT, and credit transfer can only lead to low-level practical skills, which all the trends suggest are less and less demanded by employers. Furthermore, if, as is likely, the qualifications achieved through such learner- centred methods have little currency value in terms of job opportunities, this could foster disillusion and scepticism about the value of any kind of learning.

## SUMMARY: THREE MODELS OF A LEARNING SOCIETY

In the previous sections I have distinguished between three models of a learning society and related them to three strategies for reforming post-compulsory edu- cation. In those sections I have also discussed some of the fundamental weaknesses of these models both as strategies for improving post-compulsory education in general and as ways of addressing the specific weaknesses of post-compulsory education in England and Wales, with its characteristic social divisions and voluntarist concept of the role of the state. In the final section of this chapter, I shall draw on these criticisms (in particular the failure in each of the three models to reconceptualize learning) and develop a fourth model of a learning society – the *educative model* – and suggest some of its implications for reforming post- compulsory education.

POST-COMPULSORY EDUCATION FOR A LEARNING SOCIETY: TOWARDS AN EDUCATIVE MODEL

Implicit in all definitions of a learning society is the idea of giving priority to individuals developing learning relationships throughout their lives in any activity, institution or community with which they are involved. However, in the three models of a learning society discussed so far, the focus is not on learning relationships or the learning process but on participation in institutions, gaining qualifications, and the individual as a learner. In each model the assumption is made that another process, participation, gaining a qualification, and being given choice, represents the process of learning. Unlike the schooling model, the educative model does not assume that increases in the proportion of the population engaged in full-time study or expanding the educational provision offered by specialized educational institutions such as schools and colleges necessarily leads to a learning society. Nor, as in the case of the access and credentialist models, does it reduce learning to individual processes of choosing a course or gaining a qualification. The model points to a diversification and interconnection of sites of learning and a shift in the location and role of educational specialists and their relationship with other specialists, as productive life itself becomes a learning relationship. In the last part of this chapter the implications of these ideas are discussed, albeit in a highly exploratory way; it considers four themes in the conceptualization of an educative model of a learning society and suggests some of their implications for the reform of post-compulsory education. The first three follow from my critique of the previous models and focus on the need for (a) new concepts of institutional and curricular specialization, (b) a new concept of qualification and (c) a reconceptualization of the relationship between learning and production that takes into account the changing nature of work at the end of the twentieth century. In the final section I will discuss the need to reconceptualize the concept of learning itself by drawing on Engestrom's idea of expansive learning (Engestrom, 1991, 1994).

**Institutional and curricular specialization in a learning society: beyond the schooling model**

The concept of a learning society points to the transformation of all institutions into 'learning organizations' and thus challenges the idea that learning is primarily associated with specialist educational institutions. Such 'learning organizations' would be characterized by a developing research capacity which would be the basis of a *learning* relationship between institutions and their environment (Morgan, 1988), and a human resource development strategy that linked the 'continuing re-professionalization' of all staff to the primary goals of the organization and was the basis of a learning-centred internal structure. The fact that such a development involves more and more organizations in different sectors taking on an *educational* role does not imply a diminution of the role of schools and colleges as specialist teaching organizations, or the role of universities as specializing in the research and teaching of advanced courses. That would be a reversal of the achievements of specialization of the last century. Rather it implies a change in *internal relationships*, so that schools and colleges themselves develop their research and human resource strategies, and in *external relationships* between educational institutions and their environment. This change would be from the *insulated* (and in many cases *divisive*) *specialization* which has characterized the relationships between educational institutions and the wider society in the past to relationships between different kinds of organisations based on new forms of *connective specialization* and negotiated understandings about common purposes and futures. Examples of possible shared future concepts would be ideas of sustainable growth and international collaboration which individual organizations would be unable to realize on their own. These shared concepts of the future would not only shape relations between schools/colleges/universities and the industrial and service sectors, but between the different specialist pedagogic and curricular skills of teachers in different fields and lines of study. The concept of connective specialization, therefore, is also a basis for a new model of the curriculum.

The curricular possibilites of a shift from insulated to connective specialization are profound and only beginning to become apparent. One example is the way the new programme for the Swedish upper secondary schools distinguishes between sixteen lines of study. Each line makes links between discipline-based knowledge and some aspect of productive life, and each line includes common or core and specialist areas of study, many of which are inconceivable unless based on new kinds of relationships between schools and organizations involved in commercial, community and manufacturing activities. Breadth of learning and new combinations of study are possible in such a model both through the core entitlement for all students and through the design of the specialist areas. Inevitably the old divisions will still remain, and those going to university will tend to cluster in a small number of the lines. However, the possibility is there for students to develop conceptual skills in the food, construction or business administration lines as much as it is through the lines in the natural or social sciences.

## Qualifications in a learning society: beyond the credentialist model

Qualifications in the credentialist model remain gateways to employment or future study as they have since the nineteenth century. They function primarily, therefore, as mechanisms of selection, and secondarily, through such a selection process, as guarantors of standards. Such a concept of qualifications is based on a static model of society in which it is assumed that the occupational division of labour only evolves slowly. It bears little relationship to a society of the future when people are likely to change their jobs and re-qualify several times in their lives. In a static model it is not surprising that sudden increases in opportunities to gain qualifications, as when developing countries become independent, can lead to credential inflation and the disvaluing of qualifications. The tension in the credentialist model is between the selective role of qualifications in a division of labour based upon a minority of the population being qualified and the demands in a learning society for the majority to be qualified in newly flexible ways. The shift needed would be to a focus first on *qualifying as a continuous process*, rather than a qualification terminating the qualifying process, and second on a shift from a concept of a qualification as certifying that certain standards have been achieved – what I will call *standard-setting* – to the qualification process as part of standard development. Such a shift would involve new relationships between those involved in course design and the moderation of assessment and the different groups involved in the use of qualifications – employees, employers and their respective organizations. It would also involve new approaches to quality assurance and standards. The crucial change would be in the new kinds of relationships, between various kinds of qualification users and providers, that would need to be developed to guarantee standards and underpin the focus on their development (Young, 1994b).

## Learning and production in a learning society?

Most attempts to conceptualize a learning society have one striking weakness. They invariably refer to skills for employment, and it is largely business rather than educational interests that have argued for the emphasis on skill ownership. However, not only is the typical concept of the learner buying her or his skills in a training market and selling them in the labour market (CBI, 1991, 1993) highly individualized, but it detaches learning from the specific production or work processes where it might be important. There is no explicit connection with production in such a model – how it is changing and the implications these changes may have for how knowledge about production is learned and what knowledge and skills may be needed by those involved in production. Hales (1984) writes about the 'pre-conceptualization of production' which is a consequence of the increasing sophistication of electronic control engineering, but the changes in work organization are not just about the impact of new technologies. The more general point is that as processes of production change faster and become less accessible to direct experience, the need increases to replace traditional models of apprenticeship, not, as has happened in the 1980s, just by new forms of full-time learning, but by developing new ways of linking work-based learning and conceptual learning (Young and Guile, 1994). Examples of new relationships between learning and production are suggested in the new European Union programmes, Socrates and Leonardo, which aim to support employees in finding ways of transforming declining industries, and in the Ford (UK) EDAP scheme, which provides workers with learning credits to follow any course of study they choose. Such examples of connective relationships between education and production are still rare, especially those that might apply to full-time students in school or college.

The threat posed to many employers, especially those brought up in the Anglo Saxon tradition, by employees who begin to demonstrate conceptual understanding, is well described in Zuboff's study of paper mills in the USA (Zuboff, 1988). Such threats are probably the core contradiction at the heart of the business enthusiasm for the idea of learning society. The tension in the possibilities of new relationships between learning and work is also at the heart of the crisis in the post-compulsory curriculum and the difficulty even the most egalitarian societies have in overcoming divisions between academic and vocational learning (Young, 1993b, 1995b). The educational literature of the last decade is strewn with attempts to conceptualize the problem – connective skills and knowledge, intellective skills, cultural practice, critical vocationalism, technological literacy, symbolic analysis and cognitive apprenticeship are but some of the attempts. The French and the Germans are in a better position to take the debate further with the concepts of 'building' and 'formation' for which we have no translation in English. Creating new links between learning and production remains one of the crucial unresolved issues for the learning society of the future. It is an educational problem, in that it requires educationalists to go beyond their traditional distinction between instrumental rationality and the development of the whole person, that has dominated liberal educational discourse. On the other hand, it is not just a problem of curriculum design that can be solved by educationalists alone. It is a production issue about the meaning and viability of what is becoming known as 'intelligent production', and the new kinds of relationships between work and education that such models of production necessitate. The globalization that is expressed in the location of Japanese and Korean factories in the UK has depended on the vulnerability (to unemployment) of many workers in Wales and the North East of England, as well as the restrictive trade union legislation introduced in the last fifteen years. Unless the question of links between learning and production is addressed, there is little chance of developing the more autonomous possibilities of globalization which will be the dominant basis for production in the future.

## Re-conceptualizing learning

None of the models of a learning society examined in the previous sections problematizes the central concept of learning itself. In the schooling model learning is equated with participation, in the credentialist model with gaining qualifications and in the access model with individual choice. Only the last of the three challenges the conventional notion of learning being dependent on teaching as transmission. However, the *access model* ends up by replacing a teacher-dominant model by one which has no place for teaching at all and individualizes learning, as if it could ever be separated from the social contexts where it is practised. The *educative model* starts with a recognition that all social life involves learning, whether conscious and planned or not. It then goes on to distinguish different types of learning and argues that it is the dominant type of learning that distinguishes different types of societies from others. Engestrom (1994) makes the useful distinction between three orders of learning: *first order learning*, which includes conditioning, imitation and rote learning; *second order learning*, which includes trial and error or 'learning by doing' and problem-solving or investigative learning; and *third order learning*, or what he refers to as *expansive* learning, in which the learner questions and begins to transform the context or 'community of practice' where the learning begins.

The idea of learning taking place in a 'community of practice' does not preclude schools or colleges from being such communities, but nor does it restrict learning to those specialized contexts. The criterion for a learning society becomes: how far, in both specialized and other learning contexts, is the object or focus of learning expanded? In highly integrated societies, (Durkheim's *mechanical solidarity*), most learning is first order and second order, and it is unlikely that there is any expansive learning. The move towards a learning society, in which expansive learning was dominant, would mean a shift from the insulated societies of today to a society based on more connective relationships between sectors and institutions. Engestrom's proposed strategy for expanding learning consists of three steps, each of which develops different kinds of higher-level skills, as follows:

- *through the context of criticism* (both of the practice of the school and of the tension between a 'school view' of the world, as expressed in textbooks, and that expressed in the media)
- *through the context of discovery* (through using new concepts)
- *through the context of practical social application*

This is not another top-down model of the curriculum strategy; as a learning strategy, it can only start with teachers and learners, whether in school/college or not. Following through its implications can enable schools, colleges or training programmes to help students, teachers and people in the community to design and implement their own futures, as their prevailing practices show symptoms of crisis. The strength of the model is the extent to which it is, as Engestrom claims, built on the contradictions of current practice, rather than on some utopian ideal. What is undoubtedly true is that anyone involved in a project based on such ideas will, as two American educationalists quoted by Engestrom express it, be 'working at the edge of (their) competence'.

## A CONCLUDING NOTE

In this chapter I have attempted to engage with the theme of *reforming post-compulsory education*. I began with the UK system which, it is widely acknowledged, is urgently in need of reform, and explored different models of a learning society in order to develop reform criteria. My preferred model of a learning society I termed *educative*, and I suggested that it would involve four sets of reconceptualizations: the form of specialization, the nature of qualifications, the relations between learning and production, and the concept of learning itself. These are very preliminary suggestions, and what is needed next is to explore possible usefulness with a variety of practitioners in the institutions and agencies involved in post-compulsory education. My hope is that these concepts will be of use in giving practical reality to two important ideas: first that a society of the future will embody an education-led economy rather than an economy-led education system; and second that instead of protecting young people from the dangers of work, work in its most human sense will become, as Gramsci hoped, the educational principle.

# Chapter 17

# The Limitations of the New Social Democratic Agendas

*Richard Hatcher*

## CLASS AND AGENCY: THE 'LEARNING SOCIETY'

In this chapter I want to discuss alternatives to New Labour's approach. Questions of equality and agency are central themes of a new book, *Encouraging Learning: Towards a Theory of the Learning School* (1996) by Nixon, Martin, McKeown and Ranson, which develops the argument put forward by Stewart Ranson in his book *Towards the Learning Society* published in 1994. They reject the Conservative agenda but are also critical of current programmes for reform. Ranson rejects the paternalist welfarism of the social democratic tradition, in which 'The good society or an educated public were to be *delivered* by knowledgeable specialists rather than lived and created by the public with the support of professionals' (p. 102). The task now is to renew the purposes and institutions of democracy to create active citizens for a 'learning society'. Of course, the notion of education for a learning society features in Labour Party documents too. *Opening Doors to a Learning Society* (1994) begins with a vision of 'a genuinely learning society – a society in which all individuals can fulfil their potential as active citizens in a prosperous, civilised and caring community'. Indeed, it is becoming the common currency of educational modernization in the European Union. (See the European Commission White Paper *Education and Training: Towards a Learning Society* published in December 1996). For a critique of 'the myth of the learning society' see Hughes and Tight, 1995).

But the vision of Ranson, Nixon, and their colleagues is based on critiques of the policies of the Labour Party, the Institute for Public Policy Research (a pro-Labour think-tank) in their 1993 pamphlet *Education: A Different Version* and the National Commission on Education book *Learning to Succeed* (1993). They argue that, whatever their merits and in spite of their differences, these statements share four fundamental weaknesses. They fail to grasp the magnitude of disadvantage; they tend to reduce educational change to its relationship to the labour market;

they are over-preoccupied with the instrumental and economic dimensions of learning; and they need a deeper analysis of the causes and consequences of disadvantage, and a more radical conception of learning in the context of structural transformations in society. On that basis, Ranson and Nixon *et al.* put forward a detailed vision of an alternative, based on the principles of education for the public good, popular participation, progressive decentralization, and multiple accountability, which is significantly different from the policies of New Labour and its advisers in a number of respects (for example, the rejection of economic instrumentalism, the concern for the learner and the process of learning, the antipathy to selection).

The scope of the argument of Ranson and Nixon *et al.* is wider than the reform of education alone. It envisages a new moral and political order of citizenship within a participative democracy based on 'practical reason'. Their argument belongs to a body of current thinking for which notions of democracy and citizenship are the key political terms of a new perspective for the left, and for which the centrality of the concepts of capitalism and class have been displaced by those of postmodernity and identity. It is exemplified by a recent book edited by David Miliband and published by the IPPR, Labour's think-tank, called *Reinventing the Left* (1994). The book begins with a proposal by Anthony Giddens for a new framework for radical politics, 'beyond left and right', the key concept of which is the construction through 'dialogue' of a 'common agenda' for citizenship (Giddens, 1994a). In a response in the same volume, Perry Anderson insists that democracy is primarily an arena of interests, not a field of discourse, and that therefore it is ultimately power that decides, not reason. In consequence, there can be no common agenda as the basis for citizenship: a radical agenda is inevitably divisive, because it challenges the control of resources by the powerful (Anderson, 1994). I want to trace the implications of Anderson's comments for the case of Ranson and Nixon *et al.*

Ranson and Nixon *et al.* propose a society which has learning as its organizing principle. Its utopian flavour is conveyed by this passage:

> In the new order of things, the periphery should be perceived as the centre, with all the other tiers of government seen as circles of enabling support radiating out from the defining purpose of it all: ordinary people individually and together devoting their energies to developing their own powers and capacities but also those of the local community.
>
> (Ranson, 1994, p. 128)

What is absent from their vision is the recognition that society already has an organizing principle, production for profit in the market, to which everything else is subordinate; that this generates social classes with conflicting interests; and that the state acts to maintain the dominant order. Furthermore, those conflicting but asymmetrical interests express themselves within the education system, not just conjuncturally, as a result of the excesses of the Conservatives, but structurally. It is significant that the question of social class, which is prominent in Ranson's critique of Conservative education policy, disappears entirely in his discussion of the alternative. Ranson and Nixon *et al.*'s model of partnership between parents, employers and the wider public acknowledges no structurally based conflict of interests. But in education there is no classless universal interest around which a national consensus can be constructed because, as Bob Connell says, 'Disadvantage is always produced through mechanisms that also produce advantage . . . No one should imagine that educational change in the interests of the poor can be conflict-free' (1994, p. 144).

Ranson and Nixon *et al.*'s stance gives distinctive shape to their two central themes, those of working-class equality and popular agency. It leads to an explanation of working-class underachievement in education as the product of a failure of the system to value difference equally. Their plea is for cultural pluralism, where culture is seen as a complex process of symbolic classification constructed through discourse. They reject the tradition of materially based cultural contestation associated with Raymond Williams. While they are right to stress that outcomes and processes in education are not socially predetermined in a mechanically reproductionist way, either at the level of the school as an institution or at the level of the individual pupil, what is missing from their analysis is the sense that, for Williams and certainly for Bourdieu (in spite of the way they interpret his work), resisting the dominant culture means continually thinking – and acting – against the grain (Nixon *et al.*, 1996, pp. 62–5).

The consequence of their argument is that the reform programme they put forward does not take account of the obstacles to transforming the school, in terms of its stratificatory and ideological functions, to which I referred earlier. One of the features of the 'learning school' is that it 'is deeply committed to equality and eschews any form of social, cultural or intellectual selection' (p. 86). This provides the basis for a radical internal regime of pedagogy and organization, but what it ignores is the powerful influence on the school of the highly unequal and selective capitalist division of labour. It may be possible to postpone the operation of formal selection to late on in the school, perhaps even until the school-leaving examination, but its shadow lies over the whole of schooling, bringing into play powerful processes of differentiation by teachers, parents and pupils themselves.

As to the ideological function of schooling, for Ranson and Nixon *et al.* the content of learning centres on the notion of valuing difference. But are all cultures to be valued equally, including the dominant culture itself? Nixon and his co-authors advocate 'a comprehensive curriculum of social, cultural, practical and political education as well as cognitive development' (p. 80). They give the example of how teaching about water can raise issues of 'economics, power, social structure and gender'. Are there no constraints imposed upon the school when reason questions the prerogatives of power?

The ability of the school to resist the pressures of the dominant power structure, whether in terms of selection or curriculum content, raises the central question of agency in a way that reveals the inadequacy of Ranson and Nixon *et al.*'s conception. They reject the Conservative agenda and also that of Labour, on the grounds that they are insufficiently radical. The question then is, what government will implement their programme? It would require a broad popular movement capable of exerting enough political pressure to push through the reforms they propose and defend them against reaction. Yet their conception of agency shows no recognition of this need and contains no strategies capable of translating their vision into practice. Their concrete proposals for democratic participation are no more radical than those of the Labour leadership. They propose an extension of processes of consultation very similar to those in *Diversity and Excellence* which leave the existing power structure of school management and local and national government control intact. Ironically, Ranson and Nixon *et al*'s belief in the possibility of a national consensus and a neutral state undermines the need for powerful popular agency that is their starting point.

## CLASS AS INEQUALITY – CLASS AS AGENCY

I want to end by outlining an alternative approach to the agendas for reform I have been discussing. It is based on the premise that the struggle for working-class *equality* in education is inextricably linked with the struggle for working-class *agency*. My starting-point is the relationship between class cultures and school cultures. At the centre of this relationship is, as I have suggested, the curriculum. As Bob Connell says:

> When progress in the mainstream curriculum is taken as the goal of intervention, that curriculum is exempt from criticism. However, the experience of teachers in disadvantaged schools has persistently led them to question the curriculum. Conventional subject matter and texts and traditional teaching methods and assessment techniques turn out to be sources of systematic difficulty. They persistently produce boredom. Enforcing them heightens the problem of discipline, and so far as they are successfully enforced, they divide pupils between an academically successful minority and an academically discredited majority.

> (1994, p. 137)

Connell sees the mainstream curriculum as the 'hegemonic' curriculum, historically constructed to represent dominant interests and marginalize other experiences and other ways of organizing knowledge.

> Each particular way of constructing the curriculum (i.e. organising the field of knowledge and defining how it is to be taught and learned) carries social effects. Curriculum empowers and disempowers, authorises and de-authorises, recognises and mis-recognises different social groups and their knowledge and identities.

> (p 140)

Connell proposes that a concept of curricular justice, which he defines as 'the development of abilities for social practice', should be at the heart of strategic thinking on education and disadvantage.

There is nothing exotic about this idea. It is implied in a great deal of practical teaching that goes on in disadvantaged schools, teaching that contests the disempowering effects of the hegemonic curriculum and authorizes locally produced knowledge (p. 141).

It is worth exploring what Connell means by 'locally produced knowledge'. It does not mean restricting the curriculum in working-class schools to the horizons of the neighbourhood. On the contrary, it is based on the recognition that real learning, which necessarily includes access to universal forms of thought, takes place through the dialectic of, in Vygotsky's terms, spontaneous concepts drawn from everyday experience and non-spontaneous concepts derived from elaborated systems of thought. That process is an active one – the making of knowledge, not just the taking. By 'local' is meant not the individual in isolation but the individual as an ensemble of social relationships, rooted in the cultures of family, peer group and community, shaped by class, gender and ethnicity. So 'locally produced knowledge' becomes the expression of collective experience and concern. This provides the basis for what Connell calls a programme of 'common learnings' (Connell, 1993). This is more than the pluralism of 'valuing difference'. 'The ultimate objective of a "common learnings" educational strategy is to seek the generalised diffusion throughout the whole system of schooling of counter-hegemonic knowledge based on the experiences and perspectives of the disadvantaged' by reconstructing the dominant curriculum (McCarthy, 1993, p. 300).

Connell's ideas draw on his practical involvement in the Disadvantaged Schools Project in Australia (Connell *et al.* 1991). The DSP was set up by the Whitlam Labor government in 1975. It placed resources and decision-making power in the hands of those close to the classroom, bypassing the cumbersome state bureaucracies. Projects had to be collectively planned and implemented at school level. Decisions about funding were made by regional DSP committees on which teachers and parents had a major voice.

Behind this movement was a political alliance that included a modernizing Labor Party, a parent movement that had developed new organizational skills in the campaigns around increased funding for public education, teacher activists who were extending the boundaries of teacher unionism beyond the traditional industrial model, and an emerging strand of sociological educational studies that provided an intellectual rationale for a more radical, interventionist programme of reform (Johnston, 1993, p. 109).

In recent years the move to the right by the federal Labor government, and in 1996 its defeat in the general election, has posed a threat to the DSP, but it embodies a valuable experience. 'These collaborative processes gave people within the DSP the opportunity to contest the dominant ideology of schooling and its explanation of inequality' (White and Johnston, 1993, p. 107). Teachers and parents developed their own understandings of the relationship between education and poverty. In Sydney and Melbourne, teachers and parents formed associations to highlight the problems of the inner-city schools. A real debate took place within the Project on an alternative model of the curriculum that responds to the cultural contexts of working-class children and empowers them with appropriate skills and knowledge. One discourse within it drew upon a language of social class and collective action. 'It sees the DSP as a strategy for collective social change rather than one which rescues individuals from poverty and equips them to be socially mobile' (White and Johnston, 1993, p. 113).

I have referred to the experience of the DSP in Australia because it shows in practice that popular activity in education at grassroots level is possible, and that it can lead to challenges to dominant interests in education (Apple, 1993). It demonstrates how the struggle for working-class *equality* in education and the struggle for working-class *agency* are two sides of the same coin. And it is far in advance of what is envisaged in terms of popular participation by the Blair-led Labour Party and the educationists who advise it.

Comparable examples are rare in this country. The strength of the statist social-democratic tradition has hegemonized much of the rest of the Left, which has tended to respond with its own more militant version of statism. (This statist culture is exactly the opposite of that found in Marx, incidentally. In fact, in Marx's comments on education, in *Critique of the Gotha Programme*, he insisted that the workers' movement should place no confidence in the state's adminis-tration of education.) However, in the last few years there have been two issues which have generated local popular activity – struggles around opting-out and against cuts in education spending. These are important developments, but they are essentially defensive struggles against attacks by the Conservative government. Their limitation is that they do not require any alternative programme or strategic orientation, though they do provide potentially fertile ground for developing in that direction. A partial exception is the third important campaign in recent years, against national testing, during which teachers not only won widespread support from parents and school governors but also, as Ken Jones has shown, took the opportunity to begin a dialogue with parents about the purposes of assessment and about alternative approaches. However, the most advanced experiences we have, certainly in the post-war period, of an educational movement with a popular base that challenged the hegemonic curriculum, are the campaigns for 'race' and gender equality in the 1970s and 1980s. Social class was not central to these developments: while there was a widespread basis of popular support for gender and racial equality which sustained teachers and made LEA support possible, there was no such similar pressure with regard to class. The reason was not, as Arnot (1991) suggests, because action on class was paralysed by the fatalism of reproduction theory. Many of those active on issues of 'race' and gender were also committed to challenging class inequality in education, and developed innovative curricula and teaching methods (see Chris Richards, 1966). The difficulty lay in developing a programme and a political project comparable to and capable of replacing that of equality of access, which had culminated in the comprehensive reforms of the 1960s but which had failed to resolve the question of class inequality. The root of this difficulty lies in the fact that class is not equivalent to 'race' and gender. As Ellen Meiksins Wood argues (1990), while all oppressions may have equal moral claims, class inequality has a more strategic location at the heart of capitalism. Notions of gender or racial equality in capitalist societies are not in themselves meaningless, though they may be unrealizable in practice, but class inequalities are by definition constitutive of capitalism: the notion of class equality is a contradiction in terms. There was much more political space for reforms on gender and 'race' in education in the 1980s, but the movement still came up against the limits of permitted reform, and was unable to develop a political strategy, with self-activity and collective organization at both local and national levels at its centre, to go beyond them.

## PROMOTING SELF-ACTIVITY IN EDUCATION

Let me summarize my argument. My starting-point is the reproduction of class inequality in the teaching and learning process. A conflict of class interests is inherent in the imposition of the 'hegemonic curriculum'. To it I counterposed the notion of locally constructed and authorized knowledge. This process requires forms of popular political-educational self-activity and organization capable of releasing the creativity of teachers, school students, parents and their communities and of defending radical innovations against attempts to suppress or co-opt them. The imposition of uniformity by the state tends to demotivate grassroots activity, offering only restricted room for individual independent activity by teachers and parents, and collective action at best limited to campaigns about access and funding. Of course, local initiatives on their own are not enough; they need to be co-ordinated in a coherent national political-educational project.

The implications of this argument need elaborating. The politics of school education can be thought of as defined by two axes, of content and control. The axis of control ranges from centralized state control to power at school level. The axis of content ranges from national uniformity to local diversity. The most obvious expression of dominant class interests in state education this century has been diversity of provision. State intervention to secure uniformity of provision, in the form of the comprehensive school and a common core curriculum, has historically been seen by the left to be the most effective guarantee of equality. In the current context of a renewed offensive by the Conservatives against comprehensive education, the comprehensive principle needs to be reaffirmed. But on its own that is not enough. Thirty years of experience of comprehensive schools have demonstrated that they continue, as do primary schools, to be sites of social reproduction of inequality. To challenge that requires, I have argued, local self-activity both inside and outside the class room.

A shift along the axis of control from a reliance on state management of uniformity of provision towards a strategy of stimulating local self-activity has profound implications for the content of education. Unlike in idealized consensual notions of 'partnership' and 'community', people have different, and often conflict-ing, ideas and interests. This is particularly the case in education because on many issues, even apparently 'technical' ones like how best to teach reading, there is no consensus even among professionals. People will only invest their energies in the schools if they believe that the schools can be responsive to their concerns. Given the power to choose, they will not all make the same choices.

What would it mean for the participants? For school students, in ways appropri-ate to their ages, it would mean much greater active participation both in learning, through the realization of the idea of the 'negotiated curriculum', freed from the dead hand of the present National Curriculum, and as a citizen in the society of the school, with democratic rights and responsibilities. For teachers, it would mean empowerment and 'upskilling'; a redefined professionalism emancipated from the constraints imposed by the Right. As Connell argues, 'If the education of children in poverty is to be changed, teachers will be the work force of reform' (1994, p. 143. See also Weiner, 1994). Teachers should be centrally involved in not just implementing but designing strategies for reform, enabled by appropriate initial training, in-service education and support, and working conditions. The dominant management model of 'strong leadership' by head-teachers, taken for granted by both the Right and the 'school improvement' movement, needs to be put into question, as Gerald Grace (1995, chapter 11) has begun to do, and earlier more democratic models of school organization within the comprehensive tradition need to be recovered (Benn and Chitty, 1996, chapter 8). In that context, teachers' professional skills would be freed to develop educational projects, in dialogue with the community and responsive to their concerns. Taking the notion of 'active citizenship in the learning society' seriously entails opening up all social institutions to educational activity (levered open by a combination of incentives and legislation), so that the neighbourhood and the city become a network of resources for learning managed by the school, aided by new information technology.

For parents and the school community there would be the opportunity to set new agendas in partnership with teachers and school students. A model is provided by the Australian DSP, in which representative bodies involving parents and teachers allocated funding to collaborative school-community proposals. Local moves to increase the self-management of schools by their communities, within the national policy framework, going far beyond current notions of 'partnership', would be encouraged. The participation of parents needs to be facilitated by an enhancement of democratic rights, including time off work with pay and the opening up of governing bodies and their effective accountability to those they represent.

At local authority level, the priority woud be to assert the representative democratic function of LEAs, at present marginalized by both the erosion of powers by government policy and the rise of a new technicist ideology of management within local government. Mechanisms have to be found to ensure both effective political control by properly informed elected members and much greater opportunities for direct input into policy by parents, teachers, school students, governors and the community, through for example local elected Education Councils with the right to submit proposals directly to Education Committees. Similar representative bodies would be needed at national level.

I do not underestimate the difficulties in increasing participation (I discuss this with reference to school governors in Hatcher, 1994), nor the reactionary directions it may take (as the experience of Croxteth School illustrates: see Carspecken, 1991). But they are not grounds for dismissing the practical potential of democratic self-management for a popular politics of education. As an example of what is possible I want to refer briefly to an experience in Canada. Malcolm Levin (1987) describes the creation of 21 'alternative' public community elementary and secondary schools in Toronto in the 1970s and early 1980s. Like the DSP in Australia, these were based on an alliance of teachers and parents. Again the opportunity was made possible by a social democratic party, in the case of Toronto through the city's Board of Education, which stimulated and supported community participation. Levin describes the conflicts over the ownership of the schools that were endemic in the process of constructing an alliance between parents and teachers. But in spite of these tensions, the alliance was strong enough to successfully put up a joint teachers' union–parent slate in elections for the Board of Education, and to defend its perspective for education against attacks by the Board. It successfully opposed teacher lay-offs and attempts to restrict politics in the curriculum and in school governing bodies.

It would be wrong to describe the approach I have briefly outlined as a new settlement in education. The notion is too static and closed. Rather, it is a strategic political-educational orientation based on the organizing principle of equity through self-activity, supported by state guarantees. It is not a question of a simple displacement of the state by the local, of uniformity by diversity, but of reorganizing these parameters in terms of a combination of a strategic orientation towards stimulating self-activity with a national policy framework of common entitlements which would prevent the exploitation of diversity to sustain inequality. In this bottom-up version of the 'pressure plus support' model, action through 'constitutional' mechanisms would need to be complemented by local and national campaigning by coalitions of interests, within which the role of the teachers' unions would be vital in making and defending progress. By definition, local self-activity cannot be programmed in advance, so while enabling procedures are essential, what is decisive is the commitment to encourage and support the growth-points of self-activity, however small. The criterion we should apply is what works, in terms of high standards of achievement, the development of social and moral values based on co-operation, a critical curriculum, the reduction of inequality and the promotion of popular self-activity. In this perspective, 'school effectiveness' would be freed from the built-in conservative bias resulting from its restriction to the narrow limits of what is currently permitted to exist. The school improvement movement, released from its subordination to New Labour's project for managing capitalism better than the Tories, could at last realize its potential in a flowering of educational innovation, combining a democratic impetus with rigorous evaluation.

It would be profoundly mistaken to respond to the Right's agenda, based on differentiation through the market to widen social inequalities, by clinging to a social-democratic statist model which serves fatally to depoliticize and demobilize those popular energies which alone are capable of effectively challenging the reproduction of social class inequality in education. Yet there are only two alternatives to the Right's agenda: a statist model, or a perspective based on stimulating and supporting popular collective self-activity, with all the difficulties that entails, at school, local and national levels. The danger that the opening up of schools to local democratic activity will release reactionary as well as progressive dynamics is a real one, but the outcome is not inevitably unfavourable. It's where a democratic politics of education starts.

# Chapter 18

# Only Charybdis: The Learning Society Through Idealism

*Glenn Rikowski*

## INTRODUCTION

The major British political parties, the Confederation of British Industry and some leading educationalists have come to share the view that the creation of a 'learning society' is essential for national well-being. In May 1994, the UK Economic and Social Research Council (ESRC) launched a research programme designed to explore barriers preventing the development of a 'learning society' within the United Kingdom, but also to stimulate the growth of such a society (ESRC, 1994). Meanwhile, the Commission of the European Union (1995) has published a White Paper on the learning society, and other European countries are also taking active steps towards creating a learning society (Gleeson, 1996).

Although the notion of the 'learning society' has clearly 'arrived' as a significant organizing idea for economic, social and educational policy-makers, it is not particularly new. Hutchins (1968) and Husén (1974) kick-started the concept many years ago. Thus, the question of why the 'learning society' notion resurfaced in policy positions and educational theorizing and research in the early 1990s is well worth pursuing, though on this occasion it will be left alone. The aim of this chapter is more modest; to show how the idea of a 'learning society' can fall prey to a particular form of critique which casts it as an example of hopeless pie-in-the-sky idealism.

There are a number of different and competing conceptions of the 'learning society' (Edwards, 1995b; Young, 1995b). Hughes and Tight (1995) provide a useful and succinct working definition where the 'learning society' can be viewed as a society 'which places education and training at the centre of its concerns' (p. 290), or, as Ranson (1996) puts it, learning is 'at the centre' (of educational research, of public policy, and of the social formation). Generally though, theorists, researchers and analysts who use the learning society concept are still largely engaged in a process of concept construction. Even the ESRC acknowledged that one of the tasks of the Learning Society Programme was to provide greater understanding of the *nature* of the 'learning society' (ESRC, 1994, para. 3.1). However, although the processes of defining and characterizing the learning society are still in their early stages, a few analysts and commentators (Edwards, 1995b; Gleeson, 1996; Hatcher, 1995, 1996; Hughes and Tight, 1995) have recently started to provide pertinent criticisms of the learning society concept becoming, on the one hand, a form of idealism (a fanciful idea, a utopia, a project with no firm basis in existing social reality), and, on the other hand, the learning society project degenerating into just another capitalist social form. The Learning Society, therefore, as concept and as 'emerging' social project, has to skip around the whirlpool of Charybdis as watery Idealism and also around Scylla as monstrous Materialism. This chapter deals only with the former type of critique; it is only concerned with Charybdis. It explores the notion that the whole learning society project (as concept, and as hoped-for social form) is essentially idealist in nature. In the watery grave of Charybdis, the learning society can only ever become a wish, a hope or a dream.

The first section of the chapter explores some cameos, sketches and outline perspectives on the learning society. It acts as a resource and grounding for discussion throughout the rest of the chapter. The second section provides a brief outline of the idealist outlook in general and, through the work of Harris (1994), educational idealism in particular. Using the resources and analysis of the first two sections, the third section provides the main fare with a critique of the 'learning society' as *idealist form*; that is, as a concept which has no purchase on actually existing (capitalist) social reality. In particular, it locates some specific aspects of idealist educational discourse embedded within conceptions of the learning society explored in the first section. The concluding section suggests a possible route for escape out of the idealist whirlpool for promoters of the learning society concept/project.

## LEARNING SOCIETY: CAMEOS, SKETCHES AND FRAGMENTS

Apart from the work of Ranson (1990, 1992, 1993a, b, 1994, with Stewart 1994) there has been no sustained writing on the theory of the learning society in Britain.[1] All we have are a series of cameos, sketches and fragments and this section concentrates on examples of these cameos and sketches of the 'learning society' provided by Young (1995b), Ranson *et al.* (1995) and Edwards (1995b). Examination of these sketches establishes some of the key motifs incorporated within much discussion and debate concerning the learning society of the future.

As Young (1995b) has noted, there are many definitions of and perspectives on the learning society; it is an essentially 'contested concept' (p. 4). He provides three models of the learning society. The differences between these models reflect different interests and visions of the future (incorporating different models of social and economic development) and 'different strategies for getting there' (ibid.). First, Young describes the 'schooling model' of the learning society. Here, the stress is on high participation in post-compulsory education and training which aims to ensure that as many people as possible reach some minimum education and training targets. Historically, Young's 'schooling model' of the learning society seems to point towards quantitative developments such as the raising of the school-leaving age in the early 1970s, increased staying-on rates in the 1980s and the emergence of mass higher education in the 1990s.

Young's second model of the learning society – the 'credentialist model' – seems to be conflated with his first model as it is hard to envisage a 'schooling model' that does not imply increased credentialism. Young seems to abstract qualifications from schooling, which makes little sense in terms of the later years of compulsory schooling (GCSE, GNVQ Part 1), and even less sense in relation to post-compulsory schooling (A Level, GNVQ etc.). These forms of schooling are substantially about gaining academic credentials. However, this second model 'gives priority to ensuring that the vast majority of the population have qualifications or certified skills and knowledge and that the qualifications people achieve are related to their future employment' (p. 5). The credentialist model allows for qualifications being gained beyond academic institutions (through work-based learning, for example) and also relates to wealth creation and economic growth.

The third, 'access' model, relates closely to lifelong or lifetime learning. It points towards a society where learning after compulsory education is commonplace and increasingly takes place beyond formal academic institutions. Again, it seems to overlap with the 'credentialist model' on this last point. Economically, Young views the model as being tied to a vision of de-industrialism or post-industrial society, where education becomes another consumer choice. It stresses breaking down barriers to learning, supporting learners (in a learner-led curriculum) rather than teaching and (through the use of computer technology) cutting learning costs.

Young rejects all three models and argues instead for an 'educative model' of the learning society. This perspective involves the recognition that learning is involved in all social interaction (p. 11). Young provides a description of three *levels* of learning (first–third order learning) and designates a 'learning society' as being a society where the third order of learning predominates in all social interactions. This third order level of learning is 'expansive learning in which the learner questions and begins to transform the context or "community of practice" where the learning begins' (p. 11). Young's 'educative model' points to social transformation without specifying how the abstract individual learner will 'transform the context', or, in conjunction with other 'expansive learners', how collectivities of 'new humans' will ensure the material, institutional, political and social transformations necessary for maintenance of this mode of existence. Second, Young provides no theory of the *emergence* of these specimens of new humanity. Rather, he views 'emergent properties' of the new educative paradigm as arising spontaneously. Short of teleology, Young's 'educative' model provides no account of how political, social and economic processes will yield up the 'expansive learner'. However, his 'educative model' is closer to a vision of a learning society than the other three, stunted, 'straw models' he sets the former against. The first three models all stress the *learning* aspect at the expense of any real analysis of the society within which it is embedded.

Ranson *et al.* (1995) locate a triad of perspectives on the learning society within the literature. First, the learning society can be viewed as being largely concerned with skill development for the labour market. This is the narrow, economistic version much favoured by the Confederation of British Industry (1989) with its 'skills revolution' and commentators who view the learning society mainly as a vehicle for regenerating the British economy. The 'society' element in this conception gets substituted by 'economy'.

The second perspective is on useful knowledge for work (Ainley, 1993, 1994a; Cooley, 1993). Here, the potential for new information technologies to create satisfying work and for workplaces to be infused with democratic processes (where workers have more control over all aspects of work, but especially over human–machine interaction) is highlighted. This conception is more expansive than the first in so far as it acknowledges the interests of labour as well as those of capital. However, Ranson *et al.* see this perspective as tending towards a narrow economism.

The third perspective views the learning society as being a society which incorporates *learning for citizenship* (Husén, 1974; Ranson, 1992, 1994). This form of learning is 'active' in the sense that the processes of learning are embedded within active participation in the community and in wealth creation. It is learning for life through active participation in social life itself and throughout the lifetime of the learner. Thus, it goes beyond the economism of the first two perspectives and also breaks down the barrier between the 'economy' and extra-economic institutions, process and practices. Finally, it links social and economic innovation to active, agency-manifesting behaviours of citizens. Therefore, it views the learning society not as a static social formation but as an ever-changing social aggregation of processes of unfolding or *becoming* (Sztompka, 1991). In a series of publications, Ranson (1990, 1992, 1993a, 1994) has provided criteria for evaluating the extent to which a society can be designated a 'learning' society, the presuppositions, principles, values and purposes comprising the key components of a learning society, models which set out strategies for reconstructing society towards becoming a learning society (1992, pp. 72–4) and the personal and social conditions for learning within a learning society.

Hayes *et al.* (1995) argue that viewing the learning society as a conglomeration of 'learning organizations' is insufficient and set out some institutional preconditions for the growth and maintenance of a learning society. Their notion of a 'learning polity', which seeks to provide a social foundation for the learning society to flower and develop, has similarities with Ranson's decentralized, bottom-up and democratic perspective. Like Ranson, they also acknowledge that national strategies for framing a supportive infrastructural environment, in order for local community-centred initiatives to develop, form an essential element.

Edwards (1995b) also provides three perspectives on the learning society. First, he argues, the learning society can be viewed as the *educated society*. On this view, active citizenship, liberal democracy and equal opportunities are stressed within a lifelong learning trajectory. It is education for social and economic change. This has similarities with Ranson's third perspective outlined above and can be viewed as a liberal democratic model.

Edward's second perspective on the learning society focuses on the *learning market*. It is an economistic model. The emphasis here is on educational and training institutions providing individualized learning services within a lifelong learning outlook where the whole process is premised upon enhancing the compet- itiveness of the British economy.

The third perspective views the learning society as being an aggregate of *learning networks* (with local, national, European and global dimensions) where learners adopt a 'learning approach to life' (p. 187); learning 'with attitude'! The process is powered by access to new technology and is consonant with a postmodern consumer model of the learning society where learners are 'empowered' through viewing learning as a pleasurable, individualized and student-centred activity. Again, all this takes place within a lifelong learning framework.

Many criticisms could be launched at all of these conceptions of the learning society. Indeed, the authors themselves provide critiques of the versions which they do not favour. Edwards (1995b) points to contradictions and tensions within *all* currently available perspectives on the learning society. He particularly high- lights the inequalities which are masked by appeals to a learning society based on 'learning markets', 'the empowerment of lifelong learning', 'learning networks' or 'learning in the community'. Thus, argues Edwards, 'we need to look closely at the front of the banner of the learning society before we walk behind it.' (p. 189).

When the banner of the 'learning society' is examined through the lens of the cameos, sketches and fragments outlined above, at least four observations can be discerned. First, some of these sketches are embedded within a discourse where the 'learning society' is viewed as being essentially concerned with raising the quality of human labour power (relative to that of other national capitals) throughout the British capital. This prognosis also includes a secondary *quantitative* aspect where 'skills' become more abundant throughout the national capital.

A second observation is that there is a further quantitative emphasis on more, longer periods, even lifetimes of 'learning', 'schooling' or 'education' *sui generis*, where 'learning', 'schooling' or 'education' are viewed as practices apart from economic missions and quests. This 'purist' perspective comes close to 'learning- for-its-own-sake'. At the extreme, it incorporates an incipient credentialism where 'learning' becomes umbilically tied to the piling up of qualifications and education credits.

Third, there is a transcendental moment, especially within Ranson *et al.*'s (1995) third option and Young's (1995b) fourth perspective on the 'learning society'. This is where the 'learning society' banner is used as catalyst for social transformation. For Young, the 'learning society' provides the foundation for a movement towards a new social formation permitting the emergence of 'expansive learners'. For Ranson *et al.*, it provides rich soil for moving towards a rejuvenated democracy with enhanced rights and responsibilities encircling a 'new citizenship'.

The second and third observations are closely allied to a fourth which points to the abstraction of 'learning', 'schooling' and 'education' from the *form* of society. Even in the economistic versions of the 'learning society', both the form and nature of this 'new' society and an analysis of the form and nature of *existing* society are underdeveloped, one-sided or (typically) absent. Of course, uncharita- bly, it could be argued that, in these discourses, 'learning society' becomes synonymous with a taken-for-granted 'capitalism'. At least some view the form and nature of the 'learning society' as an issue for comment. Hayes, *et al.* (1995), for example, posit the learning society as 'a new form of society' (p. 3), but without saying either how it differs from capitalism or providing an anlysis of how the 'learning society' will emerge from within the bowels of capital. The materialist outlook of Rikowski (forthcoming) explores the 'learning society' as capitalist social form, and these strands of analysis will be elaborated there. Here, the task is to confront the concept of the learning society with the charge of watery idealism.

## THE IDEALIST OUTLOOK

In order to locate idealism within conceptions of learning it is necessary to say something about the idealist outlook in philosophy. Of course, idealism has a long philosophical pedigree. It would be foolhardy to attempt to embark on a major exposition of idealism through the millenia at this juncture. The task here is to provide a general account as the basis for locating forms of idealism which pose the most wide-ranging problems for conceptions of the learning society. The discussion resolves itself into analysis of: the *general* forms of idealism – idealism as such and idealism in educational discourse; and the *specific* aspects of idealist theorizing, with some exploration of how these relate to conceptions of the learning society.

### Idealism

Harris (1994) views idealism as a philosophical approach which incorporates 'essentialism' and the drive to establish eternal truths and 'timeless social, moral and personal values and ideas' (p. 8). Idealist thinking involves a divorce of the thinker from the objects of knowledge, experience and sensuous activity (McCarthy, 1994). Those who tread the idealist path situate themselves, *qua* knowers and thinkers, as being ontologically riven from the objects of their knowledge (which involves a radical bifurcation between the 'subjectivity' of the knower and the 'objectivity' of the known).

Derek Sayer (1989) provides a radical re-interpretation of Marx's base–superstructure metaphor which constitutes an explanation of the existence of idealist thinking in its modern form within capitalist society. According to Sayer, Marx's base–superstructure metaphor is not a model of capitalist social reality. To view it as such, argues Sayer, leads to a crude economic determinism which has been the curse of Marxist theory since Marx's 'Preface' to his *A Contribution to the Critique of Political Economy* (1859), where this devilish metaphor first surfaced. Simply, the 'economic base' (economy) determines the 'ideological superstructure' (family, law and so on). Education is typically placed in the 'ideological superstructure' and hence is viewed as being 'determined' by the 'economic system', as in the work of Bowles and Gintis (1976). Of course, the crude economic determinism of the standard rendition of the metaphor has led to a number of attempts to escape the fatalism and mechanistic view of social development it entails – such as the Althusserian 'relative autonomy' (of base from superstructure) alternative which still finds favour amongst some educational theorists (such as Apple, 1985; Fritzell, 1987). Sayer cuts through all of this by alerting us to what Marx actually said in the 1859 'Preface' and arguing that 'Thus "superstructure" . . . is simply the "ideal" form in which the totality of "material" relations which make up the "base" itself are manifested to consciousness, not a substantially separable order of reality at all' (Sayer, 1989, p. 84). As Marx held that 'consciousness is determined by life', argues Sayer, then the superstructure becomes the ideas about capitalist social reality that people draw from their everyday, common-sense experience. This applies to the ideas of political economists and idealist philosophers as much as anyone else. Idealist thinkers do not (or refuse to) accept this point. Thus, idealist theories of society, in their primordial phase, come uncritically to reflect capitalist social reality. Social theory merely 'maps' what is socially given through observation and empirical study – and there it rests. The problem with this – as Marx showed with his analysis of commodity fetishism – is that social phenomena in capitalist society are not always as they present themselves to consciousness.

However, Sayer (and Marx) points to a second moment (Stage Two) of idealist social theory. Here, ideas originally derived from the capitalist form of society as it *presents* itself to consciousness come to take on 'a life of their own'. They are reified within discourse and attain the status of 'objects'. Thereafter, idealist theorists, when referring to these reified concepts, take the stance that they are establishing the 'essence' of things within 'pure thought', or the relations between social entities. This is the mystical moment of idealist theory. As Sayer points out 'Consciousness is precisely not a thing in itself, and the fundamental error of the idealists is to treat it as such, to attribute to "*conceptions, thoughts, ideas, in fact all the products of consciousness . . . an independence*"' (Sayer, 1989, p. 86; *ital.* Marx, 1846, p. 30 – with Sayer's emphasis).

Sayer, *pace* Marx, argues that the starting-point for analysis is 'the real living individuals themselves, and consciousness is considered solely as their consciousness' (Marx, 1846, p. 38, in Sayer, 1989, p. 86 – Marx's emphasis). Thus, Marx and Sayer advocate a social theory which does not separate consciousness from subjects. Sayer summarizes the two moments, or phases, within idealist theorizing in the following way: 'Idealism's historical subjects are constituted by *first* abstracting, *then* reifying what is in face merely a predicate – consciousness – of real subjects' (ibid, my emphasis). The same double movement can also be found in idealist thinking about social institutions and social collectivities. Conceptions about, say, education, are uncritically derived from 'education as known' by those who live in a particular society. Then (Stage Two), these conceptions become reified so that the thinker talks about 'the education system' and 'training' and then attempts to 'conceptually articulate' their relationship(s). Reading Hatcher's (1995, 1996) criticisms of the learning society concept it seems that something like this has occurred in the work of Ranson (1994), where the latter talks about the relations between 'learning', 'the learning society', 'citizenship', 'agency', 'self-creation' and so forth – largely in abstraction from key features of capitalist society. These key features *are* discussed at length in Ranson, 1994, *prior* to a discussion of determinate features of the learning society in the final chapter. On Sayer's analysis, Ranson effects the idealist sundering of the examination of forms of sociality and historical development from 'consciousness'; the careful analysis of social and educational trends fails to connect with the conceptual framework in the last chapter of *Towards the Learning Society*.

Before moving on to explore educational idealism it is worth briefly mentioning moral or ethical idealism, as some conceptions of the learning society incorporate this strain of idealism. Idealism in the 'moral' or ethical sense also involves the separation of 'the ideal' from social reality, but in a slightly different form from the idealist-as-social-theorist account presented above. On McCarthy's account of idealist ethics, the first moment is the same as with our previous account. The second moment involves the *imposition* of 'ideals' by the theorist, working within theoretical space, upon individuals and whole societies as 'objects' within theory. In this way 'ideals are disembodied forms that are abstracted from existence and *imposed* upon individuals from the outside' (McCarthy, 1994, p. 308, my emphasis). This is the case with some aspects of learning society discourse. Individuals are placed under a moral imperative *to learn*! The government's strategy on lifetime learning (DfEE, 1996b) comes close to this; failure to become a 'lifetime learner' means that the quality of British labour-power is lower than it might have been had learning opportunities been taken up – to the detriment of British capital and national economic well-being. The learning society 'learning imperative' also becomes a form of ethical idealism; it is seen as something we *ought* to strive to attain. Many of the conceptions of the learning society explored in the first section were concerned with breaking down barriers to learning, making learning more accessible, more student-centred and so on. Who could possibly be *against* these things? At the extreme, who could be against a *learning* society? The concept carries a huge moral depth charge within it. *In extremis*, to argue against the 'learning society' could be construed as simultaneously arguing *for* ignorance and/ or against 'learning' – or at least for downgrading learning in relation to other activities.

This might seem to be a strength of the learning society concept. That is, whilst it is clearly possible to argue that Britain or some other society cannot make the *practical* movement towards becoming a learning society (because of cultural and social factors), or, more modestly, that a particular society is not, in fact, moving along a learning society trajectory (or it is – but only at a snail's pace), it is quite another thing to suggest that the learning society is somehow *undesirable* as a 'goal' or as a social trajectory. The totalitarian ethic involved here is that to argue against the learning society exposes the antagonist to the charge that, if they 'care' about education and learning, then they cannot, consistently, argue against the learning society, a society which places 'learning at the centre'. The moral depth-charge of the learning society concept is its totalitarian form of idealist ethic, which explodes whenever a hapless theorist attempts to question the desirability of a society where learning is at the heart of all social relations, institutions and social development

A key feature of idealist thought, as summarized above, is its *conceptual distance* from a consideration of concrete social processes within society. In its most acute form, Sayer–Marx's Stage Two, there is no attempt at sustained and sober analysis of the society within which a reified 'theoretical object' – such as the 'learning society' – is being theorized. The concepts 'take on a life of their own' and the problem becomes one of *externally* relating them (how does 'education' relate to 'training', for example) through a forced conceptual analysis (conceptual common-alities, differences, logical relations) in *abstraction* from social relations, processes and practices.

## Educational idealism

Kevin Harris (1994) has provided a comprehensive account of idealist thinking as it is encountered in educational research and theory. Harris's work on idealism in educational theory is a useful staging post for an assessment of conceptions of the learning society as specifically idealist concoctions. The fundamental aspect of educational idealism, argues Harris, is that it 'denies, ignores, misconceptualizes, and renders unproblematic certain important factors about the real world of daily experience and practice' (p. 10). It abstracts from, and then leaves behind, material existence as lived and breathed by people in capitalist society. Harris locates five major aspects which relate to this general observation about educational idealism:

1 It assumes (implicitly or explicitly) an atomistic stance to social relations where actors within the education system (especially teachers) appear as free, autono-mous individual agents (p. 10).
2 It conflates concrete social institutions with abstract ideals – e.g. schooling with education – which mystifies the functions of the former (p. 11).
3 It concenctrates on abstract notions such as 'democracy', 'equality' and 'personal autonomy' whilst suggesting either that the society and institutions under scrutiny are actually 'democratic' and 'egalitarian' and so on, or (less reprehen-sibly) that they have the *potential* to become so without fundamentally altering the social relations of society – typically through offering distributive justice *within* these social relations (pp. 11–12).
4 Educational idealism 'exhorts moral and intellectual prescriptions which have a nice ring to them and read well as a projection of what things might be like in the best of all possible worlds.' Yet 'These same prescriptions ... can emerge as empty rhetoric in particular social conditions and historical periods' (p. 12).
5 Idealist educational theory relies on a-historic accounts of human nature and social development in 'attempting to justify its observations and conclusions' (pp. 12–13).

Harris provides an account of how educational idealism emanates from the 'legacy of Plato'. This account shows how Plato's idealism (through such constructs as the educational philosophy of Hirst and Peters in England) informed educa-tional theory, discourse and research up to the 1960s. Harris then charts the various reactions and adaptations to this idealist educational theory which challenged the idea that 'education was the essence of schooling' (pp. 21–34). He feels that he is on safe ground when he argues that idealism has 'provided the background and basic presuppositions for most past and contemporary educational theory and practice' (p. 8). Such a theory, argues Harris, can be comforting and attractive to teachers and educational theorists in times of relative social advancement, such as the post-war boom era, as capitalism appears to offer some genuine opportunities for greater autonomy, more democracy and equality (p. 19). However, in the harsh economic climate of the mid-1970s onwards, idealist educational theory appears to have become increasingly out of synch with what society can offer. The failure to develop a materialist alternative leaves a clear path for nihilistic, cynical, retro and absurd social-theoretical constructions (postmodernism) to fill the gap. As Cole and Hill (1995) put it, theoretical 'games of despair' and radical posturing within theoretical space become attractive alternatives in these hard times.

Harris's general observation on educational idealism – that it 'renders unproblematic certain important factors about the real world of daily experience and practice' – can be viewed as a background to Hatcher's (1995, 1996) critique of the learning society. For Hatcher, appeals to create a 'learning society' stumble over two key features of capitalism.

First, there is its *class* basis – where abstract idealist talk about 'the learner' and a 'society of active learners' founders on the fundamental organizing principle of capitalist society: 'production for profit in the market, to which everything else is subordinate' and which generates 'social classes with conflicting interests' (Hatcher, 1996, p. 46) – and with *opposed* and different relationships to 'learning'.

Second, idealist appeals to the concept of individual *agency* founder on inequalities in power. Hatcher (1996, pp. 48–51) argues that only *class agency* can make inroads into class *equality*. The reluctance of learning society theorists to relate the learning society concept to capitalist social realities cannot evade points 3 and 4 in Harris's outline of some of the specifics of idealist theorizing.

## THE 'LEARNING SOCIETY' AND IDEALIST EDUCATIONAL DISCOURSE

Some of the specific aspects of idealist educational discourse, as they surface within conceptions of the learning society, will now be explored. These are:

a The utopian element in much theorizing on the learning society – theorizing which degenerates into an ideology (Ainley, 1994b);

b the normative aspects of some conceptions of the learning society;

c how conceptions of the learning society can be viewed as ungrounded abstractions;

d how the learning society concept can be viewed as simultaneously unhistorical and 'survivalist', summarized as: society 'X' exists; therefore, collective/individual learning must have taken place in order for it to exist; hence, as long as it exists it must be a 'learning society';

e and, finally, how the learning society concept becomes endist and absolutist when set within a teleology involving a social statics as its end-point.

## Utopia to ideology

A number of writers (Ainley, 1994b; Edwards, 1995b; Young, 1995b) have pointed to a strong utopian strain running through conceptions of the learning society. As Olson (1982) has argued, utopianism – the process of rendering fictional, idealized worlds into finished forms or 'blueprints' within text and other forms of discourse – is 'the search for the good pattern of life in an a-historical cosmos.' (p. 143). This last point is highly significant, as conceptions of the learning society seem to be suspended above and beyond time, for they typically fail to temporally locate this transcendent form of society. To posit the learning society as a 'society of the future' without showing the dynamic through which it could develop out of presently existing capitalist society makes it nothing short of an act of faith.

Olson (1982) notes that the process of unveiling a utopia can be perceived primarily as a rational process for 'the best pattern of life is rational and is discovered rationally', and thus it 'is the result of a human penetration of the plane of eternal truth' (pp. 143–4). Idealist proponents of the learning society could argue that it is not so much a utopia but more an 'ideal type', and hence the significance of critera (Ranson, 1992) for judging the extent to which a society is progressing towards, or regressing away from, the ideal. There is nothing new in this stance. This is the way that classical utopians have viewed the situation, argues Olson (p. 145).

As a utopia the learning society falls into three forms. First, in classical utopian fashion, the learning society becomes a new form of society altogether (Hayes *et al.*, 1995). It transcends capitalism; thus, a *transformation* from capitalism to the new society becomes essential.

Second, many of the conceptions of the learning society pose a quasi-Nietzschean 'eternal return of the same' (capitalism) but with an enhanced emphasis on knowledge/skill/competence attainment and the drive to enhance *human* – as opposed to other – forms of capital. Here, there is no question of *transcending* capitalism at all. Movement towards a new form of capitalism might be posited – through the neutered concepts of globalization (Edwards, 1995b) for example – or the democratization of capitalism (Ranson, 1994) might be on offer. But capitalism remains the centre of gravity around which these versions revolve, and, in this sense, they degenerate into apologetics, holding out false hopes of a *capitalism as Learning Utopia*. A number of writers in recent years (Brosio, 1994; Carnoy and Levin, 1985; Wood, 1995) have pointed to the essential antagonisms between democracy and capital. Within this bifurcation, some versions of the learning society (the 'learning market' model in Edwards, 1995b, for example) show how it becomes eternally encased within a capitalist framework. In this guise it partially becomes a *retropia*. This involves appealing to general features of a crude, unregulated, de-statized, unreconstructed, pure and hyper-competitive, socially atomized and individualized capitalism which harks back to a mythical 'golden age' of capital. This *retro* moment is then overlaid with rhetoric about individual-ized learning, the application of computer technology, the need for lifetime learning and so on, which gives these versions of the learning society some appeal beyond the boardroom and corporate culture, and something to whet the appetites of radical educationalists.

Third (in Ranson, 1992, for example), there is a kind of agnosticism where the learning society is largely theorized without raising the question of the form (as opposed to abstract stipulations about institutional arrangements) of society necessary for its realization. Although those taking this position make many criticisms of current education and training provision, democratic forms and business culture, nevertheless the issue of the learning society as a celebration of capital or its transcendence is left alone. The learning society becomes a free-floating utopia.

The second type of 'learning society as Utopia', its capitalist celebratory form, is the most interesting. First, this is because it is the dominant form in terms of its salience within policy debates (Edwards, 1995b, p. 187). Second, as it celebrates capital and poses the resolution of its contradictions and tensions it degenerates into an ideology (Ainley, 1994b). Its utopian element – that capitalism in its 'learning society' form abolishes class conflict and inequalities – has been high-lighted by Young (1995b). Young argues that the emphasis on skill ownership and education and training markets provokes a vision of society where formally equal, free and skill-seeking individuals spend a lifetime of learning in a social formation where social divisions are not based on ownership of property and wealth. Skill-and knowledge-seeking and competence-enhancement within individuals ground the new forms of social division (p. 3). In this model, some purely self-interested and self-serving individuals will gain more or better – i.e. marketable – skills than others. But that, following the ideological flow, will be either through good or bad luck, judgement or display of (market) responsibilty (through doing the 'right' subjects, gaining the most marketable skills). It is at this point that the ideological attraction of the concept of the 'learning society' becomes most clear for those in currently dominant positions within contemporary capitalism, for 'As an ideology it provides a justification for inequalities by masking the extent to which modern societies, as well as depending on the population's knowledge and skills, are also based on inequalities of power and wealth' (Young, 1995b, p. 3).

This is especially so for the 'market' models or versions of the learning society. As Ranson (1993b) has noted, although all are formally free and equal within the market, nevertheless the acts of exchange within it mask differences in the degree of social power the exchanging participants possess (p. 72). The market reproduces inequalities which consumers and producers bring to the marketplace (ibid). The utopian vision of lifelong learners subsuming their wills under the imperative to enhance their market and earning power through frenzied activity in learning markets also glosses over the question of whether the gains of this activity are equal for capital and labour. In effect, the utopian strand within the 'market model' of the learning society is based on a wishing away of some aspects of capitalism (class division, social inequalities and power differentials) whilst cele-brating and highlighting others (the independence, self-investment and continual restless and manic skill-enhancement, knowledge-induction and competence development of 'learners'). It is 'capitalism without tears'.

Kumar (1995) has argued that Utopia is not mainly about 'providing detailed blueprints for social reconstruction' (p. 219). Rather, reflecting upon utopias performs the function of making us think about social possibilities, possible types of world and social existence. Utopias are about 'educating our desires' in ways which make us think about social life as lived now. This interpretation of the notion of Utopia can pose serious questions about the nature of society without proposing some idealist blueprint as ultimate goal, argues Kumar. However, strong proponents of the 'market' view of the learning society would no doubt find this position too weak, as the imperative to compete on the international stage through enhancing the nation's human capital stock takes on a greater urgency than using the learning society concept as a springboard for the critique of capitalism.

### Normative theory without political agency

The theory of the learning society involves a number of normative aspects which place it within an ethical idealist framework. First, its proponents view it as a better form of society towards which we, as rational humans, ought to work. Second, some of the specific elements of various forms of the learning society are taken as intrinsically good things which we should all work towards – for example, lifelong learning. Third, normative goals, such as enhancing the competitiveness of the economy, are frequently embedded within conceptions of the learning society.

These normative aspects are typically transformed into a form of idealism, as they rarely connect with theorizations of actually existing capitalist society in terms of their realization. They become normative goals suspended above society as constituted today. Political programmes, regarding how we get to a learning society from where we are now, are avoided. Thus the question of political agency, of which social and political forces will create the learning society, also becomes problematic.

An example given by Edwards (1995b) brings out many of the normative questions left hanging by theorists of the learning society. Drawing upon the work of Ranson (1994), where there is an emphasis on the conditions making for creative wealth accumulation, active learning leading to 'self-realization', community involvement (especially at the local level) and liberal democratic forms of citizenship, Edwards shows how these normative goals become cast adrift from social reality:

> [For Ranson] ... The learning society is both a condition for and an outcome of participation in liberal democratic societies. What is left unspecified is the precise nature of the forms of participation and by whom. Lifelong education is to support that learning and participation. The emphasis is highly normative, apparently divorced from an analysis of the specifics of power in the social formation. Its emphasis is on the provision of education, very much situated within a view of the assumed inherent worth of liberal education.
>
> (p. 188)

In calling for the specifics regarding the institutions, forms of participation on so on, which he, Edwards, believes Ranson has omitted, Edwards is, in effect, calling for a blueprint of the learning society. However, making this move takes us from one form of idealism to another. Edwards is calling for utopian specifications from Ranson. On the other hand, Ranson explores the social conditions, institutions and education and training reforms which must be put in place if there is to be movement *towards* the learning society at considerable length in *Management for the Public Domain* (with Stewart, 1994). Given the significance of the open and democratic nature of the *concrete* institutions in Ranson's vision of the learning society, it would be inappropriate to set its form with detailed precision.

What Edwards's example points to, though, is that notions of the learning society, theorized in abstraction from capitalist society, become primarily normative constructions. As forms of idealism the 'ideals' (such as liberal education) are essentially contestable.


**Ungrounded abstraction**

The concept of the 'learning society' as opposed to, say, 'feudalism' or 'capitalism', can be seen as an essentially indeterminate concept. In effect the ESRC (1994) asked researchers interested in doing work on its Learning Society Programme to write research proposals aimed at studying a *society which did not exist*. The learning society concept is an 'ungrounded abstraction'. Rikowski (1994) has demonstrated how the concept of 'modernisation' (in relation to the sociology of development and educational theory) is also an essentially ungrounded abstraction. It is impossible to 'fix' the concept ontologically in terms of any actual social processes, social forms or sets of institutional arrangements. As Rikowski explains, '"Modernisation" is an ungrounded abstraction as it refers to nothing over-and-above social processes and change that can be described in other . . . [and better: GR] ways' (p. 84). Thus, 'modernisation' is an ungrounded abstraction in a second sense, as it is arbitrary and redundant, for other concepts (calling on capitalist social forms and processes) can *explain* socio-economic developments in contemporary society more adequately. To stamp out social and educational processes as instances of 'modernisation' merely involves a forced and impressionistic labelling process, what Sayer (1989) would call 'violent abstraction'. It labels certain social developments as 'modernising' ones without exposing the social dynamic of the movement of social forms (temporally, spatially and transformationally).

The concept of the 'learning society' is also an ungrounded abstraction. All societies 'learn' in some minimalist way – both collectively, and individuals within them. The idealism here results from the fact that the basic concept of the 'learning society' *can* be detached from all (possible) societies. In itself, it is not embedded within any particular form or type of previous or present society. It is temporally and spatially detached. Attempts to 'fix' *this* concept, as previously seen, lead to either a utopia or an apologia (for capitalist social forms). Or, alternatively, it can be fixed as a set of ideals, goals and norms – but then its relations with existing social reality must in turn be fixed (in a non-teleological fashion) if it is to move beyond being a moral imperative or pious hope. It is hard to escape the idealist whirlpool.

### Unhistorical and 'survivalist'

The previous section points to the inherently *unhistorical* nature of the concept of 'learning society', its temporal promiscuity. Readings of Nietzsche's early works might lead the reader to conclude that the 'learning society' was alive and well thousands of years ago in ancient Greece. As the 'learning society' has not been theorized in relation to capitalism in any systematic way, then it becomes an unanchored, floating theory in relation to the *now*. This also makes its *future* relationship to capitalism problematic, as the limits to the learning society within capitalism have not been set. A-historicism is a key feature of idealist theory, as we saw earlier. Materialist theories, on the other hand, situate social phenomena within specific forms of society, particular social formations; phenomena are provided with historical roots, whilst at the same time their forward infinity is denied (as the fundamental nature of the social formation may change). Ranson (1994) has indicated that the 'marketisation' of education and training is a serious threat to the development of the learning society as the market places 'collective welfare beyond the reach of public deliberation, choice and action' (p. 98). Markets systematically undermine the participative, *collective* and democratic aspects of Ranson's vision of the learning society. It could be argued, that, in the British context, the marketization of education and other public services too is increasing and hence, in some respects, we are getting further away from any 'learning society'. This seems to start to frame discussion of the learning society within a discernible social formation: capitalism. However, this is misleading, as discussion about the 'market' itself tends not to be solidly based within a theorization of capitalist totality. The market is an old institution. The Greeks had markets. Thus, talk about 'the market' (and this is common within educational discourse) becomes divorced and dislocated from an overall analysis of markets in capitalism.

The opposite pole to a-historicism in discourse about the learning society is *survivalism*. Unless the concept of 'learning society' can be grounded in terms of the trajectory and development of existing society, then there is nothing to stop the malicious theorist from applying 'learning society' to all previous societies on the basis that they survived *as* societies – so they must, collectively, have learnt something. All societies *necessarily* 'learn'. Without grounding the 'learning society' in the form of society we have now – capitalism – then it appears that it can be everywhere or nowhere in temporal terms.

### Teleology, endism and absolutism

In the light of what has been said so far, one refuge for an idealist version of the learning society might be teleology. It could be held that the learning society is a fixed, end-state, phenomenon towards which we are moving. When the learning society is finally reached, it attains an absolutist form; at a certain point in time the learning society will *be* whereas previously it *was not*. Accepting this position is a desperate way of trying to break out of, or to transcend, the idealist whirlpool.

Whilst no theorist of the learning society takes on such an extreme position as that outlined above, nevertheless, there has been weaker talk of a 'need' or 'imperative' (Howard, 1990) to create such a society, either in order to compete more effectively on the economic stage – as in the 'market' conceptions of the learning society – or as part of a process of regenerating a tired, centralized and bureaucratic democracy (Ranson, 1992, p. 75). However, these weaker versions collapse into a normative form of the argument for a learning society, bringing ethical idealism in its wake. This is because perceived 'needs' for – or imperatives to create – a learning society must be justified as societal aims. The idealist nature of this enterprise is only cut short when the justification comes to rest upon unassailable moral values and principles, which, if we live in a 'postmodern age' with its associated 'relativism' and neo-Nietzschean 'perspectivism', will no doubt be difficult to establish. Idealism is hard on conceptions of the learning society.

## CONCLUSION: OUT OF THE WET AND INTO THE DRY?

The set of problems for conceptions of the learning society encountered within the idealist whirlpool as delineated above seem debilitating. However, given the general reluctance to see the learning society in materialist, historical and form-determined ways, then idealist versions are set fair for predominance. The self-enforcing nature of the idealist whirlpool is its deadliest consequence; through attempting to banish one type of idealist problem the theorist is often hurled into another one. Idealist theorists of the learning society should be left to their own whirligig theorizing. It would seem that there is no breaking of the watery circle, only its complete dissolution through adopting a materialist approach towards the learning society. A materialist theory of the learning society at least holds out the promise of a new form of society emerging out of existing capitalist society. However, as the companion paper to this chapter shows (Rikowski, forthcoming), the dangers for the learning society from materialism are at least as great as they are from idealism. A possible route between idealism and materialism may well exist, however, but this path rests upon a particular perspective on *social becoming* which will be explored in Rikowski and Ranson (forthcoming). Otherwise, it seems that supporters, promoters and protagonists of the learning society are in for double trouble – either Charybdis or Scylla.

## NOTES

1 This body of work will be explored in Rikowski and Ranson (forthcoming)

# Chapter 19

# On the Myth of the Learning Society

*Michael Strain and John Field*

## INTRODUCTION

Projections of a learning society mount a powerful challenge to conventional ideas of education. At the same time, they draw on and are developed through a critical account of existing education systems (Ranson, 1994). As a project, therefore, the learning society, is probably a good example of an inherently contestable concept. Its significance seems to lie in the recognition that the social demand for learning is spread across the life span; that the learning challenges characteristic of late modernity frequently do not arise in a simplistic and linear fashion in accordance with age or stage of life; and that the social contexts for learning encompass a wide and increasingly complex range of settings and processes. In their recent article 'The Myth of the Learning Society', Hughes and Tight (1995) seem to misdirect their criticism of the learning society. Social life and the historical dilemmas confronted there are much too complex to be illuminated by reduction to a series of unexamined dualisms: between myth and rationality, between individual and community, between structure and agency. Though Hughes and Tight appear to accept the pervasive and influential operation of myth in social processes, and base their arguments on a concern for the autonomy of individuals within working and learning communities, they end up almost endorsing the economistic perspective on social life which they oppose. Given the contemporary condition of societal dissolution and the historical tendency of educational institutions to resist pressures for social change, it is surely premature to ask 'What comes after the learning society?' Yet this is precisely how Hughes and Tight conclude their paper.

The path by which Hughes and Tight reach this quizzical conclusion can be briefly summarized. Conceding the widespread interest in the idea of a learning society as an answer to many contemporary ills, they combine a call for critical caution with a treatment of the learning society as 'a modern day myth'. In turn, the learning society myth, they argue, rests on two previous 'levels or stages of myth development': it makes use of the myths of productivity and change from the first stage/level and builds on the myths of lifelong education and the learning organization from the second. The consequence is 'an unhappy and unstable compromise' between vocationalism and individual/community growth, based on 'an alliance between state, professions and capital' which will tend to push individual self-development to one side. In practice, Hughes and Tight believe that the learning society myth is harmful. It assumes relations between learning and well-being which deny the possibility of other, more effective solutions to our ills; there is a mismatch between the rhetoric and the actual levels of participation in adult learning, so that the idea of a learning society lacks empirical validity. The myth functions to disguise the real interests and intentions of the powerful.

Theirs, then, is potentially a highly destructive critique. If we accept its premises and logic, the idea of a learning society must be abandoned as having little but harm to bring to the project of human emancipation through education. In what follows, we first examine critically the use made by Hughes and Tight of the four 'myths' upon which the learning society is said to build. Subsequently, an alternative rationale is explored, exposing implications for learning in the concept of an emergent 'risk' society.

## PRODUCTIVITY

Not all imperfectly rational social discourse should be categorized as myth. Hughes and Tight conflate myth with ideology, a more insidious form of distortion of discourse, frequently exploited by social groups exercising a privileged grip on power. Much public rhetoric depends for its persuasiveness on exploitation of self-evident 'realities' masquerading as truths. Productivity is not a myth, but an enduring empirical concept employed, amongst others, by economists. Much economic theory is itself a form of rhetoric (McLoskey, 1983, pp. 481–517). For example, neo-classical economics has popularized the notion of Man the Maximizer – a rational agent who can be relied upon to choose the course of action best suited to secure his or her individual interests. This process of popularization was assisted almost from the outset by the notion's loose association with a general misunderstanding of Darwins's theory of natural selection.

Darwinian adaptationism attempts to explain how events in the natural world took place; it is a 'because' theory. Scientists (rightly) eschew teleological explanations, refusing to concern themselves with what things 'are for'. But human beings in general

> are forever wanting to know what things are for, and we don't like having to take Nothing for an answer. That gives us a wonderful head start on understanding the psychology of ourselves and our conspecifics, but it is one of the (no doubt many) respects in which we aren't kinds of creatures ideally equipped for doing natural science.
>
> (Fodor, 1996, pp. 19–20)

Neoclassical economics was influenced by the powerful and wide-ranging explanatory capability of this general 'because' theory and used it to account for the organization and behaviour of markets. Later still, spurred on by the hope of its predictive capabilities, the logical form of the 'because' theory was adapted to become a functional ('what for') theory of individual as well as collective forms of human motivation, exhibited in the behavioural responses of the Skinnerian 'reward seeker' and the neoclassical economist's rational, maximizing consumer. In this way, the concept of productivity derives from a more general model of calculating, self-interested human action. Though inadequate as a characterization of human endeavour, it still has a value as a basis for information gathering, appraisal and policy-making. With limited explanatory and predictive power, it has been, for particular investigative and planning purposes, a useful concept and heuristic tool of empirical research.

## CHANGE

Hughes and Tight are surely right to be sceptical about widespread assumptions regarding the irreversibility and pervasiveness of contemporary change. It is arguable that the social changes (demographic, technical, political, social), which were widespread by 1850, following the first wave of industrialization (1780–1830), were more radical and affected a greater proportion of the population in European countries than those brought about by the development of information technology (IT) since 1970. But change is not just, in Fodor's terms, an *as if* concept to be used for purposes of prediction upon the basis of rightly specified hypothetical conditions. Here Hughes and Tight appear to confuse analytical, historical and sociological uses of the same term. Following Kant, 'change' may be considered as an absolute entity, an inherent concomitant of 'time', analytically (Giddens, 1995, p. 17) separable from, but co-ordinate with space (and place). But 'change' is also an aspect of the human experience of nature and of social life, deriving from awareness of our own mortality and historical understanding of the human condition. Additionally, it is intrinsic to our capability as agents to imagine and act purposively, in pursuit of imagined, feasible, future states (Shackle, 1979). Finally, and more particularly in the modern era, 'change' may be understood as social process, as the phenomenon of 'detraditionalisation', that decisive shift which is one of the primary characteristics of modernity.

Husén (1974) and others have subsequently portrayed IT as one of a number of closely related changes that have destabilized the family in its role as (traditional) agency of primary socialization. Others include the growth of personal consumption and the transfer of domestic labour from the 'gift' to the 'exchange' economy (Gorz, 1989, pp. 47, 156). These in turn destabilize the school in its (modern) role of secondary socialization. On these grounds they believe that there is a *radical and irreversible* discontinuity in the nature of learning challenges emerging in late modern society. Of interest here too is Elster's (1983) discussion of Neo-classical, Schumpeterian, Evolutionary and Marxist theories of change, where he reverts in several places to a view of change as accidental, 'qualitative and discontinuous' and to be distinguished from dissemination which proceeds by small, adaptive steps:

> [Innovation] is that kind of change arising from within the system which so displaces its equilibrium point that the new one cannot be reached from the old one by infinitesimal steps. Add successively as many mail coaches as you please, you will never get a railway thereby.
>
> (Schumpter, 1934, p. 64)

Projections (by Husén, Ranson and others) of a learning society assume that the introduction and dissemination of information technology *does* entail that kind of radical discontinuity with past practices and requires consequential changes in the composition, characteristic mode of delivery and distribution of learning opportunities. If this premise is accepted, it is hard to see the significance of objections raised by Hughes and Tight under this heading. There is nothing deterministic in the assumptions underlying the learning society.

## MYTH IN CONTEMPORARY SOCIETY

Though Husén's (1974, p. 230) 'Illustrative exercise' (*räkneexempel*), based upon the research programmes drawn upon extensively in his book *The Learning Society*, has not yet materialized, there is no cause to obstruct such developments by mislabelling a 'model of the future educational system' as myth. Myths are both necessary (Anderson, 1983) and dangerous (Strain, 1995); they are pervasive in contemporary societies (Meyer and Rowan, 1978, pp. 340–63). The growth of 'organization' in post-industrial societies has led to faster and more widespread creation of 'rationalizing myths' essential for economic growth and stability and a minimum level of acceptable public order:

> Many of the positions, policies, programmes, and procedures of modern organizations are enforced by public opinion, by the views of important constituents, by knowledge legitimated through the educational system, by social prestige, by the laws, and by the definitions of negligence and prudence used by the courts. Such elements of formal structure are manifestations of powerful institutional rules which function as highly rationalised myths that are binding on particular organizations.
>
> (Meyer and Rowan, 1978, p. 343)

Rationality itself is frequently exploited for sectional purposes and mythologized. Its rule-guided and universalizing attributes (so illuminating upon questions of equity and justice) are given strong public emphasis – what, in principle, could be more fair and socially beneficial than a policy of 'targeting' social security 'scroungers' or ensuring that all schools are funded by a generally applicable formula? Schools themselves, formerly mythologized as 'gardens' supporting and developing organic forms of individual and community life, are now, post-local management of schools (LMS), delivery centres governed by mechanisms and, increasingly, norms concerned with efficiency and effectiveness. However, rationality's weaker and ancillary relation to questions involving moral choice, which must consider consequences, is given less attention. In the moral sphere, exercise of personal autonomy claims the possibility of absolution (Bauman, 1993, p. 60) from the calculating and controlling hand of means-end rationality. It is just such a prioritization of what is calculable and universalizable in schooling that has precipitated a tendency to deprofessionalize teachers (Ozga, 1995, pp. 21–37; Hargreaves, 1994) and brought us nearer to fulfilment of Weber's pessimistic forecast of a world in which material progress crushes individual creativity and autonomy (Giddens, 1990, p. 7)

The autonomy of teachers in the British context has been progressively removed by the imposition of centrally specified curriculum and assessment procedures. The full force of this new imposition has been partially obscured by the parallel decentralization of detailed financial control. LMS has detached schools from a diminished public domain and introduced a process of marketization by delegation of entrepreneurial freedom to senior staff who may now manage resources and attract pupils in a quasi-market driven by parental choice among competing institutions. Publicly financed rights of entry are increasingly being supplemented by private parental resources (Levacic, 1995, pp. 157–8). These developments are legitimized publicly (and receive considerable support from individual practitioners) in a rhetorical discourse which parades shallow governmental jargon (DfE, 1992) as the markers for unassailable public verities and universally desirable social goods. No clearer example need be sought of the workings of ideology to secure institutional change, pungently typified by Eagleton (1991, pp. 4–5) as a phenomenon of discourse where:

> A dominant power may legitimate itself by *promoting beliefs* and values congenial to it; naturalising *and universalising* such beliefs to render them self-evident and apparently inevitable; *denigrating* ideas which might challenge it: *excluding* rival forms of thought.

The deprofessionalization of teaching and the de-publicization of schooling are morally, politically and educationally objectionable acts. Both exemplify in the educational sphere loss of individual autonomy resulting from exploitatin of 'traditional' social values which provide convenient ideological cover for the furtherance of functionalist and socially instrumental policies. Yet the grounds for securing their reversal must be argued on a stronger basis than generalized pleadings about loss of professional autonomy or the insidious nature of social myth when expropriated by 'an alliance between the interests of educators, employers and politicians' (Hughes and Tight, 1995, p. 302). As Gray has so incisively argued (Gray, 1996, p. 54), 'We cannot restore a seamless monoculture animated by the liberal ideal of "autonomy"'. Exactly the same could be said of traditional beliefs about the rights of parents and teachers as well as our inherited concepts of 'community', whether embodied in localities or in 'the community of educated people' (Pring, 1995, pp. 125–45).

## CONCERN FOR THE INDIVIDUAL AND THE COMMUNITY

This seems to be the main impetus of concern underlying Hughes and Tight's paper. They acknowledge the need which the learning society recognizes for 'the effective development and availability of all human resources' and for 'the growth of the individual and the community' (Hughes and Tight, 1995, p. 297). Yet they claim to see behind these objectives 'an unhappy compromise' masking an unholy 'alliance' between powerful interests 'likely to marginalise [those] of the individual in pursuing learning for their own self-fulfilment'. Hughes and Tight seem here to be protecting a much older myth or ideological construct, one which postulates the individual as monadic, whose moral autonomy is inalienable but may be enhanced by social conditions which encourage the pursuit of learning for its own sake, unrelated to the needs of society or the requirement to sustain individual practical life. The four 'myths' attacked by Hughes and Tight for their contribution to the learning society proposition evoke two underlying concepts regarding the nature of human experience: the presuppositions that individual conscious life is socially constructed and that it is irradiated by change. These assumptions are, in their view, tarnished and by implication made unsafe by having been adopted at some time by 'both totalitarian and liberal regimes'.

Plato also gave those concepts a severe mauling in his arguments for an ideal, liberal model of knowledge and learning, one appropriate to the 'good' life and unhampered by materialistic encumbrances. For Plato, the *polis* was, at best, a necessary evil and change synonymous with decay; only 'the good', embodied in unchanging forms, remained constant amid the inherently decadent processes of change with which all material and organic life is suffused:

> For if the starting point of all change is perfect and good, then change can only be a movement that leads away from the perfect and the good; it must be directed towards the imperfect and the evil, towards corruption.
>
> (Popper, 1966, p. 36)

In their conceptual allegiances Hughes and Tight seem to take sides with Plato and to oppose Aristotle's contrasting formulation of the inescapably political and social foundation of 'all worth-while human existence'. His conception of the *polis* makes it the central, formative institution of social life, the hallmark of humanity: 'Man is by nature an animal intended to live in a *polis*. He who is without a *polis* . . . is either a poor sort of being or a being higher than man (Popper, 1966, p. 6). Aristotle's advocacy of practical wisdom (*phronesis*) underpins the work of Ranson (1992, pp. 68–79; 1994) which has provided some of the intellectual foundations from which the 1995 ESRC initiative has sprung, a project centrally concerned with complex issues of community, individual capabilites and political and economic participation. It is surprising that Hughes and Tight have not drawn on Ranson's work. Ranson projects conditions in which a good society is secured through harnessing the reflexive capabilities of individual agents, empowered and encouraged to discover and enhance their moral identity as persons in and through their commitment to others and face-to-face participation in the life of a local community (Ranson, 1992, pp. 76—7). These relations and their local institutionalization become the *raison d'être* and object of care for all larger units of social organization which promote the ordering and political direction of society. The values and practices which might sustain these bonds are now threatened more directly by globalizing pressures to solitarize the individual (Bauman, 1994) than by any speculative or theoretical formulations embedded in the learning society 'project'.

## IS ANYTHING CHANGING?

If we abandon the sharp separation of myth from reality as our conceptual foundation, then one obvious question is whether the learning society project is indeed no more than a cloak for self-interest. Empirically, it is relatively easy to provide evidence of a significant societal shift towards patterns of lifelong learning. For example, following a national survey in 1995 the US Department of Education estimated that some 76 million Americans had taken part in at least one adult education activity during the previous twelve months. At 40 per cent of the adult population, this represents substantial growth from the 32 per cent level reported in a similar survey in 1991, which in turn indicated an equally remarkable and sustained rise since the early 1980s (Kim *et al.*, 1995, p. 4). UK figures are not sufficiently comprehensive for a direct comparison with the US surveys. Nevertheless, the evidence available to us does seem to be congruent with the hypothesis of a general rise in learning during adult life. Thus Alison Park (1994) notes that the proportion of employers reporting recent participation in adult learning activities in 1994 at 60 per cent, represents a substantial rise since the Training in Britain survey was undertaken in the mid-1980s. Labour Force survey data are also consistent with this general view, as are Family Expenditure survey findings on the average family spending on education and training costs. Resting on more substantial research evidence, Albert Tuijnman (1996) has noted similar tendencies in European countries as culturally disparate as Turkey, Finland and France, reaching the somewhat optimistic conclusion that '[Adult] education is no longer seen in terms of social costs which must be minimised but as a strategic investment' (p. 36)

In so far as there appears to be a general and substantial growth in the scope and volume of adult learning in the advanced capitalist world, then we can speak of a significant shift in the direction of the learning society. Certainly this is evidence that is directly relevant to Hughes and Tight's critique, given their preoccupation with adult continuing education. Moreover, the increase appears to be fuelled in large part by precisely those concerns for individual growth which Hughes and Tight seek to define – a point we will return to later. But this is to accept too narrow and superficial a definition of the learning society. Husén's original preoccupation, remember, was with the need to renew and strengthen the traditional agencies of initial socialization (family and school) which he believed to be at risk from an uncontrolled explosion of alternative sources of information and know-how. Adult education, for Husén, was a desirable consequence of school reform. Henceforward, he proposed, the central mission of the school will be to teach the pupils to learn, to train them to assimilate new knowledge of their own (1974, p. 23).

Development since the early 1970s should have encouraged further reflection on the implications for schools (and family) of the forces which are prompting such rapid growth in learning later in the life span. In fact, the boundaries between initial socialization and adult learning are much as they were when Husén was writing *The Learning Society*. Peter Scott suggests in his study of mass higher education in the 1990s that the language of the learning society is significant because it suggests 'a growing affinity between hitherto incommensurate worlds' (Scott, 1995, p. 32). Yet though there have been striking and radical enlargements of the educational enterprise in non-educational settings, this developing affinity remains in its embryonic stages.

## LEARNING IN A 'RISK' SOCIETY

New societal strategies for individual learning are predicated on the need to preserve human and social values in the face of certain irreversible social re-figurations, leading to the institutionalization of what Giddens has termed 'manufactured uncertainty' and the formation of what Beck (1994) has characterized as a 'risk' society, that is, one in which:

- time and space have been 'distanciated' by electronic mediation. The historical and local 'embeddedness' of individual life and experience have thereby been disjoined;
- face-to-face encounters among individuals and groups are increasingly replaced by depersonalized and electronically mediated encounters;
- historically obligated and locally practised relationships within communities are eroded and, in their place, exclusive commitments to 'pure' relationships between individuals are encouraged;
- in a complex and global social order, individual agents are increasingly required to place trust in symbolic tokens and expert systems, and to judge the sometimes conflicting and competing claims of different sets of symbols or groups of experts;
- the knowledge produced by the social sciences (including applied social sciences such as marketing, counselling, as well as education itself, of course) feeds back into actors' consciousness of their own situation, and is then used in reordering and reinterpreting their own thought and behaviour.

As a result, 'risk society' is characterized by a high level of 'institutionalised reflexivity' – a process of questioning and scrutiny that must touch all forms of social organization, including intimate relations and each person's sense of their own identity and biography. However, when traditional forms are defended not 'dialogically' but through use or threat of violence (within which should be included the fundamentalist's withdrawal from dialogue and independent assertion of 'irredeemable' truths) the legacy of the 'tradition' may become a 'relic', 'a memory-trace shorn of its collective framework' (Giddens, 1994c, p. 102). In the case of learning, it is possible that this trend may come to stifle demand for organized learning, except for those courses upheld as necessary by regulatory force or profitable by virtue of employer or market demands.

Another consequence of these tendencies has been to weaken the distinctiveness of the 'public domain', requiring representative institutions increasingly to be 'tasked' and organized as rival suppliers of commodities demanded by individuals (consumerism), and cause the processes of public policy formation to rely increasingly upon sampling (market surveys and opinion polls) and exit polls (buy/vote – yes/no), instead of evocation and expression of plural voices, to satisfy the requirements for popular participation in matters of public policy the 'Charter' and referendum mentality. Considered from the point of view of their social efficiency, these changes seem to lessen the need for individuals to learn, at least in any sense which implies the capability to introduce or create novelty, a seemingly under-examined aspect of competence-based education and training (Hutchinson, 1996). If citizens are expected merely to be responsive consumers and diligent enforcers of their chartered entitlements, a much more limited kind of learning will be necessary, sufficient to ensure 'prudent' responses to market-based and other signals.

The influence of consumer culture over education and training is pervasive. This influence is at its most visible at present in adult education and training – an area whose direct dependency on and stimulation of the learning market has grown markedly since the 1970s (Edwards 1995a; Field 1995). Increasingly, though, the marketization of the education system more generally has now led to a profound blurring of the boundaries between entertainment and learning. Many – not only postmodernists – have welcomed this development. Thus the UK government's Technology Foresight (1995, p. 40) panel on leisure and learning predicted a growing convergence between the two areas, for the following reasons:

- the same technologies will deliver both into the home;
- with more time out of work, leisure and learning will no longer be either/or choices; and
- providers are expanding into each other's territory.

This development, though, is hardly a simple or unproblematic one. For example, the director (Schank, 1994, p. 5) of the Institute for the Learning Sciences at Northwestern University has described how he attempts to design multimedia programmes for 'the student who would rather be home watching televison', leading to packages that 'impart incidental information while engaging the user in a fun and interesting task'. Such faith in the application of technological solutions to societal learning challenges is misplaced. At the very least, it begs a range of practical questions over the pedagogic approaches needed to support learning through technologies which are fungible as between education and other purposes, but whose primary social use is for play; it also risks, as the European Commission among others has noticed, the intensification of existing inequalities by creating a new inequality around the question of access to the new technologies. Yet the belief that boundaries between learning and other social practices such as leisure and work should become more blurred is an important aspect of the learning society literature.

However, Giddens' analysis points to a more fundamental threat arising from the diminution of the public domain and a corresponding reliance upon opportunism, entrepreneurship and objectified 'skill'. In traditional society, supported by belief in authority and idealized conceptions of good order, moral choice exposed the agent to possible implication in disorder, arising through loss of friends or family, or through exclusion from community and civic participation. Late modern society has lost the sureties which underwrote those social institutions and has become increasingly reliant upon concentrated formations and wide dissemination and deployment of technical expertise residing with 'experts'. The individual's scope for exercising moral choice becomes restricted to acquisition of knowledge to secure escape from meaninglessness, part of a search for personal confidence in the face of loss of identity as a 'self'. Ambiguity is coming to replace disorder as the threat precipitating moral choice; choosers must now reduce uncertainty by recourse to 'expert knowledge' and a calculation of identifiable costs and benefits so as to establish the measure of a knowable risk.

These phenomena of social change are directly related to Ranson's (1994) deprecation of what he sees as the retreat from public to private space. Ranson's prescription aims to establish conditions to fuller political participation and enhancement of the moral life of individuals, envisaging a learning society which will cultivate the necessary critical understandings and caring practices among both individuals and collectivities. Fraser (1995), in a perceptive theoretical treatment of pluralism and anti-discrimination policies, has argued that much more than prohibition and redistribution of opportunities is required. A plural society requires recognition of the equivalence of plural and competing value systems and identities which may derive from differences of gender, caste, religion or life-style. This emerging demand calls for a concerted policy on social learning. Accordingly, the learning society postulates that the implementation of new forms of learning among both individuals and all forms of collectivity (governmental bodies, companies, community groups, self-help alliances) is a prerequisite for the establishment of a moral and socially equitable foundation for human existence in the face of radical, irreversible, universalizing social change. Hughes and Tight seem to have averted their gaze from this spectre.

## CONCLUSION

In their trenchantly argued attack on the project of the learning society, Hughes and Tight seem to hark back to a simplistic reassertion of the Enlightenment hope that human happiness will be ensured by replacing the rule of custom with the application of reason. The twentieth century has eroded that visionary faith. From the ruins of that flawed project the philosophers of late modernity confront an urgent need to reconstruct a basis of morality and social purpose. Within that broader agenda, the learning society project redefines educational needs and refurbishes the institutional forms by which these are provided within the polity.

Its aims are much broader and more transformative than the more narrowly instrumental and economistic ones implied by Hughes and Tight. They are essentially those formulated pragmatically by Husén (1974) and more philosophically by Illich (1973a, p. 57):

> I believe that a desirable future depends on our deliberately choosing a life of action over a life of consumption, on our engendering a life-style which will enable us to be spontaneous, independent, yet related to each other, rather than maintaining a life-style which only allows us to make and unmake, produce and consume – a style of life, which is merely a way station to the depletion and pollution of the environment. The future depends more upon our choice of institutions which support a life of action than on our developing new ideologies and technologies. We need a set of criteria which will permit us to recognize those institutions which support personal growth rather than addiction, as well as invest our technological resources preferentially in such institutions of growth.

The project may indeed come to be subverted, hijacked by corporatist, instrumentalist, universalist interests embodied in national governments and globalized financial institutions, of which the World Bank is a signal example (George and Sabelli, 1994). But democratic conditions still make possible a formative discourse from which much stands to be gained. We should not give up so easily and on such a superficial and limited critique. There is 'out there' a real society in which knowledge and other resources are unequally distributed, to a degree that is not only inimical to the fulfilment of individual capabilities and freedoms but, arguably, detrimental to the collective survival and development of human society.

# Chapter 20

# A Reply to the Critics

*Stewart Ranson*

Within public policy as well as the academic community, the concept of the learning society has achieved considerable recognition as an aid to interpreting and responding to the transformations of our time. Inevitably there is a healthy critical debate about both the value of the concept and the way that it is typically defined. A number of critics reject its validity, believing that it lacks credibility (Hughes and Tight, 1995), or clarity (Edwards, 1995b), or critical analysis (Gleeson, 1996), or is just utopian. Others believe that the concept of the learning society has value but needs significant reformulation if it is to thrive (Hatcher, 1996; Rikowski, forthcoming; Young, 1995b).

Hughes and Tight argue that 'the idea of the learning society has no current empirical validity ... and doubt that it can be practically developed in the foreseeable future' (1995, p. 301). The learning society is a myth which proposes a palatable story of opportunities for individuals which merely masks the way powerful groups pursue their interests at the expense of the powerless, who become blamed for their own failure. The learning society, moreover, builds an analysis which is no more than a pack of mythical cards. For example, that we are living in a period of unprecedented change; that there is a linkage between training and financial benefit or economic performance; that learning organizations are more successful than others. These myths, argue Hughes and Tight, 'offer only a partial or inadequate basis on which to understand the complex relations between learning, work and life, and to plan policy and practice in these areas' (p. 293).

While the discussion elaborated by Hughes and Tight provides a helpful challenge, there is a danger that the term 'myth' is used so broadly as to collapse distinctions which are essential to the clarity of the analysis required. Whether there is 'unprecedented change' or a linkage between skill acquisition and performance are *empirical* questions; whether there should be lifelong education is a *normative* judgement; the relationship between change, organization and learning in society is a matter of *theoretical* hypothesis and analysis. Applying the same term to such different orders of proposition dissolves distinctions which are crucial to making sense of the social and political world generally and of public policy in particular.

Hughes and Tight thus fail to acknowledge the complexity of the learning society as an analytical or theoretical construct that comprises empirical propositions, conceptual analysis and normative values. The learning society does presuppose unprecedented change (empirical) and therefore the importance of learning about the meaning of this change (normative) and that solutions to these presuppositions will depend upon the creation of certain institutional conditions (theoretical and evaluative proposition). While the idea of the learning society begins with the world as it is, it proposes reforms that constitute aspirations for individual and collective well-being.

It is an inescapably evaluative concept. But whether it has value in shaping public policy will depend upon examining the validity of the empirical components of its presuppositions and evidence of the progress made towards realizing the value-laden proposals for change. The stories about making a new world need endlessly to be checked against the practice of creating it. The integrity of the story-makers will need to be explored as well. The stories may be myths – imaginary fictions which, as in the ancient world, serve to develop an understanding of the deep structures of experience. Or they may be ideologies (sets of beliefs which may include fictions) that are used to promote the interests of particular groups.

But myths and ideologies fulfil different functions in the world and to imply, as Hughes and Tight do, that they are the same introduces a confusion at the heart of their argument. They cannot at the same time argue that 'x' as a myth is empty, a vacuous fiction with no source, location or future in the world, and then argue that 'x' as an ideology has extraordinary potency as an instrument in bolstering the power of capital and the state while manipulating the consciousness of the powerless and marginalized.

Hughes and Tight fail to acknowledge what Edwards (1995b) understands. While he also remains sceptical about the value of the concept of the learning society, he recognizes that the common banner of the learning society masks very different agendas, only some of which are 'ideological'. Post-war liberal conceptions of the learning society emphasized lifelong learning to create 'an educative society' (Abrahamsson, 1993) which would provide learning opportunities for adults to meet needs for their personal development in a changing society. But since the 1980s this social need has been superseded by an economic imperative and a conception of the learning society as 'a learning market' which seeks to respond to the demands of individuals and employers for updating skills and competences for a changing labour market. However, the emphasis on choice and competition can fragment opportunities and accentuate inequalities. As society has become more differentiated under the pressures of globalization and cultural change, Edwards (1995b, p. 189) argues that the idea of 'learning networks' is more appropriate than the idea of a homogeneous, national society.

'Society', if it is to have meaning at all, might be reinscribed in the local communities networked into the globe – a position epitomised in the slogan, 'think globally, act locally'. In this conception adults may more readily be said to participate in a variety of 'learning networks' than in an educated society as such. Learning networks reflect the structured heterogeneity of contemporary social formations rather than the homogeneity of society and the individuation of the market.

If society has become more differentiated under the pressures of globalization and cultural change it may have been transformed, but this should not lead us to believe, as others have notoriously done, that there is no such thing as society – that instead there are social structures of power, wealth and cultural difference. Indeed, the challenge for contemporary society is precisely to learn to address and reconcile the ostensibly incommensurable differences which it faces within organizations, communities and the polity (Gray, 1996).

Nevertheless, Edwards is right to invite us 'to look closely at the front of the banner of the learning society before we walk behind it' (p. 189). There is a need for greater clarity in defining the meaning of the learning society, and for establishing criteria which allow some rather than all usages to be interpreted as legitimated.

For other commentators, the idea of the learning society has analytical and normative potential, but its current formulations need significant correction. Young (1995b) argues plausibly that the learning society, if it is to gain in cogency, must develop a theory of the relationship between education and economic life in the context of the changing nature of work at the end of the twentieth century; second, it must conceptualize 'education–economy relationships in the context of a view of society as a whole' (p. 2); and third, it must develop a theory of learning which conceives of productive life as a learning relationship, with 'priority to learning as a feature of the society as a whole being a condition for a successful economy of the future' (p. 3). Such a 'learning-led' or 'learning society' would provide criteria for evaluating institutions, particularly the post-compulsory phase of education.

Young's 'educative model' of the learning society is grounded in a theory of learning that builds upon the work of Engestrom (1994), who proposes orders of learning that increase in scope, culminating in 'expansive learning in which the learner questions and begins to transform the context, or "community of practice" where the learning begins' (p. 11). This higher level of learning, argues Engestrom, enables students, teachers and individuals in the community to 'design and implement their own futures as their prevailing practices show symptoms of crisis'.

Young is right to argue that any adequate grasp of the learning society must grow out of a theory of learning, and Engestrom's model provides a valuable framework for understanding learning. Yet while Young searches for a concept of the learning society defined in terms of education-economy relations, Engestrom's theory of learning provides a much deeper ontology of being in the world – of developing a sense of agency and the capability to design and transform a community of practice. Learning to develop a capacity for agency in this sense (cf. Ranson *et al.*, 1996) is the most expansive form of learning, which brings with it the confidence and competences to 'make' the communities in which citizens are to live as well as work; it is the most comprehensive capacity of practical reason, which subsumes work as one significant dimension of that making and becoming. Learning cannot influence the economy in the way that Young desires without the ontological change which is presupposed in his theory of learning.

The condition for this ontological growth in expansive learning lies in 'the context of a view of society as a whole', the political and constitutive structures which shape the relation of citizens to their society. These are foundational structures, the institutional structures of the polity, which constitute the conditions for personal development within and beyond the world of work. It is mistaken, therefore, to construct and analyse the learning society as being solely about values. It is about institutional structures which provide the conditions for a new, active citizenship, and when it is about values these are both material (about justice) as well as moral and political. The values are about *making* the world – economic, social and political – although it is true that the economic aspect of the theory of active citizenship needs considerably more elaboration.

It is this alleged neglect of the economic infrastructures in the argument which is picked up by critics such as Hatcher (1996). In order to discover alternative educational agendas to those of New Labour, he critically evaluates the body of work that 'envisages a new moral and political order of citizenship within a participative democracy based on practical reason' (p. 46) as the route to a learning society that realizes equality and agency. It is against this new discourse (cf. Giddens, 1994b; Miliband, 1994) that Hatcher argues. Drawing upon Anderson (1994), he maintains that there can be no common agenda based upon citizenship because 'democracy is primarily an arena of interests, not a field of discourse and therefore it is ultimately power that decides, not reason ... A radical agenda is necessarily divisive, because it challenges the control of resources by the powerful' (p. 46).

What these new social democratic agendas fail to recognize, in their analysis of the learning society, is the structural conflict of class interests in a society driven by the deep organizing principle not of learning but of the capitalist division of labour, while the state acts to maintain the dominant order using its power to reproduce the structured asymmetry of interests. There is thus no classless universal interest around which a national consensus on the learning society can be constructed. Any adequate theory must recognize the obstacles to equality and agency, especially the hegemony of the capitalist division of labour, and thus the need for struggle against the grain of dominant culture.

Hatcher's alternative proposes that taking 'active citizenship in the learning society seriously' would 'require a broad popular movement capable of exerting enough political pressure to push through ... reforms ... and defend them against reaction' (p. 48). Yet the social democratic agendas fail to grasp this understanding of agency and do not develop strategies to carry the vision into practice. The struggle for working-class equality and the struggle for working-class agency are two sides of the same coin.

Having acknowledged the constraints of the capitalist division of labour which determine the codes of schools, Hatcher nevertheless focuses his alternative for a real learning society upon schools and constructs an analysis which appears to be the same as the social democratic agenda – apart from the language, which reflects a different theoretical tradition:

- a sense of agency is generated through a curriculum which, following Connell (1994), 'authorises locally produced knowledge' (p. 141), a process which is an active making rather than taking of knowledge, and builds upon and develops local 'common learnings' (see Nixon *et al*'s (1996) active learning for citizenship in which 'citizens individually and together find themselves through making their communities' (p. viii);
- 'local political alliances' of parents and teachers (see Nixon *et al*'s collaborative partnerships);
- participation in a real local debate responding to cultural contexts of working-class children, recognizing different and often conflicting ideas and interests (participation in discourse and recognition of difference);
- local decision-making power close to the classroom with projects collectively planned and implemented locally (the constituting of local forums).

Thus an interesting similarity of analysis appears across the boundaries of traditions. The alternative to a capitalist hegemony must lie not in statist solutions but in local popular participative struggles within locally created arenas that allow local discourse to enable the agency of making local communities based upon justice and equality.

So, having begun by rejecting a democracy of participation and discourse, this becomes the strategy for realizing working-class agency and equality to achieve a learning society. For where there are differences and conflicts of interest in society, then democracy is the only just means of deciding among them if the statist imposition of power is to be avoided. Democracy must address conflicts of interest, but cannot impose class power as Anderson implies. Democracy searches for the *public interest*, which is the interest of the whole, above sectional claims.

Given the vulnerability of schools in the face of the wider structural constraints in society which Hatcher recognizes, it is odd that he believes that school-level democracy can be sufficient to challenge this hegemony. There is a need rather to build institutions for a more robust democracy in the locality as a whole, to create a learning democracy for the public domain. Hatcher strangely omitted from his critical analysis Ranson and Stewart's (1994) exegesis of the political institutions necessary to develop a participative democracy for the public domain. But even this political strategy requires a theory of redistributive justice in the state to provide the constitutive conditions for a citizenship of equality and fairness, if the conditions for participation are to be underpinned and the hegemonic economic structures are to be shaken.

Hatcher's argument, together with those of others, contends that the advocates of the learning society are vulnerable to the charge of idealism. Rikowski seeks to make explicit this philosophical critique of the idealist nature of the learning society in its present forms. The challenge proposes that the learning society, like other idealism, is a fanciful idea, utopian, a perspective which seeks to make of ideas timeless truths detached from their bases in social reality. Ideas come to take on a life of their own, become reified in thought: 'consciousness is precisely not a thing in itself, and the fundamental error of the idealists is to treat it as such', to attribute to 'conceptions, thoughts, ideas, in fact the products of consciousness ... an independence' (D. Sayer, 1989, p. 86). This idealist critique, Rikowski proposes, comprises a number of arguments:

(a) the theory of the learning society contains *normative* aspects which make it idealist because 'they rarely connect with theorisations of actually existing capitalist society in terms of their realisation'. They become value-laden ideals suspended above society, without analysis of the political agency which can make them real.
(b) the learning society expresses *utopian* values which degenerate into ideology. Utopianism, as Olson (1982) has argued, is 'the process of rendering fictional-ised, idealised worlds into finished forms or "blueprints" ...' is '... the search for the good pattern of life in an a-historical cosmos' (p. 143)
(c) the learning society is an *ungrounded abstraction*. It is impossible to fix the concept ontologically in terms of any actual social processes, social forms or set of institutional arrangements. It is temporally and spatially detached. To posit the learning society as a society of the future, without showing the dynamic through which it could develop out of presently existing capitalist society, makes it nothing short of an act of faith.
(d) the nature of the learning society is inherently *unhistorical*, unlike materialist theories which situate social phenomena within specific social formations and historical roots. This structural location is necessary to prevent the application of the learning society to any society.
(e) the learning society is a *fixed end-state* phenomenon towards which we are moving; when it is reached it becomes *absolutist in form*.

However, while recognizing these distinctions, Rikowski seems to collapse them and apply the same critique to all, when the different models have different weaknesses which require different criticisms. He, like Hughes and Tight, focuses his critical guns upon what Edwards defined as the 'market model' of the learning society, with its distinctive emphasis upon individual, lifelong reskilling for the labour market. But this model, which Rikowski believes is a materialist extension of capitalism, cannot at the same time be idealist, or be the focus of the same criticisms as a democratic model which seeks to change the capitalist form.

This model of the learning democracy (to be developed further in Chapter 21) can be defended against a number of the points which make up the idealist critique:

*Normative.*    But public policy is inescapably normative, as I shall develop in the last section of this chapter. The learning democracy cannot be accused of being normative and avoiding consideration of political agency. Indeed, political pro-grammes are at the centre of the normative constructions. Nor can the learning democracy be accused of being *agnostic* and normative. The promotion of the democratic model is certainly not agnostic and it builds a substantive model of material institutions.

*Utopian.* Kumar (1995), as Rikowski acknowledges, 'has argued that utopias perform the function of making us think about social possibilities, possible types of world and social existence. Utopias are about "educating our desires" in ways which make us think about social life as lived now. This interpretation ... [allows us to pose serious questions about the nature of society] without proposing some idealist blueprint as ultimate goal'(p. 226, this volume). Other Marxists (for example, Meiksins Wood (1995) have argued that it is the political institutions of democracy which present the best opportunity for transforming the capitalist form. The model of learning democracy, furthermore, cannot degenerate into an ideology, as in the materialist reskilling model, because it opens ideas to public scrutiny and criticism. Only those policies and projects which are in the public interest will survive. Nor is the learning democracy a blueprint, because democracy defines processes rather than substantive outcomes. Rikowski understands this, recognizing that the appropriate account of the open and democratic nature of concrete institutions which deny prior prescription of detail, was given in *Management for the Public Domain* (Ranson and Stewart, 1994).

*Ungrounded.* The learning democracy cannot be accused of being idealist, 'pie in the sky', and with no possibility of grounding the ideas. The vision of a new form of democracy has been grounded in the dilemmas constituted by societal transformation which cannot be resolved within the dominant concepts of the present polity or form of society. Innovative ideas are important and do have a dynamic, but it is not a dynamic disassociated from material considerations. The vision grew out of the real world and specifies the institutional arrangements and the material conditions of justice as necessary for realizing the vision. The learning democracy seeks to be sophisticated about the conditions for learning; these are material as well as institutional.

*Endist.* The learning democracy cannot be absolutist because the democratic frame recognizes and values difference. It cannot be endist or static because democratic form is always intended to allow and enable change. The learning democracy is static neither in its origins nor in its end-point. The need for it grew out of the uncertainties of a period of transition, creating problems and issues that cannot be solved without societal and therefore public learning.

*Unhistorical teleology.* This is a contradiction in terms. The argument for a learning democracy has grown out of a precise theorizing of the form and characteristics of historical periods. An historical analysis has been the foundation of proposals for change. Nor are these proposals teleological, suggesting the inevitable movement towards their realization. To argue the need for a learning democracy is not to show that it will happen. Whether it happens will depend upon sources of agency, and these depend upon a mobilization of those publics aroused by the problems created by the dominant polity. New but diverse social movements emerge. Cultures of difference confront the problems and issues produced by the incongruence between policy and issue. Because the movements gain strength in locality and are diverse in form and nature, they are less easily appreciated by those who seek uniformity. Yet a learning democracy depends upon the politics of difference – as Aristotle acknowledged, 'a city is composed of different kinds of people, similar people cannot bring a city into existence. One learns from difference more than uniformity.'

A number of the critiques discussed in this chapter suggest there are differences of understanding and lack of agreement about the philosophical presuppositions which underlie the study and nature of public policy. Drawing upon Ranson (1995), a number of organizing principles for a theory of public policy are set out, before we turn in the concluding chapter to further develop our substantive understanding of a learning democracy.

## PRINCIPLES FOR THE STUDY OF PUBLIC POLICY

The fissiparous tendencies of theorists, striving to emphasize the virtues of a particular perspective, can fragment the task of explanation, which requires some critical interrelating of those different approaches. An adequate understanding of public policy demands a multi-theoretic and multi-disciplinary analysis. A number of theoretical and methodological presuppositions can form the basis, it is argued, for a more integrated approach to explanatory analysis. Theoretical analysis of public policy should accommodate:

*Historical location.*   Only an interpetative analysis of the transformations of our time can make sense of the temporal and structural context of public policy development. Barraclough (1967) believed that if contemporary history was to become a heavyweight discipline, able to offer more than a superficial discussion of events, then it had 'to clarify the basic structural changes which have shaped the modern world. These changes are fundamental because they fix the skeleton or framework within which political action takes place' (1967, p. 16; quoted in Ball, 1990, p. 1). An in-depth discussion of these changes is presented in the chapter by Strain and Field.

What Barraclough, reinforced by Hobsbawm (1994) takes to be the prerequisite for history, Gellner (1964, 1988) conceives as the subject matter for the contemporary social sciences – to interpret the structural transformation of our time, though this injunction was typically to study the impact of the Industrial Revolution rather than the contemporary post-Industrial Revolution. The economic, social and political transformations of our time (Ranson, 1992) are fundamentally altering the structure of experience: the capacities each person needs to flourish, what it is to live in society, the nature of work, and the form taken by polity. The changes raise deep questions for the governing of education and for the polity in general about: *What is it to be a person?* Is a person a passive being or one possessed of powers that define his or her essential agency? *Is there any such thing as a society?* What is it? An aggregation of individuals or some form of social and linguistic community? *What should be the nature of the polity?* What does it mean to be a member? What are the rights and duties? What distribution of power and wealth is consistent with justice and freedom? Who should take decisions and how? What forms of accountability and representation define our democracy?

*Theorizing action and structure.*   Much theoretical writing has created a mistaken opposition between agency and structure in explaining change, when arguably only a theorizing of their necessary interrelationship can make sense of social and political reality. Turner (1981) has emphasized the considerable overlap in the work of Weber and Marx in their analysis of capital formation and accumulation. The characterization of Weber's work as 'subjectivist', in some phenomenological and Marxist perspectives, neglects his emphasis upon the dual interplay of agency and structure in the creation of historical periods, such as the increasing rationalization of social forms in the modern world.

> The type of social science in which we are interested is an *empirical science* of concrete reality [*Wirklichkeitswissenschaft*]. Our aim is the understanding of the characteristic uniqueness of the reality in which we move. We wish to understand on the one hand the relationships and cultural significance of individual events in their contemporary manifestations and on the other the causes of their being *so* and not *otherwise*.
>
> (Weber, 1949, p. 72)

The work of Giddens (1976, 1984) and Archer (1982) acknowledges, from different points of view, that while individuals and groups strive to construct their worlds to reflect chosen values and interests, they are nevertheless also constrained by the structures of power and domination. Theorizing the interconnection of action and structure presupposes a number of interrelated forms of analysis (Ranson *et al.*, 1980): *phenomenological* to understand the meanings which actors create to make sense of their worlds; *comparative* to explore the underlying regularities of which actors may be unaware; and *temporal*, to explore how actors choose to construct and change social forms over time in the face of the constraints which confront them. These analyses enable explanations to be developed which are adequate at the levels of meaning and cause across different contextual conditions and have the capacity to explain change over time. Such a framework suggests the need to examine the creation over time of education policy in the context of broader structural processes of social, cultural and economic reproduction (Power, 1992; Whitty, 1985, 1992).

*Theory, practice and value.*   Perceived as mutually reinforcing by revealing the underlying relationships. Theory can guide action, while the monitoring of practice informs theory. Because the task of theory is not only to explain why public policy is as it is within the polity, but also to theorize the conditions for a different form of polity and public policy, it is inescapably normative, driven by 'strong evaluation' of the moral and political order. Public policy analysis must describe, explain and propose public values. The personal values and political commitment of the critical policy analyst, argues Prunty (1985), would be 'anchored in the vision of a moral order in which justice, equality and individual freedom are uncompromised by the avarice of a few'.

Thus policy analysis must be committed to the critical analysis of values within current policies as part of the process of clarifying the values which the analyst believes should inform educational and public policy (Troyna, 1994). The literature on policy analysis, however, has lost a sense of the 'strong values' which provide the meaning and purpose for public policy. These values, it is argued, are needed to regenerate a democratic public domain for the learning society.

## A philosophy of public purpose

The task of theory is to explain why public policy is as it is within the polity, but also to theorize the conditions for a different form of polity and public policy. Theorizing the conditions for an alternative public domain requires a philosophy of its values and purposes (Ranson, 1992, 1994). Policy analysis is inescapably a normative as well as a conceptual and theoretical activity. Policy analysis, which is about changing practice in the public domain, needs to follow clear public values.

The education policy literature lacks a framework of the values about the public domain which it brings to its analysis. The appropriate values for public policy and its analysis are those of democracy and citizenship for the learning society. The transformations of the time require a renewed valuing of and commitment to learning – as the boundaries between languages and cultures begin to dissolve; as new skills and knowledge are expected within the world of work; and, most significantly, as a new generation, rejecting passivity in favour of more active participation, requires to be encouraged to exercise such qualities of discourse in the public domain. A learning society, therefore, needs to celebrate the qualities of being open to new ideas, listening to as well as expressing perspectives, reflecting on and inquiring into solutions to new dilemmas, co-operating in the practice of change and critically reviewing it. There is a need for the creation of a learning society as the constitutive condition of a new moral and political order. It is only when the values and processes of learning are placed at the centre of the polity that the conditions can be established for all individuals to develop their capacities, and that institutions can respond openly and imaginatively to a period of change.

The theory which can provide the common language of agency to enrich a new moral and political order is that of citizenship within the learning society. The notion of 'a citizen' captures our necessary duality as an individual and as a member of the public. The deliberative agency of the citizen is exercised in judgement, in choice and in action, so that his or her powers and capacities are actively and reflectively expressed through the creative development of the self, through civic virtue within the community, and through discourse within the polity. This agency of citizens can only be supported and sustained through the institutional structures of a participative democracy. It is to develop a clearer elaboration of the purposes, tasks and conditions of such a learning democracy that we turn in the last chapter.

*Part 4*

---

# Conclusion

# Chapter 21

# The Learning Democracy[1]

## Stewart Ranson and John Stewart

## PRESUPPOSITIONS

The chapters in this book reveal that the idea of the learning society has been adopted by diverse traditions and used to communicate very different understandings of the way society is changing and the forms of response appropriate to a changing world. When taken together these different conceptions can present quite contradictory beliefs: on the one hand, for example, a belief in individual lifelong learning for the changing labour market; on the other, collective learning for a changing polity. Such definitional generosity will leave the concept of the learning society without clarity of meaning, as Edwards (1995a) has argued. There is a need to establish a definition which can dissolve contradiction and sharpen meaning, because without public learning societal learning will be restricted to sectional learning.

Many of those who write under the rubric of the learning society, we propose, are operating within a limited frame of reference. They write about new forms of learning for individuals rather than about learning for new forms of society. We regard such an approach as inadequate. Implicitly it assumes the present forms of society. While in one sense any society can be called a learning society in that it has some capacity for adaptation to changing circumstance, for us the phrase 'a learning society' denotes a different form of society. If all societies are learning societies then the phrase is effectively devoid of meaning. For us, a learning society is one which has to learn to become a different form of society if it is to shape the transformation which it is experiencing.

A society facing a period of structural change will require individuals to acquire new skills to contribute to civil society as well as to a changing labour market. Such a society also faces deep dilemmas, often described as 'wicked' issues because they cannot be adequately dealt with by, or even understood within, the conceptual framework dominant in present society. The degradation of the environment, or the growing exclusion and erosion of the bonds of civil society, exposes the inadequacy of understanding and response. The case for a learning society is thus grounded in the uncertainties of the present. Society can only develop through learning, and the learning must be public learning shared through institutions of democratic governance.

In this context of change a learning society will be characterized by:

- a society which must learn how it is changing;
- a society must change what it has to learn;
- a society which must learn how to change;
- a society which must change the way it learns;
- a society which involves all its members in learning:
  - what they are learning
  - what demands are placed on the person who engages in this kind of learning?
- a society which learns to change the (institutional) conditions of learning:
  - what are the characteristics of effective learning systems?
  - what are the forms and limits of knowledge that can operate within the processes of societal learning?

The quality of our future in periods of change, therefore, will depend upon our capacity to learn. Only if learning is placed at the centre of our experience will individuals continue to develop their capacities, institutions be enabled to respond openly and imaginatively to change, and the differences within and between communities become a source for reflective understanding. A new vision is needed to express the value of and conditions for a learning society which will have the following substantive characteristics:

- *collective change*: a society which learns about itself, how it is changing and how it needs to change how it learns;
- *agency*: a society which encourages the active participation of citizens in the making of their communities and that 'our most urgent common need at present is to learn how to act together more effectively' (Dunn, 1992);
- *dialogue*: a society which enables a conversation that brings to the surface differences in values and beliefs for critical evaluation;
- *democracy*: a society which learns that the conditions for active citizenship lie in creating the institutional forms of participative democracy.

A learning society, therefore, if it is to address the transformation it faces, will learn to become a different form of society, one that places active citizenship as the organizing principle of learning. By creating the conditions for a new participatory democracy, citizens will be enabled to find themselves, individually and together, through making the common wealth of their communities.

Such a society will recover the *agency* of the learner as the key to personal and social development. We learn when we have a sense of purpose, and such motivation is most likely to grow out of our active participation in creating the projects which are to shape our selves as well as the communities in which we live. Such a perspective emphasizes our dual responsibility as citizens for making our private and public worlds, and for our mutual dependence and accountability as best supported through the deliberative processes of democratic decision-making. We learn about ourselves and others through deliberating with others and reasoning practically about change.

In this concluding chapter we build upon the argument we set out in 1994 in *Management for the Public Domain: Enabling the Learning Society*. We present our interpretation of a changed world, the nature of the learning that follows, and the challenge of remaking a democratic polity for citizenship.

## LIVING IN A DIFFERENT WORLD: THE SPECTRE OF USELESSNESS

The social and economic changes which have been accelerating since the mid-1970s imply structural transformations for our society. The changes are not cyclical. Our world has become different in form and will not return to what it was before. The very language now being created to characterize these transformations – 'postmodern', post-industrial', post-Fordist' – anticipates an historic juncture taking place. Understanding these changes is not only a precondition for interpreting educational purpose but, more deeply, for understanding what it is to live a life at the turn of the century.

What makes the changes we are experiencing quite historic is that the restructuring – driven by what Edward Luttwak (1995) has called technology powered, deregulated, globalizing 'turbo-charged capitalism' – will remove secure employment as the central experience from most citizens' lives, leaving them to lead chronically vulnerable risk-taking lives unless society learns ways of overcoming that vulnerability. Successful companies sell, but also buy, parts more cheaply than they can make them, on the world market. This, together with the accelerated computerization of the entire administration of production and assembly, makes surplus to requirement whole hierarchies of clerks, supervisors and managers. This structural change accelerates the 'downsizing' of firms, flexible labour demands and declining income. The less-skilled are condemned to a life-time of declining earnings; many of the low-paid respectable jobs that once allowed a striving sector of the underclass to rise into the working class have been eliminated. What some have failed to grasp is that these upheavals and disruptions condemn most working people of all skill levels to lives of chronic economic insecurity. For Richard Sennett (1995), the issue is the spectre of uselessness:

> Many working people are experiencing a heightened sense of personal failure, believing themselves to be useless, peripheral, or over the hill at an early age. Fear of sudden vulnerability infects even those making their way in the new economy, reinforcing the sense that work is no secure framework for the self. The imagined corollary of uselessness is a dispensable self; someone without value.

Exclusion from work and well-being leaves many living outside the routines and structures which the included take for granted. Disadvantage isolates individuals and communities and sets them apart. They feel themselves, and are believed, to live 'in a different world' – a world apart. The experience of alienation excludes.

Living in poverty typically influences how young people think of themselves: with low self-esteem, eroded belief in what they can achieve and thus low expectations and withered motivation to learn. What can be the point of it all? Individuals and their communities can feel beleaguered by their sense of 'otherness'. The task for the learning society is to learn how to overcome this impoverishment.

**Worlds of difference**

This material difference grows within a world typically characterized by clashes of cultural traditions, whose values, histories and identities are said to be chronically agnostic and thus rival and incommensurable, compounded by a poverty of recognition and mutual understanding (Gray, 1995; MacIntyre, 1981). Traditions shape 'critical points of deep and significant *difference* which constitute "what we really are", or rather – since history has intervened – "what we have become"' (Hall, 1990). Many schools, in this context, are a microcosm of the predicament facing the postmodern polity. The challenge for an institution, as for society, is to discover processes which can reconcile the valuing of difference with the need for shared understanding and agreement about public purpose that dissolves prejudice and discrimination.

   The experience of cultural difference can also be one of otherness and exclusion. Cultures codify the essential boundaries of social classification. To be placed in a different world is thus to experience the deepest codes of classification: who is to be included and excluded set the boundaries of the social order. The identities of self and other, of sacred and profane are defined within the moral order, while the relations of power, of super- and subordination, constitute the political order. Systems of social classification so embody the relations between communities that to be regarded as other, outside, profane is to experience the greatest disadvantage – to be denied the dignity, and thus the sense of agency, that derive from being acknowledged as a fellow citizen with shared rights and responsibilities. Yet because these classifications of who we are and what we can become, can be recognized as social constructions, we can also learn that they are amenable to revision.

**Collective action dilemmas**

The trends towards fragmentation implied in the postmodern society threaten to undermine the co-operation and trust that define a community and thus the possibility of co-operative action, upon which any society depends. The most serious 'collective action problem' is the predatory exploitation of the environment with its dramatic consequences. Mounting litter, growing crime, traffic congestion and the prospect of global warming reveal the unintended collective consequences of our individual choices: self-interest can be self-defeating. The seductive yet ultimately irrational compulsion of some to 'free-ride' presents perhaps the most significant challenge for future society. Parfit (1984, p. 62) succinctly describes the dilemma:

> It can be better for each if he adds to pollution, uses more energy, jumps queues and breaks agreements; but if all do these, things can be worse off for each than if none do. It is very often true, that if each rather than none does what will be better for himself, this will be worse off for everyone.

The conditions for co-operation have to be learnt through an understanding of these dilemmas and of societal interdependence.

## Legitimacy

What will be the nature of work in the future, who will be required to work, and how and when will they work: Do individuals need to work to express their identities, develop their capacities, acquire status and contribute as citizens to the common wealth of the community in which they live? Will those who remain outside work be regarded as 'members', as 'citizens' by others in the community? Will they be accorded equal rights and status and power in the community? Social, economic and political changes have, through the uncertainty they have generated, raised the most fundamental questions for a society to cohere during a period of transition: What is it to be a person? Is there any such thing as society? What form should democracy take in the postmodern polity? Answers to these questions have to be learnt. The effect of these structural changes and the questions to which they have given rise has been to cause a fundamental re-examination of the social democratic polity and the manangement of the public sector. Has our society the political resources to create a new framework of justice about rights and duties which acquires legitimate authority across a fragmenting society?

## WHAT IS TO BE LEARNED: RENEWING THE PUBLIC DOMAIN

In periods of transition learning becomes central to our future well-being. Only if learning is placed at the centre of our experience will individuals continue to develop their capacities, institutions be enabled to respond openly and imaginatively to change, and the differences within and between communities become a source for reflective understanding. (Ranson, 1992, 1994). Learning is needed for the transition but learning will also constitute the new domain. The transformation is through but also to a learning society.

Yet the key issue is, which learning do we have to learn? The predicaments of our time are public (collective) problems and require public solutions, yet the public institutions required to support the resolutions have all but eroded; our society has developed institutions that are not constituted for an active public domain. The characteristics of structural change in society (fragmentation, privatism and sectionalism) and the qualities of the neo-liberal polity (competitive individualism) mutually reinforce the erosion of public life and thus the conditions for personal development, as well as collective well-being. If the task for the time is to re-create a public domain that can support society through an historic transition, then the challenge will be to learn, re-learn two indispensable capacities: the capacity for co-operative action and the capacity for action, for agency.

## Learning the capacity for co-operative action

The predicaments of our time – whether in understanding how to sustain the environment or how to reconcile the rights and well-being of diverse communities – cannot be determined by individuals or groups in isolation, nor by 'exit' because we cannot stand outside them. The predicaments of our time are faced by communities and societies as a whole: 'They are urgent problems for human beings together and in common ... If we are so much as to survive as a species ... we clearly need to think about well-being and justice internationally, and together' (Nussbaum, 1990). What each individual or group experiences as separate concerns, has actually to be faced together and can only be tackled through public institutions that enable us to share understanding and act together. 'Facing the obscure and extravagantly complicated challegnes of the human future, our most urgent common need at present is to learn how to act together more effectively' (Dunn, 1992).

## Learning as the cultural reconstruction of agency

The post-war social democratic polity emphasized a passive public, taking its lead from professional experts and distant elected representatives. While much was achieved, excluding the public from participating in the development of society led in time to a withering of identification and support. The vacuum in the polity was the absence of public engangement. The neo-liberal polity also denied the need for such engagement. Public consent and legitimacy have atrophied as a result. Understanding of this predicament has been widespread but differences surround the appropriate response.

Learning requires individuals to progress from the post-war tradition of passivity, of the self as spectator to the action on a distant stage, and the neo-liberal role of customer whose concerns are limited to immediate choices in the market, to a conception of the self as agent both in personal development and active participation within the public domain. Such a transformation requires a new understanding from self-development for occupation to self-development for autonomy, choice and responsibility across all spheres of experience. The change also presupposes moving from our prevailing preoccupation with cognitive growth to a proper concern for development of the person as a whole – feeling, imagination and empathy, and practical and social skills as much as the life of the mind. An empowering of the image of the self presupposes unfolding capacities over (a life-) time. This implies something deeper than mere 'lifelong education or training' (referred to as 'access institutions'). Rather it suggests an essential belief that people develop comprehensively throughout their lives both as individuals and as members of society and that this should be accorded value and supported.

## THE CHALLENGE OF REMAKING

Thus the challenge for our society at the turn of the century to remake itself is a task of cultural renewal, requiring a culture of co-operative action if we are to find ourselves by remaking the communities in which we are to live. This makes the central task of our time to transform the way people think of themselves and others and what they are capable of. It is only by changing the sense citizens have of themselves as learners that they will begin to develop their capacities and realize their potential.

Where is the motivation for such a project of cultural renewal to come from? What conditions will provide the sense of purpose, so that each person is motivated to release this agency to contribute to this historic role? This will depend upon the development of a learning society: more people, learning in different locations, to develop more extended capacities, over a longer period of their lives. But, much more significantly, a learning society is one which nurtures the sense of agency amongst its citizens to enter into the remaking of the communities in which they are to live. The values and conditions of this learning society are: citizenship, democracy, justice.

### Citizenship

Social and political theorists in search of perspectives which might illuminate and resolve the puzzles presented by the postmodern politics of difference have drawn upon theories of citizenship and civil society to offer interpretative analyses of a changing democracy at the turn of the century. Traditional models of 'entitlement citizenship', which emphasize membership of the nation-state and formal legal rights (Marshall, 1977; Plant, 1990), have been subjected to critical analysis because they ignore the contemporary condition of plurality (Parekh, 1988) and neglect the tradition of participation, exercise of agency and deliberation which also informed classical traditions of citizenship (Barber, 1984). The task has been to reconstruct a theory of citizenship which is grounded in the experience of hetero-geneity and elaborates the need for different groups to enter a discourse in which they voice claims for their identities and interests to be recognized and accommo-dated in the public space. Theorists (Mouffe, 1992, 1993; Phillips, 1993, 1995; Young, 1990) point to the mistaken illusion of a unified polity, of homogeneous communities which form a universal citizenry and civic public, which is required in order to leave behind particularity and difference in the public domain. Traditional models of citizenship imposed a univocal understanding of what should count as 'universal' values, which excluded and silenced the voices – whether they are gendered, ethnic or class – of 'other' traditions. A conception of citizenship is needed, Yeatman (1994) argues, which acknowledges the contested nature of public purposes and enables the different voices to re-present their cultural traditions and material class interests (Coole, 1996) in the public space in conditions of unconstrained dialogue.

The motivation of members of society to acknowledge mutuality, to deliberate with others and to search for shared understanding is more likely to succeed if they regard each other as citizens with shared responsibility for making the communities in which they are to live. This makes the *agency* of citizens central to personal and social development. Our active participation in creating the projects which are to shape our selves as well as the communities in which we live provides the sense of purpose to work together with others and to secure trusting relations with them. There is no solitary development or learning. We can only create our worlds together. The unfolding agency of the self always grows out of the interaction with others. *It is inescapably a social and creative making.* The self can only find its identity in and through others and the membership of communities. The possibility of shared understanding requires individuals not only to value others but to create the communities in which mutuality, and thus the conditions for learning, can flourish.

The *telos* of citizenship is to learn to make the communities without which individuals and others cannot grow and develop. The presupposition of such making is *openness* to mutual recognition: we have to learn to be open to different perspectives, alternative life-forms and views of the world, to allow our pre-judgements to be challenged; in so doing we learn how to amend our assumptions, and develop an enriched understanding of others. The key to the transformation of prejudice lies in what Gadamer (1975) calls '*the dialogic character of understanding*': through genuine conversation the participants are led beyond their initial positions, to take account of others and move towards a richer, more comprehensive view, a 'fusion of horizons', a shared understanding of what is true or valid. Conversation lies at the heart of learning; learners are listeners as well as speakers. The concept of *bildung* describes this process through which individuals and communities enter a more and more widely defined community of shared understanding – they learn through dialogue to understand other views, leading to a wider, more differentiated view, and thus acquire sensitivity, subtlety and capacity for judgement.

## A participative democracy for communicative action

We can only make ourselves and our communities when empowered by a public domain which recognizes the distinctive contribution each has to give. For Habermas (1984, 1990), the processes of a discursive democracy provide the conditions for differences to be brought into the public sphere and negotiated through procedures of fair, equal and unconstrained discussion undistorted by power. Identities are respected and compromises, if not consensus, reached between rival traditions.

Such a view of democracy recognizes an understanding, effaced by rights-based models, of the duality of citizenship: that citizens are both individuals and active members of the whole, the public as a political community. Citizenship in this view is not a passive status (Turner, 1990) nor the status of the customer: membership brings with it a sense of responsibility on the part of citizens to become involved and to speak out in the public sphere, exercising their agency to deliberate with other traditions in search of a good for the community as a whole. For Clarke (1996) this deep 'democratic citizenship' requires, for the recovery of collaborative participation, the establishing and strengthening of the spaces – the intermediary institutions of civil society – in which such active citizenship can be practised (Cohen and Arato, 1992; Cohen and Rogers, 1995; Hirst, 1994; Keane, 1988a, b). A domain is formed in which private meets public, providing the conditions for what Mouffe (1993) argues strong democracy needs: an articulation between the particular and the universal; a sphere which recognizes and mediates, through the arts of association, a diversity of particular interests for the public good. By providing forums for participation the new polity can create the conditions for public discourse and for mutual accountability, so that citizens can take each other's needs and claims into account and learn to create the conditions for each other's development (cf. Dunn, 1992).

### Justice: a contract for the basic structure

The conditions for agency of self and society depend upon agreement about its value as well as about allocating the means for private and public self-determination. Freedom rests upon justice, as Rawls (1971) and Sen (1992) argue. But this makes the most rigorous demands upon the polity, which has to determine the very conditions on which life can be lived at all: membership, the distribution of rights and duties, the allocation of scarce resources, the ends to be pursued. The good polity must strive to establish the conditions for virtue in all its citizens: material (for example, clean public water); social (tolerance, compassion); institutional (for example, education); and moral (a civic ethic). These issues are intrinsically political and will be intensely contested, especially in a period of transformation that disturbs traditions and conventions.

## REMAKING INSTITUTIONS FOR PUBLIC LEARNING

Institutions matter! They are powerful human constructions. Their distinctiveness lies in the intensity of their function: they are constituted to shape human nature, to form the person – its dispositions, powers and capacities. An institution, in conception, leaves its mark on 'a life', in the identity, thinking, feeling of the person. Even the body is marked: the confidence or deference of carriage and gesture, can find its origins in 'a schooling'. Institutions frame: they shape the horizons of their members and thus their sense of place. They mediate the relationship people have to their society through social time and space. At the same time, what institutions become, the values and interests they embody, are shaped by the agency and power of those that come to control them. Institutions constrain yet open up possibilities. Thus the 'keying' of educational institutions, as Goffman (1974) might call it, can tell us much about the emerging shape of the social order and its patterns of control. Institutions carry the past into the future but yet allow the possibility of the future.

Public institutions must express those values and purposes which reflect their historic role of enabling citizens to remake their society. This will necessitate institutional reform to create a public domain for public learning. We need to reconstitute a public domain based on active citizenship, which will be an arena for public learning, for seeking responses to new problems.

The case for a public domain based on public learning is grounded in the government of uncertainty. The need for public learning has always been present, but has recently been highlighted by the transformations of our times, which now pose problems imperfectly understood, that require us to search for a response. Out of that response will come further learning, for public learning is a search which should never reach an end-state.

The polities of the post-war era neglected the need for public learning. It was assumed too readily that government understood the problems faced and could deliver a solution through reliance on professional expertise. A system of government was built for certainty, which required no place for public learning and hence for an active citizenship. In reaction, attempts were made to establish the neo-liberal polity, although never so successfully as its advocates sought. There was no concern for public learning, because the market would spontaneously produce responses to perceived needs. It is now realized that markets do not replace the need for public learning, but reveal it in the problems markets create and in the issues they cannot resolve. The reality of the government of uncertainty has now replaced the apparent government of certainty or the assumption that the market will resolve public problems.

Reconstituting the public domain as an arena for public learning must involve the public as citizens, otherwise it merely reconstitutes the government of certainty in new forms. The argument for a public domain based on public learning is in effect an argument for strengthening the democratic base through active citizenship.

## Public learning for democracy

The British system of government is based on representative democracy, but on an attentuated conception of representation. It is as if the act of being elected constitutes the representative without the need for any further action, beyond making onself available through local surgeries to hear individual problems. This is a passive concept of being a representative, rather than an active process of representing or re-presenting the views of those represented.

The passive concept of representation leaves little or no place for participatory democracy or the active involvement of citizens in the process of government. There is a tendency therefore to see representative democracy and participatory democracy as opposed. Given an active process of representation, however, representative democracy requires and is strengthened by participatory democracy; and by participatory democracy more is meant than collecting the views of individual citizens. It involves informing, discussing and listening. Participatory democracy makes the role of the elected representative more important.

The public does not and will not speak with one voice, but with many voices, making different demands. Within any area there are many communities, and lines of conflict as well as co-operation. The development of participatory democracy, if successful, should extend the range of voices beyond those normally heard. The importance of discussion in participatory democracy is to establish an awareness of different positions, to test them against other and against wider concerns, and to see whether through discussion new positions can be reached which can reconcile differences, or at least explore how far they can be reconciled. It is the role of the elected representative to aid that process, and in the end, if required, to balance and to judge differing views.

If there has been an attenuated conception of representative democracy, there has also been an attenuated conception of citizenship. In the welfare state, the role of citizen was that of elector, but beyond that little more than that of client. In the neo-liberal polity the Citizens' Charter as an expression of a market philosophy defines the citizen as customer, and in so doing limits the role of citizens or even their concerns. Even if I am not a customer of education, as a citizen I have views on education and a right to express them, as I have a duty to listen to the views of others.

The attenuated state of democracy has led to and is constrained by a centralist culture. While many countries have come to appreciate that one cannot govern a complex and changing society in the certainty of centralism, centralization has proceeded apace in Britain, weakening local government. Geographical and organizational distance separate central government and citizen.

Of course it will be said that citizens are apathetic. Examples will be quoted of attempts to involve citizens that have failed. The low turnout in local elections will be quoted in confirmation of that apathy. But too often attempts to involve citizens are on the organization's terms. Little attempt is made to work with the grain of how people behave. Old, tired forms of public meeting are hardly likely to generate public involvement. New approaches have to be developed, based on an understanding of the reality of people's attitudes and behaviour.

*Innovation in democratic practice*

There is a need for innovation in democratic practice. While much has changed in policy and management, there has been little innovation in democratic practice. For example, while concern has been widely expressed about local electoral turnout, there has been no attempt to improve it. Even the notice that announces an election remains as unreadable as it was when the design was first laid down many years ago. It is a symbol of the general lack of innovation in British democratic practice. Innovations to enhance citizen participation are possible in democratic practice (Stewart, 1995, 1996). Public bodies should recognize the need to develop citizen participation, and develop a repertoire of approaches to nurture the habit of citizenship.

## The informed citizen

This section takes as its main illustration the possibilities of a family of approaches that are designed to find the informed views of a representative group of citizens. These are not the only approaches, and the range of possibilities will also be discussed. There are three main defining characteristics of these approaches. They involve a group of citizens deliberately chosen as a representative sample of citizens generally, as the modern equivalent of the Athenian principle of selection by lot. In that way people from all sections of the population are involved, avoiding the danger that only the articulate and the joiners take part. They also ask from citizens not a continuing involvement (impossible to sustain) but a particular commitment over a limited period of time.

The approaches ensure that citizens only give their views after hearing about the issue in depth, with an opportunity to question and challenge. There is a fundamental difference between these approaches and opinion polls, which can be merely a device for obtaining the uninformed and often unconsidered views of citizens. Recently the Local Government Commission for England sought citizens' views on local government reorganization in most counties. Generally opinions were divided, although there was a tendency to favour 'no change' in many areas. However, on one issue there was general agreement – about 80 per cent on average said they knew nothing or very little about the issues on which they were giving their view. One might consider that this robbed their views of some of their value.

These approaches also ensure that the citizens involved have discussed the issues amongst themselves. Democracy, if it is to be meaningful, must be more than a recording system for individual views. It should involve discourse in which citizens explore views together, test ideas, seek agreement, yet become aware of difference. These approaches bring deliberation by citizens into the process of government. As Fishkin (1991) has argued:

> The distinction between the inclinations of the moment and public opinions that are refined by 'sedate reflection' is an essential part of any adequate theory of democracy. Political equality without deliberation is not of much use, for it amounts to nothing more than the power without the opportunity to think about how that power could be exercised. Although the numbers involved are small they are a microcosm of the citizenry at large.

## Citizen's juries

Citizens' juries are an example of these approaches. Citizens' juries were developed independently in Germany, where they are called planning cells, and in the USA. A group of citizens representing the general public meet together to explore a policy issue or to discuss a particular decision. Witnesses present information and jurors ask questions. They then deliberate amongst themselves before making their conclusions public.

Normally, both in Germany and the USA, citizens' juries last about four to five days. In that time, it has been found that citizens develop a good understanding of the issues involved and effective discussion develops. Jurors find it a rewarding experience and can become advocates for its further development. Citizen's juries are not used as decision-making bodies. They are a source of advice and guidance for decision-makers on issues about which they seek to learn the views of informed citizens. Normally the decision-maker will easily learn the views of interested parties, at least if they belong to groups having ease of access to government. They can learn through opinion polls the, too often, uninformed views of citizens. They do not readily have access to the informed views of citizens.

There are issues on which elected representatives are uncertain how to proceed. They may be unconvinced by the professional advice they receive, but be uncertain of the public's attitude. They may be aware of a conflict of views among interested parties or the pressure of particular parties, and will wish to know what the views of the public generally would be if informed about the issue. In fields of policy where new issues are arising they may seek ideas from an informed public.

In all these circumstances and others, decision-makers may seek the views of a citizens' jury. In Germany, where the use of citizens' juries is more developed, Professor Peter Dienel and the Research Institute for Public Participation and Planning Procedures at the University of Wuppertal accept commissions from local authorities, the *Länder* and the federal government. The authority commissioning the citizens' jury does not undertake to accept its views. It will, however, undertake to consider the views expressed and to respond to them. This emphasizes that the role of the citizens' juries is not decision-making itself, but rather to inform decision-making, in the same way as participatory democracy generally has been presented as informing, not replacing, representative democracy.

Citizens' juries were used to consider the designs for development in and around Cologne City Square, and led to reconsideration of the proposals of the council's professional advisers. One wonders whether some town centre developments in Britain would have survived appraisal by citizens' juries. In Grevelsburg a citizens' jury examined alternative approaches to traffic problems in a historic town centre. Citizens' juries have also been used to explore broader policy issues on which they may well produce guidelines rather than specific recommendations. In Germany they have considered the social consequences of new technology and in Greater New Haven in the USA they have explored the problem of at-risk children.

The phrase 'citizens' juries' commands attention and connects the development with an established tradition involving citizens in the process of government. It can mislead, however, because the process differs from the formality of courts of law and indeed the phrase is not used in Germany. There is no judge, but rather a moderator, whose role is to facilitate discussion and certainly not to maintain quasi-legal procedures. The jury does not have to reach agreement, but only record its different views if agreement is not reached. Importance is attached to discussion, which can take place throughout the process. In Germany, with juries of 25, some of the discussion takes place in groups of five, before coming back to the wider group. The emphasis is on informality in order to make discussion easier.

Since the publication of the Institute of Public Policy Research's work on citizens' juries there has been considerable interest in their potential in local authorities. The Local Government Management Board has sponsored a series of pilot projects. Over forty authorities expressed interest in the projects and six were chosen to proceed. The issues covered include the impact of new technology, drugs issues and the improvement of a specific area of a town. There has also been interest among health authorites. This is seen as, in part, a means of enhancing their own accountability, as concern with the accountability of appointed boards has grown. The Institute of Public Policy Research and the King's Fund are supporting a number of citizens' juries in health authorities, focusing on such issues as health rationing.

The citizens' juries in Britain are being formed as this chapter is being written. There will be evaluations of their success and their impact on authorities. For the purpose of this chapter they have been used as an example of innovation in democratic practice. Citizens' juries are not *the* approach to building participatory democracy, but *one* approach amongst a repertoire of approaches designed to find the informed views of citizens. Here, more briefly, are several others.

*Deliberative opinion polls*

Deliberative opinion polls also seek the informed views of citizens. However, while citizens' juries take the jury system as their starting-point and then modify it, the deliberative opinion poll takes as its starting-point the ordinary opinion poll and seeks to overcome its weakness. Fishkin, its main advocate, has argued: 'An ordinary opinion poll models what the public thinks, given how little it knows. A deliberative opinion poll models what the public would think, if it had a more adequate chance to think about the questions at issue.' Deliberative opinion polls differ from citizens' juries in that they involve larger numbers and can involve less time and less intense discussion. They differ from normal opinion polls in that opinions will be tested after the participants have had an opportunity to hear witnesses, ask questions and discuss the issue although, for the purpose of comparison, views may also have been tested at the outset of the process.

Fishkin piloted a deliberative opinion poll on issues of law and order in Britain through Channel 4 television and the *Independent* newspaper. In January of this year a National Issues Convention was held in the USA which included a deliberative opinion poll based on 600 voters selected as a representative sample of the American population. They discussed key issues facing America, including the economy, America's role in the world, and the state of the family.

*Citizens' panels*

Citizens' panels are representative panels of citizens called together as sounding boards. In 1993, eight health panels, each consisting of twelve people selected to be a representative sample of the population, were set up by the Somerset Health Commission to discuss the values that should guide health resource allocation decisions. The panels held four meetings over the following year. At the first meeting panel members were asked to bring their own health issues. At the succeeding meetings they discussed issues raised by the health authorities. These included whether the health authority should pay for coronary artery by-pass operations for people who smoke, and whether certain treatments should be given at all. The topics chosen were issues being actively considered by the authorities.

There is an emphasis on deliberation: 'An important rationale of our approach to consultation was that those involved should have the opportunity to explore issues in some depth. Most people need a period of listening to the views of others and talking about issues themselves in order to clarify their thoughts on any complex question.' After discussion, panel members complete a series of decision sheets, in effect voting on the issue. The research team organizing the project prepared reports for the health authority using the discussion as well as the results from the decision sheets, to convey the flavour of the panel meeting. The panels are continuing, with four members replaced at each meeting.

The same principle has been suggested for a local authority, but with a panel of from 200 to 300, to meet once a month, as a sounding board for the authority, again with a percentage changing each month. The panel would again be a representative panel, ensuring that sections of the public from whom the authority rarely heard views were represented.

*Consensus conferences*

Consensus conferences are another variant. They were designed to incorporate public interests and concerns into processes of policy making on science issues, which has often been seen as a matter for experts but increasingly raises ethical or environmental issues. This approach was developed in Denmark. A consensus conference on plant biotechnology was organized in Britain by the Science Museum in London. Simon-Joss and John Durant (1994) define consensus conferences as 'a forum in which a group of lay people put questions about a scientific or technological subject of controversial political and social interest to experts, listen to the experts' answers, then reach a consensus about this subject and finally report their findings at a press conference'.

In Denmark, subjects have included air pollution, childlessness, food irradiation and electronic identity cards; the cost has been from £35,000 to £50,000 per conference. The procedure is well-established in that country, and differs from citizens' juries in having a less representative method of selection, one based on written applications. Consensus conferences are a variation on the theme of the informed citizen.

*A range of innovation*

These are not the only possible innovations. Other examples include:

- mediation groups, which bring together groups which are in conflict over, for example, environmental issues, to see if through discussion differences can be reconciled or at least reduced
- new forms of public meetings, designed to enable discussion in groups rather than to structure meetings around platform and audience
- community forums, in which authorities can reach out to diverse communities, remembering that as well as communities of place there are communities of interest
- stakeholder conferences, in which all interested in an issue can be brought together in a variety of forms of discussion designed to identify areas for action
- teledemocracy, which as time passes may have an increasing role in providing access for the public and involving the public
- involvement of citizens in scrutiny panels, village appraisals, environmental assessments.

All of these can enhance participatory democracy and strengthen representative democracy. There is also a case for direct democracy on specific issues. There is more of a tradition of referendums at local level than is often appreciated. There is a long history of referendums on libraries, local licensing options, Sunday opening of cinemas, and private Bills. Although most of these are in the past, the right of electors to call parish polls remains and what are, in effect, referendums have been instituted by the Conservative government for parents on options for grant-maintained status and for tenants on the transfer of local authority housing stock. Some local authorities have recently held referendums on local issues such as the Sunday opening of leisure centres. The use of referendums on issues of community concern that lie outside the main framework of party political divides can be an exercise in citizenship, encouraging public discussion.

The point lies not in particular approaches but in the range of approaches. Innovation opens up opportunities through which a habit of citizenship can be built. Participation can be used to encourage further participation. Possibilities are opened up through the creation of arenas for discourse.

*Towards decentralization*

Strengthening democracy and public learning requires a learning government. The capacity of central government to constitute the basis for a learning system of government is limited. Many tiers in organizational hierarchies separate ministers from action and impact. Central government cannot easily encompass diversity of circumstance or achieve diversity in response. Yet learning comes from a recognition of diversity of need, diversity of aspiration and diversity of response. From uniformity one may learn little, except of the scale of one's failure. One learns from diversity of relative success and relative failure. A central government can achieve learning if it uses the diversity of local government as its base.

Participation is built more easily at local level than at national level, and the evidence is that citizens are more ready to participate at that level. A commitment to the strengthening of participatory democracy is a commitment to decentralization within the system of government, both to local authorities and within local authorities. Within local government, too, decentralization and more effective local democracy involve a commitment to strengthen participatory democracy through innovation in democratic practice, for which a repertoire of approaches is being and can be developed.

This section has discussed a family of approaches for re-constituting the public domain for public learning and active citizenship. This creation of a learning local democracy provides the context for renewing educational institutions for citizenship and the remaking of civil society.

## Towards a pedagogy of co-operative making

The central task for local institutions is to develop pedagogies of active learning which support the reconstruction of agency. To learn is to develop understanding which leads into, and grows out of, action; to discover a sense of agency that enables us, not only to define and make ourselves, but to do so by actively participating in the creation of a world in which, inescapably, we live together. Realizing this will require institutions to dissolve the boundaries of otherness and to establish cultures of learning which value difference (Nixon *et al.*, 1997a).

Learning itself begins with a sense of discovery of new knowledge or skills. But the deeper significance of learning lies through its forming of our powers and capacities, in our unfolding agency, in our understanding of who we are and what we can do as a person. The purpose and outcome of active learning may be a particular 'competence' which alters our capacity to intervene in experience. But the central purpose of learning is to enable such skills to develop our distinctive agency as a human being. Learning is becoming. It is an unfolding through which we learn not only what makes us unique – what individuates us – but how we can learn to make that distinctive agency work in the world. Learning involves becoming aware of our difference but also, significantly, how to enact its distinctiveness. Learning to develop the agency of the person is inescapably a temporal process: it takes time.

Learning leads into action and grows out of the experience which action enables: it creates the capacity for *self-creation*. Understanding only lives and has meaning through our agency in the world. For Dewey (1958) this notion of learning expresses a philosophy of being in the world: through active experience we come to understand the world and to change it.

There is, however, no solitary learning: we can only create our worlds together. The unfolding agency of the self always grows out of the interaction with others. It is *inescapably a social creation*. We can only develop as persons with and through others; the conception of the self presupposes an understanding of what we are to become and this always unfolds through our relationship with others; the conditions in which the self develops and flourishes are social and political. The self can only find its identity in and through others and the membership of communities. The possibility of shared understanding requires individuals not only to value others but to create the communities in which mutuality, and thus the conditions for learning, can flourish. The *telos* of learning is to learn to make the communities without which individuals and others cannot grow and develop.

We need to recover what the Anthenians understood: that human development requires recognizing the duality of values that are central to human development. A person is also a citizen whose responsibility to contribute to the well-being of the whole is matched by the obligation to acknowledge the freedom of its members. Autonomy depends upon the quality of co-operative interdependence that values the difference of others. The personal exercise of a virtue cannot be separated from the same persons making a world which recognizes such values.

## CONCLUSION

Reaching shared understanding and agreement is the condition for the co-operative inter-dependence which releases the agency of citizens (Nixon and Ranson, 1997). Such understanding can no longer be taken for granted and new forms of governance must be constituted to allow democratic participation, agreement and consent. By developing the strategies for a new democracy discussed in this chapter, the new polity can create the conditions for public discourse and for mutual accountability so that citizens can take each other's needs and claims into account. By doing so they will learn to create the conditions for each other's development. Learning as discourse underpins the learning society.

The values of the learning society, enabling all people to make a purpose for their lives, can create the conditions for working through the transformations of our time. A learning society encourages individuals to value their active role as citizens and thus their shared responsibility for the common wealth. Active learning within institutions and the community needs, therefore, to be informed by and lead towards citizenship within a participatory democracy. Professionals and managers with their understanding of the processes of learning can, we believe, play a leading role in enabling such a vision to unfold across the public domain (Nixon *et al.*, 1997b; Ranson and Stewart, 1994).

Thus are the conditions for a learning society to be developed. Such a society is needed for the transformations of our times, but there is more to it than that. The transformation required is not just *through* a learning but *to* a learning society.

## NOTE

1. This chapter draws directly on Ranson (1997) and Stewart (1997).

# References

Abrahamsson, K. (1993) Concepts, organisation and current trends in lifelong education in Sweden. *International Journal of Lifelong Education*, 32 (3), 47–69

Abram, I. (1984) Permanent Leren in de joodse samenleving (Lifelong Learning in the Jewish Community. In H. Van der Zee (ed.), *Volwasseneneducatie: dilemma's en perspectieven (Adult Education: Dilemmas and Perspectives)*. Meppel: Boom

Ainley, P. (1993) *Class and Skill: Changing Divisions of Labour and Knowledge*. London: Cassell

Ainley, P. (1994a) *Degrees of Difference: Higher Education in the 1990s*. London: Lawrence & Wishart

Ainley, P. (1994b) Two roads to modernisation: two versions of the learning society. Unpublished paper, University of Kent at Canterbury

Aitken, R. (1983) *Comprehensive Education For Life*. Coventry City Council

Anderson, B. (1983) *Imagined Communities*. London: Verso

Anderson, P. (1994) Power, politics and the Enlightenment. In D. Miliband (ed.), *Reinventing the Left*. Cambridge: Polity Press

Apple, M. (1985) *Education and Power*. London: Ark Paperbacks

Apple, M. (1993) *Official Knowledge: Democratic Education in a Conservative Age*. London: Routledge

Archer, M. (1982) Morphogenesis versus structuration: on combining structure and action. *British Journal of Sociology*, 33 (4), 455–83

Argyris, C. (1993) *On Organisational Learning*. Oxford: Blackwell

Argyris, C. and Schön, D. (1978) *Organizational Learning: a Theory of Action Perspective*. Reading, MA: Addison-Wesley

Arnot, M. (1991) Equality and democracy: a decade of struggle over education. *British Journal of Sociology of Education*, 12 (4), 447–66.

Ashton, D., Maguire, M. and Spilsbury, M (1990) *Restructuring the Labour Market: Implications for Youth*. London: Macmillan

Ashton, J. (ed.) (1992) *Healthy Cities*. Buckingham: Open University Press

Attwood, M. and Beer, N. (1988) Development of a learning organisation. *Management Education and Development* 19 (3), 201–14

Avis, J., Bloomer, M., Esland, G., Gleeson, D. and Hodkinson, P. (1996) *Knowledge and Nationhood: Education, Politics and Work.* London: Cassell

Bagnall, R. (1990) Lifelong education: the institutionalization of an illiberal and regressive concept? *Educational Philosophy and Theory,* 22 (1), 1–7

Ball, C. (1990) More means different: wider participation in better higher education. *Royal Society of Arts Journal,* October, 743–57

Ball, C. (1991) *Learning Pays: The Role of Post-Compulsory Education and Training.* London: Royal Society of Arts

Barber, B. (1984) *Strong Democracy: Participatory Politics for a New Age.* Berkeley: University of California Press.

Barber, M. (1996) *The Learning Game: Arguments for an Education Revolution.* London: Gollancz

Barcelona (1990) *The Educating City.* Barcelona: Adjuntament de Barcelona

Barcelona (1991) *First International Congress of Educating Cities.* Barcelona: Adjuntament de Barcelona

Barnett, R. (1994) *The Limits of Competence: Knowledge, Higher Education and Society.* Buckingham: Open University Press

Barnett, R. (1997) *Higher Education: A Critical Business.* Buckingham: Open University Press

Baron, S. (1989) Community education: from the Cam to the Rea. In S. Walker and L. Barton (eds), *Politics and the Processes of Schooling.* Milton Keynes: Open University Press

Barraclough, G. (1967) *An Introduction to Contemporary History.* Harmondsworth: Penguin

Barry, B. (1989) *Theories of Justice: Volume 1: A Treatise on Social Justice.* London: Harvester/Wheatsheaf

Bateson, G. (1972) *Steps to an Ecology of Mind.* London: Paladin

Bauman, Z. (1993) *Postmodern Ethics.* Oxford: Blackwell

Bayman, Z (1994) *Alone Again: Ethics after Uncertainty.* London: Demos

Beck, U. (1994) The reinvention of politics: towards a theory of reflexive modernisation. In U. Beck, A. Giddens and S. Lash (eds), *Reflexive Modernisation: Politics, Tradition, and Aesthetics in the Modern Social Order.* Cambridge: Polity Press

Bell, D. (1973) *The Coming of Post-industrial Society: A Venture in Social Forecasting.* New York: Basic Books

Benn, C. (1992) Common education and the radical tradition. In A. Rattansi and D. Reeder (eds), *Rethinking Radical Education.* London: Lawrence & Wishart

Benn, C. and Chitty, C. (1996) *Thirty Years On: Is Comprehensive Education Alive and Well or Struggling to Survive?* London: David Fulton

Bennett, R., Wicks, P. and McCoshan, A. (1994) *Local Empowerment and Business Services.* London: University of London Press

Berger, P. (1980) *The Heretical Imperative.* New York: Anchor Press/Doubleday

Blaxter, L. and Tight, M. (1994) Juggling with time: how adults manage their time for lifelong learning. *Studies in the Education of Adults,* 26 (2), 162–79

Bolton, E. (1990) *Standards in Education 1988–89: The Annual Report of HM Senior Chief Inspector of Schools.* London: DES

Boshier, R. *et al.* (1980) *Towards a Learning Society: New Zealand Adult Education in Transition.* Auckland: Learning Press

Boswell, J. (1990) *Community and the Economy.* London: Routledge

Bottomley, D., McKay, S. and Walker, R (1997) *Unemployment and Job Seeking: A National Survey* Research Report No. 62, Department of Social Security. London: HMSO

Boud, D. (ed.) (1988) *Developing Student Autonomy in Learning.* London: Kogan Page

Bowles, S. and Gintis, H. (1976) *Schooling in Capitalist America.* London: Routledge and Kegan Paul

Brighouse, T. (1996) Learning networks: a glimpse of the future. *Birmingham Governor,* Autumn, p. 3.

Brookfield, S. (1987) *Learning Democracy: Eduard Lindemann on Adult Education and Social Change.* London: Croom Helm

Brosio, R. (1994) *A Radical Democratic Critique of Capitalist Education.* New York: Peter Lang

Carnegie Commission on Higher Education (1973) *Towards a Learning Society: Alternative Channels to Life, Work and Service.* New York: McGraw-Hill

Carnoy, M. and Levin, H. (1985) *Schooling and Work in the Democratic State.* Stanford: Stanford University Press

Carspecken, P. (1991) Parental choice, participation and working-class culture. In Education Group II (ed.) *Education Limited.* London: Unwin Hyman

Castells, M. (1989) *The Informational City.* Oxford: Blackwell

CBI (1989) *Towards a Skills Revolution.* London: CBI

CBI (1991) *The Skills Revolution.* London: CBI

CBI (1993) *Routes for Success.* London: CBI

CBI (1995) *Realising a Vision: A Skills Passport.* London: CBI

CERI/OECD (1993) *City Strategies for Lifelong Learning.* Gothenburg: Education Committee

Clark, D. (1996) *Schools as Learning Communities.* London: Cassell

Clarke, P. (1996) *Deep Citizenship.* London: Pluto

Cochinaux, P. and de Woot, P. (1995) *Moving Towards a Learning Society.* Geneva: Association of European Universities

Coffield, F. (ed.) (1995a) *Higher Education in a Learning Society* (Report for DfEE, ESRC, HEFC). Durham: School of Education.

Coffield, F. (1995b) One vision beyond the barriers. *Times Educational Supplement,* 3 March, p. 19

Coffield, F. (1997a) Prophets of the true God. *Times Educational Supplement,* 24 January

Coffield, F. (1997b) The value of one daring question. *Times Educational Supplement,* 31 January.

Coffield, F. (1997c) *Can the UK become a learning society?* Fourth Annual Education Lecture, King's College, University of London, 26 June

Coffield, F. (1997d) A tale of three little pigs: building the learning society with straw. *Evaluation and Research in Education,* 11, 1–15.

Cohen, J. and Arato, A. (1992) *Civil Society and Political Theory.* Cambridge, MA: MIT Press

Cohen, J. and Rogers, J. (eds) (1995) *Associations and Democracy*. London: Verso

Cole, M. and Hill, D. (1995) Games of despair and rhetorics of resistance: postmodernism, education and reaction. *British Journal of Sociology of Education*, 16 (2), 165–82

Commission of the European Union (1995) *Teaching and Learning: Towards the Learning Society*, White Paper on Education and Training. Brussels: Commission of the European Union

Commission on Post-Secondary Education in Ontario (1972) *The Learning Society*. Toronto: Ministry of Government Services

Connell, R. W. (1993) *Schools and Social Justice*. Philadelphia: Temple University Press

Connell, R. W. (1994) Poverty and education. *Harvard Education Review*, 64 (2), 125–49

Connell, R. W., White, V. M. and Johnston, K. M. (eds) (1991) *Running Twice as Hard: The Disadvantaged Schools Programme in Australia*. Geelong: Deakin University

Coole, D. (1996) Is class a diference that makes a difference? *Radical Philosophy*, 77, 17–25

Cooley, M. (1993) Skills and Competence. Paper presented at the ILTD 24th National Conference, Galway

Cropley, A (1979) Introduction. In A. Cropley (ed.), *Lifelong Education: A Stocktaking*. Hamburg: UNESCO Institute for Education

Cropley, A. (ed.) (1980) *Towards a System of Lifelong Education: Some Practical Considerations*. Oxford: Pergamon Press

Cross, K. P. (1986) *Adults as Learners: Increasing Participation and Facilitating Learning*. London: Jossey-Bass

Department of Education (1963) *Higher Education*. London: HMSO

Department of Education and Science/Department of Employment (1991) *Employment and Training for the Twenty-first Century*. London: HMSO

Department for Education (1992) *Choice and Diversity: A New Framework for Schools*. London: HMSO

Department for Education and Employment (1995a) *Lifetime Learning: A Consultation Document*. Sheffield: DfEE

Department for Education and Employment (1995b) *Secondary School Performance Tables 1995*. London: DfEE

Department for Education and Employment (1995c) *Financial Control of Payments Made Under the Training For Work and Youth Training Programmes in England*. London: HMSO

Department for Education and Employment (1996a) *Lifetime Learning: A Summary of Responses to the Government's Consultation Document*. London: DfEE

Department for Education and Employment (1996b) James Paice Publishes a Framework for a Learning Society. Press Release 203/96. London: DfEE

Department for Education and Employment (1996c) *Training Statistics 1996* London: HMSO

Department for Education and Employment (1997) *Basic Skills for Life*. London: DfEE

Department of Employment (1994) *The Civil Service: Continuity and Change.* London: HMSO

Department of Trade and Industry/Employment Department (1996) *Competitiveness: Creating the Enterprise Centre of Europe.* London: HMSO

Delors, J. (1996) *Learning: The Treasure Within.* Paris: UNESCO

Dewey, J. (1915) *Democracy and Education.* New York: Free Press

Dewey, J. (1935) Liberalism and social action. In J. Boydston (ed.), *John Dewey: Later Works: 1925–53, Vol. 11.* Carbondale: University of Southern Illinois Press

Dewey, J. (1958) *Experience and Nature.* New York: Dover.

De Zeeuw, G. (1984) Verborgen vaardigheden (Hidden skills). In H. Van der Zee (ed.), *Volwasseneducatie: dilemma's en perspectiven* (Adult Education Dilemmas and Perspectives). Meppel: Boom

De Zeeuw, G. (1985) Problems of increasing competence. *Systems Research,* 2 (1), 13–19

Dreze, J. and Sen. A. (1989) *Hunger and Public Action* Oxford: Clarendon

Duffy, H. (1995) *Competitive Cities: Succeeding in the Global Economy.* London: Spon

Dunn, J. (1992) *Democracy.* Oxford: Blackwell

Eagleton, T. (1991) *Ideology: An Introduction.* London: Verso

Economic and Social Research Council (1996) *The Learning Society: A Research Programme.* Swindon: ESRC.

Edwards, R. (1995a) Different dicourses, discourses of difference. *Distance Education,* 16 (2), 241–55

Edwards, R. (1995b) Behind the banner: whither the learning society? *Adults Learning,* February, 187–9

Elster, J (1983) *Explaining Technical Change.* Cambridge: Cambridge University Press

Engestrom, Y. (1991) Non scolae sed vitae discimus: towards overcoming the encapsulation of school learning. *Learning and Instruction,* 1, 243

Engestrom, Y. (1994) *Training for Change.* Geneva: ILO

ESRC (1994) *Research Specification for the ESRC Learning Society: Knowledge and Skills for Employment Programme.* Swindon: ESRC

Etzioni, A. (1968) *The Active Society: The Theory of Societal and Political Processes.* New York: Free Press

Etzioni, A. (1988) *The Moral Dimension: Toward a New Economics.* New York: Free Press

European Commission (1996) *Teaching and Learning: Towards the Learning Society.* Luxembourg: EC

Evans, N. (1985) *Post-Education Society: Recognising Adults as Learners.* London: Croom Helm

Fauré, E., Herrera, F., Kaddowa, A., Lopes, H., Petrovsky, A., Rahnema, M. and Ward, F. (1972) *Learning To Be: The World of Education Today and Tomorrow.* Paris: UNESCO/Harrap

FEU (1991) *A Basis for Credit.* London: Further Education Unit

Field, J. (1995) Globalisation, consumption and the learning business. *Distance Education,* 16 (2), 270–83

Finegold, D., Keep, E., Miliband, D., Raffe, D., Spurs, K. and Young, M. (1990) *A British Baccalauréate: Ending the Division Between Education and Training*. London: Institute of Public Policy Research

Finegold, D. and Soskice, D. (1988) The failure of training in Britain. *Oxford Review of Economic Policy* 4

Fishkin, J. (1991) *Democracy and Deliberation: New Directions for Democratic Reform*. New Haven: Yale University Press

Fletcher, R. (1984) *Education in Society: The Promethean Fire*. Harmondsworth: Penguin Books

Flude, R. and Parrott, A. (1979) *Education and the Challenge of Change: A Recurrent Education Strategy for Britain*. Milton Keynes: Open University Press

Fodor, J (1996) Peacocking: a review of R. Dawkins *Climbing Mount Improbable*. *London Review of Books*, 18 April, 19–20

Forrester, K., Payne, J. and Ward, K. (eds) (1993) *Developing a Learning Workforce: Conference Proceedings*. Leeds: University of Leeds, Department of Adult Continuing Education

Fraser, N. (1995) From redistribution to recognition? Dilemmas of justice in a post-socialist age. *New Left Review*, 212, 68–93

Friedman, J. (1987) *Planning in the Public Domain: From Knowledge to Action*. Princeton: Princeton University Press.

Fritzell, C. (1987) On the concept of relative autonomy in educational theory. *British Journal of Sociology of Education*, 8 (1), 23–5

Gadamer, H. G. (1975) *Truth and Method*. London: Sheed and Ward

Gallie, W. B. (1964) *Philosophy and Historical Understanding*. London: Unwin

Gardner, H. (1984) *Frames of Mind*. London: Heinemann

Gardner, H. (1991) *The Unschooled Mind*. London: Fontana

Gellner, E. (1964) *Thought and Change*. London: Weidenfeld and Nicholson

Gellner, E (1988) *Plough, Sword and Book*. London: Collins

George, S. and Sabelli, F. (1994) *Faith and Credit: The World Bank's Secular Empire*. Harmondsworth: Penguin

Giddens, A. (1976) *New Rules of Sociological Method*. London: Hutchinson

Giddens, A. (1984) *The Constitution of Society*. Cambridge: Polity Press

Giddens, A. (1990) *The Consequences of Modernity*. Cambridge: Polity Press

Giddens, A. (1991) *Modernity and Self-Identity: Self and Society in the Late Modern Age*. Cambridge: Polity Press

Giddens, A. (1994a) Brave new world: the new context of politics. In D. Miliband (ed.), *Reinventing the Left*. Cambridge: Polity Press

Giddens, A. (1994b) *Beyond Left and Right: The Future of Radical Politics*. Oxford: Polity Press

Giddens, A. (1994c) Living in a post-traditional society. In U. Beck, A. Giddens and S. Lash (eds), *Reflexive Modernization: Politics, Tradition and Aesthetics in the Modern Social Order*. Cambridge: Polity Press.

Giddens, A. (1995) *A Contemporary Critique of Historical Materialism* (2nd edn) London: Macmillan

Gilligan, C. (1986), Remapping the moral domain. In T. Heller, M. Sosna and D. Wellbury (eds), *Reconstructing Individualism: Autonomy, Individuality and the Self in Western Thought*. Stanford: Stanford University Press

Gleeson, D. (1996) Not so much the learning society. *Curriculum Studies*, 4 (1), 149–56.

Glennerster, H. and Low, W. (1990), Education and the welfare state: does it add up? In N. Barr *et al.* (eds), *The State of Welfare: The Welfare State in Britain Since 1974*. Oxford: Clarendon Press

Gokulsing, K., Ainley, P. and Tysome, T. (1996) *Beyond Competence: The National Council for Vocational Qualifications Framework and the Challenge to Higher Education in the New Millenium*. Aldershot: Avebury

Goffman, E. (1974) *Frame Analysis*. Harmondsworth: Penguin

Gorz, A. (1989) *Critique of Economic Reason*. London: Verso

Grace, G. (1995) *School Leadership: Beyond Education Management*. London: Falmer

Gray, J. (1995) *Enlightenment's Wake*. London: Routledge

Gray, J. (1996) *After Social Democracy*. London: Demos

Green, A. (1996) Towards the learning society. *History of Education*, 26 (1), 117–20

Green, A. (1997) *Education, Globalisation and the Nation State*. London: Macmillan

Habermas, J. (1972) *Knowledge and Human Interests*. London: Heinemann

Habermas, J. (1984), *The Theory of Communicative Action: Volume One: Reason and the Rationalization of Society*. London: Heinemann

Habermas, J. (1990) *Moral Consciousness and Communicative Action*. Cambridge: Polity Press

Hales, M. (1984) *Living Thinkwork*. London: CSE Books

Hall, S. (1990) Cultural identity and diaspora. In J. Rutherford (ed.), *Identity: Community, Culture, Difference*. London: Lawrence & Wishart

Handy, C. (1984) *The Future of Work*. Oxford: Blackwell

Handy, C. (1989) *The Age of Unreason*. London: Arrow Books

Handy, C. (1994) *The Empty Raincoat*. London: Hutchinson

Hagreaves, A. (1994) *Changing Teachers, Changing Times*. London: Cassell

Hargreaves, D. (1984) *Improving Secondary Schools*. London: Inner London Education Authority

Hargreaves, D. (1997) A road to the learning society. *School Leadership and Management* 17 (1), 9–21

Harris, K. (1994) *Teachers: Constructing the Future*. London: Falmer Press

Harrow, J. And Willcocks, L. (1990) Public services management: activities, initiatives and limits to learning. *Journal of Management Studies*, 27 (3), 281–304

Harrow, J. and Willcocks, I. (1992) Management, innovation and organisational learning. In L. Willcocks and J. Harrow (eds), *Rediscovering Public Service Management* London: McGraw-Hill

Harvey, D. (1989) *The Condition of Postmodernity*. Oxford: Blackwell

Hatcher, R. (1994) Culture, consent and contestation. In A. Thody (ed.), *School Governors: Leaders or Followers?* Harlow: Longman

Hatcher, R. (1995) *Class, Equality and Agency: the Limitations of the New Social Democratic Agenda*. Paper presented at the Symposium of Post-Conservative Programmes of Reform, at the European Conference on Educational Research, 14–17 September, University of Bath

Hatcher, R. (1996) The limitation of the new social democratic agendas: class, inequality and agenda. In R. Hatcher and K. Jones (eds), *Education After the Conservatives: The Response to the New Agenda of Reform*. Stoke-on-Trent: Trentham Books

Hayes, C., Fonda, N. and Hillman, J. (1995) *Learning in the New Millennium*. NCE Briefing, New Series No. 5. London: National Commission on Education, Paul Hamlyn Foundation

Held, D. (1989) *Political Theory and the Modern State*. Cambridge: Polity Press

Held, D. (ed.) (1993) *Prospects for Democracy*. Cambridge: Polity Press

Hirsch, E. D. (1988) *Cultural Literacy: What Every American Needs to Know*. New York: Vintage Books

Hirst, P. (1994) *Associative Democracy*. Cambridge: Polity Press

Hobsbawm, E. (1994) *Age of Extremes: The Short Twentieth Century 1914–1991*. London: Michael Joseph

Holly, P. and Southworth, G. *The Developing School*. London, Falmer

Holmes, M. (1988) The fortress monastery: the future of the common core. In I. Westbury and A. C. Purves (eds), *Cultural Literacy and the Idea of General Education*. Chicago: University of Chicago Press

Holt, J. (1970) *How Children Learn*. Harmonsworth: Penguin

Holt, J. (1977) *Instead of Education*. Harmondsworth: Penguin

Houle, C. O. (1972) *The Design of Education*. London: Jossey-Bass

Howard, R. (1990) Introduction. In R. Howard (ed.), *The Learning Imperative*, Boston: Harvard Business School

Hughes, C. and Tight, M. (1995) The myth of the learning society. *British Journal of Educational Studies*, 43 (3), 290–304

Husén, T. (1974) *The Learning Society*. London: Methuen

Husén, T. (1986) *The Learning Society Revisited*. Oxford: Pergamon

Husén, T. (1990) *Education and the Global Concern*. Oxford: Pergamon Press.

Hutchins, R. (1968) *The Learning Society*. Harmondsworth: Penguin; reprinted (1970) London: Pall Mall Press

Hutchinson, B. (1996) Work, autonomy and democracy: competence in what? *Curriculum*, 4 (1), 67–90

Hyland, T. (1994) *Competence, Education and NVQs: Dissenting Perspectives*. London: Cassell

Illich, I. (1971) *Deschooling Society*. New York: Harper and Row

Illich, I. (1973) *After Deschooling, What?* London: Writers and Readers Cooperative

Illich, L. (1973a) *Deschooling Society*. Harmondsworth: Penguin Books

Institute for Public Policy Research (1993) *Education: A Different Version*. London: IPPR

Jarvis, P. (1983) *Adult and Continuing Education: Theory and Practice*. London: Croom

Johnston, K. (1993) Inequality and educational reform lessons for the disadvantaged schools project. In B. Lingard, J. Knight, and P. Porter (eds), *Schooling Reform in Hard Times*. London: Falmer.

Jones, A. and Henry, G. (1992) *The Learning Organization: A Review of Literature and Practice*. London: HRD Partnership

Jordan, B. (1989) *The Common Good: Citizenship, Morality and Self-Interest*. Oxford: Blackwell

Kanter, R. (1989) *When Giants Learn to Dance: Mastering the Challenges of Strategy, Management and Careers in the 1990s*. New York: Simon & Schuster

Keane, J. (ed.) (1988a) *Civil Society and the State*. London: Verso

Keane, J. (1988b) *Democracy and Civil Society*. London: Verso

Kelly, K. (1994) *Out of Control*. London: Fourth Estate

Kennedy, H. (1997) *Learning Works: Widening Participation in Further Education*. Coventry: Further Education Funding Council

Kidd, J. R. (1983) Learning and libraries: competencies for full participation. *Library Trends*, 31 (4), 525–42

Kim, K, Collins, M. and Stowe, P. (1995) *Forty Percent of Adults Participate in Adult Education Activities 1944–95*. Washington: Department of Education

Kingdom, J. (1992) *No Such Thing as Society?* Milton Keynes: Open University Press

Kinvinen, O. and Rinnie, R. (1992) *Educational Strategies in Finland in the 1990s*. Turku: Research Unit for the Sociology of Education, University of Turku

Kohn, R (1982) *Enforced Education: Enforced Leisure*. London: Fabian Society (Tract 479)

Kolb, D. (1973) *Organisational Psychology*. Englewood Cliffs: Prentice-Hall

Kolb, D. (1984) *Experiential Learning* Englewood Cliffs: Prentice Hall

Kumar, K. (1995) Apocalypse, millennium and utopia today. In M. Bull (ed.), *Apocalypse Theory and the Ends of the World*. Oxford: Blackwell

Labour Party (1994) *Opening Doors to a Learning Society: A Policy Statement on Education*. London: Labour Party

Lawton, D. (1992) *Education and Politics in the 1990's: Conflict or Consensus*. London: Falmer

Le Goff, J. (1994) *La vieille Europe et la notre*. Paris: Editions du Seuile

Lengrand, P. (1989) Lifelong education: growth of the concept. In C. Titmus (ed.), *Lifelong Education for Adults: An International Handbook*. Oxford: Pergamon

Lessem, R. (1993) *Business as a Learning Community*. London: McGraw Hill

Levacic, R. (1995) *Local Management of Schools: Analysis and Practice*. Buckingham: Open University Press

Levin, M. A. (1987) Parent-teacher-collaboration. In D. Livingstone (ed.), *Critical Pedagogy and Cultural Power*. Basingstoke: Macmillan

Lukes, S. (1974) *Power*. London: Macmillan

Lunneborg, P. (1994) *OU Women: Undoing Educational Obstacles*. London: Cassell

Luttwak, E. (1995) Turbo-charged capitalism and its consequences. *London Review of Books*, 22 November, 6–7

McCarthy, G. (1994) *Dialectics and Decadence: Echoes of Antiquity in Marx and Nietzsche*. Lanham: Rowman & Littlefield

McCarthy, M. (1993) After the canon: knowledge and ideological representation in the multicultural discourse on curriculum reform. In C. McCarthy and W. Crichlow (eds), *Race, Identity and Representation in Education*. London: Routledge

McEwan, I. (1984) *Een gesprek met Milan Kundera* (Talking to Milan Kundera). *De revisor*, 6, 26–32

McGivney, V. (1990) *Education's For Other People: Access to Education for Non-Participant Adults*. Leicester: NIACE

McGivney, V. (1992) *Motivating Unemployed Adults to Undertake Education and Training*. Leicester: NIACE

McLoskey, D. (1983) The rhetoric of economics. *Journal of Economics*, 21 June, 481–517

MacIntyre, A. (1981) *After Virtue: A Study in Moral Theory*. London: Duckworth

Maden, M. (1994) Blair's braver game. *Times Education Supplement*, 30 September

Marshall, T. (1977) *Classes, Citizenship and Social Development*. Chicago: University of Chicago Press

Martin, I. (1992) New times: new direction? *Community Education Network*, 12 (9), 1–15

Martin, I. (1994) *Community Education: The School*. Adult and Continuing Education, Unit 4. Canterbury: YMCA National College

Martin, W. J. (1988) The information society: idea or entity? *Aslib Proceedings*, 40 (11/12), 303–9

Marx, K. (1846) *The German Ideology* (with F. Engels). Moscow: Progress Publishers (1968)

Marx, K (1859) *A Contribution to the Critique of Political Economy*.

Marx, K. (1875) *Critique of the Gotha Programme*.

Mayhew, L. (1992) Political rhetoric and the contemporary public. In R. Colomy (ed.), *The Dynamics of Social Systems*. London: Sage

Meyer, J. and Rowan, B. (1978) Institutionalised organizations: formal structures as myth and ceremony. *American Journall of Sociology*, 83 (2), 340–63.

Mik, K., Collins, M. and Stowe, P. (19950 *Forty Percent of Adults Participate in Adult Education Activities: 1944–95*. Washington: Department of Education.

Miliband, D. (1994) *Reinventing the Left*. Cambridge: Polity Press

Mills, C. W. (1959) *The Sociological Imagination*. Oxford: Oxford University Press

Moore, R. (1990) Knowledge, practice and construction of skill. In D. Gleeson (ed.), *Training and its Alternatives*. Milton Keynes. Open University Press

Morgan, G. (1988) *Images of Organisation*. London: Sage

Mouffe, C. (ed.) (1992) *Dimensions of Radical Democracy*. London: Verso

Mouffe, C. (1993) *The Return of the Political*. London: Verso

Münch, R. (1992) The dynamics of social communication. In R. Colomy (ed.), *The Dynamics of Social Systems*. London: Sage

Murphy, J. (1993) A degree of waste: the economic benefits of educational expansion. *Oxford Review of Education*, 19 (1), 9–31

National Advisory Council for Education and Training Targets (1996) *Skills for 2000*. London: NACETT

National Commission on Education (1993a) *Learning Succeeds*. London: Heinemann

National Commission on Education (1993b) *Briefings*. London: Heinemann

National Commission on Education (1996) *Success Against the Odds*. London: Routledge

National Committee of Inquiry into Higher Education (1997) *Higher Education in the Learning Society (The Dearing Report)*. London: HMSO

National Institute for Adult Continuing Education (1994) *What Price the Learning Society?* Leicester: NIACE

Neehal, J. and Tough, A. (1983) Fostering intentional changes among adults. *Library Trends* 31 (4), 543–53

Nietzsche, F. (1983) *Waarheid en cultuur* (Truth and culture): A selection from Nietzsche's Early Work. Meppel: Boom

Nijk, A. J. (1985) *De mythe van de zelfontplooiing (The Myth of Self-Development)*. Meppel: Boom

Nisbet, J. and Shucksmith, J. (1986) *Learning Strategies*. London: Routledge & Kegan Paul

Nixon, J. and Ranson, S. (1997) Theorising 'agreement': the bases of a new professional ethic. *Discourse: Studies in the Cultural Politics of Education*, 18 (2), 197–214

Nixon, J., Martin, J., McKeown, P. and Ranson, S. (1996) *Encouraging Learning: Towards a Theory of the Learning School*. Buckingham: Open University Press

Nixon, J., Martin, J., McKeown, P. and Ranson, S. (1997a) Confronting 'failure': towards a pedagogy of recognition. *International Journal of Inclusive Education*, 1 (2), 121–41

Nixon, J., Martin, J., McKeown, P. and Ranson, S. (1997b) Towards a learning profession: changing codes of occupational practice within the new management of education. *British Journal of Sociology of Education*, 21 (1), 5–28

Noble, D. (1993) Let them eat skills: Essay review of Marshall and Tucker's Thinking for Living (unpub)

Nussbaum, M. (1990) Aristotelian social democracy. In G. Mara and H. Richardson, (eds), *Liberalism and the Good*. New York: Routledge

Offe, C. (1996) *Modernity and the State*. Cambridge: Polity Press

Okins, S. M. (1991) Gender, the public and the private. In D. Held (ed.), *Political Theory Today*. Cambridge: Polity Press

Olson, T. (1982) *Millennialism, Utopianism, and Progress*. Toronto: University of Toronto Press

Organisaton for Economic Cooperation and Development (1992) *Education at a Glance: OECD Indicators*. Paris: OECD

Ozga, J. (1995) Deskilling a profession: professionalism, deprofessionalisation and the new managerialism. In H. Busher and R. Saran (eds), *Managing Teachers as Professionals in Schools*. London: Kogan Page

Parekh, B. (1988) Good answers to bad questions: review of R. Dahrendorf, *The Modern Social Question. New Statesman and Society*, 28 October

Parfit, D. (1984) *Reasons and Persons*. Oxford: Oxford University Press

Park, A. (1994) *Individual Commitment in Lifetime Learning: Individuals Attitudes*. Sheffield: Department of Employment

Pateman, C. (1987) Feminist critiques of the public/private dichotomy. In A. Phillips (ed.), *Feminism and Equality*. Oxford: Blackwell

Pedler, M., Burgoyne, J. and Boydell, T. (1991) *The Learning Company: A Strategy for Sustainable Development*. London: McGraw-Hill

Penland, P. R. and Mathai, A. (1987) *The Library as a Learning Service Center*. New York: Dekker

Perkin, H. (1989) *The Rise of Professional Society: England Since 1880*. London: Routledge

Phillips, A. (1991) *Engendering Democracy*. Cambridge: Polity Ptress

Phillips, A. (1993) *Democracy and Difference*. Cambridge: Polity Press

Phillips, A. (1995) *The Politics of Presence*. Oxford: Oxford University Press

Piore, M. (1995) Local development on the progressive political agenda. In C. Crouch and D. Marquand (eds), *Reinventing Collective Action: From the Global to the Local*. Oxford: Blackwell

Plant, R. (1990) Citizenship and rights. In R. Plant and N. Barry (eds), *Citizenship and Rights in Thatcher's Britain: Two Views*. London: Institute of Economic Affairs

Popper, K. (1966) *The Open Society and its Enemies* (5th rev. edn). London: Routledge

Power, S. (1992) Researching the impact of education policy: difficulties and discontinuities. *Journal of Education Policy*, 7 (5), 493–500

Pring, R (1995) The community of educated people. *British Journal of Educational Studies*, 43 (2), 125–45

Prunty, J. (1985) Signposts for critical education policy analysis. *Australian Journal of Education*, 29 (2) 133–40

Quicke, J. (1997) Reflexivity, community and education for the learning society. *Curriculum Studies*, 5 (2), 139–61

Raggatt, P., Edwards, R. and Small, N. (eds) (1996) *The Learning Society: Challenges and Trends*. London: Routledge

Ranson, S. (1986) Government for a learning society. In S. Ranson and J. Tomlinson (eds), *The Changing Government of Education*. London: Allen and Unwin

Ranson, S. (1988) From 1944 to 1988: education, citizenship and democracy. *Local Government Studies*, 14 (1), 1–19 (Special issue on the Education Reform Bill)

Ranson, S. (1990) Towards education for citizenship. *Education Review*, 42 (2), 151–66

Ranson, S (1991) Towards the learning society: an inaugural lecture, University of Birmingham

Ranson, S. (1992) Towards the learning society. *Educational Management and Administration*, 20 (2), 68–79

Ranson, S. (1993a) *Local Democracy for the Learning Society*, NCE Briefing No. 18, July. London: NCE/Paul Hamlyn Foundation

Ranson, S. (1993b) Markets or democracy for education. *British Journal of Educational Studies*, 41 (4), 333–52

Ranson, S. (1994) *Towards the Learning Society*. London: Cassell

Ranson, S. (1995) Theorising education policy. *Journal of Educational Policy*, 10 (4), 427–48

Ranson, S. (1996) The future of educational research: learning at the centre. *British Educational Research Journal*, 22 (5), 523–35

Ranson, S. (1997) For citizenship and the remaking of civil society. In R. Pring and G. Walford (eds), *Affirming the Comprehensive Ideal*. London: Falmer

Ranson, S., Hinings, B. and Greenwood, R. (1980) The structuring of organizational structures. *Administrative Science Quarterly*, 25 (1), 1–18

Ranson, S., Martin, J., McKeown, P. and Nixon, J. (1996) Towards a theory of learning. *British Journal of Educational Studies*, 44 (1), 9–26

Ranson, S., Rikowski, G., Nixon, J. Mckeown, P. and Butterfield, S. (1995) Institutional systems, capacity for agency and wealth creation in a learning society. Research Proposal for the ESRC Learning Society Programme. University of Birmingham, School of Education

Ranson, S. and Stewart, J (1994) *Management for the Public Domain: Enabling the Learning Society*. Basingstoke: Macmillan

Rawls, J. (1971) *A Theory of Justice*. Oxford: Clarendon

Reich, R. (1991) *The Work of Nations: Preparing for 21st Century Capitalism*. London: Simon and Schuster

Reid, L. A. (1986) *Ways of Understanding and Education*. London: Heinemann

Resnick, L. B. (1987) Learning in school and out. *Educational Researcher*, 16 (9), 13–20

Revans, R. (1982) *The Origins and Growth of Action Learning*. Chartwell: Brett

Richards, C. (1996) Labouring to learn. In R. Hatcher and K. Jones (eds), *Education After the Conservatives*. Stoke on Trent: Trentham Books

Rikowski, G. (1994) Modernisation through education? primary school reforms in Mexico and Chile. Unpublished Paper, University of London, Institute of Education.

Rikowski, G. (forthcoming) *For Scylla: A Materialist Critique of the Learning Society*.

Rikowski, G., Ainley, P. and Ranson, S. (1996) The learning society for the learning city. Paper presented at the annual conference of the Royal Geographical Society and Institute of British Geographers, University of Strathclyde, 3–6 January

Rikowski, G. and Ranson, S. (forthcoming) *The Third Eye: Social Becoming, New Demos and the Learning Society*

Roberts, K., Dench, S. and Richardson, D (1990) Youth labour market processes. In D. Gleeson (ed.), *Training and its Alternatives*. Milton Keynes: Open University Press

Robinson, E. (1968) *The New Polytechnics: The People's Universities*. Harmondsworth: Penguin

Rorty, R. (1989) *Contingency, Irony and Solidarity*. Cambridge: Cambridge University Press

Roszak, T. (1986) *The Cult of Information: The Folklore of Computers and the True Art of Thinking*. New York: Pantheon Books

Sargent, N. (1991) *Learning and Leisure: A Study of Adult Participation in Learning and its Policy Implications*. Leicester: NIACE

Saunders, P. (1979) *Urban Politics: A Sociological Interpretation*. London: Hutchinson

Sayer, D. (1989) *The Violence of Abstraction: The Analytic Foundations of Historical Materialism*. Oxford: Blackwell

Sayer, D. (1979) *Marx's Method: Ideology, Science and Critique in Capital*. Hassocks: Harvester Press

Sayer, J. (1989) The public context of change. In J. Sayer and V. Williams (eds), *Schools and External Relations*. London: Cassell

Schank, R. (1994) Changing the way people learn. *Applied Learning Technologies in Europe*, (7), 4–7.

Schön, D. (1971) *Beyond the Stable State: Public and Private Learning in a Changing Society*. New York: Norton

Schön, D. A. (1987) *Educating the Reflective Practitioner: Towards a New Design for Teaching and Learning in the Professions*. London: Jossey-Bass

Schopenauer, A. (1851) *Parrerga und Paralipomena*. I have used a selection from *De wereld een hel (The World is a Hell)*. Published by Boom in 1981

Schuller, T. (1992) Towards a learning society. *Adults Learning*, 4 (2), 53–4

Schumpeter, J. (1934) *The Theory of Economic Development*. Cambridge, MA: Harvard University Press

Scientific Council for Government Policy (1986) *Basisvorming in het onderwijs* (Basic Forming in Education). The Hague: State Publishing House

Sciulli, D. and Bould, S. (1992) Neocorporatism, social integration, and the limits of comparative political sociology. in R. Colomy (ed.), *The Dynamics of Social Systems*. London: Sage

Scott, P. (1995) *The Meanings of Mass Higher Education*. Buckingham: Open University Press

Scottish Community Education Council (1995) *Scotland as a Learning Society* SCEC

Scottish Office Education Department (1994) *Higher Still: Opportunity for All*. Edinburgh: SOED

Sen, A. (1990), Individual freedom as social commitment. *New York Review of Books*, 14, June

Sen, A. (1992) On the Darwinian view of social progress. *London Review of Books*, 5 November

Sennett, R. (1995) Something in the City. *Times Literary Supplement*, 22 September, 13–15

Shackle, G. (1979) *Imagination and the Nature of Choice*. Edinburgh: Edinburgh University Press

Shackleton, J. (1992) *Training Too Much? A Sceptical Look at the Economics of Skills Provision in the UK*. London: Institute of Economic Affairs

Shank, R. (1994) Changing the way people learn. *Applied Learning Technologies in Europe*, 7, 4–7

Shotter, J. (1993) Psychology and citizenship: identity and belonging. In B. S. Turner (ed.), *Citizenship and Social Theory*. London: Sage

Simey, M. (1985) *Government by Consent: The Principles and Practice of Accountability in Local Government*. London: Bedford Square Press

Simon-Joss, J. and Durrant, J. (1994) *Consensus Conferences*. London: Science Museum Library

Smith, R. M. (1982) *Learning to Learn: Applied Theory for Adults*. Milton Keynes: Open University Press

Sparkes, J. (1995) *The Education of Young People in Learning for Success*. London: Royal Academy of Engineering/National Commission on Education

Spours, K. (1995) Post 16 Participation, Attainment and Progression, Post Education Centre Working Paper, No 17, Institute of Education, University of London

Spours, K. and Young, M (1990) Beyond vocationalism. In D. Gleeson (ed.), *Training and its Alternatives*. Milton Keynes: Open University Press

Steadman, H. and Green, A. (1993) *Widening Participation in Further Education and Training*. London: Centre for Economic Performance.

Steffy, B. E. and Lindle, J. C. (1994) *Building Coalitions*. New York: Sage

Stewart, J. (1995) *Innovation in Democratic Practice*. Institute of Local Government Studies

Stewart, J. (1996) *Further Innovation in Democratic Practice*. London: Institute of Local Government Studies

Stewart, J. (1997) *Thinking Collectively in the Public Domain*. Birmingham: University of Birmingham

Stewart, J., Kendall, L. and Coote, A. (1994) *Citizens' Juries*. London: Institute of Public Policy Research

Strain, M. (1995) Autonomy, schools and the constitutive role of community: towards a new moral and political order. *British Journal of Educational Studies*, 43 (1) 4–20

Strain, M. and Field, J. (1997) On 'The myth of the learning society'. *British Journal of Educational Studies*, 45 (2), 141–55

Swedish Ministry of Education and Science (1993) *The Swedish Way Towards a Learning Society*. Stockholm: Ministry of Education and Science.

Sykes, A. (1965) Myth and attitude change. *Human Relations*, 18 (4), 323–37

Sztompka, P. (1991) *Society in Action: The Theory of Social Becoming*. Cambridge: Polity Press

Taylor, C. (1985), *Philosophy and the Human Sciences: Philosophical Papers 2*. Cambridge: Cambridge University Press

Taylor, C. (1994) *Multiculturalism*. Princeton: Princeton University Press

Technology Foresight (1995) *Progress through Partnership 14: Leisure and Learning*: Office of Science and Technology

Thomas, A. (1991) *Beyond Education: A New Perspective on Society's Management of Learning*. San Francisco: Jossey-Bass

Tight, M. (1994a) Crisis, what crisis? Rhetoric and reality in higher education. *British Journal of Educational Studies*, 42 (4), 363–74

Tight, M. (1994b) Utopia and the education of adults. *International Journal of University Adult Education*, 33 (2), 29–44

Tillyard, E. (1962) *Myth and the English Mind*. New York: Collier

Titmuss, R. M. (1971) *The Gift Relationship: From Human Blood to Social Policy*. London: Allen and Unwin

Toffler, A. (1970) *Future Shock*. London: Bodley Head

Troyna, B. (1994) Critical social research and education policy. *British Journal of Education Studies*, 41 (1), 70–84

Tuijnman, A. (1996) The expansion of adult education and training in Europe: trends and issues. In P. Raggatt, R. Edwards and N. Small (eds), *The Learning Society: Challenges and Trends*. London: Routledge/Open University Press

Turner, B. (1981) *For Weber: Essays on the Sociology of Fate*. London: Routledge

Turner, B. (1990) Outline of a theory of citizenship. *Sociology*, 24 (2), 189–214

Turner, B. (ed) (1993) *Citizenship and Social Theory*. London: Sage

Uden, T. (1996) *Widening Participation: Routes to a Learning Society: A Policy Discussion Paper*. Leicester: NIACE

Unterhalter, E. and Young, M. (1995) Human resource development in post-apartheid South Africa. In *World Year Book of Education, 1995*. London: Kogan Page

US Congress (1983) *A Nation at Risk: The Imperative for Educational Reform*. Washington: Congress

Watkins, K. and Marsick, V. (1992) Building the learning organisation: a new role for human resource developers. *Studies in Continuing Education*, 14 (2), 115–29

Weber, M. (1949) *The Methodology of the Social Sciences*. New York: Free Press

Weber, M. (1978) *Economy and Society*. Berkeley: University of California Press

Webster, F. (1995) *Theories of the Information Society*. London: Routledge

Weiner, G. (1994) Equality and quality: approaches to changes in the management of gender issues. In P. Ribbins and E. Burridge (eds), *Improving Education: Promoting Quality in Schools*. London: Cassell

Westwood, S. (1992) When class became community: radicalism in adult education. In A. Rattansi amd D. Reeder, (eds), *Rethinking Radical Education*. London: Lawrence & Wishart

White, J. (1997) *Education and the End of Work: A New Philosophy of Work and Learning* London: Cassell

White, V. and Johnston, K. (1993) Inside the disadvantaged schools program: the politics of practical policy-making. In L. Angus (ed.), *Education, Inequality and Social Identity*. London: Falmer Press

Whitty, G. (1985) *Sociology and Social Knowledge: Curriculum, Theory, Research and Politics*. London: Methuen

Whitty, G. (1992) Education, economy and national culture. In R. Boocock and K. Thompson (eds), *Social and Cultural Forms of Modernity*. Cambridge: Polity Press

Wood, E. M. (1990) The uses and abuses of 'civil society'. In R. Milliband and L. Panitch (eds), *Socialist Register 1990: The Retreat of the Intellectuals*. London: Merlin Press

Wood, E. M. (1995) *Democracy against Capitalism: Renewing Historical Materialism*. Cambridge: Cambridge University Press

Woolhouse, W. (1993) Towards a world class system. In W. Richardson, J. Woolhouse and D. Finegold (eds), *The Reform of Post-16 Education and Training in England and Wales*. Harlow: Longman

Yeatman, A. (1994) *Postmodern Revisionings of the Political*. London: Routledge

Young, I. (1990) *Justice and the Politics of Difference*. Princeton: Princeton University Press

Young, M. (1993a) Bridging the academic/vocational divide; two Nordic case studies. *European Journal of Education*, 28 (2)

Young, M. (1993b) A curriculum of the 21st century: towards a new basis for overcoming the academic/vocational divisions. *British Journal of Education*, 40 (3)

Young, M. (1994a) Post-compulsory education for a learning society. Paper presented at a Conference on Reforming Post-Compulsory Education and Training, Griffith University, Queensland, Australia

Young, M. (1994b) Qualifications for a high skill future? *Education for Production*, 10 (3)

Young, M. (1995a) *Evaluation Report on the Experiments in Upper Secondary Education in Finland*. Helsinki: Ministry of Education

Young, M. (1995b) Post-compulsory education for a learning society. Unpublished paper, University of London, Institute of Education

Young, M. and Guile, A. (1994) Work-based learning and the teacher/training of the future. Report of a National Development Project, Post-16 Education Centre. London: Institute of Education, University of London

Zee, van der, H. (1991) The learning society. *International Journal of Lifelong Education*, 10 (3), 213–30

Zijderveld, A. C. (1983) *De culturele factor; een cultuursociologische wegwijzer (The Cultural Factor: A Cultural/Sociological Guide)*. The Hague: VUGA

Zuboff, S. (1988) *In the Age of the Smart Machine*. London: Heinemann

# Name Index

# Subject Index